In Memory
of
Frank S. Mead
(1898–1982)

CONTENTS

xi

ALPHABETICAL TABLE
OF CONTENTS
FOR RELIGIOUS GROUPS

1

2

3

6

In the text that follows (e.g., see page 31), an asterisk (*) next to the name of a denomination indicates that there is a main entry about the denomination or denominational family.

PREFACE

For over half a century Frank Mead's *Handbook of Denominations in the United States* has been one of the most used reference books for the topic of religion in America. This is the twelfth edition of the *Handbook*, and like its predecessors, it attempts to portray some of the depth and breadth of the major religious traditions in the United States. It is not a comprehensive guide to American religion, however. That would require several volumes. Neither is it merely a comparison of church statistics or listing of fact. Rather it is a narrative of American religious life that includes brief descriptions of about two hundred bodies in the broad Abrahamic religious tradition in the U.S. I hope that this volume excites the curiosity of readers. A list of suggested readings is provided to assist further investigation.

The title of this *Handbook* reflects a distinctly American (and modern) understanding of religion. The word denomination means simply "name." It is a way we identify things, such as the denomination of money. It is a neutral term that is applied to religious communities that identifies them without passing judgment on their validity. Terms such as church, sect, and cult, for instance, have an implied judgment. No one considers their religious organization a "sect" or a "cult"; those terms are reserved for others. As used in this *Handbook*, a denomination is merely a self-conscious religious organization that includes but is greater than a local community of faith. Since the term was developed to describe different Christian bodies, it can only be used very loosely for non-Christian religions. Properly speaking, the various branches of Judaism and Islam are not denominations.

9

When churches use the word denomination to describe themselves and others, there is an implicit acknowledgment or even acceptance of the legitimacy of other churches. Because of this implicit acceptance of pluralism, at least within the broad Christian tradition, many churches do not use the word to describe themselves. Other Christian bodies do not use the term because it is not a biblical term. Many newer communities of faith avoid the word "denomination" because it is associated with national corporations. In an interesting transformation, the term denomination that once implied an acceptance of pluralism has come to mean administrative authority and control. Some church officials and sociologists even claim that denominationalism is dead.

Future editions of the *Handbook* may require a different title, but we have retained the familiar title to emphasize the continuity of this edition with its predecessors. Despite reservations about the term "denomination," this *Handbook* attests to the continuing power and influence of denominations. The drive toward establishing national organizations remains strong, and immigrant religions tend to follow the American model of denominational organization.

The most difficult editorial decision concerns the scope of this volume. The diversity and complexity of American religion is amazing and daunting. Rather than treat the many world religions in America superficially, or drastically limit the space given to various denominations, I chose to include only those religions stemming from the Abrahamic-monotheistic tradition. Therefore the religious bodies presented here in some way claim allegiance to the faith of Abraham. They share many similarities in their approaches to ethics, worship, and sacred texts.

Most newer religions, such as Scientology, new age belief systems, and groups often termed "cults" are thus excluded either because of their size or because they are not in the Abrahamic tradition.[1] This focus on Christianity, Judaism, Islam, and their branches is not meant to suggest that they alone are real or important religions; it is intended to give the work conceptual coherence and to set definite limits. The Abrahamic traditions have been by far the dominant forms of religious expression in America, but readers should be aware that this situation is changing rapidly.

---

[1]For more information on groups not included in this Handbook, see J. Gordon Melton, *Encyclopedia of American Religions*. 7th ed. 3 vols. (Detroit: Gale Research, 2003); the Religious Movements homepage of the University of Virginia (www. religiousmovements.lib.virginia.edu).

Every year the most religiously diverse country in history becomes even more diverse. The "Pluralism Project" at Harvard University is demonstrating that non-Western religions are daily becoming a more visible and vibrant part of American religion and culture.[2] The old Protestant hegemony that was present when Frank Mead wrote the first edition of the *Handbook* has disappeared. America is now home to most branches of Sikhs, Jains, Hindus, Buddhists, Taoists, Confucianists, and a host of new religious movements. Americans spend millions of dollars each year on spellbooks, crystals, charms, and guides for meditation. Some follow ancient Eastern or neo-pagan religions strictly, while others combine Eastern ideas or practices with traditional Christian or Jewish theology and rituals.

The religious bodies described in this edition of the *Handbook* are grouped in family categories that help tell the story of American religion both historically and typologically. The large headings, such as "Judaism," "Christianity," and "Islam" are arranged chronologically. The family groupings within the major traditions are also arranged chronologically. This way the reader can gain a better sense of the development and changes within Western religion through the centuries. An alphabetical table of contents is provided to make it easier to look up organizations by name rather than by category. A star (*) next to a term indicates that there is a separate entry by the name in the *Handbook*.

The family groupings are not intended to be prescriptive or normative. In many cases, one church could be placed in two or more categories, and I apologize to any who feel that they have been "misplaced." A number of denominations have been moved to more appropriate categories than they were in the previous *Handbook*. With few exceptions, the religious organizations included here have at least five thousand active members. Some smaller bodies are included because of their historical or social importance.

There are over thirty new entries in this edition of the *Handbook* reflecting trends in American religion. Some of the fastest growing religious groups are entrepreneurial rather than bureaucratic and hierarchical; therefore they lack typical denominational structures.

---

[2]The Pluralism Project, Harvard University (www.pluralism.org); Diana Eck, *A New Religious America: How a "Christian Country" Has Become the World's Most Religiously Diverse Nation.* San Francisco: HarperSanFrancisco, 2001.

Many of these expanding groups have embraced the most recent communication technologies and focus on a younger demographic than traditional religious organizations. Even established denominations now make effective use of the Internet, and so I have provided Web site addresses with most entries.

It is important to recognize that this *Handbook* is based on information provided by the religious organizations themselves. As such, it focuses on the doctrines, statistics, and histories of institutions. Such information is valuable and helpful in making sense of our culture and our neighbors, but much of the inner life and meaning of each denomination is omitted from such a presentation. Most of the statistics used in the *Handbook* are self-reported from the various religious organizations directly to me or appear in the *Yearbook of American and Canadian Churches*.[3] Reports of religious adherence are not always reliable, especially for comparative purposes. Some denominations report all baptized persons whether or not they attend services; others report only those who have made an adult profession of faith. Many religious bodies do not keep membership records at all. All statistics in this *Handbook* are merely the best estimate currently available.

This is the twelfth edition of the *Handbook,* and numerous individuals have generously contributed to its production through the years. It is unfortunate that they cannot all be named. Dr. Mead regularly updated the work several times during his long career, and after his death the task of revision fell to Samuel Hill, the leading scholar in the area of religion in the southern United States. Dr. Hill expanded the scope of the *Handbook* as well as updated it. Some of the work of professors Mead and Hill remain in this edition of the *Handbook,* as does the work of numerous anonymous writers who submitted information on their denominations through the years.

---

[3]Eileen W. Lindner, *Yearbook of American and Canadian Churches 2004* (New York: National Council of Churches of Christ; published by Abingdon Press, 2004). Also valuable is the demographic, geographical, and historical materials in Edwin Scott Gaustad and Philip L. Barlow, *New Historical Atlas of Religion in America* (New York: Oxford University Press, 2001). See also American Religion Date Archive (ARDA) of Pennsylvania State University (www.TheARDA.com); the Hartford Institute for Religion Research of Hartford Seminary (www.hirr.hartsem.edu); Institute for the Study of American Evangelicals (ISAE) at Wheaton College (www.wheaton.edu/isae); Institute for the Study of American Religion (www.americanreligion.org).

A number of people offered very helpful critiques of the 11th edition and gave suggestions on what religious bodies to add to this edition. Particularly worthy of gratitude are Roger Olson, Albert W. Wardin, Scott Thumma, Edwin Gaustad, and Julia Corbett. I would like to express my thanks to Jane Shore for her administrative assistance and to Home Moravian Church for allowing me time to devote to this project. Most especially I wish to thank my wife, Julie, for her charm, wisdom, and patience.

—Craig Atwood, Winston-Salem, NC, November 2004

RELIGION IN AMERICA

Craig D. Atwood

Religion is one of the most powerful human forces. Religion lifts the heart, challenges the mind, and inspires great achievements. A disproportionate number of Nobel Peace Prize winners have been people whose religious convictions led them to confront injustice and seek to reconcile warring enemies. Religion plays a role in much that is noble and good in the world. It is impossible to understand American (or world) history and culture without a knowledge of the religious fabric of our society.

The *Handbook of Denominations* was written to help individuals navigate the confusing and shifting waters of American religion. It is hoped that this volume will help readers better understand not only American religion in all its diversity but also their neighbors who are of a different faith community. Readers should remember that each of these religious organizations is made up of flesh-and-blood individuals who voluntarily gather to sing, chant, pray, work, teach, and learn. In every church, synagogue, and mosque births are celebrated; children are taught to be virtuous and compassionate; adults learn to enjoy what is beautiful, good, and true; parents grow in wisdom and patience; the hungry are fed; the naked are clothed; and the lonely are redeemed from their isolation. Rabbis, imams, pastors, priests, and lay leaders bless marriages, bury the dead, comfort those who mourn, and challenge their flocks with a vision of a more peaceful and just society.

But the terrorist attacks on September 11, 2001, were a harsh reminder that religious beliefs can be twisted into tools of hatred and murder. No religion is exempt from the type of fanaticism that

15

inspired 9/11. People of every faith face the choice once presented by the prophet Moses: "I have set before you life and death, blessings and curses. Choose life so that you and your descendants may live" (Deut. 30:19, NRSV). This 12th edition of Frank Mead's *Handbook of Denominations in the United States* is dedicated to life.

Millions of Americans drew upon their faith after the terrorist attacks and found the courage to reach beyond the boundaries of their own religious communities and embrace their neighbors in love. Across the country there were reports of Jews, Christians, Muslims, and others joining hands to protect mosques and synagogues from vandals. People of all faith traditions performed unheralded and heroic acts of mercy and charity. Millions of Americans discovered that people with different religious beliefs love their families, work hard, care for their neighbors, love their country, and can be good friends. In the process, many Americans discovered how little they really know about what is most important to their neighbors: their religious faith. This book is one of many tools to help people discover more about their friends, neighbors, and themselves.

However, the terrorist attacks and aftermath also challenged many Americans' tolerance of other religions and even their commitment to the First Amendment. The great American experiment in religious freedom has always been a challenge, but it is especially challenging since 9/11. It is easy for fear and suspicion to rob us of our reason and ethics. Now, more than ever, we need greater knowledge of other faiths and a greater understanding of the distinctiveness of American religion. The United States is the most religious industrialized nation in the world and is also the most religiously diverse. It is important to have some sense of the reasons for these facts and the tensions inherent in the American system in this new millennium.

What is it that makes American religion so diverse and confusing? Why was it in the United States that the idea of "denominations" emerged so that we can speak of different religious groups without using the often pejorative word sects? How does religion relate to social change in America? In order to answer those questions, we need to take a step back in history and review some factors that are central to American religious experience.

First of all, we must be aware that until modern times—indeed, until the rise of the United States—it was assumed that civic harmony depended on religious conformity. There should be "one king, one faith, one law," in the famous phrase of Louis XIV. Religion was seen as the warp of the social fabric, the glue that held different estates together and balanced conflicting interests. Religious diversity was equated with civic unrest and upheaval. The idea that a nation could tolerate not only different Christian churches but also radically different religions was considered lunacy until the American Revolution. Modern Americans who have always lived under the Bill of Rights and its guarantee of freedom of worship have difficulty realizing what a truly radical experiment the First Amendment was when proposed by James Madison and Thomas Jefferson.

Once the Bill of Rights was ratified, the federal government was forbidden to intervene in matters of personal faith. There have been notable cases in which local and national authorities have indeed impinged this civil right, but for the most part the spirit of freedom of religion has prevailed in the United States for over two centuries. This meant that no force other than popular opinion could prevent the formation of new religious organizations, new churches, and even new religions. Anyone who could gather followers could be the founder of a new denomination. Sometimes these new religions have been dismissed by the public and have become what might be termed cults, but some of them have developed into very popular and dynamic faith traditions.

Rather than leading to the demise of religion, as many detractors (and a few supporters) of the First Amendment expected, this freedom of religious expression led to a marked increase in religious belief and practice in the United States during the last two centuries. In contrast to other industrialized nations, the United States continues to have high levels of personal belief, membership in religious organizations, and participation in religious activities.

It may appear ironic that the world's first completely secular government has fostered one of the most religious societies, but the reason why is rather simple. In the free-enterprise system of American religion, denominations have always had to compete for the hearts and minds of the masses. Denominations in the United States have had to present their message in a way that appeals to current and potential members. Even those churches that stress hierarchical and traditional values have had to adopt the methods of conversion-oriented churches in order to retain members.

Free competition has made American religion unusually responsive to changes in society as denominations adapt popular culture, especially music, for the purpose of attracting members. Each generation has seen the creation of new religious bodies and the transformation of older bodies as religious leaders have tried to address the anxieties of their age and offer hope for the perceivable future. This process of adaptation and change has often led to splits within denominations, with one party embracing new techniques, such as revival meetings, and the other party promoting traditional approaches, such as belief in the classical creeds and use of ancient liturgical forms. New denominations may be innovative or traditionalist, but even the traditionalists have to "sell" members and potential members on the virtues of tradition. The pages that follow will trace the way new churches develop out of older churches. For instance, the majority of Pentecostal churches developed out of the older Holiness churches, which in turn had come out of the Methodist churches, which had themselves originated in the Anglican Church.

The free-enterprise approach to religion has also encouraged experimentation with worship forms, doctrines, and even Scriptures. Nineteenth-century America was the birthplace of some of the most dynamic religious movements of modern times. Many of these denominations emerged during the heady days of the Second Great Awakening in the days of the early Republic (1800–30), when it seemed that the common person could achieve any dream. If backwoodsmen could serve in the Congress and farmers create a new government, why shouldn't an angel appear to an ordinary man and reveal a new Scripture? Why couldn't a former housewife be the new incarnation of Christ?

Since most of these new religious movements, like the Shakers and the Mormons, have roots in traditional Christianity, they are not considered new religions; however, some of them are indeed radical variations on ancient Christian themes. Even among those that stayed closer to traditional Protestantism, there was a widespread sentiment that religious authorities could be ignored and that common people could recreate the church based on their own understanding of the Bible. Out of this conviction arose the denominations associated with Alexander Campbell and Barton Stone. Later Pentecostals, Adventists, and even the Jehovah's Witnesses would also draw upon this idea of remaking the church according to one's own understanding of Scripture. The old Reformation slogan of "Scripture alone" produced a cornucopia of denominations in the United States as ordinary individuals took up the challenge of interpreting the Bible and judging religious authorities.

A **second** major factor in the diversity of American religion is immigration. Each wave of immigration brought different national churches. In fact, by the time the Constitution was written there were so many denominations that it would have been difficult, if not impossible, to have created a state church. Among the English colonists there were Congregationalists in New England, Quakers in Pennsylvania, Anglicans in New York, Presbyterians in Virginia, and Roman Catholics in Maryland. In addition, there were Dutch, Swiss, and German Reformed; Swedish and German Lutherans; French Huguenots; and Sephardic Jews, just to name the most prominent faiths.

Even within the same church, most noticeably the Roman Catholic and Lutheran churches, the United States has been home to an impressive array of ethnic communities that have often posed a challenge to church hierarchies trying to maintain institutional unity. This process continued in the twentieth century as traditional denominations, such as Presbyterians and Methodists, have had to make room for Korean- and Swahili-speaking congregations. Moreover, as many as twelve million American Catholics speak Spanish as their first language.

Religion has provided each immigrant group with an identity in a foreign land, a way of being grounded in the old culture while adjusting to a new and confusing society. Ethnic culture in the United States is inseparable from ethnic religious tradition. Over the decades, though, these ethnic denominations gradually have adapted to the American setting as they struggled to win the allegiance of third and fourth generations. The transition to English in worship is one benchmark of the Americanization process. Gradually immigrant churches grow to resemble their neighboring churches more than the national churches that gave them birth. Some denominations, most notably Eastern Orthodoxy, aggressively resist this process of assimilation, but in doing so they also adopt American techniques of marketing and group formation. Only in America do you see bumper stickers that say "Orthodoxy: Proclaiming the truth since AD 33."

In the second half of the twentieth century, immigration from Asia and the Caribbean basin has brought the religions of the world, including folk religions such as Santeria, to American shores. This dramatic increase in religious diversity will be one of the major factors of religious life in the United States during the twenty-first century. No longer will the symphony of American religion be composed of variations on the Christian theme.

A **third** distinctive feature of American religion has been interchurch cooperation in the midst of competition. Again, one can use an economic analogy and point to the American penchant for large corporations and mergers. Interdenominational, para-church, and cooperative ministries have brought together believers from different backgrounds throughout American history. In times of disaster it is not at all surprising to see Catholics, Protestants, Jews, and Muslims working hand in hand. The individuals helping are motivated by their religious values, which have been nurtured in a particular faith tradition. But in working together, they learn to respect other faiths.

Sometimes these cooperative efforts have led to the creation of new denominations, such as the United Church of Christ, and sometimes to interchurch agencies, such as the National Association of Evangelicals. More generally, such efforts have increased religious toleration on the local level. This is the essence of denominationalism: Diverse religious traditions and organizations openly compete for adherents while respecting other religious organizations as valid. It is rare, for instance, to hear a Presbyterian in the United States declare that Methodists are not really Christian. Further, as the presence of world religions increases in the United States, one sees this sense of toleration being extended beyond Christian boundaries. Of course, as with every movement, the ecumenical trend has also led to the creation of new denominations that reject this perspective and insist on doctrinal or ecclesiastical conformity and exclusiveness.

Sociologists have noticed the strength of this ecumenism in American religion and have concluded that we are now in a "post-denominational" period when religious identity has lost its place in individuals' lives. It is relatively easy for an Episcopalian to join a Lutheran church. Even the conversion from Catholic to Protestant or vice versa no longer carries the weight it did fifty years ago. There has been a tendency toward homogenization of religion as churches learn from each other and adopt successful practices. Most Americans have an eclectic faith stitched together from many different threads of tradition and contemporary ideas and attitudes. Even so, denominations remain vibrant because they provide a form of religious identity amid the pluralism of belief. They also provide needed resources for local communities of faith, such as facilities for training ministers, for publishing curriculum resources, and for overseeing certification procedures.

Although the character of denominations continues to evolve, there is little indication that they will disappear. It is noteworthy that as denominations unite splinter groups always form, thus acknowledging the usefulness of denominational structures even while they are rejecting the authority of the parent organization. It is interesting as well that many non-denominational churches gradually evolve their own denominational structures. In this edition of the *Handbook*, there are entries on "mega-churches," which are congregations that actually function as small denominations.

A **fourth** characteristic of American culture that affects religious institutions and belief is the close connection between politics, popular culture, public morality, and religion. The disestablishment clause of the Bill of Rights did not remove religion from the "public square." Throughout the past two and a quarter centuries people have been motivated by their faith to participate actively in the political process and in the social arena. This was most evident in the abolition movement, women's suffrage, and many campaigns for humane treatment of prisoners, human rights, voting rights, police reform, public education, and economic justice. The Prohibition movement in the early twentieth century was one of the most successful "crusades" politically and least effective socially.

Each of these campaigns was fought in the public square and in the pulpit. Each created new divisions in American religion and new alliances. Denominational identity became less important than political identity for many Christians, but by and large the different denominations allowed for a diversity of political opinions among clergy and laity. It was rare for religious organizations to identify with a particular politician or political party. By the end of the twentieth century, there were signs that the old assumptions no longer held. President George W. Bush claimed a divine mandate for the invasion of Iraq and won re-election on the strength of Protestant evangelical voters. Religious leaders established lobbying organizations, political action committees, and participated enthusiastically in campaigning for candidates who supported their positions on issues such as abortion, gay rights, and private schools. By 2004 it was increasingly evident that denominations were dividing over the related issues of ordination of homosexuals and the blessing of gay marriages.

21

Politics, they say, makes strange bedfellows, and that is particularly true when religious leaders enter the political fray. In the 1960s and '70s radical Catholic priests shared jail cells with atheist political activists. In 2004, some Roman Catholic bishops urged Catholics to vote for a "born again" Southern evangelical rather than a Roman Catholic senator because he had opposed efforts to outlaw abortion. It is likely that in the future denominational affinity and political opinion will grow closer together.

A **fifth** major factor in American religion at the beginning of the twenty-first century is the Internet. The potential of the Internet to reach individuals and to spread the word about a particular faith was quickly realized. Religion is one of the major topics discussed in chat rooms and on Web sites. The Internet has even allowed for the creation of new denominations that gather primarily in "cyberspace." The factors discussed above all figure in the Internet's influence on American religion. Denominations use it to compete for followers; individuals use it as a resource in building their personal belief system; and immigrant churches use it as a resource to keep scattered members of the flock connected with the ethnic tradition.

American religion is complex, and will grow increasingly so. This *Handbook* merely presents some of the "objective" aspects of religion to assist the reader in making sense of our world. It is no substitute for the lived experience of the different communities of faith where people find joy, strength, and hope day after day. If this book helps readers to get to know their neighbors, join a worshiping community, and better appreciate the intricate social fabric of America, then it has fulfilled its purpose.

Suggestions for Further Reading:

Ahlstrom, Sydney E. *A Religious History of the American People.* 2 vols. New Haven: Yale University Press, 1972.

Bowden, Henry W., ed. *Dictionary of American Religious Biography.* 2nd. ed. Westport, Conn.: Greenwood, 1993.

Corbett, Julia Mitchell. *Religion in America.* 3rd ed. Upper Saddle River, N.J.: Prentice Hall, 1997.

Eck, Diana. A New Religious America: *How a "Christian Country" Has Become the World's Most Religiously Diverse Nation.* San Francisco: HarperSanFrancisco, 2001.

Gaustad, Edwin Scott and Philip L. Barlow. *New Historical Atlas of Religion in America.* New York: Oxford University Press, 2001.

Hatch, Nathan O. *The Democratization of American Christianity.* New Haven: Yale University Press, 1989.

Hill, Samuel S, ed. *The South and the North in American Religion.* Athens: University of Georgia Press, 1980.

James, Janet W., ed. *Women in American Religion.* Philadelphia: University of Pennsylvania Press, 1980.

Lincoln, C. Eric, and Lawrence H. Mamiya. *The Black Church in the African-American Experience.* Durham, NC: Duke University Press, 1990.

Lippy, Charles H., and Peter W. Williams, eds. *Encyclopedia of American Religious Experience: Studies of Traditions and Movements.* 3 vols. New York: Scribner, 1988.

Marty, Martin E. *Modern American Religion.* 2 vols. Chicago: University of Chicago Press, 1986.

Melton, J. Gordon. *Encyclopedia of American Religions.* 7th ed. 3 vols. Detroit: Gale Research, 2003.

Moore, R. Laurence. *Selling God: American Religion in the Marketplace of Culture.* New York: Oxford University Press, 1994.

Noll, Mark A. *A History of Christianity in the United States and Canada.* Grand Rapids, Mich.: Eerdmans, 1992.

Noll, Mark A. *America's God: From Jonathan Edwards to Abraham Lincoln.* New York: Oxford University Press, 2002.

Porterfield, Amanda. *The Transformation of American Religion: The Story of a Late Twentieth-Century Awakening.* New York: Oxford University Press, 2001.

Raboteau, Albert J. *Slave Religion: The "Invisible Institution" in the Antebellum South.* New York: Oxford University Press, 1978.

Roof, Wade Clark. *Spiritual Marketplace: Baby Boomers and the Remaking of American Religion.* Princeton, NJ: Princeton University Press, 1999.

Ruether, Rosemary Radford, and Rosemary Skinner Keller, eds. *Women and Religion in America.* 3 vols. San Francisco: Harper & Row, 1981.

Wuthnow, Robert. *The Restructuring of American Religion: Society and Faith Since World War II.* Princeton, NJ: Princeton University Press, 1988.

ABRAHAMIC TRADITIONS

According to ancient tradition, the story of Western monotheism began in Mesopotamia (modern day Iraq) when a virtuous man named Abram answered a summons from the Creator. Abram and his wife, Sarah, left their home and journeyed westward to the land of Canaan, which today is known to millions as "the holy land." God, the Creator, sealed a covenant with Abram that was passed down through many generations. According to the covenant, Abram and his descendants would worship only the one God, study his teachings, and try to live according to his laws of justice and mercy. God, in turn, would bless those who worshiped and followed him. God changed Abram's name to Abraham, and he fathered two sons: Ishmael, son of Hagar, and Isaac, son of Sarah.

Judaism, Christianity, Islam, and their numerous branches all trace their ancestry to Abraham and his children. For Jews, Isaac and his son Jacob (also called Israel) were the heirs of the covenant. The ritual of circumcision marked the descendents of Jacob as a Chosen People, a priestly nation serving the one God. The early followers of Jesus believed that he was the promised Jewish messiah who fulfilled the original covenant and gave a new covenant sealed by his own death and resurrection. Gentiles (people who are not Jewish) could become children of Abraham through "adoption" because they had faith in the one God revealed in Jesus the Christ. Six centuries after the time of Jesus, Muhammad proclaimed to the Arabs that they were also children of the covenant given to Abraham and his elder son, Ishmael. All who submit to the rules of righteousness given to Abraham were the true children of Abraham. They were Muslims (those who submit to God) just as Abraham was.

The history of Western civilization is bound up with this story of those who claim to be children of Abraham by birth, adoption, or obedience. There has been much conflict between and within the Western religions as each fought to promote and protect their understanding of the covenant with God. Some modern scholars argue that monotheism is intrinsically violent because of its exclusivism and drive to uniformity of belief and practice. There is truth in that observation, but that is not the whole story. As this book demonstrates, the Abrahamic tradition has itself produced great diversity of beliefs, practices, and communities of faith. Through the centuries the three great Abrahamic religions have learned much from each other despite frequent strife.

The Abrahamic religions share many features that have profoundly shaped Western society. For example, they teach that God is concerned about ethics and that the ethical life is a happier life. They are all religions "of the book," which means that their sacred writings provide the norms for doctrine, rituals, and daily living. To varying degrees, each encourages believers to devote themselves to study as well as work in the world. Each shares a basic conviction that the physical world is a product of God's goodwill and that nature works according to God's laws. Through reason, one can discern the presence of God in creation and understand God's instructions for right living. More profoundly, through faith, one can experience the presence of God in one's life and learn both to love God and one's neighbors. Each Abrahamic religion offers its followers hope for a better tomorrow, either in this world or the world to come.

The Abrahamic religions differ in many significant ways. Jews and Muslims proclaim the unity and oneness of God and resist all attempts to create images of God. Christian churches, with a few exceptions, proclaim that God is three as well as one and that Jesus the Christ was the incarnation of God the Son. Those called the Latter-day Saints believe that Jesus was God, but that the faithful can also become divine in the way Jesus is divine.

Jews and Muslims agree that living according to the laws of God is central to following and loving God, but they disagree over the details of those laws. They also disagree over whether Muhammad was a prophet of God. Christians, by and large, place greater value on faith, love, and forgiveness than righteousness. Christians and Muslims believe that God has entrusted them with the sacred task of convincing all the people of the world that there is one God whom they should love and serve, but they disagree on the nature of God and what it means to serve God. Jews, for the most part, feel no need to bring outsiders into their covenantal relationship with God, but they do call for Gentiles to live justly as God demands.

The Abrahamic religions, therefore, share a common "world-view," but it is important to look at each religion and denomination in their particularity or individuality. Each elaborates on the basic tradition in important ways that give meaning and guidance to their followers. In the pages that follow, we will look at each of the Abrahamic traditions according to when they appeared on the world scene.

Suggestions for Further Reading:

Armstrong, Karen. *A History of God: The 4,000-year Quest of Judaism, Christianity, and Islam.* New York: Knopf, 1993.

Armstrong, Karen. *The Battle for God: A History of Fundamentalism.* New York: Ballatine, 2001.

Corrigan, John, Frederick M. Denny, Carolos M. N. Eire, and Martin S. Jaffee. *Jews, Christians, Muslims: A Comparative Introduction to Monotheistic Religions.* Upper Saddle River, NJ: Prentice Hall, 1998.

Eck, Diana. *Encountering God: A Spiritual Journey from Bozeman to Banares.* Boston: Beacon, 1993.

Feiler, Bruce. *Abraham: A Journey to the Heart of Three Faiths.* San Francisco: HarperCollins, 2002.

Kimball, Charles. *When Religion Becomes Evil.* San Francisco: HarperSanFrancisco, 2002.

Neusner, Jacob, ed. *World Religions in America: An Introduction.* Louisville: Westminster/John Knox, 1994.

Occhiogrosso, Peter. *The Joy of Sects: A Spirited Guide to the World's Religious Traditions.* New York: Image, 1996.

Oxtoby, Willard G., ed. *World Religions: Western Traditions.* New York: Oxford University Press, 1996.

Smith, Huston. *Why Religion Matters: The Fate of the Human Spirit in an Age of Unbelief.* San Francisco: HarperSanFrancisco, 2001.

Smith, William Cantwell. *Patterns of Faith Around the World.* Oxford: Oneworld, 1998.

Wuthnow, Robert. *Growing Up Religious: Christians and Jews and Their Journeys of Faith.* Boston: Beacon, 1999.

JUDAISM

Judaism is one of the oldest religions of the world. All Western religions trace their origins in some way to Judaism. Today there are about twelve million Jews in the world, half of whom live in the United States. Judaism can refer to both a religion and an ethnicity, and there are, of course, disagreements among Jews as to what truly makes a person Jewish—whether it is a matter of birth, cultural heritage, or religious observance. Perhaps as many as half of the Jews in the United States are not observant.

Unlike Christianity, which is generally defined in terms of doctrines and beliefs, Judaism as a religion is defined primarily by practices and ethics. Put briefly, Jews understand themselves as the people to whom God gave the commandments to observe as their obligation to God. By following God's instructions, the Chosen People in turn become a blessing to the entire world as they help to establish God's realm of justice and peace (*shalom*).

History. Jews trace their heritage back to the patriarch Abraham, who answered the call of God and left his home in Mesopotamia to seek a promised land beyond the Jordan River. According to tradition, Abraham's grandson was Jacob, whose name was changed to Israel after he wrestled with an angel. The twelve sons of Jacob/Israel became the fathers of the twelve tribes of ancient Israel.

The defining event for the Israelites and their descendents was the Exodus. After many years serving as slaves to Pharaoh in Egypt, a prophet named Moses was called by God to lead the people to freedom. Moses parted the waters of the Sea of Reeds (or the Red Sea) and led the people to Mt. Sinai. There he established the priesthood and gave instructions on how they should live.

Israel's obligations to God became known as the Torah ("Law" or "Instruction"). Torah is the centerpiece of all forms of Judaism down to the present day.

Around 1000 B.C.E. the second king of Israel, David, established a strong and prosperous centralized government with a standing army and efficient bureaucracy. He captured the Canaanite city of Jerusalem and made it the capital of his realm. Despite his personal flaws and failings, David was heralded as the perfect king, God's own son. Prophets and priests alike proclaimed that God had made a special covenant with the house of David so that there would always be a son of David on the throne in Jerusalem. Jewish kings were known as the Lord's Anointed, which in Hebrew is *messiah*. David's son Solomon expanded the kingdom and built a large central temple in Jerusalem. Jerusalem was proclaimed to be the holy city, the dwelling place of God. Centuries after the destruction of the Temple, Jerusalem is still viewed as the holy city by most Jews, and the Temple Mount is the most holy land in the Holy Land.

After Solomon's death, there was a rebellion against the Davidic kings, and the kingdom divided into two unequal parts. The smaller southern kingdom of Judah consisted primarily of the tribe of Judah, and its capital city was Jerusalem, where the descendents of David ruled until the sixth century B.C.E. The words *Judaism* and *Jew* come from "Judah." The northern kingdom was known as Israel, and its capital was Samaria. In the early eighth century this kingdom was destroyed by the Assyrians. The people were dispersed, never to reunite. From that time on, the southern kingdom assumed the heritage of Israel. Around 587 B.C.E. the kingdom of Judah was conquered by the Babylonians. The temple was destroyed and thousands of citizens were taken into captivity. During the forty years of exile, the prophets, priests, scribes, and scholars began the process of codifying the writings that became the sacred Scripture.

Eventually the Jews were allowed to return to the land of the patriarchs and built a nation under Persian and later Greek control. There was no longer a king; instead the high priest served as the chief administrator of Judea. In the second century B.C.E. their Hellenistic overlord, the Syrian Emperor Antiochus IV, tried to crush the Jews and their religion in order to make them more subservient to his rule. Copies of the Torah (the scrolls of the first five books of the Bible) were burned, Jews were forbidden to circumcise their boy babies (the physical sign that one is in the covenant), and the temple was desecrated by the sacrifice of an unclean animal to a pagan deity. Rather than crush the spirit of the Jews, these measures led to open revolt. This revolt of the Maccabbees on behalf of the right of Jews to observe the commandments of God is commemorated each year at Hanukkah.

Within a hundred years of the revolt against foreign domination, though, Judea fell into Roman hands and at the time of Jesus was administered by a Roman governor. Rebellion again broke out in 66 C.E., but this time the Jews were defeated. Jerusalem and the temple were destroyed in 70. By that time, there were Jewish communities throughout the Roman and Persian worlds, and they grew in importance when the heart of Judaism was destroyed. The Diaspora, or scattering, of the Jews was facilitated by the development of a mobile form of religion that was based in the family and small community. In diaspora Judaism, it takes only ten men to form an assembly and conduct worship. Even without a synagogue, Judaism can be observed in the home, in secret if need be.

As Christianity* emerged as the religion of the Roman Empire, anti-Semitism grew in the Empire. But with the rise of Islam,* which has many affinities to Judaism, Jews met with a measure of toleration in the new Islamic Empire. Jews often had positions of great power and influence, particularly in the learned professions, such as medicine. Jews in the Islamic world generally spoke Arabic or other local languages and even translated the Torah into Arabic. They assimilated outwardly while maintaining Jewish observance and theology. These Jews of the Mediterranean basin would eventually be called Sephardic, from the Hebrew word for "Spain." Spain had a thriving Jewish community until Isabella and Ferdinand consolidated their rule over the Iberian Peninsula. In 1492, the year Columbus sailed west, the Jews were forced to leave Spain or face the wrath of the Spanish Inquisition. Many Sephardic Jews made their way to the New World, settling in Brazil, New York, and Rhode Island.

Jews in the Christian kingdoms of the West had a more tenuous existence than did those in Islamic lands. During the struggle to define Christianity as separate from Judaism in the patristic period, much anti-Semitism found its way into Christian theology and practice. Throughout the Middle Ages, Jewish communities were subject

31

to harassment by Christian mobs. In the thirteenth and fourteenth centuries Jews were expelled from England and France. Many made their way eastward into the sparsely settled lands of Germany, Poland, Hungary, and Russia. There they established separate communities, often building entire farming villages, where they could observe the Torah in relative peace. These Jews became known as Ashkenazi, from the Hebrew word for Germany, and they developed a unique German dialect known as Yiddish, which is written in Hebrew letters. The Ashkenazi were generally less sophisticated and less secular than were the Sephardim.

Persecution of the Ashkenazi Jews in Eastern Europe began in earnest in the nineteenth century, and thousands emigrated to the U.S. Soon anti-Semitism increased in Germany and throughout Central Europe. Hatred of Jews reached a fever pitch in the first half of the twentieth century. When the National Socialist (Nazi) Party came to power in Germany through popular elections, they encouraged violence against Jews. Adolf Hitler (1889–1945) and his aides put in place a series of anti-Jewish laws that stripped Jews of their rights. Soon, they began shipping Jews to concentration camps, where as many as six million Jews, along with millions of gypsies, Slavs, and other hated groups, were brutally tortured and murdered. This Holocaust marked a watershed in Jewish history that continues to affect Judaism in profound ways. Never before had the threatened destruction of the Jewish people been so close to fulfillment. Perhaps half of the world's Jewish population died during the Nazi era.

The founding of the State of Israel in 1948 was connected with the horrors of the Holocaust. Since the nineteenth century, when many peoples of Europe had agitated for their own nations, there had been calls for a Jewish nation. This Zionist, or Jewish nationalist, movement was led by Theodor Herzel (1860–1904), who laid the groundwork upon which the Jewish homeland would be erected. Initially a rather small movement among secularized Jews, many of whom had socialist convictions, Zionism grew in power as Jews learned the truth about the Holocaust. A Jewish state free from Gentile control seemed to be the best solution to Jewish survival. In the 1960s and 1970s, religious Jews became firm supporters of the Jewish state as well; and many people perceived a link between the future of Israel as a nation and the establishment of the long-hoped-for messianic age. In the last quarter of the twentieth century there was a growing fundamentalist movement focused on Zionist goals.

Jews in the United States. Sephardic Jews arrived early in American history. During the colonial period synagogues were established in New Amsterdam (1654), Newport, R.I. (1670s), Savannah, Charleston, and Philadelphia (1730s and '40s); however, the first official rabbi did not arrive until the middle of the 19th century.

President Washington was able to assure a delegation of Jewish leaders that the new constitution of the United States guaranteed freedom of worship and conscience to all people, not just Christians. Because of this guarantee of freedom from persecution, America gradually became a second "promised land" for world Jewry. In the 19th century, some Jews embraced American culture so completely that they redefined Judaism in terms familiar to liberal Protestants. Hebrew was dropped except in special services; the rules of ritual observance were relaxed, and organs were added to synagogues. Some synagogues even began worshiping on Sunday rather than on the Sabbath. Other Jews rejected this extreme assimilation to the Protestant American mainstream and retained traditional elements of worship and observance.

The massive influx of Eastern European Jews, the Ashkenazi, profoundly affected the American Jewish community. Millions of immigrants settled in the major Northern cities, creating large Jewish neighborhoods where they could maintain much of their Old World identity in the midst of industrial America. There were about 500,000 Jews in the U.S. in 1900. By 1940 there were over four million, and they made a significant impact on American popular culture. The Ashkenazi tended to be more conservative than the Sephardic Jews who had lived in the U.S. for decades. Over time, much of this Yiddish culture has fallen away, but many of the most famous American entertainers came out of this Yiddish culture, with its distinctive foods and traditions. By the end of the twentieth century, Judaism was so well established in American society that an observant Jew, Joseph Lieberman, could be nominated for vice president in 2000.

While the local synagogue is very important to Jewish life in the U.S., there are hundreds of Jewish organizations that help to define and defend Judaism. They range from those focused on Jewish rights to youth societies. There are some two hundred periodicals and newspapers and two news syndicates dedicated to Judaism. The

American Jewish Committee is organized to protect the civil and religious rights of Jews around the world. It seeks equality in economic, social, and educational opportunities and gives aid and counsel in cases of intolerance and persecution.

Jewish institutions of higher learning, affiliated with the various movements, serve the community nationwide, not only training rabbis, but also providing general Jewish learning for all interested people. The most important are (Orthodox) Rabbi Isaac Elchanan Theological Seminary of Yeshiva University in New York City; (Reform) Hebrew Union College—Jewish Institute of Religion in New York, Cincinnati, Los Angeles, and Jerusalem; (Conservative) Jewish Theological Seminary in New York City; and Reconstructionist Rabbinical College in Philadelphia. Yeshiva University in New York City is the only Jewish college that awards a B.A. degree; Brandeis University in Waltham, Massachusetts, is the only nonsectarian Jewish-sponsored college or university in the U.S.

Theology and Practice. Rabbinic Judaism was the only form of Judaism to survive ancient times. It actually developed at the same time that Christianity was being formed. In fact, in the first century, Christianity was simply one of many forms of non-rabbinic Judaism. By the sixth century, the two religions had developed the basic structures, theology, and practices that define each to the present.

Judaism as a religion is based on the Hebrew Scriptures (for Christians, the Old Testament), but it is distinct from the form of religion described in those texts. The ancient religion of the Israelites focused on cultic observances, particularly animal sacrifice, and revelation given by prophets. Priests were in charge of seeing that cultic rites were properly performed and that ritual purity was maintained. Prophets served social and religious functions as well. They were men (and occasionally women) through whom God spoke, especially in judgment. Prophets challenged the leaders of society, even the king, to live by the ethical demands of the covenant. Justice for the poor, the outcast, and the oppressed was a major theme of the prophetic judgment.

Over time, scribes codified the pronouncements of the prophets and the laws of the priesthood, producing an enormous body of legal and ethical material that has profoundly shaped Western society. However, many of the laws and instructions contained in the Scriptures clearly reflect the world of an ancient agricultural people.

First the priests and later the rabbis helped people understand and apply the Torah in radically different historical and social contexts.

Rabbinic Judaism grew out of the Pharasaic movement. The Pharisees in the first century C.E. were a Jewish party that controlled most of the synagogues in and around Palestine. They differed from the priests and other Jews by their strict interpretation of the demands of the Torah: It should be observed as faithfully as humanly possible. To make observance of the Torah easier, the Pharisees taught, Jews should keep themselves separate from Gentiles, especially at meals, when it would be hard to observe the dietary restrictions of the Torah. Marriage to Gentiles was also generally forbidden. The Pharisees de-emphasized temple observances and the sacrifice of animals and focused on the demands of the Torah in day-to-day living. Justice, not sacrifice, was what God demands, the prophet Micah had said, and the Pharisees agreed. For the rabbis, prayer and study of Torah served the religious needs that the priests had once met.

One of the key concepts of rabbinic Judaism is that there are two Torahs. The written Torah was given to Moses and is contained in the scrolls of Moses (Genesis, Exodus, Leviticus, Numbers, and Deuteronomy). These writings were revealed by God through the prophetic lawgiver, but the written Torah can be very confusing and difficult to observe unless you live in a small agricultural society. Here is where the second Torah of the rabbis comes in. This is the oral Torah, which was also communicated to Moses by God on Mt. Sinai. The oral Torah is the key to understanding Scripture and to applying the teachings of Scripture to one's daily life. The written Torah says to observe the Sabbath and keep it holy. The oral Torah tells you how to do this. According to tradition, this oral Torah was passed down by a succession of prophets and scribes, such as Ezra.

After the destruction of the temple, though, it became necessary to codify and clarify this oral tradition and preserve it in written form. This culminated in the production of the Talmud around 600 C.E. The Talmud is one of the masterpieces of world literature and intellectual history. It contains the debates of the rabbis on questions of biblical interpretation and how to understand and apply the Torah. There are, in fact, two Talmuds, one produced in Babylon by the descendents of Jews who had not returned to Israel, and one produced in Palestine centuries after the destruction of the temple.

The Talmud has two main parts, one of which, the *Haggadah,* deals with biblical interpretation, customs, legends, and edifying stories. The other part concerns *Halakah,* the rules of the covenant with God. *Halakah* involves the 613 commandments that Jews are to obey and practice in their daily lives. This can be difficult as the world changes, so the Talmud also provides guidelines for the rabbis to continue the tradition of interpreting *Halakah.* This process of interpretation, adaptation, and even disagreement over the meaning of Torah is the thread that runs through the history of Judaism.

There are some features of Jewish theology and observance that are common throughout the various branches of Judaism. The core of Jewish theology is the concept of the oneness of God. There is only one God, and God's will is known in the covenant. Every day the practicing Jew repeats the ancient verse that introduces the Ten Commandments in Deuteronomy: "Hear, O Israel! The Lord is our God, the Lord alone" (Deut 6:4 NJPS). There is but one creator, who ultimately controls the destiny of humankind and the world.

Humankind, created by this one God, is inherently good. There is no idea of original sin in Judaism. Humans are made in God's image and are endowed with an intelligence that enables them to choose between good and evil. Torah assists in this process of choosing good over evil, but all people, Jews and Gentiles alike, will be judged. The righteous (or just) will be rewarded and the wicked punished. However, concern for life after death is an issue of minor significance for most Jews. More important is the way one lives in this life. Judaism looks forward to the establishment of a divine kingdom of truth and righteousness on the earth. Orthodox Jews believe the time will come when God sends the Messiah, the descendent of David who will restore the kingdom. Other Jews speak of a messianic age. To work toward the divine kingdom, Jews have been established by God as "a kingdom of priests and a holy nation," the "servant of the Lord."

Judaism follows a liturgical calendar, dating from ancient times. It is based on the lunar year rather than the solar year, so the dates vary from year to year. The year begins in the autumn with Rosh Hashanah, a new year festival that begins the High Holy Days. For ten days, Jews are encouraged to examine their lives and make reconciliation with those they have wronged, including God, in preparation for Yom Kippur, the Day of Atonement. On this day, God judges the sins of the people and provides for atonement.

Some weeks after Yom Kippur is Succoth, the Feast of Tabernacles or Booths, during which Jews relive the years of wandering in the wilderness. Hanukkah, in December, commemorates the purification of the temple during the Maccabean revolt. This feast day has grown in importance in the U.S. because of the commercial power of Christmas. Pesach, or Passover, in the spring is a memorial of the liberation of Jews from Egypt. Shabuoth, also known as the Feast of Weeks or Pentecost, follows Passover in late May or early June. It was once a harvest festival but now commemorates Moses' receiving of the Torah.

Other observances follow the life cycle of the individual. These include the circumcision of male children on the eighth day after birth, the *bar/bat mitzvah* (a rite of entry into adult accountability for the covenant), weddings, and funerals. Also important in Judaism is the observance of the Sabbath (sundown Friday until sundown Saturday) as a sacred day of rest and study of the Torah. Most synagogues have Sabbath services, although Sabbath observance is actually a home obligation.

Local congregations have full independence. There are no synods, assemblies, or hierarchies of leaders, but there are rabbinical councils and organizations that make rulings about the law and establish credentials for rabbis. Jewish worship varies according to theology and culture. Traditional Orthodox synagogues, for instance, have no instrumental music, the congregation worships with covered heads, and the men and women sit separately. In Reform, Conservative, and Reconstructionist houses of worship, sermons are in English, and there is no segregation by sex.

At the head of the congregation stands the rabbi, trained in seminary and fully ordained. He (in some cases, she) officiates at marriages and grants divorce decrees in accordance with Jewish law after civil divorce has been granted by the state. Rabbis conduct funerals and generally supervise burial as Jewish law requires. Orthodox rabbis may supervise the slaughtering of animals and validate other aspects of dietary law. Many congregations engage readers, or cantors, who lead most of the service.

Suggestions for further reading:

Eisen, Arnold M. *The Chosen People in America: A Study in Jewish Religious Ideology.* Bloomington: Indiana University Press, 1983.

Handlin, Oscar. *Adventure in Freedom: Three Hundred Years of Jewish Life in America.* New York: McGraw-Hill, 1954.

Idel, Moshe. *Hasidism: Between Ecstasy and Magic.* Albany: SUNY Press, 1995.

Meyer, Michael A. *Response to Modernity: A History of the Reform Movement in Judaism.* New York: Oxford University Press, 1989.

Neusner, Jacob. *An Introduction to Judaism: A Textbook and Reader.* Louisville: Westminster/John Knox, 1991.

Neusner, Jacob. *The Way of Torah: An Introduction to Judaism.* 4th ed. Belmont, Calif.: Wadsworth, 1988.

Rosenthal, Gilbert S. *The Many Faces of Judaism: Orthodox, Conservative, Reconstructionist, and Reform.* Edited by S. Rossel. New York: Behrman House, 1978.

Sklare, Marshall. *Conservative Judaism: An American Religious Movement.* New ed. New York: Schocken, 1972.

Steinberg, Milton. *Basic Judaism.* New York: Harcourt Brace, 1986.

ORTHODOX JUDAISM

ORTHODOX UNION

Founded: 1898
Membership: est. 600,000 in 1,500 synagogues (2000)

Roughly 40% of the synagogues in the U.S. are identifed as Orthodox, but only about 10% of the Jews in America identify themselves as such. Orthodox Judaism was an attempt to maintain traditional European Judaism in opposition to the rise of what would be called Reform Judaism* in the nineteenth century. The Orthodox sought to preserve synagogues from what they viewed as theological corruption and to maintain traditional forms of worship and observance of *Halakah*. This often included preservation of Eastern European customs as well as a strict observance of dietary laws. For the Orthodox, the Torah is binding on all Jews and is not subject to interpretation or change.

The Orthodox Union in America was founded by Dr. Henry Pereira Mendes (1852–1937), a Sephardic leader in New York. He hoped that this union would unify traditionalists, promote the observance of the Torah, and halt Jewish assimilation. Initially the Union focused on protecting Jewish children and immigrants from Protestant missionaries and promoting the strict observance of the Sabbath. Another concern was the difficulty of maintaining the rules of *kashrut* (kosher laws) in the U.S. In 1924 the Orthodox Union created the first non-profit kosher certification program, which now certifies over 200,000 products and supervises over 2,000 corporations with 4,000 certified plants in fifty-six countries. The Orthodox Union also helps American soldiers to follow *kashrut,* even on the battlefield, and educates the public about Jewish dietary restrictions.

The Orthodox view intermarriage and assimilation as threats to the survival of Judaism. The National Conference of Synagogue Youth (NCSY), an outreach ministry for teenagers, stresses Jewish identity and the need to marry within the faith. The NCSY spurred the birth of the North American Teshuva movement as well. Following the social disruptions of the 1960s, there was a revival of interest in traditional Jewish faith and practice among American youth. Many Conservative synagogues moved more toward Orthodox observance. Orthodox Jews have been particularly active in working with Russian Jewry and have been strong supporters of the State of Israel.

For more information: www.ou.org

Headquarters: 11 Broadway, New York, NY 10004-1003

HASIDIC JUDAISM

LUBAVITCHER COMMUNITY

Founded: roots to the 1700s
Membership: est. 165,000 (2000)

Hasidic Jews are often confused with the Orthodox; however, they represent one of the most distinctive types of Judaism. Like the

Amish* among Christians, the Hasidim are so conservative that they generally wear the same style of clothing as their ancestors did in the nineteenth century. By choice they live in segregated communities and clearly define themselves against the dominant culture. They are similar to the Orthodox in their strict observance of *Halakah* and literal approach to the Torah, but theologically and liturgically they are often far removed from Orthodoxy.

Hasidic Judaism developed in Eastern Europe during the early 1700s when groups of pious laypersons began reading the Kabala (medieval Jewish mystical writings) and following the Torah strictly. In doing so they developed a number of controversial practices, such as rocking back and forth during prayer, that set them off from others in the synagogue. The key figure in early Hasidism was Israel b. Eliezar Ba'al Shem Tov (ca. 1700–60), known as the Besht, who would enter into an ecstatic state and be guided by the Spirit of God. The Besht was a charismatic figure who attracted a large following of disciples, for whom he served as an adviser and guide. His visions and revelations soon took on the force of truth among his followers.

In 1780 Jacob Joseph wrote *Toledot Ya'akov Yosef,* a memoir that included many sayings of the Besht. This was the first attempt at any kind of theoretical formulation of Hasidic beliefs. Among these beliefs are that the separation between the creator and the creation is merely an illusion; God is hidden in the creation, but is present in this hiddenness; there is only one God, and God is all, and God is completely in creation; therefore, we are all one with God.

The key to the religious life and to understanding the Torah is to understand and experience the reality of union with God. This mystical idea undergirds all of the life of the Hasidim. Rituals are not meaningless if the mind and heart are properly prepared. The proper attitude for devotion and life is joy rather than melancholy. Melancholy and despair are the great enemies of faith because these emotions deny the reality of God's presence in the world. If God is all, then the faithful must be joyful. Distinctive Hasidic practices, such as dancing in worship, flow from this burning desire for a joyful union with God through celebration of creation.

The key to the spread and development of Hasidism was the Zaddikim, the holy men, who continued to demonstrate the real presence of God in the world through their own experience and activities. These Zaddikim were seen as mediators between God and the community, offering people vicarious fulfillment through their spiritual accomplishments. Now known as Rebbes, these charismatic figures continue to shape Hasidism. The most influential Rebbe in the U.S. was Menachem Schneerson (1902–94), the Lubavitcher Rebbe in New York City. Since Schneerson's death in 1994, there has been a bitter split among the Lubavitcher over whether he was the expected Messiah.

For more information: www.lubavitch.com

Headquarters: 770 Eastern Parkway, Brooklyn, NY 11213.

RECONSTRUCTIONIST JUDAISM

JEWISH RECONSTRUCTIONIST FEDERATION

Founded: 1954
Membership: est. 100,000 in approx. 100 synagogues (2000)

Originating in 1934 under the leadership of Mordecai M. Kaplan (1881–1983) of the Jewish Theological Seminary in New York City, Reconstructionism is a movement indigenous to the United States. Reconstructionism defines Judaism as an evolving religious civilization, and it attempts to assure the physical and spiritual survival of Judaism by demonstrating that a maximum Jewish life can be lived within the setting of a modern democratic state. Viewing Judaism as a civilization, Reconstructionists have strong commitments both to Jewish tradition and to the search for modern meaning.

Reconstructionists accept that Judaism has evolved over the centuries. Rabbinic Judaism is not identical to the Judaism of King David, for instance. However, they do not want to break with the historical process. Instead, "the past has a vote" in determining what the present and the future will be. The whole Jewish heritage, not just the Talmud, is embraced as a resource for building a Jewish civilization in the midst of modern culture. As such, the Zionist cause figures prominently in Reconstruction, but so too does an energetic scholarly program endeavor to give laypersons resources for understanding the Jewish heritage.

41

Theologically, Reconstructionists believe it is the duty of all Jews to question and to study in order to find unique paths to the divine. They believe in a God who inhabits this world and especially the human heart. This God is the source of generosity, sensitivity, and concern for the world.

For more information: www.jrf.org

Headquarters: 7804 Montgomery Ave., Suite 9, Elkins Park, PA 19027

REFORM JUDAISM

UNION OF AMERICAN HEBREW CONGREGATIONS

Founded: 1873
Membership: est. 1,500,000 in approx. 890 synagogues

The earliest roots of Reform Judaism can be traced to the Hashalah movement in Europe during the Enlightenment. In the 1740s Moses Mendelsohn (1729–86) urged his fellow Jews to learn from the secular world and speak the languages around them instead of Hebrew or Yiddish. He translated and published the Scriptures in German and encouraged others to translate the Talmud so that both Jews and Gentiles would be able read and understand them. Those in the Hashalah movement advocated that Jews fully assimilate into their local culture: that they speak, dress, act, and even eat like those around them. This would be the path of emancipation from persecution; Jews would overcome cultural alienation and be able to participate fully in life around them. Some of the more religious in the movement sought to reform Judaism from what they considered an archaic past, thus they are known as Reform Jews.

Rabbi Isaac Mayer Wise (1819–1900) brought the Hashalah movement to the U.S. when he emigrated in the 1840s. His American plan (*Minhag America*) included new liturgies for use in the congregations. The prayers dropped all mention of rebuilding the temple in Jerusalem, for example. Wise attempted to unify Judaism in the U.S. by convoking a Cleveland Conference, where he called for an "American Judaism, free, progressive, enlightened, united, and respected." In 1873

Wise founded Hebrew Union College in Cincinnati, one of the most important Jewish schools in the U.S., and for many years he was a leader in the Union of American Hebrew Congregations.

Since Wise's time, Reform Judaism has continued to understand Judaism in terms of "ethical monotheism," in which the ethical demands of the Torah are vital rather than the ceremonial and dietary aspects. Reform Judaism promotes assimilation into American culture in part as a way to move this nation toward the pursuit of justice and peace.

For more information: www.uahc.org

Headquarters: 6333 Third Ave., New York, NY 10017

CONSERVATIVE JUDAISM

UNITED SYNAGOGUE OF CONSERVATIVE JUDAISM

Founded: 1913
Membership: est. 1,500,000 in 800 synagogues (2000)

More religious Jews identify themselves as Conservative than anything else (more than 40%), and the number of Conservatiave synagogues appears to be on the rise. The basic conviction of Conservative Judaism is that the whole Jewish community should be united in a type of Judaism that is based on the North American experience and adapted to modern living, but still devoted to the Torah and *Halakah*. In other words, Conservative Judaism is willing to make changes in Jewish custom, such as segregated seating for men and women, but strives to observe the requirements of the Torah as closely as possible in a modern setting.

Solomon Schechter (1847–1915), head of the Jewish Theological Seminary in New York and founder of the United Synagogue of Conservative Judaism, provided the Conservative movement with its intellectual and organizational foundation. Education has been a major focus of the Conservative movement. The oldest department of Schechter's United Synagogue is the department of education, which produces and sets standards for textbooks and Jewish school curricula. The United Synagogue congregational religious school system had over one hundred thousand students in 1996. There is also a Solomon Schechter Day School system, a network of sixty-eight schools throughout the continent with a combined enrollment of over seventeen thousand children. Youth programs are designed to help Jewish teens and young adults learn to live as Jews in a Gentile world.

Conservative Judaism emphasizes observance of the Sabbath, Jewish holy days, and *kashrut* ("rules of purity"). Synagogues are encouraged to have schools for children and follow the *Halakah*. Each congregation is free to accept changes in *Halakah* observance recommended by the Committee on Jewish Law and Standards if and when they so decide. Many Conservative rabbis find they have a great deal in common with the Orthodox, while others relate better to the Reformed.

For more information: www.uscj.org

Headquarters: 155 Fifth Ave., New York, NY 10010-6802

MESSIANIC JUDAISM

MESSIANIC JEWISH ALLIANCE OF AMERICA

Founded: 1915
Membership: est. 100,00 in over 200 synagogues

The MJAA is the largest organization for Jews who believe that Yeshua (Jesus of Nazareth) is the messiah and savior of the world. It is primarily a network of synagogues that proclaim faith in Yeshua while maintaining their Jewish identity. Such synagogues are not recognized as Jewish by the main Jewish bodies. The MJAA was founded for three primary purposes: to provide visible testimony to the growing numbers of Jewish people who believe in Yeshua as the messiah and savior; to provide an organization for Jewish and Gentile Christians to work together for Jewish revival; and to introduce the Jewish people to Yeshua.

In addition to the Tanach (the Torah, Prophets, and Writings) of the Old Covenant, the MJAA teaches that the *B'rit Chadasha,* or the New Covenant Scriptures, is the inspired and authoritative Word of God. Messianic Jews believe in one God as declared in the Sh'ma (Deut. 6:4), but they teach that God is Echad (a compound unity) and eternally existent in three forms: Father, Son, and Holy Spirit. They accept the basic teachings of the Apostles' Creed about

Jesus, but they also believe in God's eternal covenant with Abraham, Isaac, and Jacob. Therefore they continue to follow the traditional Jewish calendar and religious observances, as did Yeshua himself.

For more information: www.mjaa.org

Headquarters: P.O. Box 274, Springfield, PA 19064

JEWISH FUNDAMENTALISM

Founded: 1940s
Membership statistics unavailable

"Fundamentalism" is a term borrowed from Protestant Christianity to describe many conservative movements in religion. Unlike other Jewish movements that emphasize strict observance of the traditional Torah, such as Hasidism* and Orthodoxy,* Jewish fundamentalism is closely connected to the reclamation of the Land of Israel and the establishment of the messianic kingdom. As with other fundamentalist movements, Jewish fundamentalists established separate schools and printing presses to promote their vision.

One of the earliest theorists of Jewish fundamentalism was Rabbi Abraham Yitzak Kook (1865–1935), who immigrated to Palestine in 1904 as rabbi for a community of European settlers who were inspired by Theodore Herzl's vision of a Jewish state. Kook was influenced by Jewish Kabalah, and he longed for the completion of Jewish redemption in the messianic kingdom. He rejected the secularism of Zionism and offered instead a mystical/theological vision of Israel restored. The son of Rabbi Abraham Kook, Rabbi Zvi Yehuda Kook, emerged as the leading voice of Jewish fundamentalism in the 1960s and 1970s. Unlike his father, Zvi Kook justified violence against the perceived enemies of the Jews, and he welcomed the Six Days War as a significant event in the expected redemption of Israel.

The failure of the State of Israel to use its military might to reclaim all of the land promised to Abraham led the Kookists to become more extreme. In 1974 the most militant Kookists formed the "Bloc of the Faithful" or Gush Emunim, which quickly became one of the most strident fundamentalist organizations. It began to attract support in the United States, where similar separatist movements were established.

The most visible voice for Jewish fundamentalism in the U.S. was Rabbi Meir Kahane, who had established the Jewish Defense League in response to racial tension between Jews and blacks in New York City. In 1974 Kahane immigrated to Israel, where he became the spokesman for a militant fundamentalism that denied that the "enemies of the Torah" had human rights. The Dome of the Rock was to be destroyed and the temple rebuilt. Until that happens, the messiah can not return. In 1994 a follower of Kahane gunned down twenty-nine Palestinians worshiping in a mosque in Hebron. When Prime Minister Yitzhak Rabin attempted to make peace with the Palestinians, he was assassinated by a former soldier inspired by the teaching of Gush rabbis.

For more information: www.kahane.org

CHRISTIANITY

Christianity is the largest religion in the world today, but it began as a small sect of Judaism two thousand years ago. Around 26 C.E. a Galilean Jew named Jesus of Nazareth was baptized by John the Baptist and began a ministry of healing and teaching. Many of those who followed him believed that he was the long-awaited Jewish messiah, but he did not re-establish the kingdom of David. Instead he was crucified by the Roman governor of Judea. Three days after his death, he appeared to some of his followers, who proclaimed that he was not just a prophet or messiah. They went out into the world with the message that Jesus was the Son of God who had overcome death and had ascended into heaven. Those who had faith in him and followed his way of truth and life would also pass from death into eternal life.

Under the guidance of an early teacher and missionary named Paul, Christians welcomed Gentiles into their fellowship, and slowly a new religion was born. Christians continued to use the Jewish Scriptures, but they added a New Testament that focused on the life, teachings, death, and resurrection of Christ, and what Christ means for the church and the world.

As Christians moved from the synagogue to the church, they adapted many Jewish practices to reflect their new understanding of salvation. Passover became the Eucharist or Holy Communion and was celebrated each Sunday rather than once a year. It retained some of its connection to the story of the Exodus from Egypt, but it was primarily a celebration and remembrance of the sacrifice of Jesus on the cross. His body and blood indicated a new Exodus from sin and death to life with God.

The annual Passover celebration was transformed into a remembrance of the crucifixion on Good Friday and a celebration of the resurrection of Jesus on Easter morning. Baptism replaced circumcision as the sign that one had entered the new covenant, having died to one's old life and risen to a new life in Christ. Gradually, Sunday rather than the Sabbath became the Christian holy day in honor of the resurrection of Christ, but the church followed the basic outline of worship in the synagogue: prayers, psalms, Scripture reading, and a sermon.

As it spread around the world, Christianity was remarkably adept in incorporating beliefs and practices from the traditional ("pagan") religions of the people who converted. Early Christian theologians believed that all truth comes from God; therefore they used the insights of pagan philosophers like Plato to formulate Christian theology. Missionaries and bishops often transformed traditional shrines into Christian churches or shrines. Local religious calendars were adapted to promote belief in Jesus. For instance, the old Roman saturnalia festival in December was transformed into a celebration of Christ's birth, and the Celtic Samhain became a time to remember all the saints who had given their lives in devotion to Christ.

Within a century of Jesus' resurrection, a basic structure of leadership emerged in the church. Some men and women took ascetic vows and lived lives of perpetual prayer and service. Others, called priests, were set aside to be pastors of local congregations. They administered the sacraments and proclaimed the gospel. Deacons assisted priests in acts of service and mercy in the congregation. Bishops were overseers of all the congregations in a region and were responsible for establishing doctrine and discipline. Bishops of major urban centers, such as Alexandria, Antioch, Constantinople, and Rome, were called archbishops or patriarchs.

As the church spread geographically and developed theologically, conflicts and divisions arose. Councils of bishops decided that some theological movements within early Christianity, such as Gnosticism, Montanism, and Arianism, were heretical and forbidden. Modern scholarship is recovering the actual teachings and practice of some of the excluded groups.

Some of the most significant divisions of the early church, though, were primarily the result of growing divisions between the Latin-speaking West, the Greek-speaking East, Coptic-speaking Egypt, and Syriac-speaking Asia Minor. The first official separation of the church took place in the middle of the fifth century. The final break between the Catholic* and Orthodox* churches was formalized in 1054.

The Roman Catholic* Church became the dominant social institution in Western Europe. During the Middle Ages, many zealous reformers established religious orders, such as the Franciscans, that attempted to institutionalize the reformer's vision for the church and world. Some of those who attempted to reform church and society, though, were deemed heretical. Such was the case of the Cathars and the Waldensians.

In the sixteenth century (beginning around 1517), several vigorous reformers, such as Martin Luther and Ulrich Zwingli, called for a more radical reform of the church's doctrine and structure based on Scripture more than tradition. As a result, Christianity in Western Europe was divided between Roman Catholicism and Protestantism. The Protestants, in turn, were divided into four major camps: Lutheran,* Reformed* (see Congregational and Presbyterian churches), Anglican,* and the radicals (see Mennonite and Anabaptist Churches).

The common ideas shared by the Protestants were a rejection of the papacy, the priority of Scripture over tradition, a greater role for laity in the church, and the use of national languages rather than Latin in worship. Otherwise there were great differences among the Protestant churches, and there was almost as much conflict among the Protestant groups as between Catholics and Protestants. Some of the most horrifying European wars were fought in the name of religion following the Reformation. The Peace of Westphalia (1648) brought an end to major military conflict over religion in Europe and established Protestant and Catholic territories. The development of Christianity in different regions of America depended in part on the nationality of the settlers.

Christianity came to America around the same time that the Protestant Reformation was taking place. When Columbus sailed West in 1492, he saw himself as an agent of God destined to bring Christianity to the Indies. Of course, the "Indies" he discovered were a New World rather than Asia. Undeterred, he and his successors established Catholicism in the Spanish and Portuguese colonies. British, Dutch, Swedish, and German settlers in the British colonies established their Protestant churches. Radical Protestant groups, like the Society of Friends, also came to the colonies. Russian Orthodox priests served in California in the 1700s. Each wave of European immigration brought other types of Christian churches. As Christianity adapted to American culture, new forms of Christianity were created.

When one considers the diversity of Christian churches, each with its own forms of worship and doctrinal traditions, it is hard to imagine that they are part of a single religion. How could the sensually rich liturgy of the Orthodox church be related to the silence of an unprogrammed Friends* meeting? How could the Catholic Stations of the Cross be related to a Pentecostal healing service? Yet, in the midst of diversity, confusion, and conflict, the various Christian churches see the Old and New Testaments as authoritative Scripture and proclaim Jesus Christ as Lord. This proclamation of faith in Christ was the basis for the ecumenical movement of the twentieth century.

Suggestions for further reading:

Atwood, Craig D. *Always Reforming: A History of Christianity Since 1300.* Macon, Ga.: Mercer University Press, 2001.

Cameron, Euan. *The European Reformation.* Oxford: Clarendon, 1991.

Gonzalez, Justo L. *The Story of Christianity,* 2 vols. San Francisco: HarperSanFrancisco, 1984.

Hatch, Nathan O. *The Democratization of American Christianity.* New Haven: Yale University Press, 1989.

Irvin, Dale T. and Scott W. Sunquist, *History of the World Christian Movement. Vol. 1: Earliest Christianity to 1453.* Maryknoll, NY: Orbis, 2001.

MacHaffie, Barbara J. *Her Story: Women in Christian Tradition.* Philadelphia: Fortress, 1986.

Malone, Mary T. *Women and Christianity,* 2 vols. Maryknoll, NY: Orbis, 2001.

Marty, Martin E. *Protestantism in the United States: Righteous Empire.* 2nd ed. New York: Scribner, 1986.

Noll, Mark A. *A History of Christianity in the United States and Canada.* Grand Rapids, Mich.: Eerdmans, 1992.

Pelikan, Jaroslav. *Credo: Historical and Theological Guide to Creeds and Confessions of Faith in the Christian Tradition.* New Haven: Yale University Press, 2003.

Walker, Williston, et al. *A History of the Christian Church.* 4th ed. New York: Scribner, 1985.

ORTHODOX AND ORIENTAL ORTHODOX CHURCHES

With more than 200 million members around the world, the Orthodox churches represent one of the three major branches of Christianity (the others being Roman Catholic and Protestant). Though there are over four million Orthodox in the U.S., their churches remain mysterious to most Americans.

Unlike the Roman Catholic Church*, the Orthodox churches (also known as the Eastern churches) do not have a single hierarchical institution. Instead, there are dozens of national bodies, each of which worships in its native language with its own independent (autocephalous) hierarchy. Each Orthodox church thus reflects its own national heritage and ethnic customs in its liturgy. Unlike the Protestant churches, which also demonstrate a wide variety of institutions and forms, most of the Orthodox churches are in communion with one another and hold to the same basic theology based on the ancient creeds of Christianity.

A few of the main Eastern bodies, however, reject the statements of the Council of Chalcedon (451 C.E.), in particular the phrase relating to Jesus Christ being one person in two natures, divine and human. These are known as non-Chalcedonian or Oriental Orthodox Churches. Included among these bodies are the Armenian Church, the Coptic Church, the Ethiopian Church, the Eritrean Church, the Syrian Church of Antioch, and the Syrian Indian Church of South India. A few Orthodox bodies are in communion with the Roman Catholic Church and are known as Uniate* churches.

Orthodox church services are elaborate, ritualistic, and beautiful. Virtually every architectural feature of the sanctuary, every movement of the priest's body, and every word spoken by the worshipers has symbolic value. The liturgy is an ancient drama that celebrates Christ's incarnation, crucifixion, and resurrection. Lighting, clerical vestments and altar adornments, icons, music, and consecrated bread and wine bring the kingdom of God into the present. The word *orthodox* means "true glory" as well as "straight teaching." "Giving glory to God is the purpose of life" is the keynote of this tradition. Praising God, giving God thanks, and receiving God's presence in the sanctified gifts capture the heart of worship. Through worship, and in God-informed relationships and responsibilities, these Christians mean to move toward sanctification. The Christian goal is *theosis,* "perfection" or "deification," living in genuine unity with God in the here and now and for eternity.

History. Western history books will often state that the Orthodox churches of the East separated from the Catholic Church* of the West, but that is not an accurate presentation. The Eastern Orthodox tradition claims direct descent from Christ and the apostles. For centuries, Christianity was primarily Eastern in orientation, with most of the episcopal sees of the early church being in Greece, Turkey, Egypt, and Syria. Greek, not Latin, was the language of the New Testament, early Christian liturgy, and early theology. The ecumenical councils that continue to define the beliefs of most of the world's Christians were held in the East and were attended primarily by Eastern bishops and theologians.

Of the five ancient patriarchal Sees (Rome, Alexandria, Antioch, Constantinople, and Jerusalem), only Rome was in the West. For centuries these five patriarchs, guided by councils of bishops, governed the worldwide Christian church. It is still the practice in the Orthodox churches that no one patriarch is responsible to any other patriarch. The bishops of the two capitals of the Roman Empire after 330, Constantinople and Rome, had the greatest authority, but in 1054 the bishops of Constantinople and Rome mutually excommunicated each other along with their followers, creating a formal breach in Christianity that has only recently begun to heal.

Long before the official schism between East and West, the two churches had already developed certain basic differences. The East was primarily Greek in speech and attitude, while the West was Latin and Roman. The transference of the imperial capital from West to East meant a shifting of the center of political, social, and intellectual influences. The church in the East was integrally related to the Byzantine Empire, and the great cathedral of Hagia Sophia ("Holy Wisdom") in Constantinople was the center of both the church and the empire.

As the Roman Empire decayed in the West and the Germanic tribes began pouring into Italy and Gaul, the bishop of Rome became a symbol of unity and stability for Westerners. When the pope crowned Charlemagne as Holy Roman Emperor in 800, it marked a clear break with the Roman Empire in the East (commonly called the Byzantine Empire). Conflict deepened between the pope at Rome and the patriarch at Constantinople. One major point of controversy was the addition of the words "and the son" (*filioque*) to the Nicene Creed in referring to the procession of the Holy Spirit.

A number of the schisms in the East were both political and theological in nature, the most important of which involved the understanding of the person of Christ. In Syria, some churches embraced the views of Nestorius (b. after 351; d. after 451), who held that there were two separate persons in the incarnate Christ, one divine and one human. In Egypt and Armenia other churches accepted the teaching of Cyril of Alexandria (d. 444), as expressed in the phrase "one Incarnate nature of the Word." Most of the Eastern churches, though, remained in communion with the patriarch of Constantinople.

As the Byzantine Empire expanded to the west and north, Orthodox missionaries, such as the celebrated brothers Cyril (826–69) and Methodius (ca. 815–85), converted the Slavic peoples of Bulgaria, Serbia, and Russia to Christianity. The Divine Liturgy and holy books were translated into Slavic tongues, and monasteries and schools were established throughout Eastern Europe. As these peoples gained political independence, national Orthodox churches were gradually established, the first being the Bulgarian Orthodox Church.

The Orthodox churches were profoundly affected by the dramatic rise and spread of Islam in the seventh century. Three of the ancient patriarchal sees (Antioch, Alexandria, and Jerusalem) quickly came under Muslim control and were effectively separated from Constantinople. Christianity in Muslim countries continued to exist as a minority faith living under severe restrictions. As a result, those churches were unable to grow numerically or exert influence on the surrounding culture. Relations with the Catholic Church in the West were nearly destroyed by the sack of Constantinople in 1204 by Latin crusaders in the Fourth Crusade.

The harshest blow to Orthodoxy came when the Turks captured Constantinople in 1453 and put an end to the Byzantine Empire. Hagia Sophia was converted into a mosque, and the Ecumenical Patriarch was forced to give allegiance to the Muslim rulers. For centuries the Orthodox churches in the Balkans struggled for existence under Turkish rule. During this time, the Russian Orthodox Church rose in power and prestige until Moscow was declared to be "the third Rome." As the Ottoman Empire declined in the 19th century, other Slavic churches asserted their independence from Greek and Russian rule while still remaining in communion with the Ecumenical Patriarch.

The Russian Revolution of 1917 and the spread of Communism to Eastern Europe following the Second World War led the Eastern Orthodox churches in Poland, Finland, Estonia, and Latvia to assert their independence. The Orthodox Church managed to survive Communist rule despite persecution. After World War II, Estonia and Latvia were reintegrated into the Russian Orthodox Church.

Nearly all European and Asiatic bodies of this ancient church have established dioceses in the United States; some are governed by one of the five patriarchates, while others have declared themselves independent and self-governing (autocephalous). In the U.S. today, Albanian, Bulgarian, Greek, Romanian, Russian, Serbian, Ukrainian, Carpatho-Russian, and Syrian churches are under the supervision of bishops of their respective nationalities and usually are related to their respective mother churches in tradition and spirit, if not in administration. The patriarch of Moscow and the patriarch of Alexandria each has jurisdiction over a few parishes. In recent years a number of churches of Protestant origin moved into the Orthodox orbit.

Beliefs and Practices. The Nicene Creed in its original form is central to the Orthodox faith in all its branches. It is recited whenever the Divine Liturgy is celebrated and is the heart of Orthodox theology and mysticism. For the Eastern churches a creed is "an adoring confession of the church engaged in worship;" faith is expressed more fully in liturgy than in a doctrinal statement.

It is the long tradition of the church, not the pronouncements of individual theologians or canon law, that defines what is orthodoxy. This tradition includes the decisions of the seven Ecumenical Councils as well as the tradition of the Divine Liturgy itself. Many of the doctrines and practices of the Roman Catholic and Protestant churches are rejected as inappropriate innovations. For instance, the dogma of the pope as the sole "vicar of Christ on earth" is rejected, together with papal infallibility. Members of Orthodox churches honor the Virgin Mary as *theotokos* ("the bearer of God") but do not subscribe to the dogmas of the immaculate conception and the assumption. They show reverence to the cross, the saints, and nine orders of angels but reject the teaching of the treasury of merits of the saints and the doctrine of indulgences.

Icons (consecrated pictures) of revered persons and events are central to Orthodox devotion, and Protestant iconoclasm or opposition to icons is condemned. Orthodox Christians hold that since God became incarnate in Christ, God's human nature may be depicted in a sacred image. Refusal to venerate an icon is seen as denying the concrete reality of the Incarnation; however, the Orthodox reject three-dimensional statues as being too close to "graven images" forbidden in Scripture.

The mysteries, or what are called sacraments in the Western church, are central in Orthodox life. These are physical items or actions that communicate spiritual reality. The seven that are definitive in the Roman Catholic Church (baptism, confirmation, the Eucharist, penance, extreme unction, holy orders, and matrimony) are important in the Orthodox tradition as well, but there is little disposition to restrict the number of mysteries formally to seven. Other rites have a sacramental character. In fact, for the Orthodox, worship itself is a mystery or sacrament. For some Orthodox theologians and mystics, even creation is a sacrament since creation communicates the presence of God to all people.

The Holy Eucharist, or Communion, is the "mystery of mysteries." It is the chief service on all Sundays and holy days and is treated with great reverence. All Orthodox churches teach that the bread and wine are the body and blood of Christ, but this is not described as transubstantiation. Mysteries cannot be defined by human intellect. Purgatory is denied, but prayers are offered for the dead. It is believed that the dead can and do pray for those on earth. Both faith and works are considered necessary for salvation.

Polity. The government of all Orthodox churches is episcopal and hierarchical to a degree. There is usually a synod of bishops over which an elected archbishop, metropolitan, or patriarch presides. In the U.S., each jurisdiction is incorporated with a church assembly of bishops, clergy, and laity. The three orders of ministry are deacons (who assist in parish work and in administering the sacraments), priests, and bishops. Deacons and priests may be either secular or monastic. Candidates for the diaconate and priesthood may marry before ordination but are forbidden to marry thereafter. Bishops are chosen from members of the monastic communities and, therefore, are under lifelong vows of poverty, chastity, and obedience.

The history of the Orthodox in North America is primarily the story of immigration and ethnic identity. The church was a way for immigrants to keep a connection with their homeland, their language, and their customs. Membership statistics are confusing and often unreliable, however, inasmuch as membership is based on baptismal records rather than communicant status. There are at least 3.5 million Orthodox in the U.S.

After a century or so of "creeping disunity" within U.S. Orthodoxy, during the period of heavy immigration and the formation of various Orthodox communities of faith, there have been movements toward closer cooperation. One such movement was the organization in 1960 of the Standing Conference of Canonical Orthodox Bishops in the Americas, which is composed of nine jurisdictions that represent the majority of the Orthodox in North America. Another was the formation of two pan-Orthodox seminaries.

There are a number of so-called Orthodox churches in the U.S. that are not recognized as canonically "Orthodox." These irregular Eastern churches might be called autogenic, or self-starting, but they cannot properly be called Orthodox, since Orthodox churches must be in canonical relationship with the Patriarch of Constantinople and with one another. These autogenic churches are to be distinguished from the ancient non-Chalcedonian Orthodox Churches, such as the Coptic Church.

Suggestions for further reading:

Constantelos, Demetrios J. *Understanding the Greek Orthodox Church: Its Faith, History and Life.* Brookline, Mass.: Hellenic College Press, 1998.

Erickson, John H. *Orthodox Christians in America.* New York: Oxford University Press, 1999.

Fitzgerald, Thomas E. *The Orthodox Church.* Westport, Conn.: Greenwood, 1999.

Meyendorff, John. *The Orthodox Church: Its Past and Its Role in the World Today.* Crestwood, NY: St. Vladimir's Seminary Press, 1981.

Ware, Kallistos T. *The Orthodox Way.* Crestwood, NY: St. Vladimir's Seminary Press, 1995.

AFRICAN ORTHODOX CHURCH

Founded: 1921
Membership: est. 5,000 (1999)

This body is not in communion with Orthodox churches generally, but it claims to be in apostolic succession through the West Syrian

Church of Antioch. It was established in 1921 by George Alexander McGuire (1866–1934), who was an immigrant to the United States from Antigua. McGuire had served as a priest in the Protestant Episcopal Church but left that body because of racial prejudice. This quest for equality led him to Marcus Garvey's (1887–1940) Universal Negro Improvement Association. Once McGuire founded the African Orthodox Church, Garvey used his periodical, *The Negro World,* to disseminate news about the denomination throughout Africa. The periodical also carried the story of McGuire's consecration by a white bishop named Joseph Rene Vilatte (1854–1929). In 1924 the church was established in South Africa, where it became a potent force among the black population.

The church puts strong emphasis on the apostolic succession and historic sacraments and rituals; it celebrates the seven sacraments of baptism, confirmation, Eucharist, penance, extreme unction, holy orders, and matrimony. Its worship is a blend of Western and Eastern liturgy, creeds, and symbols, though the liturgy is usually Western with a mingling of Anglican,* Greek, and Roman patterns. The common creeds, Athanasian, Nicene, and Apostles', are used. Bishops are in charge of dioceses, or jurisdictions; and groups of dioceses form a province, each led by an archbishop and a primate. The primate, in turn, presides over the provincial synod. At the head stands a primate archbishop metropolitan, general overseer of all the work of the church, which now extends over the U.S. into Canada, Latin America, and South Africa.

For more information: There is no denominational website, but information may be found at http://www.pitts.emory.edu/Archives/text/rg005.html.

Headquarters: 137 Alston St., Cambridge, MA 02139

ALBANIAN ORTHODOX ARCHDIOCESE IN AMERICA

Founded: 1919
Membership: est. 40,000 (1999)

The Albanian Orthodox Archdiocese in America has been part of the Orthodox Church of America* since 1971, but its bishops and clergy continue to minister to the special needs of the Albanian community in the U.S. The history of the church in Albania is complex, filled with a series of persecutions and changes in the religious and political struggles of the Balkans. Christianized by both Latin and Greek missionaries, Albania, as part of Illyricum, had both Latin- and Greek-rite Christians and was at various times under the authority of the patriarch of Constantinople and the pope. When the Turks conquered Albania in 1478–79, half of its people became Muslim. The Christian minority remained divided between Latin-rite Christians in the North and Greek-rite Christians in the South.

When Albania became an independent nation in the twentieth century, its people demanded a liturgy in their language rather than in Greek. They turned to the Russian Orthodox Church for assistance, and in 1908 the Russian Orthodox Church in America set up an Albanian diocese under an Albanian archimandrite-administrator, Father Theophan S. Noli (1880–1965), who translated the liturgy into Albanian.

With the outbreak of the Russian revolution, the ties with the Russian Church were severed, and Noli was consecrated the bishop in 1923 at the Korche Cathedral in Albania as the Archbishop and Metropolitan of Durres. In doing so, he became the first bishop of a completely independent Albanian Archdiocese, a "mother church" that, strangely enough, spread its influence back into Albania. Noli returned home to establish a metropolitan throne with its See in Boston. Because of the official closing of all religious institutions in Albania in 1967, communication between the American church and the Albanian church was not possible until the collapse of communism. Another body, the Albanian Orthodox Diocese of America, was established in 1950 under the authority of the Ecumenical Patriarchate of Constantinople. It has two parishes with about 2,275 members.

For more information: www.orthodoxalbania.org

Archdiocese Office, 523 East Broadway, South Boston, MA 02127

AMERICAN CARPATHO-RUSSIAN ORTHODOX GREEK CATHOLIC CHURCH

Founded: 1938
Membership: 13,650 in 80 parishes (2004)

The Carpatho-Russian people derive their name from the Carpathian mountain region of eastern Europe, where they have resided for centuries. For many years the mother church endured strife between Orthodoxy and Roman Catholicism. Under political pressure in the seventeenth century, it became a Uniate* church, with Eastern rites and customs, but recognized the supremacy of the Roman Catholic pope.

The struggle to separate from Rome and become completely Eastern was transferred to North America when large numbers of members emigrated to the U.S., especially to the coal-mining and industrial areas of the northeast. In 1891 Alexis Toth, a Carpatho-Russian Uniate priest, led his Minneapolis parish back to the Orthodox Church. Along with several other pastors and parishes they were absorbed into the Russian Orthodox Church in the U.S.

In 1938 a new American Carpatho-Russian Orthodox Greek Catholic diocese was established and canonized by Benjamin I, the ecumenical patriarch of Constantinople. Orestes P. Chornock (1883–1977) became its first bishop. Both the diocesan headquarters (Christ the Saviour Cathedral) and Christ the Saviour Seminary are located in Johnstown, Pennsylvania. The diocese maintains a youth camp, a retreat, and a conference center in Mercer, Pennsylvania.

For more information: www.goarch.org (Greek Orthodox Archdiocese website)

Headquarters: 312 Garfield St., Johnston, PA 15906

ANTIOCHIAN ORTHODOX CHRISTIAN ARCHDIOCESE OF NORTH AMERICA

Founded: 1975, with roots to 1895
Membership: est. 380,000 in 230 parishes (2002)

Antioch, in Syria, was one of the first cities to be evangelized by the apostles and in the early church was one of the most important ancient patriarchal Sees. The faithful managed to maintain the existence of the church through centuries of Muslim rule, even adopting Arabic as a liturgical language, but as the Ottomon Empire collapsed in the late nineteenth century, thousands of Antiochene Christians emigrated to North America. Their spiritual needs were first met through the Syro-Arabian Mission of the Russian Orthodox Church

59

(now called the Orthodox Church in America*). In 1895 a Syrian Orthodox Benevolent Society was organized by Antiochian immigrants in New York City, with Dr. Ibrahim Arbeely, a prominent Damascene physician, serving as its first president.

Arbeely convinced Raphael Hawaweeny, a young Damascene clergyman serving as Professor of the Arabic Language at the Orthodox Theological Academy in Kazan, Russia, to come to New York to organize and pastor the first Arabic-speaking parish on the continent. Hawaweeny was consecrated as a bishop in New York in 1904, making him the first Orthodox bishop of any nationality to be consecrated in North America. He crisscrossed the United States and Canada, gathering the scattered immigrants into parish communities. He founded *al-Kalimat* (*The Word*) magazine in 1905 and published many liturgical books in Arabic for use in his parishes, in the Middle East and in immigrant communities around the world.

The mission suffered because of the early death of Hawaweeny in 1915, the disruptions of the First World War, and the Russian Revolution. The Syro-Arabian Mission fell into divisiveness until 1975, when jurisdictional and administrative unity was restored with the merger of the Antiochian Orthodox Christian Archdiocese of New York and the Antiochian Archdiocese of Toledo. The resulting Archdiocese is divided into four chancellories located in New Jersey, Ohio, Kansas, and California. The General Assembly, the largest legislative body of the Archdiocese, consists of all the pastors and representatives of every parish and mission. It meets in convention every other summer.

There are nearly four hundred priests and deacons who minister at the local level. Candidates for ordination complete an undergraduate program and then receive their theological education at either St. Vladimir's Orthodox Theological Seminary in New York or St. John of Damascus Orthodox Theological Academy near Tripoli, Lebanon. Their program is augmented by specialized courses offered annually by the Antiochian House of Studies, held for two weeks at the Heritage and Learning Center in Ligonier, Pennsylvania. Twenty-four established departments and commissions deal with specific needs of the Archdiocese, such as communications, translations, clergy education, and parish development.

A pioneer in the use of the English language in the Orthodox churches, since the 1930s the church has translated and published liturgical and devotional works into English. The Antiochian Village, a 280-acre property located in southwestern Pennsylvania, serves as a retreat center and popular summer camp that attracts children and young adults from throughout North America. The St. John of Damascus Sacred Art Academy is also headquartered at the Village.

For more information: www.antiochian.org

Headquarters: P.O. Box 5238, Englewood, NJ 07631

APOSTOLIC CATHOLIC ASSYRIAN CHURCH OF THE EAST, NORTH AMERICAN DIOCESE

Founded: ca. 50 C.E.
Membership: statistics not available, 14 parishes

This church traces its origins to the apostles Peter, Thaddaeus, Thomas, and Bartholomew. St. Mari is one of the key figures in the founding and spread of this church in the Persian Empire. Missionaries went as far as India and China, but the Mongol invasions of the 13th century decimated the church. The Nicene Creed is central to this church's liturgy and theology. The church insists that Christ had two natures (human and divine) in one person (Nestorianism); therefore it rejects the phrase *Theotokos* or "Mother of God" for the Virgin Mary. Instead, they pray to the "Ever Virgin Blessed Mary Mother of Christ" or *Christokos*. The current Catholicos Patriarch, Mar Dinkha IV, resides in Baghdad, Iraq.

For more information: www.cired.org

Media Contact: 7201 N. Ashland, Chicago, IL 60626.

APOSTOLIC EPISCOPAL CHURCH

Founded: 1980s
Membership: est. 18,000 in 300 parishes (2002)

The Apostolic Episcopal Church is one of the many bodies that separated from the Episcopal Church* because of changes in the 1928 *Book of Common Prayer* and the admission of women to the ordained ministry. Like many of the Continuing Churches,* the Apostolic Episcopal Church moved more toward Eastern Orthodoxy than toward Roman Catholicism because of the Orthodox Church's policy of autocephalous national bodies. In 2000 the AEC signed concordats with several Orthodox bodies in the U.S. and became a Western Rite Orthodox Church under terms first established by the Holy Synod of St. Petersburg in 1905.

Headquarters: 80-46 234 St., Jamaica, NY 11427-2116.

ARMENIAN APOSTOLIC CHURCH, DIOCESE OF AMERICA

Founded: 301 C.E.; came to the U.S. in 1887
Membership: est. 774,000 in 127 parishes (2004)

Armenia is generally recognized as the first nation to become Christian, when Christianity became the state religion in 301. Tradition holds that the apostles Thaddeus and Bartholomew first brought the message of Christ to Armenia. Saint Gregory the Illuminator became the first head of the national church in 314 and was given the title Patriarch Catholicos of All Armenians. A translation of the Scriptures by St. Sahag and St. Mesrob and their students in the early part of the fifth century is accepted as the authoritative Armenian version of the Bible. The translators created an Armenian alphabet in order to give the Armenians the Scriptures in their own language.

The Armenian Church administers seven sacraments: baptism, confirmation or chrismation, eucharist, penance, matrimony, ordination, and extreme unction or order of the sick. Baptism, ordinarily of infants, is administered by immersion. Chrismation (anointing with oil) and communion follow immediately after baptism. The eucharist is offered on Sundays and on special feast days of the church. At the conclusion of the eucharist, fragments of thin unleavened bread, simply blessed, are distributed to those not receiving communion.

The hierarchical organization of the Armenian Church consists of the Catholicos, the supreme head of the church, who resides in the ancient city of Etchmiadzin, Armenia, and the Catholicate of Cilicia, located in Antelias, Lebanon. The two patriarchates are Jerusalem and Constantinople. There are three major orders of clergy, according to the tradition of all ancient churches: deacon, priest, and bishop. Parish priests are ordinarily chosen from among married men, but bishops are chosen from among the celibate clergy. Widowed priests may be promoted to the episcopate. Clergy are trained in seminaries attached to Etchmiadzin, Jerusalem, and Antelias.

One of the most important aspects of the Armenian Church administration is its conciliar system. The administrative, doctrinal, liturgical, and canonical norms are set and approved by a council through a participatory decision-making process. The Council of Bishops (or the Synod) is the highest religious authority in the church.

The Armenian Church has sustained its people throughout a history marked by tragedy. It suffered in the conflict between the Byzantine Empire and Persia and sustained persecutions by the Turks, culminating in the genocide of 1915. Thousands of Armenians escaped to North America before World War I, but the bulk of emigration occurred after the war. The first Armenian Church in the U.S. was established in Worchester, Massachusetts, in 1891. The Armenian Diocese of America was organized in 1898, headed by a primate appointed by the Mother See of Holy Etchmiadzin in Armenia, under whose jurisdiction the diocese functioned.

In 1933 a dispute over matters related to the church in Soviet Armenia led to a split in the church in the United States. One group of churches, the Armenian Apostolic Church of America, chose to remain independent until 1957, when these churches placed themselves under the jurisdiction of the Holy See of Cilicia in Antelias. The other group, the Armenian Church of America, remained within the jurisdiction of the Mother See of Etchmiadzin. Dogma and liturgy were not affected by the division. Deacons, priests, bishops, and archbishops are ordained and elevated by the hierarchical authorities of the respective jurisdictions. The Armenian Church of America has seventy-two churches; the separated Apostolic Church has thirty-six.

The Armenian Church is in communion with the Oriental Orthodox Churches that did not ascribe to the doctrinal statements adopted at the Council of Chalcedon in 451 C.E. It should be noted that the Armenian Church accepts the decisions of the first three ecumenical councils. It affirms the Christological formula of St. Cyril of Alexandria (d. 444): "One is the nature of the divine Word incarnate. The union of Godhead and the manhood are without confusion, without change, and indivisibly." In 1990, the theologians and official

63

representatives of both Eastern and Oriental Orthodox churches agreed in a formal statement that their theological understanding, especially their Christology, is "orthodox." The statement called for unity and communion among the Eastern and Oriental Orthodox churches.

For more information: www. armprelacy.org

Headquarters: 138 E. 39th Street, New York, NY 10016-4885

BULGARIAN EASTERN ORTHODOX CHURCH

Founded: 1938
Membership: est. 70,000 in 23 parishes (1990)

Christianity was introduced to the Bulgar peoples in the ninth century during the reign of Tsar Boris. For centuries, the church struggled for independence from Constantinople, an independence won for brief periods. There was a schism between the Bulgarians and the Ecumenical Patriarch until the end of World War II. Before the outbreak of the Macedonian revolution in 1903, very few Bulgarians emigrated to the U.S. In 1940 there were still only about 60,000 residents. They brought with them memories of the church's long struggle for independence from Constantinople. The first Bulgarian Orthodox Church in the U.S. was built in Madison, Illinois, in 1907. In 1922 the Bulgarian Orthodox Mission of the Holy Synod of Bulgaria began attempts to organize the Bulgars. It established a bishopric in 1938.

Attached directly to the Holy Synod of Bulgaria, the membership of this church is made up of descendants of immigrants from Bulgaria, Macedonia, Thrace, Dobruja, and other parts of the Balkan peninsula. Services are in the Bulgarian and English languages, and doctrine is in accord with that of other Eastern Orthodox churches.

For more information: http://bulch.tripod.com/boc/mainpage.htm

Headquarters: Diocese of the U.S.A., Canada and Australia, 550–A West 50th Street. New York, NY 10019

COPTIC ORTHODOX CHURCH

Founded: 60 C.E., first American diocese founded in 1993
Membership: est. 300,000 in 100 parishes (2002)

The Coptic Church is one of the oldest Christian churches in the world, tracing its origins to the time of the Apostle Mark. The word Coptic refers to both the native people and language of Egypt before the Arab conquest in the seventh century. Alexandria in Egypt was one of the original patriarchal sees, and it produced some of the most significant theologians and bishops of early Christianity. Centuries later the works of Origen, Clement, Athanasius, and Cyril are still studied by Orthodox, Catholic, and Protestant theologians. Egyptian, or Alexandrian, theology was instrumental in the formation of the Nicene Creed recited weekly throughout the Christian world.

The hierarchy of the Egyptian church in Alexandria was primarily Greek, but by the year 500 Christianity had spread to the native peoples up the Nile. Coptic missionaries brought Christianity to Nubia and the Sudan over one thousand years before the great period of Protestant missions to the tribes of Africa. The story of Mary and Joseph's flight into Egypt to escape Pharaoh captured the popular imagination, and an elaborate pilgrimage route developed so worshipers could honor Jesus and the Blessed Virgin. Pagan shrines were converted to Christian worship, and the Copts developed a distinctive liturgical calendar based on the ancient Egyptian calendar.

The greatest contribution of the Egyptian church to Christianity came out of the desert. Two hundred years after Christianity was brought to Egypt, there were a few devout souls who felt that the urban churches were too comfortable with the sensuous culture of the pagan world. One of these was a wealthy man named Anthony who heard Jesus' call to "sell all you possess and give it to the poor." He did so and retreated in the desert to the mountains, where he lived alone in a cave. He is reputed to be the first such monk (from the Greek word for solitary), and his story inspired hundreds of men and women to do likewise. Monasticism and its spirituality gradually spread to the whole Christian world and was the mainstay of Christianity until the Protestant Reformation. The desert monasteries provided much of the stories of saints and miracles that nourish the Coptic faithful today.

The Coptic Church was caught up in the political struggles of the Byzantine Empire in the fifth century, and many of the bishops believed that the Council of Chalcedon was more about imperial politics than theology. The iconography, liturgy, veneration of relics, and theology of the Coptic Church is very similar to other Orthodox churches, but the Coptic church emphasizes the unity of Jesus Christ as God and human.

Despite their similarities, the Egyptian church split between the Greek hierarchy in Alexandria (Greek Orthodox) and the Coptic-speaking church of the people who were persecuted by the Empire. The monastic caves became the centers of the opposition movement. The oppression of the native population was so severe that many people actually supported the Arabic conquerors in the seventh century since they broke the yoke of Constantinople. Initially the Muslim rulers were tolerant of Coptic Christianity, but the church faced many obstacles, including the prohibition of converting Muslims. At times, though, persecution could be severe; the age of martyrs in Coptic Christianity lasted longer than in other churches.

Coptic Christianity came to America with Egyptian immigration in the twentieth century. The American Coptic Church is part of the worldwide network of Copts who continue to worship in the language of their ancestors and honor their saints and martyrs. Like most immigrant churches, the Coptic Church enjoys the freedom of worship and evangelism America offers while it tries to help its people negotiate the permissiveness of American culture. The church in America is closely connected to the worldwide Coptic Church led by Pope Shenouda III, the 117th Pope of Alexandria and the See of St. Mark. There is one monastery in the U.S. Ecumenical dialog with other Catholic and Orthodox churches has helped heal the old theological division over the nature of Christ.

For more information: www.coptic.org; ecucopt.org

Headquarters: P.O. Box 384, Cedar Grove, NJ 07009

GREEK ORTHODOX ARCHDIOCESE OF NORTH AMERICA

Founded: 1922
Membership: 1,954,500 in 555 parishes (1998)

The Greek Orthodox Church is one of the largest Orthodox bodies in the U.S. due to the massive immigration of Greeks to the U.S. between 1890 and 1929. Greece was one of the earliest and most vital centers of Christianity, but the capture of Constantinople by the Turks and the subjugation of the patriarch to Muslim rule was a severe blow to the Greek Orthodox Church. In the nineteenth century, the church in Greece established a Holy Synod independent from (but in communion with) the Ecumenical Patriarch. Orthodox priests were sent to the U.S. either by the Holy Synod of Greece or by the Ecumenical Patriarchate of Constantinople.

In 1864 the first Greek Orthodox Church in the United States was founded in New Orleans, Louisiana. By 1910 there were approximately thirty-five congregations in various parts of the country. A period of confusion existed from 1908 to 1922, during which time the jurisdiction of American churches shifted from the Ecumenical Patriarchate of Constantinople to the Holy Synod of Greece and back again. This was finally resolved with the Founding Tome of 1922, which established the Greek Orthodox Archdiocese of North and South America.

Archbishop Athenagoras Spyrou of Corfu was appointed to head the Greek Church in America in 1931, and under his leadership the church increased to 286 parishes. In 1948, Athenagoras was elected Patriarch of Constantinople and was succeeded by Archbishop Michael Constantinides of Corinth, who was enthroned in the New York Cathedral of the Holy Trinity. Since 1996 Archbishop Spyridon, appointed by Constantinople's Ecumenical Patriarch, has led the Greek Orthodox Archdiocese of North America. He oversees work in nine dioceses, each headed by a bishop. Worship, doctrine, and polity follow historical Orthodox patterns, with the service of worship being the center of congregational life. In the 1980s and '90s the church began attracting Protestants and Catholics, some of whom felt their churches were too accommodating to modern culture, others who were attracted to the artistry and depth of Orthodox worship.

The church supports eighteen parochial schools; nine summer camps; a school for orphans and children from broken homes; Hellenic College and Holy Cross Greek Orthodox School of Theology, both in Brookline, Massachusetts; three homes for teenage boys; and a home for the aged.

For more information: www.goarch.org

Headquarters: 8 East 79th St., New York, NY 10021

MALANKARA ORTHODOX SYRIAN CHURCH and MAR THOMA ORTHODOX SYRIAN CHURCH (INDIAN ORTHODOX)

Founded: in the U.S. 1978; 1988
Membership: est. 42,000 in 125 parishes (1997)

These are the two major bodies of independent Indian Christian churches in the U.S. Both bodies claim descent from Thomas the apostle, who legend says went to India as an evangelist after the resurrection of Christ. The Malankara church was named for a town where Thomas is believed to have arrived in India in 52 C.E. It uses the liturgy, calendar, language, and traditions of the Syrian Orthodox Church.

The church in India is indeed ancient and historically had close ties to the Syriac church in Persia, which was made up of Nestorian refugees from Syria. The ancient Indian churches used Syriac rather than one of the Indian languages in worship. The Persian/Syrian church is often called "Nestorian" because of its adherence to the doctrine attributed to the fifth-century theologian Nestorius of Antioch that a distinction should be made between the divinity and humanity of Christ. This idea contrasted strongly with the Alexandrian theology that Christ is a single person with a single nature ("monophysites"). Symbolic of the difference between the Nestorian churches and the Orthodox churches is that the Nestorians never refer to Mary as "the mother of God." Instead, they call her "mother of Christ." Not all of the Syriac churches were Nestorian, but the missionaries to India were.

In 1599, under the influence of Portuguese missionaries, most Malankara Christians, who lived in southwest India, rejected Nestorianism. Many united with Rome as a Uniate* church. Others, however, turned to the Syrian Orthodox Church for guidance. The Mar Thoma Church was established to preserve the native Indian church from forced Latinization by the Portuguese colonizers of the Malankara region. It is in communion with the Syrian Orthodox Church of Antioch and uses the Orthodox liturgy and calendar. In the nineteenth century, Christianity in India experienced further fracture during the period of British rule as Anglican and Protestant missionaries poured into India.

The American Diocese of the Malankara Syrian Orthodox Church was established in 1978 to serve Indian immigrants to the U.S. and their children. It includes about twelve thousand members in sixty parishes. The Mar Thoma Church is independent and is in communion with the Anglican Church. The American diocese was organized in 1988 to serve members in the immigrant community. It has about twenty-five thousand members in sixty-five parishes.

For more information: www.malankara.org; marthomachurch.org
Headquarters: 1114 Delaware Avenue, Buffalo, NY 14209

ORTHODOX CHURCH IN AMERICA
(RUSSIAN ORTHODOX)

Founded: 1970, with roots to 1794
Membership: est. 900,000 in 725 parishes (2002)

The Orthodox faith came to the New World shortly after the American Revolution by way of Alaska rather than from the East. This was because Alaska was part of Russia until 1867. Eight Russian Orthodox monks entered Alaska in 1794 and established headquarters at Kodiak. Orthodox monks and bishops created an alphabet and printed a grammar in the Aleutian language, translated portions of the Bible, and built a cathedral at Sitka.

Russia itself joined the Orthodox fold with the baptism of Grand Prince Vladimir of Kiev in 988 C.E. The church was ruled at first by metropolitans appointed or approved by the Patriarch of Constantinople, but eventually an independent patriarchate was established in Moscow, which came to be regarded by Slavs as "the Third Rome." Russian Orthodoxy was modeled on the church in Constantinople, but over the centuries it developed distinctive qualities. Russian iconography is greatly valued by art collectors, but is valued even higher by the faithful for whom the saints provide a connection to God and history. As with many churches, Russian Orthodoxy is closely connected with Russian patriotism, and many saints are national heroes. For centuries the Russian Church was governed by a Holy Synod rather than a patriarch.

Early in the nineteenth century, a chapel was built at a Russian trading post near present-day San Francisco. The Episcopal See was transferred to that city in 1872, but moved to New York City in 1905 as waves of immigration brought thousands of Slavs to the eastern states. For many years, the Russian hierarchy in the U.S. cared for immigrants from other Orthodox countries, such as Serbia, Syria, and Bulgaria. Many Eastern-rite Catholics from the old Austro-Hungarian Empire also transferred to the jurisdiction of the Russian Orthodox Church rather than accept the administration of Irish and Italian Catholic bishops.

Bishop Tikhon, who later became Patriarch of the Russian Church, founded the first Russian Orthodox Theological Seminary in Minneapolis, Minnesota, in 1905. Bishop Tikhon also transferred the

69

Episcopal See and its Ecclesiastical Consistory from San Francisco to New York City, where the Russian Orthodox headquarters for this hemisphere are still located. Under Tikhon, St. Nicholas Cathedral in New York was built in 1901. In 1919 the Russian Church in America held its first Sobor, or general council, at Pittsburgh.

The history of the church in the United States has been tied to political events in Russia. In 1917 the Bolsheviks took over the government of Russia and instituted restrictive religious policies. The patriarch and the Holy Synod resisted, but the government found some priests and bishops ready to support the new regime. These officials held an assembly that deposed the patriarch, endorsed communism, and declared itself the governing body of the Russian church.

Calling itself the Renovated, or Living, Church, this group changed the ancient disciplinary rules and instituted liturgical reforms. With the support of Soviet authorities, who hoped thus to divide and weaken the church, that body held control for several years but was never recognized by the great majority of clergy or people. The government considered opposition to the Living Church a civil offense and, on this basis, banished thousands of bishops, clergy, monks, and laypersons to labor camps.

The Living Church faction in Russia, supported by the communist government, sent an emissary to secure control of Russian Orthodox Church property in the U.S.; through action in the civil courts, it gained possession of the cathedral in New York City. In 1924 an assembly of the Diocese of North America, in an attempt to prevent further seizures, declared that, on a temporary basis, it was administratively, legislatively, and jurisdictionally independent of the church in Russia. But this independence was not recognized by the Patriarchate of Moscow or by the Russian Orthodox Church Outside Russia, headquartered at that time in the former Yugoslavia.

In 1927 the Soviet government prevailed upon Metropolitan Sergius, the *locum tenens* (that is, temporary substitute) of the then-vacant patriarchal See, to submit the policy of the church totally to the Soviet regime. Stalin engineered the meeting of a small group of bishops to elect Metropolitan Sergius as Patriarch of Moscow and All Russia. Sergius called upon his people to support the government in the defense of their country during World War II, and this marked a turning point in the Soviet policy toward the church. The Living Church was discarded, and the patriarch's authority was recognized by the state. Many surviving clergy and bishops who had been banished

70

were permitted to return, and gradually the patriarchal administration became again the sole authority in the Orthodox Church of Russia.

A body of Russian émigrés, though, formed the Russian Orthodox Church Outside Russia in 1920 under the authority of the Ecumenical Patriarch. They hold that the Moscow Patriarchate forfeited its right to be considered a true Orthodox church because it adopted a position of submission to the atheistic Soviet regime, not only in regard to politics and external matters but also with respect to its internal policies and affairs. In 1950 this church came to the U.S. It has about 175 parishes dedicated to the traditions of the pre-Soviet Russian church.

Another body to come out of the Russian Orthodox Church is the Holy Eastern Orthodox And Apostolic Church In North America, Inc., founded in 1927. It has about 4,000 members and claims to be the first Orthodox church established in North America specifically to serve English-speaking worshipers. Over the years, the church has adopted more of the Western (Catholic) rite, but remains theologically in the Eastern tradition. It is found in twelve states and has one religious order, the Society of St. Basil.

Despite the conflicts in the church in Russia, the main body of believers in the U.S. maintained their institutional life and worked to bring other Slavic peoples together into a vibrant Orthodox Church. On May 18, 1970, a delegation of hierarchs, clergy, and laity of the Russian Orthodox Metropolia in America, headed by Bishop Theodosius, went to Moscow to receive the Thomos of Authocephaly, the document of independence, from the head of the Russian Orthodox Church. Since that time, the Orthodox Church in America has been independent.

Relations between the Orthodox in the U.S. and Russia have improved greatly since the collapse of the Soviet Union and restoration of the authority of the church in Russia to govern its own affairs and doctrine. In recognition of this, one of the most venerated Russian icons, which had been smuggled to the U.S. for safe-keeping during the Soviet era, was returned to St. Petersburg in 2004. Throngs of the faithful greeted the icon as it made its procession through Russia before being enthroned in the cathedral.

From administrative offices in New York City, the primate of the Orthodox Church in America oversees the work of eleven dioceses, which are in turn headed by bishops. The primate and bishops make up the Holy Synod of Bishops, which is the highest decision-making body in the church. Church ministry units include education and community life ministries, mission and stewardship ministries, pastoral life ministries, witness and communication ministries, and church order ministries. The church administers three theological seminaries: St. Tikhon's in Pennsylvania, St. Vladimir's in New York, and St. Herman's in Alaska. The church also operates several monasteries throughout the U.S.

For more information: www.oca.org

Headquarters: P.O. Box 675, Syosset, NY 11701-0675

ROMANIAN ORTHODOX EPISCOPATE OF AMERICA

> Founded: 1929
> Membership: est. 25,000 in 55 parishes (2000)

Christianity came to Romania in the fourth century. Originally Western and Latin in orientation, the church there gradually came under the authority of Constantinople and adopted Greek liturgical practices and customs. In 1859 the church declared itself independent of Constantinople as a national church, a move that was officially acknowledged twenty-five years later. The church in the U.S. was organized at a congress convened in Detroit, Michigan, by clergy and lay representatives of Romanian Orthodox parishes in the U.S. and Canada. It remained under the canonical jurisdiction of the Romanian Orthodox Patriarchate in Bucharest until political conditions forced its separation; it is now a diocese under the autocephalous Orthodox Church in America.* The archbishop is a member of the Holy Synod of the Orthodox Church in America, and the diocese is recognized as an administratively self-governing body.

For more information: www.oca.org

Headquarters: 19959 Riopelle St., Detroit, MI 48203

SERBIAN ORTHODOX CHURCH

> Founded: 1921
> Membership: 65,000 in 140 parishes (1998)

Saints Cyril (826–69) and Methodius (815–85) were sent out by the Patriarch in Constantinople to strengthen and spread Christianity

72

among the Slavic peoples. One of their great achievements was creating the first Slavic alphabet, which they used to translate the Orthodox liturgy and the Gospels into the old Slavonic language. Most famous for their work in Moravia (the Czech Republic) and Kiev, they were also instrumental in establishing Christianity among the Serbian people.

From the seventh century until the thirteenth, the church in Serbia was under the jurisdiction of the Patriarchate of Constantinople. It became the independent National Serbian Church in 1219 during the Western occupation of Constantinople. The church made notable contributions to art and architecture during the glory days of the medieval Serbian empire until the defeat to the Turks at Kosovo in 1389. The Ottoman Turks governed their Christian subjects in part through church officials, most notably the Ecumenical Patriarch in Constantinople (now Istanbul); therefore the Serbian Church, like other Orthodox churches, became a symbol of national identity as well as religious faith. It played an important part in the Serbian struggle for independence, which was won in the nineteenth century. In 1879 the church also achieved independence from the Patriarch of Constantinople following the freedom of the nation from Turkish control.

Through the close of World War I, the ecclesiastical and political situation in the Balkans was turbulent and complicated. Attempts were made to unite several Orthodox groups into one church. The fruit of the effort came in 1920 when the union of five autonomous bodies was proclaimed. Metropolitan Dimitriji of Belgrade was appointed patriarch, uniting in himself the historic titles of Archbishop of Ipek, Metropolitan of Belgrade and Karlovci, and Patriarch of Serbs.

Serbian immigrants came to the U.S. more for political than economic reasons and began arriving in large numbers around 1890. They worshiped at first in Russian churches, accepting the ministrations of Russian priests and the supervision of Russian bishops. The Serbian Patriarchate of Yugoslavia approved the organization of the Diocese of the United States and Canada in 1921, and in 1926, with thirty-five Serbian churches making up the American Diocese, Archimandrite Mardary Uskokovich was consecrated by Patriarch Dimitriji of Serbia as the first bishop of the Serbian Orthodox Church of America.

Today the Serbian Eastern Orthodox Church has two dioceses in

73

North America: the New Gracanica Metropolinate Diocese of America and Canada, based in Libertyville, Illinois; and the Diocese of Western America, based in Alhambra, California. The cathedral of the Serbian Church, built and opened in 1945, is located in New York City.

The extended conflict in the Balkans during the 1990s brought great distress to Serbs living in North America. The Serbian Eastern Orthodox Church played an important role in conveying information to Serbs in the U.S. and Canada and in offering them spiritual and psychological support. It also sought to present a comprehensive picture of Serbian life and culture to the American public.

For more information: www.serbianorthodoxchurch.org

Headquarters: St. Sava Monastery, P.O. Box 519, Libertyville, IL 60048

SYRIAN ORTHODOX CHURCH OF ANTIOCH (ARCHDIOCESES IN THE U.S.A. AND CANADA)

Founded: 50 C.E., American Archdiocese est. 1957
Membership: est. 32,500 in 32 parishes (2004)

The Syrian Orthodox Church dates back to the apostolic age. It was in Antioch that the followers of Jesus were first called Christian, and tradition holds that Peter established the first patriarchate in Antioch. The Syrian Orthodox use the ancient liturgy of St. Mark in worship. The Syriac Scripture is one of the oldest translations of the Bible and continues to be vital for Syrian Christianity. The Syrian Orthodox Church continues to have its patriarchal See in Damascus. The Syrian Orthodox use a number of ancient liturgies in worship, the principal being that of St. James. The official liturgical language remains classical Syriac.

Christianity in Syria was divided during the Nestorian controversy. The followers of Nestorius, who taught that there were two separate persons in the incarnate Christ, one divine and one human, were persecuted and found refuge in Persia. The Syrian Orthodox Church has always held to the one-nature position of St. Cyril of Alexandria and professes the faith of the first three ecumenical councils. When the Council of Chalcedon adopted a formula that seemed to endorse Nestorius's ideas, the Syrian Orthodox refused to comply

74

with the Patriarch of Constantinople. The Syrian Orthodox experienced persecution under the Byzantine Empire, but found a degree of toleration under Muslim rule until the Mongol invasions in the thirteenth century.

Syrians were few in number in the U.S. until the turn of the twentieth century. Syrian Orthodox silk weavers from Diyarbakir, Turkey, settled in New Jersey, a major area of the silk industry. Families from Harput, Turkey, were drawn to Massachusetts. The first priest, the Very Rev. Hanna Koorie, arrived in 1907; their first patriarchal vicar, Archbishop Mar Athanasius Y. Samuel, was appointed on May 13, 1952. On November 15, 1957, Patriarch Ignatius Yacoub III set his seal upon the document officially establishing the Archdiocese of the Syrian Orthodox Church in the United States and Canada. The next year, a cathedral in the name of St. Mark was consecrated in Hackensack, New Jersey. It was relocated in 1994 to a new complex in Teaneck, New Jersey.

From the 1960s through the 1980s, new Syrian Orthodox parishes were established throughout North America. Following the death of Archbishop Samuel in 1995, the Holy Synod of the Syrian Orthodox Church of Antioch divided the North American Archdiocese into three separate Patriarchal Vicariates: the Syrian Orthodox Archdiocese for the Eastern United States under His Eminence Mor Cyril Aphrem Karim, the Syrian Orthodox Archdiocese of Los Angeles and Environs under His Eminence Mor Clemis Eugene Kaplan, and the Syrian Orthodox Archdiocese of Canada under His Eminence Mor Timotheos Aphrem Aboodi.

For more information: www.syrianorthodoxchurch.org

Headquarters: Archdiocese for Eastern U.S.A., 260 Elm Ave., Teaneck, NJ 07666

UKRAINIAN ORTHODOX CHURCH OF THE U.S.A.

Founded: 1924
Membership: est. 13,000 in 115 parishes (2000)

Around the year 862, the first Orthodox Christian community was founded on the outskirts of Kyyiv (Kiev), during the reign of two princes, Askold and Dyr. Instrumental in making Orthodox Christianity known in Rus-Ukraine was the Kyyivian Princess Olha, baptized in 975, grandmother of St. Volodymyr (Vladimir) the Great. After considerable reflection and investigation, Volodymyr (baptismal name Basil) proclaimed Orthodox Christianity the official faith of his kingdom of Rus-Ukraine in 988. Thus the introduction of Christianity to Russia came through the Ukraine.

In 1686 the Ukrainian church was forced to submit to the Patriarchate of Moscow, but after the 1917 Bolshevik revolution, the Ukrainian Orthodox Church sundered jurisdictional ties with Moscow and declared autocephaly (independence) in 1921. The June 5, 1990, Sobor (council) of the Ukrainian Autocephalous Orthodox Church in newly independent Ukraine established its own patriarchate and elected as its first patriarch Metropolitan Mstyslav, at that time Primate of the Ukrainian Orthodox Church of the U.S.A.

The Ukrainian Orthodox Church of the U.S.A. was established in 1924, when its first bishop, Metropolitan Ioan (John) Teodorovych arrived from the Ukraine. He served as leader of the church until his death in 1971. He was followed as Metropolitan by Mstyslav, who served from 1971 until his death in 1993 at age 95. In 1996 the church united with the former Ukrainian Orthodox Church of America.

The church has congregations in twenty-five states; heaviest concentration is in the New York-New Jersey-Pennsylvania area. The church maintains St. Andrew Center, a Ukrainian cultural center, in South Bound Brook, New Jersey. The center is home to St. Andrew Memorial Church, a monument to Ukrainian Cossak Baroque architecture, and to St. Sophia Seminary.

For more information: www.uocofusa.org

Headquarters: Metropolia Center, 135 Davidson Ave., Somerset, NJ 08873

CATHOLIC CHURCHES

Christians in many different churches profess their faith in "the one, holy, catholic church" using the words of the Apostles' Creed. "Catholic" in this sense does not necessarily refer to a particular religious institution but to the idea of the universality of the church. The Catholic Church is the church that exists around the world and through the ages. Obviously, though, religious institutions will have differing understandings about the institutional expression of that catholicity. In this section are included those bodies that hold most dearly to a view of the church that is universal in time and space. Although for most of its cultural and political history the U.S. has been dominated by Protestants, it is important to remember that Roman Catholicism came to the New World with Christopher Columbus. Today, the Roman Catholic Church is by far the largest religious organization in America.

Catholic churches see themselves in unbroken continuity with the institutional expression of Christian faith in the West since the days of the apostles. They differ markedly from Restorationist bodies (see CHRISTIAN CHURCHES), for example, which view most of Western history as a decline and fall of the church and thus sought to restore the New Testament church. Though there are thousands of Protestant denominations, it is important to remember that most of the world's Christians are in the Roman Catholic Church.

For Catholics, the Holy Spirit continued to work through historical development in order to bring the faith to its richest and fullest expression. In particular, the writings of the church Fathers (e.g., Jerome [c. 345–c. 420] and Augustine [354–430]) instruct the faithful in how to understand the Scripture and live a Christian life. It was during the Patristic Age (the time from the death of the apostles to the close of the eighth century) that much Catholic doctrine, polity, and devotion were established.

Catholic History: The history of the Catholic Church for a thousand years is basically the history of Christianity. There is not space in this volume to give a full account of that history, but it should be noted that during the first five centuries of Christianity there were numerous struggles over the nature of Christian doctrine and ecclesiastical authority. Gradually the lines of orthodoxy were established through the authority of creeds, especially the Nicene Creed, and the episcopacy (bishops, archbishops, and patriarchs). During this process of development there were not fundamental divisions between Eastern and Western Christianity.

The East and the West did develop some distinctive liturgical and administrative practices, however, due in part to the greater sophistication of Byzantine (Eastern) culture. Most important, the Eastern bishops and theologians tended to define the church in terms of Orthodox belief and practice (see ORTHODOX AND ORIENTAL ORTHODOX CHURCHES), while in the West institutional allegiance became paramount, particularly during the rising social chaos of the early Middle Ages.

The church in the West gained secular authority and power when it emerged as the only body strong enough to provide government after the barbarian onslaught beginning with the sack of Rome in 410 C.E. Ravaged first by Goths, Vandals, and Franks, then by Saxons, Danes, Alemanni, Lombards, and Burgundians, Western Europe found its only steadying hand in the institutional church. The church in the West was seen as a unifying force amidst the chaos of society, and thus the word *catholic* ("universal") was increasingly applied to those who were loyal to the bishop of Rome.

The first mention of the term catholic was made by Ignatius of Antioch about 110–115 C.E., but it was Augustine in the fifth century who provided the theological and philosophical structure that gave the papacy its justification and defense. The general consensus in Western Christianity was that there should be a single ecclesiastical institution with a single head who served as Christ's representative in the church. The bishop of Rome was seen as the Vicar of Christ.

Until 1054 the bishop of Rome and the bishop of Constantinople served as the heads of the Western and Eastern churches, respectively, without one asserting absolute authority over the other, but in that year each excommunicated the other. By the time the Fourth Crusade conquered Constantinople instead of Jerusalem in 1204, the break between East and West was complete. The church in the East continued to suffer decline, especially after the final conquest of Constantinople by the Turks (see ORTHODOX AND ORIENTAL ORTHODOX CHURCHES).

The Roman Catholic Church was the most significant force in Western society for most of the Middle Ages. It preserved and spread Christianity during the days of barbarian invasion; preserved and spread classical education through monasteries, convents, cathedral schools, and universities; stabilized feudal society; promoted architectural and artistic achievements; and established the basis for the Western legal system.

Schisms, heresies, and divisions began appearing in the late Middle Ages, but it was the Protestant Reformation, ignited by Martin Luther (1483–1546), that splintered Western Christianity. Roman Catholic scholars acknowledge that there were corrupt individuals within the church and that reform was necessary. Indeed, reform was underway even before the Reformation. Erasmus

(1469–1536), Thomas More (d. 1536), Savonarola (1452–98), and others wrote and preached against the corruption and worldliness of leaders and laypeople, but they tried to stay in the church. Roman Catholic historians and theologians recognize that these reformers had a point, but the church asserts that while priests and bishops may err or be corrupt, the one true church cannot err.

In some ways, the Reformation encouraged the Roman Catholic Church to reform and reorganize itself. Indeed, some historians, Catholic and Protestant alike, would date the founding of the Roman Catholic Church as a self-conscious and distinctive religious body to the great Council of Trent (1545–63), when many Catholic doctrines were officially defined for the first time and where the current ecclesiastical structure was codified. The Tridentine (or post Council of Trent) church was in many ways a stronger and more effective institution than the Renaissance church. The newly established Society of Jesus (Jesuits) led the way in winning back areas lost to Protestantism and, along with the Franciscans, in courageously bringing Christianity to the recently discovered lands east and west of Europe.

Having reformed the papacy of many of the abuses that had fueled the Reformation, the Tridentine church increasingly looked to the papacy as the guarantor of Catholic unity and continuity. As the Enlightenment took hold in Europe in the eighteenth century and revolutions convulsed the European kingdoms in the nineteenth, Catholic bishops and theologians held up the Roman pontiff as the symbol of stability, authority, and order in church and society.

This led to the declaration of papal infallibility by the First Vatican Council in 1870, a move that inspired a number of Catholics, calling themselves Old Catholics,* to separate from the Roman Catholic Church. These churches, which seek to be true to the historic Catholic Church without endorsing papal supremacy, are discussed in this section. Also, within the nineteenth–century Anglican* church, the Oxford Movement sought to restore the "High Church" ideals of the seventeenth century to the Church of England. This movement stressed the idea that the Church of England was part of the Catholic rather than the Protestant tradition. This lead to a variety of small Anglo-Catholic bodies.

Beliefs and Practices. The faith and doctrine of the Roman Catholic Church are founded upon what the First Vatican Council referred to as "that deposit of faith given to it by Christ and through his apostles, sustained by the Bible and by tradition." Thus, like other Catholic and Orthodox bodies, the church accepts the decisions of the first seven ecumenical councils; however, for Roman Catholics, the later councils of the Western church, such as the Fourth Lateran Council (1215), are also authoritative.

According to Catholic teaching, these councils, down to the Second Vatican Council, clarify and enrich without changing the "deposit of faith," and they become part of the apostolic tradition. The church also accepts the Apostles' Creed, the Nicene-Constantinople Creed, the Athanasian Creed, and the Creed of Pius IV, also called the Creedal Statement of the Council of Trent. These creeds set forth many doctrines common to most Christian bodies, such as the Trinity and the full humanity and divinity of Christ.

The creedal statements also define a number of beliefs and practices that are more distinctively Catholic. Like the Orthodox, Roman Catholics stress the sacraments more than do most Protestants; the sacraments are a visible means of receiving God's grace and are thus holy. For Catholics there are seven sacraments:

(1) Baptism, necessary for membership in the church, is administered to infants and to adults by pouring or immersion. Anointing with oil (the holy chrism) in the form of a cross follows baptism.

(2) Confirmation is by the laying on of hands, ordinarily by a bishop; but today priests also may confirm if necessary.

(3) The Eucharist, or Holy Communion, is the central act of Catholic devotion. The laity may receive the Eucharist in the forms of bread and wine. This is not a mere sign or ritual for believers. The body and blood of Christ are considered actually present in the eucharistic elements so that the worshiper communes spiritually and physically with the Savior.

(4) Through the sacrament of reconciliation (formerly called penance), post-baptismal sins are forgiven.

(5) Anointing of the sick is for the seriously ill, the injured, or the aged.

(6) The sacrament of holy orders is for the ordination of deacons, priests, and bishops.

(7) Marriage is a sacrament that "cannot be dissolved by any human power"; this rules out remarriage after divorce. However, improper marriages may be annulled.

Members are required to attend Mass on Sundays and on obligatory holy days. They should also fast and abstain on certain appointed days, confess at least once a year, and receive the Holy Eucharist during the Easter season. In addition, laity are expected to contribute to the support of the church, and to strictly observe the marriage regulations of the church.

The Roman Catholic liturgical calendar is more elaborate than that of Protestant churches, with days to remember and venerate hundreds of heroes of the faith, known as saints. Of particular importance in Roman Catholic devotion in the United States and around the world is Mary, the mother of Christ, who serves as an intercessor for the faithful.

The central act of worship is the Mass. Its two principal parts are the liturgy of the Word and the liturgy of the Eucharist. Until 1963 Latin was the only appropriate liturgical language. Now the entire Mass is recited in the vernacular by both priest and people. Many Catholics also participate in devotions such as benediction, the rosary (a cyle of prayers usually counted on a string of beads), stations of the cross (prayers occasioned by depictions of Christ's journey from Pilate's house to the tomb), and novenas (a period of nine days of public or private devotion).

Religious Orders: At least since the fourth century, religious orders have been an integral part of Catholicism. *The Official Catholic Directory 2000* lists a total of 137 religious orders for men and 441 for women. These orders differ widely in their work. Some are "contemplative," the members remaining in monasteries or cloistered convents. Those in active or mixed religious orders engage in teaching, caring for the sick, missionary work, writing, or social work. Brothers and sisters are required to take vows of poverty, chastity, and obedience but are not ordained.

Originally monks or nuns were individuals who embraced an ascetic lifestyle of poverty and celibacy as a way to share in the witness of the martyrs who died for the faith. Voluntary asceticism was viewed as a way to "take up the cross" and follow Christ. Over time more organization and discipline were provided for those who chose to serve Christ fully instead of serving family or personal ambitions. In the sixth century, Benedict of Nursia established a monastery on his estate of Monte Cassino in Italy. His rule for the men there became the basis for all Western monasticism, male and female. Among the key features of his rule were the vow of obedience to the abbot (head of the monastery) in addition to vows of poverty and chastity; moderation of ascetic excess; and participation in physical labor in addition to prayer.

Through the centuries other religious orders were established, some in an attempt to reform perceived abuses in an older order, others in response to some unmet need in the church and society. Among the most important of these orders were the Cistercians and the Carthusians, established in the twelfth century in protest against the luxury and laxity of many Benedictine houses.

With the rapid urbanization of Europe in the late Middle Ages, the mendicant orders were established to reach out to secular society. The Franciscans embraced a radical devotion to poverty and initially lived by begging. The Dominicans also stressed poverty, but they focused their efforts on preaching, especially in areas where heresy was strong. Known as friars, rather than monks, members of these orders quickly established a strong presence in the burgeoning universities of the Middle Ages. There are now 235 Roman Catholic colleges and universities in the U.S., including Notre Dame, Fordham, Georgetown, Boston College, St. Louis University, Marquette, Loyola, and Villanova, most of them closely connected with various religious orders.

Numerous orders were established during the Reformation in order to reform the Roman Catholic Church internally and to respond to the Protestant challenge externally. Chief among them was the Society of Jesus (Jesuits). Today, many priests are also members of a religious order. Parishes in the U.S. are often under the charge of a particular order, such as the Franciscans.

Religious orders have provided an important focus of ministry for women in the Roman Catholic Church for more than 1,800 years. Some of the male orders have branches for women, but in general women have established their own institutions. Among them are the Carmelites, who produced the great mystic Teresa of Avila (1515–82); the Ursulines, who embraced a mission of educating young women; and the Sisters of Mercy, founded by Mother Teresa of Calcutta (1910–97). In the U.S., women religious have been the backbone of the extensive Roman Catholic parochial school system. In the 1990s there were some 7,000 parochial and private schools in this country with about two million students, including over 1,300 Roman Catholic high schools.

Women religious have also been vital in staffing Catholic hospitals and establishing countless charitable institutions. It is indicative of the work of Roman Catholic women that the first American officially to be declared a saint of the church was Elizabeth Seton (1774–1821), noted for her sacrificial role in alleviating social misery. The National Conference on Catholic Charities helps to coordinate charity and welfare work on state and national levels; work is also conducted by several religious orders whose members devote full time to the relief of the poor in homes or institutions, and many dioceses have bureaus of charity.

The Society of St. Vincent de Paul is perhaps the largest and most effective charitable organization. But there are many others (particularly women's orders, such as Little Sisters of the Poor, Sisters of Charity, Daughters of Charity of the Society of St. Vincent de Paul, and Sisters of Mercy) that are active among the poor in Catholic hospitals, orphanages, and homes for the aged. The church operates 1,414 homes for the aged and 149 orphanages. More than seventy-seven million patients are treated annually in 593 general and special hospitals and 557 health-care centers. One of every three beds in the nation's private hospitals is provided by the Catholic hospital system.

Besides religious orders and congregations, Catholics may join secular institutions whose members also observe poverty, chastity, and obedience but do not wear distinctive garb or live together in a community. Before receiving approval as secular institutes engaged in apostolic work, these groups may operate as approved "pious unions." Some of the prominent leaders of the American labor movement and other advocates for social justice were Catholic. Among them were Dorothy Day, Thomas Merton, and Daniel Berrigen. Catholic bishops have issued a number of important statements calling for great attention to social justice in America.

Catholicism in America: Missionaries came with Coronado and other early Spanish explorers to the southern and western regions of what would become the United States. The first permanent Catholic parish was established at St. Augustine, Florida, in 1565, half a century before the first Protestant baptism in the Americas. The intrepid French explorers, voyageurs, and colonizers, such as Cartier, Jolliet, and Marquette, who live in North American lore, were Roman Catholics. They were generally accompanied by missionaries or were missionaries themselves. New France became a vicariate apostolic in 1658 with Bishop Laval at its head. The See of Quebec (1675) had spiritual jurisdiction over the vast French provinces in North America, reaching down the valley of the Mississippi to Louisiana.

In 1634 Roman Catholics from England founded Maryland in part as a refuge for Catholics during the turmoil of the English Civil War and Puritan Commonwealth. Catholic activity in the English colonies was restricted by law, however, even in Maryland, until after the American Revolution. In 1763 there were fewer than twenty-five thousand Roman Catholics in a colonial population of 2.2 million, and they were under the jurisdiction of the vicar apostolic of London. Even so, among the signatures on the Articles of Confederation, the Declaration of Independence, and the Constitution are found those of three Catholics: Thomas Fitzsimmons (1741–1811), Charles Carroll (1737–1832), and Daniel Carroll (1730–96). Religious equality became law with the adoption of the Constitution in 1787.

The status of the Roman Catholic Church in the new nation was unclear until the Reverend John Carroll (1735–1815) of Baltimore, elder brother of Daniel Carroll, was named Superior, or perfect apostolic, of the church in the new United States. In 1800, he was the head of some 150,000 Roman Catholics. By 1890 that number had grown to 6,231,417, primarily due to the flood of emigration from the Catholic countries of Europe.

Catholics faced a number of unique problems in the U.S. There is only one Roman Catholic Church worldwide, with a single head, unlike most Protestant churches, which have separate national organizations. For example, while there is an Anglican communion worldwide, it is made up of largely independent Anglican churches in the various former British colonies. Episcopalians* in the U.S. are not under the direct authority of the Archbishop of Canterbury the way Roman Catholic bishops are under the authority of the pope. Thus there has been tension in the Roman Catholic Church over the issue of Americanization: How much independence could the American bishops exert while still remaining obedient to Rome?

This was a particularly touchy problem following the First Vatican Council (1869–70), when the European bishops rejected a number of ideas, such as democratic government, that were at the core of American values. James Gibbons (1834–1921), the archbishop of Baltimore and primate of the Catholic Church in America, guided the church through these difficult issues and gained permission for Catholics in the U.S. to participate fully in American political and social life while remaining loyal to the Roman church. Ultimately, the Second Vatican Council (1962–65) approved of many proposals long advocated by American bishops.

Vatican II and Beyond, Pope John XXIII (pope 1958-1963) summoned all the bishops of the church to the twenty-first ecumenical council, which met at the Vatican in Rome. Following John's death, Pope Paul VI reconvened the council, which made the most radical changes to Catholic life in centuries. Vatican II and the papacy approved the use of the vernacular in the Mass, encouraged modern methods of biblical study and interpretation, promoted more active involvement of the laity in the life of the parish, placed the church on the side of the poor in Catholic countries, and allowed Roman Catholics to participate in ecumenical and interfaith dialogue.

Before Vatican II, Catholics had been forbidden to attend meetings of the World Council of Churches; now Catholic observers attend council sessions, and bishops of the church have entered into theological dialogue with several larger Protestant denominations. Since then, the church has been rebuilding bridges to the Orthodox* churches and has even exonerated Martin Luther of heresy. John Paul II, who was pope from 1979–2005, even made dramatic steps toward greater friendship with Judaism and Islam. Such changes alienated some conservative Catholics, however, leading to the formation of organizations dedicated to preserving pre-Vatican II Catholicism, especially the Latin Mass.

In 1968 Pope Paul VI reaffirmed the official church position against any form of artificial birth control in the encyclical *Humanae Vitae*. Many theologians, priests, and laity protested this strict interpretation of sexuality, but the bishops of many industrialized nations, such as France, Canada, Belgium, Holland, Switzerland, Austria, and West Germany, interpreted the papal position in the light of freedom of the individual conscience. Dissension has been a common feature in contemporary Catholic life in the U.S., and many Catholics make their own judgments on birth control, abortion, the role of women in the church, and the official positions of the church on political and economic matters. A sex-abuse scandal involving many priests rocked the American Catholic Church early in this century. The evidence of ecclesiastical misconduct on the part of bishops has encouraged further dissent in the church and may lead to further fractures.

John Paul II, from Poland, was the first non-Italian pope since the 1520s. With respect to human rights, democracy, and inter-religious dialogue, he was one of the most progressive leaders of any church. He was a true internationalist in itinerary and in linguistic skills and a beloved figure around the world. He was also a firm traditionalist in matters of doctrine and practice, especially on family and gender issues. During his long pontificate, the church shifted back toward a more patriarchal and authoritative church structure. For instance, he ruled out clerical marriage and the ordination of women.

At the time of his death in April 2005, John Paul II was widely acclaimed as one of the greatest popes of the Catholic Church and a beacon of hope to millions suffering oppression around the world. His legacy included efforts to amend for Christian sins against Jews, Muslims and other victims of church-sanctioned violence through the centuries. Cardinal Joseph Ratzinger of Germany, one of John Paul's closest advisors, was quickly elected as the new pope, Benedict XVI. As head of the Congregation of Doctrine of the Faith, Ratzinger distinguished himself as an opponent of modernism and liberalism in the American church. Many Catholics expect him, like previous holders of the name Benedict, to chart a strict and disciplined course for the church.

An issue facing the church world-wide, including in the U.S., is the effect of Protestant movements on Catholicism. For instance, the pentecostal movement began making inroads in Catholic parishes in the 1970s, and now the number of "Spirit-filled" Catholics—that is, those who believe in and claim charismatic gifts, such as speaking in tongues, healing, interpretation, and prophecy—is well over three hundred thousand. Many more have had some measure of contact with what is broadly called charismatic Catholicism. Politically conservative but liturgically innovative, it is not clear how these "born again" Catholics will fit into the emerging church.

Suggestions for further reading:

Bokenkotter, Thomas S. *Concise History of the Catholic Church.* Rev. ed. New York: Image, 1990.

Chinnici, Joseph. *Living Stones: The History and Structure of Catholic Spiritual Life in the United States.* New York: MacMillan, 1989.

Dolan, Jay P. *In Search of American Catholicism: A History of Religion and Culture in Tension.* New York: Oxford University Press, 2002.

Greeley, Andrew M. *The Catholic Myth: The Behavior and Beliefs of American Catholics.* New York: Scribner, 1990.

Johnson, Kevin Orlin. *Why Do Catholics Do That? A Guide to the Teachings and Practices of the Catholic Church.* New York: Ballantine, 1995.

Mann, Arthur. *The One and the Many: Reflections on the American Identity*. Chicago: University of Chicago Press, 1979.

Orsi, Robert A. *The Madonna of 115th Street: Faith and Community in Italian Harlem, 1880–1950*. New Haven: Yale University Press, 1985.

Pruter, Karl. *A History of the Old Catholic Church*. Scottsdale, Ariz.: St. Willibrord's Press, 1973.

AMERICAN CATHOLIC CHURCH

> Founded: 1989
> Membership: est. 25,000 in 100 parishes (2000)

Reacting to the conservative response after the Second Vatican Council and to papal rulings regarding birth control, ordination, and theological debate, the American Catholic Church was founded as "a progressive alternative" in 1989. This organization supports the ordination of women and married persons, sees birth control and abortion as matters of personal conscience and morality rather than church law, and is accepting of homosexuals in the church. It is a federation of independent churches served by duly ordained priests. Members of the church are committed to basic Catholic beliefs and sacramental theology, and the church stresses the importance of prayer, spirituality, community, and love for one's neighbor and self. The church affirms that authority rests in the "sensus fidelium" (the sense of the faithful) and that communion is open to all. The rite is modern but in the tradition of the Roman Catholic and Orthodox churches.

For more information: www.geocities.com/WestHollywood/4136

Headquarters: P.O. Box 725, Hampton Bays, NY 10022

APOSTOLIC CATHOLIC ORTHODOX CHURCH

> Founded: 1916
> Membership: est. 25,000 in 13 parishes (2002)

The ACOC is one of the larger Old Catholic* churches. It was established when Bishop DeLandes Berghes of the See of Utrecht consecrated Carmel Henry Carfora and William Francis Brothers.

True to Old Catholic standards, the Eucharist is the central rite of the church, and it is not denied to anyone because of race, gender, or marital status. The priesthood is open to married as well as celibate men and women. There are three orders of ministry, and the church emphasizes the importance of a loving local community that addresses spiritual and social needs of the world around.

Headquarters: 7100 Regency Sq. Suite 210, Houston, TX 77063-3202

EASTERN RITE CATHOLIC
(UNIATE CHURCHES)

Founded: various dates
Membership: est. 500,000 (2000)

The Eastern Rite churches hold a special position within the Roman Catholic Church. Historically and liturgically they are closely related to the Eastern Orthodox* churches, but each has chosen to come under the jurisdiction of the Roman Catholic Church* while preserving its own distinctive language, rites, and canon law. Most of these churches, for instance, are permitted to have married clergy and have always served both the bread and the wine of the Eucharist to the laity.

There are five major families of Uniate churches: Alexandrian (Copts and Ethiopians), Antiochene (Maronites, Syrians, Malankarese), Armenian, Chaldean (Chaldean and Malabarese), and Byzantine (Hungarian, Yugoslav, Melkites, Ukranian). The largest Eastern Rite church is the Ukrainian Catholic Church, which was formed when Ukrainian subjects of the king of Poland were united with Rome in 1596. This church was outlawed by the Soviet Union following World War II, but has resumed open activity since the collapse of the U.S.S.R. The Maronites of Lebanon established ties with Rome during the Crusades.

Each of the Eastern Rite churches is headed by its own patriarch who has jurisdiction over the bishops, the clergy, and the people of that rite. All of the patriarchs are members of the Congregation for the Oriental Churches, which governs the relations of the Vatican with the Eastern Rite Churches.

88

ECUMENICAL CATHOLIC CHURCH

Founded: 2003
Membership: est. 5,000 members in 14 churches

The Ecumenical Catholic Church is part of the Old Catholic* movement that was founded in direct response to the increasingly conservative direction of the Roman Catholic Church in the 1990s. The ECC defines itself as Catholic in doctrine and liturgy, and it considers its bishops to be in apostolic succession from Peter. However, it also sees its mission as "a response to the messianic call of the Spirit to preach the Gospel of liberation and justice; to offer a refuge in Christ for those who suffer prejudice; to stand open to dialogue with others so called and, to conform our lives to the life and teachings of the Lord Jesus Christ." In specific it promotes the ordination of women, liberal views of sexuality and birth control, and gives the laity a greater say in the life of the parish than is common in the Roman Catholic Church. About 85% of the current members were formerly Roman Catholic.

For more information: www.dioceseecc.org

Headquarters: 1111 W. Town and Country Road – Suite 14, Orange, CA 92868

MARIAVITE OLD CATHOLIC CHURCH, PROVINCE OF NORTH AMERICA

Founded: 1906 (came to the U.S. in 1972)
Membership: statistics not available

Mariavites are a unique type of Old Catholic Church.* Mariavites derive their name from the Latin *Mariae vitae imitantur,* meaning "to imitate the life of Mary," the mother of Christ. This ideal originated in late nineteenth-century Poland, a heavily Roman Catholic country. The Mariavite Order of priests and sisters was founded August 2, 1893, by Maria Felicia Kozlowska (1862–1921), a Third Order Franciscan, and Jan Kowalski (1871–1942), a diocesan priest. Kozlowska had earlier formed a community of sisters in response to visionary experiences; and

89

Kowalski took up the movement about five years later, adding a community of secular priests. The motto of the order was, "Everything for the greater glory of God and the honor of the Most Blessed Virgin Mary." From the beginning, its members endeavored to practice an ascetic/mystical religious life, in accordance with the primitive Rule of St. Francis of Assisi. Their goal was to maintain a deep inner spiritual life among themselves and their faithful by being pastors and servants, not through cloistered or contemplative communities. Candidacy requirements were firm and sacrificial, with a tendency toward the ascetic.

Ecclesiastic and civil opposition marked the early decades of the Mariavites in Poland. The Roman Catholic Church* was skeptical of their mystical claims and denied their application for recognition as a religious order. In 1906 the group formed a church independent of Rome, and in 1909 it became part of the Old Catholic Church at Utrecht, Holland. That church had been independent of Rome since 1871. At the time of Kozlowska's death in 1921, the Mariavite movement had some fifty thousand adherents. However, the group went into decline, and the Old Catholics severed communion with the Mariavites in 1924. The latter were perceived as growing more fanatical, evidenced by Kowalski's ordination of women to the priesthood. Kowalski was eventually imprisoned by the Nazis and died in a concentration camp.

Mariavites first came to the U.S. around 1930. During World War II it was impossible for the churches to maintain close contact with Europe, and by 1972 the U.S. church had become autonomous and self-reliant. Archbishop Robert Zaborowski has led the church since 1974; its headquarters are in Wyandotte, Michigan. According to its own reports, this church has grown rapidly since 1972; some reports claim as many 300,000 members. However, information is difficult to obtain from church officials and actual membership is uncertain. Worship is celebrated according to the Tridentine Rite of 1570 in Latin, English, and Polish in the U.S. The principal purpose of the Mariavite Church, which came to be known as the Work of Great Mercy, is "the propagation of devotion to the Most Blessed Sacrament and the invocation of the Perpetual Help of Mary as a means of final salvation for a world perishing in its sins."

OLD CATHOLIC CHURCHES

> Founded: 1871 (came to the U.S. in 1914)
> Membership: statistics not available

Old Catholic churches in the U.S. are an outgrowth of the Old Catholic movement, centered in the See of Utrecht in the Netherlands. Conflicts between Dutch Catholics and the papacy date to the Jansenist controversy over grace and determinism in the eighteenth century, which resulted in a schism in the Roman Catholic Church in Holland. The schismatic Dutch body continued its existence into the next century, attracting new followers when Pope Pius IX (1846–78) affirmed the First Vatican Council's statement on papal infallibility in 1870 (see CATHOLIC CHURCHES).

A significant number of Swiss, German, and Austrian Roman Catholic priests also refused to accept the doctrine of papal infallibility and were excommunicated in 1871. Ignatz von Döllinger (1799–1890) presided over a number of conferences attended by Catholics who could not accept the new dogma on papal authority and representatives of the Anglican and Lutheran churches in the mid-1870s. Old Catholic bishops were ordained by the bishops of Utrecht and were eventually welcomed into communion with the Anglican Church* and several Orthodox* bodies.

In 1889 the Declaration of Utrecht was issued as the doctrinal statement of Old Catholics. The declaration affirms the main lines of the Catholic tradition up to about the year 1000. Especially important for the Old Catholics are the first seven ecumenical councils (before the division between East and West) and most of the medieval liturgy. However, the declaration rejected more recent doctrines of the Roman Catholic Church,* especially papal infallibility, the immaculate conception of Mary, and compulsory celibacy of the priesthood. The church maintains that the five patriarchal Sees of the ancient church remain the equal heads of the church. The Slavic branch of the Old Catholic Church has a separate history (see POLISH NATIONAL CHURCH).

The Old Catholic movement in the U.S. first emerged with the work of Père Joseph René Vilatte (1854–1929) in Wisconsin near Green Bay, where several parishes were organized. A group of

English-speaking Old Catholics was also gathered together by a former Roman Catholic monk, Augustine de Angelis (William Harding), who had organized a community of men devoted to the Religious Rule of St. Benedict at Waukegan, Illinois around the turn of the century. The Old Catholic episcopacy in the United States was established in 1914 when the English Archbishop Arnold Harris Matthew (1852–1919) consecrated Bishop de Landas Berghes et de Rache (1873–1920), a prince of the house of Lorraine-Brapan. He was succeeded by Father Carmel Henry Carfora (1878–1958), an Italian Franciscan friar, who led the church until his death in 1958.

At that time, the North American Old Catholics split into several ecclesial bodies, not all recognized by Old Catholics in Europe. Perhaps as many as seventeen bodies have claimed to be Old Catholic in the U.S., but the major bodies originating in the Utrecht movement are the Old Catholic Church of America, the Old Roman Catholic Church of North America, the North American Old Catholic Church, the North American Old Roman Catholic Church (Archdiocese of New York), and the Old Roman Catholic Church (English Rite). Most of the Old Catholic churches have fewer than ten parishes in the United States.

In the U.S., the Old Catholics often represent a conservative form of Catholicism despite their early identification as "liberal." The sweeping liturgical and devotional changes of the Second Vatican Council led some conservative priests to join the Old Catholics in order to preserve the old traditions, such as prayers for the dead. Several conservative churches in the Anglican* tradition may be classified with the Old Catholic churches as well. Most of these bodies use the 1928 edition of *The Book of Common Prayer,* reject the ordination of women, and emphasize catholic ritual in worship. Most of these bodies would agree with the statement of purpose for the Holy Catholic Church (Anglican Rite): "to perpetuate the Faith, Order, Worship and Witness of Western Catholicism as it existed in the Church of England from around 200 C.E., to the time of the Great Schism, and set forth by the 'ancient catholic bishops and doctors,' and especially as defined by the Seven Ecumenical Councils of the undivided Church."

92

POLISH NATIONAL CATHOLIC CHURCH

Founded: 1897
Membership: est. 26,587 in 155 parishes (2003)

The Polish National Catholic Church, along with a few smaller Slavic national churches in the U.S., represents a different type of the Old Catholic* movement, as Eastern European immigrants sought to have parishes in their native tongue. The Polish body was formally organized at Scranton, Pennsylvania, on March 14, 1897, in protest over the lack of a Polish bishop and a desire to have more control over parish affairs. Some 250 families then began work on a new church, St. Stanislaus, and called a native Pole, Francis Hodur (1866–1953), to be their priest. A constitution for the new church was adopted by the Scranton parish in 1897, claiming the right to control all churches built and maintained by Poles and to administer such property through a committee chosen by each parish. This action was not accepted by authorities in Rome, and Hodur was subsequently excommunicated.

Other Polish parishes followed the Scranton example and began referring to themselves as "National Churches." Joining together, they held their first synod at Scranton in 1904, with 146 clerical and lay delegates representing parishes in Pennsylvania, Maryland, Massachusetts, and New Jersey. Hodur was consecrated a bishop in 1907 at Utrecht, Holland, by three bishops of the Old Catholic Church. Following the first synod, the vernacular, first Polish and then English, gradually replaced Latin as the liturgical language. A second synod at Scranton in 1909 officially adopted the church's present name. The Polish National Catholic Church adopted the "Confession of Faith," written by Bishop Hodur, at a general synod in Chicago in 1914.

There are five dioceses: Buffalo-Pittsburgh, Canadian, Central, Eastern, and Western. Polish and English are used in worship and in the educational programs of parish schools taught largely by pastors. Clergy have been allowed to marry since 1921 but only with the knowledge and permission of the bishops. Because of its opposition to the ordination of women, ties between the PNCC and the Old Catholic Church in Utrecht have been severed.

For more information: www.pncc.org

Headquarters: 1004 Pittston Ave., Scranton, PA 18505

REFORMED CATHOLIC CHURCH

> Founded: 1988
> Membership: est. 25,000 in 100 parishes (2002)

The RCC is one of several bodies that separated from the Roman Catholic Church* in the 1980s in order to promote greater openness to the modern world without denying traditional Catholic worship, spirituality, and sacramental theology. It is progressive in terms of social policies and leaves medical decisions up to individual conscience. Its rite is influenced by the Orthodox* tradition, but it considers its priests to still be in the Catholic Church.

Headquarters: Good Shepherd Rectory, P.O. Box 725, Hampton Bays, NY 11946.

ROMAN CATHOLIC CHURCH

> Founded: ca. 60 C.E. (came to the U.S. in 16th century)
> Membership: 63.4 million in 19,081 parishes (2004)

The Roman Catholic Church is the largest single religious body in the United States and has the oldest continuous institutional existence. Nearly one in four Americans is a member of the Catholic Church. It is difficult to give a precise date for the origin of this church, since there is disagreement over the distinctive nature of the church. There are indications that Christianity came to the city of Rome as early as 50 C.E., but the structure of papal supremacy that has characterized the Roman Catholic Church took centuries to develop. Officially, the Roman Catholic Church traces its beginning from the moment of Christ's selection of the Apostle Peter as guardian of the keys of heaven and earth and chief of the Apostles (Matt. 16:18-19). According to Catholic teaching, Peter, martyred in Rome under Nero, was the first bishop of Rome and thus the first pope. During the second, third, and fourth centuries its claim to the theological primacy of Rome was reinforced by practical developments in the church and Western society. Since much of the history and theology of the Catholic Church was discussed in the opening section, this section will focus on what is distinctive to the Roman Catholic Church.

Although the basic liturgy, doctrine, and organization of the Catholic Church is standard throughout the U.S., there is a great deal of diversity on the local level. Much popular Catholic devotion focuses on the praying of the rosary and the veneration of Mary, the mother of Jesus. Parishes offer a variety of groups for fostering greater devotion and personal piety. Catholicism also offers one of the most comprehensive and sophisticated theological systems of any religion, which encourages a more intellectual and inquisitive approach to faith on the part of some in the church. Moreover, the Catholic Church in the U.S. has played a very prominent role in the promotion of social justice, peace, religious toleration, and economic improvement. Many of the nation's most respected political figures were nurtured in the Catholic faith.

Structure: The government of the Roman Catholic Church is hierarchical, but the trend since Vatican II has been toward more and more lay participation. At the head of the structure stands the pope, who is also Bishop of Rome and "Vicar of Christ on earth and the Visible Head of the Church." His authority is supreme in all matters of faith and discipline.

Next is the College of Cardinals. Although laypeople once were appointed as cardinals, the office has been limited to priests since 1918. Many cardinals live in Rome, acting as advisers to the pope or as heads or members of the various congregations or councils that supervise the administration of the church. When a pope dies, cardinals elect the successor and hold authority in the interim. The Roman Curia is the official body of administrative offices through which the pope governs the church. It is composed of Roman congregations, tribunals, and pontifical councils and acts with the delegated authority of the pope.

In the U.S. there are eleven active cardinals, forty-five archbishops (seven of whom are cardinals), 336 bishops, and more than 46,000 priests; there are thirty-four archdioceses and 151 dioceses. An archbishop is in charge of an archdiocese and has precedence in that province. Bishops, appointed by Rome usually upon suggestions from the U.S. hierarchy, are the ruling authorities in the dioceses, but appeals from their decisions may be taken to the apostolic delegate at Washington, D.C., and even to Rome. The parish priest, responsible to the bishop, is assigned by the bishop or archbishop and holds authority to celebrate Mass and administer the sacraments with the help of such other priests as the parish may need. Priests are educated in theological seminaries, typically connected to Roman Catholic colleges and universities. The usual course of study covers a period of eight years—four years of philosophy and four years of theology. Those in religious orders (see below) also spend one or two years in a novitiate.

The clergy of the church also includes deacons. Since the restoration of the Permanent Diaconate in 1967 more than eleven thousand men have completed the training course and been ordained deacons. Most of these men are married and over the age of thirty-five. They are empowered to preach, baptize, distribute Holy Communion, and officiate at weddings. Most deacons support themselves in secular jobs and exercise their ministry during weekends and evenings.

Three ecclesiastical councils form an important part of the Roman Catholic system: (1) The general, or ecumenical, council is called by the pope or with his consent. It is composed of all the bishops, and its actions on matters of doctrine and discipline must be approved by the pope. (2) The plenary, or national, council is made up of the bishops of a given country; its acts, too, must be submitted to the Holy See. (3) Provincial and diocesan councils make further promulgation and application of the decrees passed by the other councils and approved by the pope.

With the most centralized government in Christendom, the Holy See at Rome has representatives in many countries of the world. Roman Catholic churches have been established in over 230 countries, with a total membership of more than one billion. The majority of Italians, Spanish, Irish, Austrians, Poles, Latin Americans, Belgians, Hungarians, southern Germans, Portuguese, French, and Filipinos are baptized Roman Catholics. The Society for the Propagation of the Faith is the overall representative missionary body. The U.S. sent about 5,800 missionaries to over 130 countries in 1998–99.

Almost every diocese publishes a weekly newspaper; more than four hundred Catholic newspapers and magazines are published in the U.S. and Canada. Some of the largest and most influential periodicals are *The National Catholic Reporter, Commonweal, America, Columbia, U.S. Catholic, St. Anthony Messenger, Catholic Digest, Catholic World, Ligourian, Catholic Twin Circle,* and *The National Catholic Register.*

Ethnic Parishes: One of the major issues that faced the Roman Catholic Church in the U.S. involved immigration. Catholics in

Europe were united in their obedience to Rome, but they were organized on national lines. Spaniards had Spanish priests, Spanish bishops, and venerated Spanish saints. Likewise, the Catholic churches of Ireland, Germany, France, Poland, and elsewhere had their own national character. There was often great tension between ethic groups, and there was a correspondingly strong impulse for these ethnic identities to determine the structure of the Catholic Church in America. In other words, there were those who wanted to recreate the old national churches on American soil with separate hierarchies for each major ethnic group. There would have been many Catholic churches loyal to Rome, but separated from each other in the U.S. This would have been similar to the Lutheran* pattern in America. Cardinal Gibbons charted the course that led to a parochial system in which local parishes could be organized on ethnic lines, but the national church would be a single American church. Thus diversity and unity were preserved.

There is much that Catholics share in common; however, it is important to note the rich diversity of traditions within Catholicism in the U.S., even in a single metropolitan area. When immigrants arrive in this country, they tend to group in neighborhoods in major cities and there re-create some familiar features of the Old World. Thus, although the basic elements of the Mass are the same in every Roman Catholic parish and the same high holy days are observed, at the local level there are many variations liturgically and in popular devotion. A sampling of a few of the major Catholic ethnic groups within the U.S. includes:

Irish. It is estimated that more than four million people fled Ireland for the U.S. during the nineteenth century, joining at least one hundred thousand more who arrived before the American Revolution. Irish emigration was connected with the subjugation of Ireland to the British crown. Once Protestantism was firmly established in England, Catholicism became a mark of national resistance for the native Irish who clung tenaciously to their faith.

In the New World, Catholicism continued to be a bond among the immigrants and to the homeland. Countless Irish benevolent and mutual aid societies were established in the U.S., often with a close connection to the church. St. Patrick's Day became a major holiday in many northern cities and an expression of Irish pride. From the time of the first American bishop, John Carroll, to the present, more dioceses and archdioceses have had prelates of Irish descent than of

97

any other nationality. In many ways, the Irish have largely defined American Catholicism, and it was a bishop of Irish descent, James Gibbons, who established the pattern for Catholicism in America.

Italians. By 1908 more than two and half million persons had emigrated from Italy to the U.S., settling mainly in the major cities of the Northeast, particularly New York City, and the upper Midwest. The Franciscans provided most of the pastoral leadership for Italian immigrants. Notable among them were Father Pamfilo da Magliano, founder of St. Bonaventure's College at Allegany, New York (1858), and Father Leo Paccillio, pastor of the first Italian parish in New York, St. Anthony's. The Franciscans were followed by the Jesuits, the Scalabrini Fathers, the Salesians, the Passionists, and the Augustinians. In some cases priests of other nationalities learned Italian in order to minister to the needs of the Italians in areas where no Italian priest was available. Italian Catholics continued to honor the patron saints of their native Italian towns, naming benevolent societies after them and holding parish festivals on the saints' days. Particularly important in this regard have been St. Anthony and St. Joseph.

Poles. Poland gradually disappeared as a political entity during the eighteenth century as Russia, Prussia, and Austria divided the territory among them. Partition, however, did not destroy Polish identity or patriotism. Particularly in western Poland, German efforts to assimilate the Poles into German Protestant culture served to heighten devotion to the Roman Catholic Church. There were Poles in the U.S. during colonial days, and some served prominently in the American Revolution; but the immigration of the Polish masses began in the 1850s. In 1851 Father Leopold Moczygemba (1824–91), a Franciscan, came to the U.S. and soon after induced nearly one hundred families from Upper Silesia to come to Panna Maria, Texas, where they built the first Polish church in the U.S. in 1855. Immigration, particularly from Polish Prussia, increased rapidly, primarily to Illinois, Michigan, and Pennsylvania. By 1890 there were some 130 Polish churches served by 126 priests. Most of the more than 120 schools were conducted by the Felician Sisters and the School Sisters of Notre Dame. The election of the first Polish pope, John Paul II, in 1978 was a great boon to Polish Catholics in the U.S.

Hispanic. Catholicism came to the New World primarily by way of Spain, whose monarchs were strong supporters of the Counter

Reformation. The first universities in the Americas were founded in the Spanish colonies, and indigenous cultures blended with the religious practices of the conquering Spaniards to create a great variety of vibrant subcultures of the faith. Missionaries to the American Southwest made some progress in converting native peoples, and by 1800 beautiful adobe missions dotted the West.

For most of U.S. history, Mexicans have been the dominant Hispanic group, and in some cities it is common to see devotion to the Virgin of Guadalupe and the spectacular Day of the Dead festival, which is celebrated around the time of Halloween. Since World War II immigration has increased from other Latin American countries, making the Hispanic population the fastest growing portion of the Roman Catholic Church in the U.S.

By 1970 a quarter of Catholics in the U. S. spoke Spanish, and in that year the first Mexican-American Catholic bishop, Patricio F. Flores, was consecrated in San Antonio. During the 1970s an organization of Hispanic priests called PADRES (Priests for Religious, Educational, and Social Rights) worked effectively to focus the church's attention to the special needs of the often neglected but rapidly growing Spanish-speaking population.

In large part due to a shortage of priests and economic distress, there has not been as great a tendency among Hispanic Catholics toward the creation of parishes along national lines as there was among Europeans in the nineteenth century. Some parishes do primarily use Spanish, and many parochial schools teach in Spanish. But in general there has been a greater blending of immigrants from different Latin American countries and cultures than was the case with European immigrants in the 19th century.

Catholic Institutions: The Roman Catholic Church has made a substantial contribution to American culture and society through its numerous educational and charitable organizations. There are almost six hundred Catholic hospitals, which had over eighty million patients in 2002 alone. The parochial school system includes nearly eighty-five hundred schools with over two and half million students, many of whom are not Catholic. Several of the 230 Catholic colleges in the U.S. are ranked among the nation's top institutions of higher education. Over seventy thousand women serve in Catholic religious orders, mainly working in education and social ministries.

The Roman Catholic Church remains a strong, vibrant, and growing religious body in the United States, but it also reflects the diversity and divisions in American society generally. In the 2004 presidential campaign Senator John Kerry of Massachusetts was opposed by some of the bishops in his own church because he had not voted to restrict access to abortion, but he was endorsed by other Catholic leaders for his commitment to workers' rights and care for the poor. By the end of the twentieth century, conservative Catholics often found they had more in common with conservative Evangelicals, despite their differing theologies, than with more liberal Catholics. Mel Gibson's highly successful movie, *The Passion of the Christ,* which reflects much Catholic devotion, found its largest audiences among Protestant Evangelicals.

For more information: www.vatican.va; www.usccb.org

Headquarters: 3211 Fourth Street, Washington, DC 20017

SOCIETY OF SAINT PIUS X

Founded: 1969
Membership: est. 20,000 in 103 chapels

The Society of Pius X views itself as a society of priests within the Roman Catholic Church rather than a separate denomination, but that claim is not recognized by the Vatican. It was founded by Archbishop Marcel Lefebvre, a priest of the Holy Ghost Order who had been bishop of Dakar before returning to his native France in 1962 as bishop of Tulle. He was a vocal opponent of the modernization of the church effected at the Second Vatican Council, and in 1968 resigned as head of the Holy Ghost Order rather than implement the changes required by the Council. The following year he established a conservative seminary, the Society of Pius X, named for the first pope of the twentieth century to be canonized. Pius X was a key figure in resisting secularization and liberalism in France. Although initially supported by Vatican officials, the society was officially suppressed in 1975. Lefebvre's defiant ordination of twelve traditionalist priests in the following year furthered the separation of the society from the Vatican.

The major focus of the society's work is promotion of the traditional Latin Mass and the decrees of the first Vatican Council through an aggressive grassroots campaign. It may seem ironic that a society that proclaims the doctrine of papal infallibility could rebel against the Vatican and criticize the pope's words and actions, but in their view, the second Vatican Council and its decrees corrupted the church and the papacy. Priests in the society attempt (and sometimes succeed) in "liberating" parishes from the modern Mass and restore the pre-Vatican II liturgy. The society has also founded many chapels around the country. Though stronger in France, Argentina and Africa, the number of priests and seminarians is growing in the U.S. There are no membership statistics for the laity since the society does not view itself as a separate church. The society operates twenty-three primary schools, one college, four retreat centers, and a seminary. It's publishing house is Angelus Press.

For more information: www.sspx.org

Headquarters: Regina Coeli House, 2918 Tracy Avenue, Kansas City, MO 64109

UNITED CATHOLIC CHURCH

Founded: 1996
Membership: Statistics not available

The United Catholic Church is a new organization of Catholic churches that was established in 1996 under the leadership of Robert Bowman, a former Air Force pilot with years of experience in space science and technology. Bowman was involved in peace and justice work for decades before accepting consecration as a bishop in the new church. The United Catholic Church grew out of the Independent Catholic movement of the Old Catholic* churches. Along with other independent Catholic churches, the United Catholic Church rejects the dogma of papal infallibility and seeks to remain true to Old Catholic teaching. It also continues in the line of Vatican II, with an emphasis on social justice, peace work, and inclusivity. It defines itself as ecumenical, non-judgmental, and inclusive; however, it makes a distinction between forgiving and condoning sin. The church was founded, in part, to maintain traditional moral standards without being legalistic, and to promote the classic Catholic teaching of the early church.

For more information: www.united-catholic-church.org

Headquarters: 5017 Bellflower Ct, Melbourne, FL 32940-1200

EPISCOPAL AND ANGLICAN CHURCHES

The Episcopal Church has been one of the most influential churches in American history and has provided many national leaders, including presidents, Supreme Court justices, and generals. Episcopalians also built numerous educational institutions, hospitals, homes for the elderly, and many of the most beautiful houses of worship in the country. The Episcopal Church and its offshoots trace their origins to the Church of England (the Anglican Church), which severed allegiance to the papacy during the Protestant Reformation. In doing so, however, the Church of England sought to maintain an unbroken historical continuity to the Christian church in England from the early fourth century.

The historical succession of bishops, or the episcopacy, is the visible sign of this long tradition of English Christianity. Bishops are recognized as important symbols of unity in the church. The other two orders of ministry are priests and deacons. The Anglican Church has often been viewed as a "middle way" between Roman Catholicism and Protestantism. Through the years, there has been tension in Anglican churches between those who favor a more Catholic stance and those who adopt more Protestant principles.

Though King Henry VIII first rejected papal supremacy in the 1530s, it was his successors, Edward VI and Elizabeth I, who made the Anglican Church clearly Protestant with the adoption of *The Book of Common Prayer* and the *Thirty-nine Articles of Religion*. In the 1600s Puritans agitated for a more Reformed* style of Christianity, but episcopacy and the prayer book were firmly established in the Anglican Church with the restoration of the monarchy after the English Civil War.

The Anglican theologian Richard Hooker (ca. 1554–1600) helped shape the Anglican approach to worship and theology. The church's sources of belief and practice are the Bible, the tradition of the church, and reason. Aesthetic in orientation, Anglicanism incorporates theology into liturgy and makes use of the senses of sight and taste as well as those of hearing and speaking. This church is distinctive in leaving undefined the exact nature of the presence of Christ in the Eucharist, regarded as a spiritual mystery.

The Anglican Church came to America along with English colonization. Francis Fletcher planted a cross and read a prayer when Sir

102

Francis Drake landed on the western coast of North America in 1578, and the first English baptisms were conducted in Sir Walter Raleigh's colony on the Outer Banks of North Carolina. In several colonies, the Church of England was the established church, but many colonists were suspicious of the state church. The Society for the Propagation of the Gospel was established in England in 1701 to help support the poorly paid American clergy and spread the work of the church westward. With this increased support, the church grew in the colonial period. The College of William and Mary in Virginia was established in 1693.

The American Revolution almost destroyed the colonial Church of England since clergy had to choose whether to flee to England or Canada, remain as Loyalists in the face of persecution, or break their vows of allegiance. The church did provide many leaders of the American cause, however, including George Washington and Patrick Henry, but in the popular mind, episcopacy was associated with the British crown rather than with independence. At war's end the church had no bishop, no association of the churches, and not even the semblance of an establishment, but the clergy who remained in the new nation reorganized the church.

In 1783 a conference of the churches met at Annapolis, Maryland, and they formally adopted the name "Protestant Episcopal Church." It was Protestant to distinguish it from Roman Catholicism and Episcopal to distinguish it from the Presbyterian and Congregational churches. Also in 1783, the clergy in Connecticut elected Samuel Seabury (1729–96) as their prospective bishop. He went to England to be consecrated but was denied. He then went to Scotland and obtained consecration there in 1784. Two other bishops-elect (from New York and Pennsylvania) were consecrated by the Archbishop of Canterbury in 1787 in recognition of the legitimacy of the American church. In 1789, the church constitution was adopted and *The Book of Common Prayer* was revised for American use.

The Book of Common Prayer and the episcopacy remained the glue that held this diverse and active church together. W. A. Muhlenberg (1796–1877) called for a wider catholicity in the Protestant Episcopal Church. This resulted in the famous Chicago Lambeth Quadrilateral on Church Unity in 1888, from which the Anglican Communion and its ecumenical dialogues continue to derive their validity.

Two sacraments, baptism and the Eucharist, are recognized by

Episcopal churches as "certain sure witnesses and effectual agencies of God's love and grace." Baptism by any church in the name of the Trinity is recognized as valid. Without defining the holy mystery, the Episcopal Church believes in the real presence of Christ in the elements of the Eucharist. The church also recognizes a sacramental character in confirmation, penance, orders, matrimony, and the anointing of the sick.

Suggestions for further reading:

Albright, Raymond W. *A History of the Protestant Episcopal Church.* New York: MacMillan, 1964.

Butler, Diana Hochstedt. *Standing against the Whirlwind: Evangelical Episcopalians in Nineteenth-Century America.* New York: Oxford University Press, 1995.

Caldwell, Sandra M, and Caldwell, Ronald J. *The History of the Episcopal Church in America, 1607-1991: A Bibliography.* New York: Garland, 1993.

Konolige, Kit. *The Power of their Glory: America's Ruling Class, the Episcopalians.* New York, Wyden, 1978.

Prelinger, Catherine M. *Episcopal Women: Gender, Spirituality, and Commitment in an American Mainline Denomination.* New York: Oxford University Press, 1992.

Prichard, Robert W. *A History of the Episcopal Church.* Harrisburg, Pa.: Morehouse, 1991.

Woolverton, John Frederick. *Colonial Anglicanism in North America.* Detroit: Wayne State University Press, 1984.

CONTINUING ANGLICAN CHURCHES

Founded: 1977
Membership: statistics not available,
but est. over 75,000 in 300 parishes

In 1977 an international Congress of Concerned Churchmen comprised of nearly two thousand Anglican bishops, clergy, and laypeople met in St. Louis to voice their opposition to changes in the Episcopal Church,* particularly the ordination of women and revisions to the prayer book. The Affirmation of St. Louis, which affirms traditional teachings as unalterable, serves as a primary doctrinal statement for several small bodies that were formed in the wake of the St. Louis meeting. They call themselves "continuing" Episcopal churches in opposition to the Episcopal Church, which they declared out of continuity with traditional Anglican teaching. The traditionalist churches promote the canon of Scripture, the creeds and statements of the seven ecumenical councils of the early church, *The Book of Common Prayer* (1928), the writings of the church fathers, and the historic succession of male bishops, priests and deacons.

These churches generally see themselves as being in communion with the Eastern Orthodox* and Roman Catholic* churches because of their common affirmation of the decrees of the ecumenical councils before the division of 1054. Despite their common affirmation of the historical episcopacy, the continuing churches have had difficulty remaining in communion with one another.

In 1968 the American Episcopal Church was founded in Mobile, Alabama, by several traditionalist clergy and laity who wished to preserve the 1928 *Book of Common Prayer.* It developed into the Anglican Province of America, and currently it is in the process of uniting or at least having full communion with the Anglican Rite Synod of the Americas, the Episcopal Orthodox Church, the United Episcopal Church, and the Reformed Episcopal Church. It has also absorbed congregations from other traditionalist churches, such as the Southern Episcopal Church.

The Anglican Catholic Church was a direct result of the 1977 St. Louis meeting. Its constitution was adopted in 1978. The Province of Christ the King separated in 1979 and has about fifty parishes nationwide. The United Episcopal Church separated in 1980 and has about twenty parishes. The Anglican Rite Jurisdiction of the Americas was established in 1991 through a merger of the American Episcopal Church and a sizable portion of the Anglican Catholic Church. Also notable is Evangelical Anglican Church of America, based in California, which draws upon the heritage of the eighteenth–century evangelists John Wesley and George Whitefield to promote both personal conversion and traditional Anglican ritual.

Many traditionalist Anglican bodies adopt much of the practice of Eastern Orthodoxy* or identify themselves as part of the Old Catholic movement.* When the Rev. James Parker Dees resigned from the priesthood of the Protestant Episcopal Church in 1963 to protest "its failure to proclaim firmly the biblical doctrine, and ... its emphasis on the social gospel and pro-communist program," he founded the Anglican Orthodox Church. Dees was consecrated bishop by Bishop Wasyl Sawyna of the Holy Ukrainian Autocephalic Orthodox Church and Bishop Orlando J. Woodward of the Old Catholic succession.

The church is headquartered in North Carolina, but is in communion with bodies in Africa and Asia. It emphasizes the doctrines of the virgin birth, the atoning sacrifice of the cross, the Trinity, the bodily resurrection of Jesus, the Second Coming, salvation by faith alone, and the divinity of Christ. A split led to the formation of the Episcopal Orthodox Christian Archdiocese of America, which came under the jurisdiction of the Anglican Rite Synod in the Americas in 1999. That body, in turn, is under the jurisdiction of the Philippine Independent Catholic Church.

Likewise, the Anglican Rite Archdiocese of the Americas is a traditional Anglican body that uses the 1928 *Book of Common Prayer* and the Anglican Missal. It is in alliance with the Orthodox Church of Canada; therefore it claims membership in the "oldest denomination in the world." The church holds to the seven sacraments and the teachings of early Christianity and believes that other churches "diminish" the true faith through "social teachings" and political correctness. The church also identifies itself as "a safe harbor" from political and theological battles in other churches.

For more information: www.anglicansonline.org; www.anglican-catholic.org; www.anglicanprovince.org; www.eoc.orthodoxanglican.net.; www.celtchristian.net; www.anglicanpck.org; www.fidelium.org

COMMUNION OF THE EVANGELICAL EPISCOPAL CHURCH

Founded: 1995
Membership: statistics not available, est. 55 parishes

The CEEC, "where the sacramental, evangelical, and charismatic converge" was founded by charismatic bishops and priests of the Episcopal Church in the 1990s. It was inspired in part by the works of Lesslie Newbigin of the Church of South India in the 1940s. Newbigin proposed that the fullness of the Body of Christ required a flowing together of "streams" of Christianity: the Catholic emphases of "incarnation and creation"; the Protestant focus on "biblical proclamation and conversion"; and the Orthodox/Pentecostal experience of "the mystical and the Spirit". Newbigin's vision played a key role in the formation of the Church of South India out of five different churchs that received apostolic succession through Anglican bishops in India.

In the U.S., Robert Webber, a professor at Wheaton College, encouraged evangelical leaders to take the early church seriously as a model for the modern church. He personally moved from a fundamentalist evangelical background into the Anglican tradition. A handful of participants in the Vineyard* movement and other liturgically-minded charismatics and evangelicals gathered in 1993 to discuss the "streams of Christianity" idea. This led to more serious discussion, and Bishop Michael Owen agreed to be the chief consecrator for the first two bishops Russell McClanahan and John Kivuva, at a service in Virginia in 1995. Soon the movement spread to other countries, and in 1997 the CEEC was incorporated. The church has grown rapidly, especially in India and the Philippines.

For more information: www.theceec.org

Headquarters: 124 Broadwell Circle, Franklin, TN 37067

EPISCOPAL CHURCH

Founded: 1789
Membership: 2,320,221 in 73,030 parishes (2002)

The largest body to come out of the Church of England in the United States has been known as the Episcopal Church since 1967. Members of the Episcopal Church profess two of the ancient Christian creeds: the Apostles' Creed and the Nicene Creed. Thirty-five articles, derived from the Church of England's thirty-nine, are accepted as a general statement of doctrine, but adherence to them as a creed is not required.

At their ordination, clergy profess their belief in the Scriptures and willingness to conform to "the doctrine, discipline, and worship of the Episcopal Church." The church expects its members to be loyal to the "doctrine, discipline and worship of the one Holy Catholic and Apostolic Church" in all the essentials, but permits great liberty in nonessentials. It allows for variation, individuality, independent thinking, and religious liberty. Some Episcopal churches are "high," with elaborate ritual and ceremony; others are described as "low," with less stylized ceremony and more of an evangelistic emphasis. Liberals, conservatives, modernists and evangelicals find common ground for worship in the prayer book. Stained-glass windows, gleaming altars, vested choirs, and a glorious ritual give the worshiper a deep sense of the continuity of the Christian spirit and tradition.

The local congregation, or parish, elects its own minister (rector or priest), who is vested with pastoral oversight of the congregation by the bishop. Lay officers administer the temporal affairs and the property of the parish along with the priest or rector. Each parish, mission, and chapel is represented in the annual diocesan convention by its clergy and elected lay delegates. Each diocese is in turn represented in the triennial General Convention of the church by its bishop (or bishops), clergy, and lay deputies. Between sessions of the General Convention, the work of the church is carried on by the presiding bishop and an executive council. The church maintains national headquarters in New York City.

All of the U.S. dioceses are self-supporting with the exception of the Church in Navajoland. The church participates actively with mission work in the Caribbean, South America, and southeast Asia. The domestic missionary program has traditionally emphasized grants and ministry for urban mission, and ministry to African American, Hispanic, Native American, and Asian American congregations and organizations. In recent years, attention and funding have turned to evangelism and the incorporation of youth in planning and decision making.

The church sponsors eleven accredited seminaries. There are eight Episcopal colleges and one university in the United States and two colleges overseas. Over 1,100 Episcopal schools and early childhood education programs are in operation. Each diocese sponsors social service and health organizations, including homes for seniors, youth care, hospitals and hospice centers, and centers for the homeless and destitute. Orders of men (eleven) and women (five) religious are scattered across the U.S.; the church also recognizes eleven Christian communities.

When Presiding Bishop John Hines called a Special General Convention in 1969 to address the problems of racial segregation and urban decay, the church entered upon a path of engagement with modernity and American culture. Since then, the church has discussed and debated issues of liturgical reform, equal access to ordination, sexuality, and ecclesiastical authority. Black Episcopalians continue to lead the church in addressing institutional racism and its complicity in the larger problem of racism in America. Women, who had so long provided the energy in labor and fund-raising for the church's missionary work, adjured their "auxiliary" status. This process opened the door to a series of profound changes in the understanding of authority, the stewardship of resources, and the full participation of the faithful in the life of the church.

After much trial and debate, the General Convention adopted a new standard of the *Book of Common Prayer* in 1979. This was the first revision of the American prayer book since 1928, and it provides alternate rites that use more contemporary usage and idiom. A new hymnal, the first since 1940, was approved in 1982. Liturgical reform led directly to a participatory theology that was finally encoded in 1988 into the church's canons emphasizing, "the development and affirmation of the ministry of all baptized persons in the Church and in the world," and the full and equal ministry of all the faithful. Liturgical reform coincided with a vigorous pursuit of women's ordination. Ordination of women to the priesthood finally passed the General Convention in 1976, and in 1989 the Reverend Barbara C. Harris was ordained the Suffragan Bishop of Massachusetts and the first woman bishop in the historic succession. The inclusion of formerly marginalized groups into the circles of governance, program and ordinary parish life begun in 1969 continues. In 2003 the church chose to ordain an openly gay bishop, V. Gene Robinson, of the Diocese of New Hampshire. The ordination of homosexuals and the blessing of same sex unions promise to be difficult tests for the cohesion of the Episcopal Church, if not its essential unity.

Through all of the controversy, members have remained focused primarily on the work of ministry in parish communities. In 2000 the General Convention approved full formal communion with the Evangelical Lutheran Church in America. Currently there is greater emphasis on domestic evangelism than in the past. Church members are also becoming more aware of and sensitive to the American church's place in the ninety million-member Anglican Communion, the majority of whom live on the African continent.

For more information: www.ecusa.anglica.org

Headquarters: 815 Second Ave., New York, NY 10017

EVANGELICAL ANGLICAN CHURCH IN AMERICA

Founded: 1986
Membership: statistics not available, but less than 5,000

Most of the Anglican denominations separated from the Episcopal Church in order to preserve the tradition, especially the 1928 prayer book. A few new bodies have formed within the Anglican tradition in order to promote a more liberal perspective than found in the Episcopal Church while maintaining the traditional ritual. The bodies are new and small, but merit mentioning because of their distinctiveness on the American scene. One example is the Universal Episcopal Church, which combines theosophical and Anglican traditions. More traditional is the Evangelical Anglican Church in America, which should not be confused with the traditionalist Evangelical Anglican Church of America. This church offers the seven sacraments "to all of the People of God with respect to the diversity of creation as the cornerstone of God's lavish love and welcome for creation." The church bases its practice and doctrine on the idea of the original blessing in creation and the call to bring the message of salvation to all people.

For more information: www.eaca.org; www.universalanglican.org

INTERNATIONAL COMMUNION OF
THE CHARISMATIC EPISCOPAL CHURCH

Founded: 1992
Membership: 600 parishes (2000)

Founded by Bishop Austin Randolph Adler, this communion seeks to combine Pentecostal*/charismatic experience with liturgical worship. It is a new and growing fellowship of charismatic churches that maintain their identification with traditional Anglicanism. Tracing its origins to an expressed desire among various evangelicals in the 1970s for connection with "historical Christianity," the church endeavors to bring the rich sacramental and liturgical life of the early church to searching evangelicals and charismatics.

The Charismatic Episcopal Church's doctrine was given explicit formulation in the San Clemente Declaration 1999. Church teaching gives priority to worship and liturgical practice in community life.

Stressing that it is not a splinter group but an intentional religious community drawing on a rich theological and liturgical heritage, the Communion intends to "provide a home for all Christians who seek a liturgical-sacramental, evangelical, charismatic church and a foundation for their lives and gifts of ministry."

The Communion maintains relations with groups in over twenty countries, reporting a worldwide communicant membership of over two hundred thousand in approximately one thousand parishes. As an Episcopal communion, the governance of the church is in the hands of bishops who are understood to be pastors of the church and who must be rectors in their own parishes. The office of the Patriarch and that of the General Secretary are in San Clemente, California.

For more information: www.iccec.org

Headquarters: 107 West Marquita, San Clemente, CA 92672

REFORMED EPISCOPAL CHURCH

Founded: 1873
Membership: est. 10,000 in 125 parishes (2004)

The Reformed Episcopal Church was organized in New York City by Bishop George D. Cummins (1822-76), eight clergy, and twenty laypersons who had been members of the Protestant Episcopal Church. This body emerged during the long Tractarian controversy in England and the United States, in which the issues of church ritual and ecclesiastical authority became prominent. Cummins was a leader of the low-church, evangelical party within the Protestant Episcopal Church. He protested what he perceived to be intolerance of other Protestant churches among those influenced by the Oxford Movement, the movement within the church of England that sought to restore pre-Reformation ideas and practices of the church.

In October 1873 Cummins participated in an ecumenical, evangelical communion service held in Fifth Avenue Presbyterian Church in New York. In the face of public criticism from other bishops, and in the conviction that the ecumenical nature and mission of the Protestant Episcopal Church were being lost, Cummins withdrew to found the new denomination. In 1873 he drew up the Declaration of Principles, which are understood to be the evangelical response to the issues of the nineteenth-century controversies.

111

Doctrine and organization are similar to those of the parent church, with some notable exceptions. Clergy are required to subscribe to the Church of England's Thirty-nine Articles of Religion, as revised by the Protestant Episcopal Church in 1801. *The Book of Common Prayer* (BCP) has been revised in accordance with the English prayer book tradition, bringing it into conformity with the English 1662 BCP and the American 1928 BCP.

Parish and diocesan units prevail in the administration of the church. The triennial General Council is like the General Convention of the Episcopal Church; however, its bishops do not constitute a separate house. The church has seven dioceses in North America (four in the U.S.) and carries out oversees work in India, France, Brazil, Liberia and Germany. There are seminaries in Blue Bell, Pennsylvania; Summerville, South Carolina; and Houston, Texas. The denomination is in process of merger with the Anglican Province of America.

For more information: www.rechurch.org

Headquarters: The Rt. Rev. Royal U. Grote, 4142 Dayflower Dr., Katy, TX 77449

LUTHERAN CHURCHES

In the early sixteenth century, a German theologian named Martin Luther (1483–1546) set out to reform the Roman Catholic Church* of his day. Although he did not intend to create a new church, his followers were nicknamed "Lutherans." These Protestants, as they were called after a famous protest in 1529, affirmed the message of the Bible as the sole authority for church life and Christian belief and practice without rejecting the historical church. To this day, Lutheranism retains much of the tradition of the ancient and medieval church, including a sense of participation in the historic people of God and in the traditional liturgy, revised to accord with Protestant biblicism. Lutherans are devoted to sound doctrine systematically developed and expressed in thoughtful preaching. Luther's teaching on justification by faith and on the universal priesthood of believers might be called the cornerstone of Protestantism.

History. The story of Luther's rebellion against the Roman Catholic Church is well known. His position, briefly, was that the church and the papacy had no divine right in things spiritual; Scripture, not the priest or the church, has final authority over conscience. "Whatever is not against Scripture is for Scripture, and Scripture is for it," said Luther. People are forgiven and absolved of their sins, he believed, not by good works or by a church rite but by turning from sin directly to God, with the help of the Holy Spirit. Justification is attained through faith, not through ceremony.

Faith, for Lutherans, is not subscription to the dictates of the church, but "the heart's utter trust" in Christ. "The just shall live by faith" was the beginning and the end of Luther's thought. He held that the individual conscience is responsible to God alone. He also held that the Bible is the clear, perfect, inspired, and authoritative Word of God and guide for humankind. Luther called this theology "evangelical" because it was rooted in the gospel (in Greek *evangelion*) message of justification by faith through grace alone.

In 1529 Luther wrote both his Large Catechism and his Small Catechism. A year later, Philip Melanchthon (1497–1560) authored the statement of faith known as the Augsburg Confession. The year 1537 brought the Schmalkald Articles of Faith, written by Luther, Melanchthon, and other German Reformers; in 1577 the Formula of Concord was drawn up. These documents, which offer an explanation of Luther's ideology and theology, form the doctrinal basis of Lutheranism. Lutheranism spread to Poland, Russia, Lithuania, Bohemia, Austria, Hungary, France, and Holland. It became the state church of Denmark, Norway, Sweden, Finland, Iceland, Estonia, and Latvia.

Lutherans in the United States. It was mainly from Germany and Scandinavia that Lutheranism came to the United States. A Lutheran Christmas service was held at Hudson Bay in 1619. The first European Lutherans to remain permanently in this country arrived at Manhattan Island from Holland in 1623. The first independent colony of Lutherans, New Sweden, was established at Fort Christiana along the Delaware River in 1638, at present-day Wilmington, Delaware. The great influx of Lutheran immigrants, however, went to Pennsylvania, where by the middle of the eighteenth century Lutherans numbered thirty thousand, four-fifths of whom were German, the remainder Swedish.

The first churches were small and poor, often without pastors. The situation was relieved with the coming of Henry Melchior Muhlenberg (1711–87) from the University of Halle. He brought about the first real Lutheran organization in 1748 by uniting the pastors and congregations in Pennsylvania, New Jersey, New York, and Maryland into what came to be called the Ministerium of Pennsylvania. Synods were formed in New York in 1786, North Carolina in 1803, Maryland in 1820, and Ohio in 1836.

Each synod adjusted itself to its peculiar conditions of language, natural background, previous ecclesiastical relationship with Lutheran authorities abroad, and geographical location. The need for even further organization was evident from the ever-increasing flood of Lutherans from Europe, resulting in the formation of the General Synod in 1820. The General Synod extended its efforts to the west, and the Missouri Synod was formed in 1847. From 1850 until 1860, one million Germans arrived in the U.S., the majority of whom were Lutheran. By 1870 Lutherans were the fourth-largest Protestant group in the country, with approximately four hundred thousand members.

The Civil War brought the first serious break in Lutheran ranks, with the organization of the United Synod of the South in 1863; three years later a number of other synods, led by the Ministerium of Pennsylvania, withdrew from the General Synod to form the General Council. To increase the complexity, Lutheran immigrants continued to arrive in larger and larger numbers. These immigrants spoke different languages and came from nations where the church was organized in different ways. From 1870 until 1910, approximately 1.75 million Scandanavians arrived, bringing a slightly different form of Lutheranism than the older, now established German congregations. Numerous small synods were organized.

At one time there were 150 Lutheran bodies in the U.S.; consolidation, unification, and federation in the twentieth century reduced that number to fewer than a dozen. In 1988 the American Lutheran Church merged with the Lutheran Church in America and the Association of Evangelical Lutheran Churches to form the Evangelical Lutheran Church in America. With each major merger, new separate churches were also formed in protest.

Groups of lay and ministerial delegates from major Lutheran churches in twenty-two countries formed a Lutheran World Federation in 1947 for the purpose of relief and rehabilitation on a global scale among Lutherans. Perhaps the most cooperative effort in the history of American Lutheranism is found in Lutheran World Relief, through which more than $300 million in cash and food (including U.S. government-donated commodities) has been distributed throughout the world.

Belief and Practices. In spite of their divisions, there has been real unity among Lutherans, based more on faith than on organization. All the churches represent a single type of Protestant Christianity built on Luther's principle of justification by faith alone. Lutherans maintain that the Bible is the inspired Word of God and the rule and standard of faith and practice. They confess their faith through the three general creeds of Christendom (Apostles', Nicene, and Athanasian), which they believe to be in accordance with the Scriptures. They also believe that the Augsburg Confession is a correct exposition of the faith and doctrine of evangelical Lutheranism, although there is disagreement over which version is preferred. The two catechisms of Luther, the Schmalkald Articles, and the Formula of Concord are held to be faithful interpretations of Lutheranism and of the Bible.

Baptism and the Lord's Supper are not merely signs or memorials, but are believed to be channels through which God bestows forgiving and empowering grace upon humankind. The real body and blood of Christ are believed to be present "in, with, and under" the bread and wine of the Lord's Supper and are received sacramentally and supernaturally. Infants are baptized, and baptized persons are believed to receive the gift of regeneration from the Holy Spirit.

Polity. The local congregation is usually administered between its annual meetings by a church council consisting of the pastor and a number of elected lay officers. Pastors are called by the voting members of the congregation. Congregations are united in synods composed of pastors and lay representatives elected by the congregations and have authority as granted by the synod constitution.

Synods (conferences or districts) are united in a general body that may be national or even international and are called variously "church," "synod," or "conference." Some of these general bodies are legislative in nature, some consultative; they supervise the work in worship, education, publication, charity, and mission. Congregations have business meetings at least annually; synods, districts, and conferences hold yearly conventions; the general bodies meet annually or biennially.

Suggestions for further reading:

Cimino, Richard. *American Lutherans Today.* Grand Rapids, Mich.: Eerdmans, 2003.

Gritsch, Eric W. *Fortress Introduction to Lutheranism.* Minneapolis: Augsburg-Fortress, 1994.

Groh, John E. and Robert H. Smith, eds. *The Lutheran Church in North America.* St. Louis: Concordia, 1979.

Huber, Donald L. *World Lutheranism: A Select Bibliography for English Readers.* Lanham, Md.: Scarecrow, 2000.

Knudsen, Johannes. *The Formation of the Lutheran Church in America.* Philadelphia: Fortress, 1958.

Neve, H. T. and B. A. Anderson, eds. *The Maturing of American Lutheranism.* Minneapolis: Augsburg, 1968.

Schlink, Edmund. *Theology of the Lutheran Confessions.* Trans. Paul F. Keohneke and Herbert J. A. Bouman. Philadelphia: Muhlenberg, 1961.

AMERICAN ASSOCIATION OF LUTHERAN CHURCHES

Founded: 1987
Membership: 15,230 in 85 congregations

The AALC was formed by laity and pastors of the former American Lutheran Church in America (ALC) who did not wish to participate in that church's 1988 merger with the Lutheran Church in America (LCA) and Association of Evangelical Lutheran Churches (see ELCA). The AALC holds to a high view of the divinely inspired, revealed and inerrant Word of God, joyfully submitting to this as the only infallible authority in all matters of faith and life. The emphasis has been on the primacy of reaching people through the ministries of evangelism and world missions through the local congregations.

The eighty-five congregations of The AALC, divided into ten regions, are distributed throughout twenty-two states of the continental United States from Long Island, NY, to San Diego, Calif. The primary decision-making body is the annual General Convention, to which each congregation has proportionate representation. The Joint Council, with three representatives from each region, governs the church body the rest of the time. The elected Presiding Pastor, along with the Executive Committee, leads from the National Office in Bloomington, Minnesota. The AALC maintains a Clergy Roster through its Clergy Commission. The Commission for Higher

APOSTOLIC LUTHERAN CHURCH OF AMERICA

Education is the board responsible for the American Lutheran Theological Seminary in Edina, Minnesota.

For more information: www.taalc.org

Headquarters: The Evangeli, 801 West 106th Street, Suite 203, Minneapolis, MN 55420-5603

APOSTOLIC LUTHERAN CHURCH OF AMERICA

Founded: 1872, 1928
Membership: est. 9,000 in 60 churches (2004)

Sometimes called the Laestadians, for Lars Levi Laestadius, (1800–61), a naturalist, a revivalist, and a minister of the state church of Sweden, this church originated with Finnish immigrants in and around Calumet, Michigan, in the middle years of the nineteenth century. The church was first incorporated in Michigan in 1928 under the name "Finnish Apostolic Lutheran Church of America."

Conservative in theology, this church stresses the infallibility of Scripture and the importance of an experience of justification by faith. Such an experience is required for voting membership in spiritual matters; supporting members may vote on temporal matters only. The church accepts the ecumenical creeds and puts strong emphasis on the confession of sins, absolution, and regeneration. Confession may be made to another Christian, but for some publicly known sins, a person "should confess them publicly before the congregation and receive absolution." Local congregations are quite free to govern themselves. The annual church convention elects an executive board which elects officers for the denomination.

For more information: www.apostolic-lutheran.org

Headquarters: 332 Mr. Washington Way, Clayton, CA 94517-1546

ASSOCIATION OF FREE LUTHERAN CONGREGATIONS

Founded: 1962
Membership: 36,431 in 252 churches (2002)

This association was formed by congregations of the Lutheran Free Church, which rejected merger with the newly formed

117

American Lutheran Church in 1962 (now part of the Evangelical Lutheran Church in America*). It has its roots in a revival movement that swept through Scandinavian Lutheran churches in the late nineteenth century. It is conservative theologically and maintains that the local congregation is subject to no authority but the Word of God. Doctrinal emphases include the inerrancy and supreme authority of the Bible as the Word of God, congregational polity, the spiritual unity of all true believers, evangelical outreach for the purpose of leading persons to an experience with and devotion to Christ, the Lordship of Christ in one's personal life, and conservatism on social issues.

The association elects a president and a coordinating committee that maintains a clergy roster and fosters cooperation between churches in ministry to youth, evangelism, parish education, and other matters. Association members also sponsor a theological seminary and a Bible school in Minneapolis, Minnesota.

For more information: www.aflc.org

Headquarters: 3110 E. Medicine Lake Blvd., Minneapolis, MN 55441

CHURCH OF THE LUTHERAN BRETHREN OF AMERICA

Founded: 1900
Membership: 13,702 in 108 churches (2001)

This is an independent Lutheran body made up of autonomous congregations scattered across the U.S. and Canada. The synod was organized in 1900 to assist in Christian education and in home and world missions. The church maintains a firm commitment to the supreme authority of the Scriptures. It accepts the basic Lutheran teachings and emphasizes the need for a personal faith in the Lord Jesus Christ that demonstrates itself in daily life. Membership in the local congregation is based on an individual's personal profession of faith. Worship services use traditional and contemporary music, lay participation, and biblical teaching and preaching that is evangelistic and personal in application. The congregations support a seminary, a Bible school, and a four-year secondary academy. These institutions, as well as the headquarters, are located in Fergus Falls, Minnesota.

Missions projects are carried on in Chad, Cameroon, Japan, and Taiwan.

For more information: www.clba.org

Headquarters: P.O. Box 655, Fergus Falls, MN 56538

CHURCH OF THE LUTHERAN CONFESSION

Founded: 1960
Membership: 8,492 in 77 churches (2002)

This confessional church was organized by clergy and laypeople who had withdrawn from several synods of the Synodical Conference of North America over the issue of uniting with other synods. The CLC holds firmly to the doctrine of verbal inspiration and inerrancy of the Bible, and it maintains that there can be no church union (even with other Lutherans) unless there is full agreement in doctrine. It holds without reservation to all the historic confessions of the Lutheran faith. Membership is concentrated in South Dakota, Minnesota, and Wisconsin. It also engages in mission work in India and Nigeria. A high school, a college, and a seminary in Eau Claire, Wisconsin, are supported by the church.

For more information: www.clclutheran.org

Headquarters: 501 Grover Rd., Eau Claire, WI 54701

EVANGELICAL LUTHERAN CHURCH IN AMERICA

Founded: 1988
Membership: 5,038,006 in 10,721 churches (2002)

The Evangelical Lutheran Church in America (ELCA) is the youngest of the large U.S. Lutheran church bodies, but it is also the oldest. The ELCA was constituted in 1987 and began operation in 1988 as a result of the union of the American Lutheran Church (ALC), Lutheran Church in America (LCA), and Association of Evangelical Lutheran Churches (AELC), but it traces its history through predecessor church bodies to the formation in 1748 of the first synod in North America, the Ministerium of Pennsylvania. The ELCA represents historical continuity for Lutherans from colonial

119

days as well as the weaving together into one body all of the threads of Lutheran history in North America.

Two of the uniting churches that formed the ELCA were the result of mergers. The ALC was formed in 1960, bringing together four churches of German, Norwegian, and Danish heritage. Subsequently, in 1962 the LCA was established in a four-way merger of German, Danish, Finnish, and Swedish heritage churches. Those mergers of the early 1960s marked a movement away from ethnic identity for U.S. Lutheran church bodies. The AELC, in contrast, resulted from a break in 1976 from The Lutheran Church–Missouri Synod in a dispute over the authority and interpretation of Scripture.

Efforts to form the ELCA formally began in 1982 when the three uniting churches elected a seventy-member commission to draft the constitution and other agreements. In August 1986, the conventions of the three churches approved the merger, and the ELCA's constituting assembly was held in May 1987. The Rev. Herbert W. Chilstrom was elected the first presiding bishop and the Rev. Lowell G. Almen, the first secretary. The ELCA's main office is in Chicago. Its congregations are grouped into sixty-five synods throughout the U.S. and the Caribbean region. Each synod is led by a bishop elected by voting members at a Synod Assembly to six-year, renewable terms.

The highest governing authority in the ELCA is the Churchwide Assembly, which includes six hundred lay voting members equally divided by gender and about four hundred clergy voting members. A 37-member Church Council, elected by the assembly, serves as the board of directors and interim legislative authority between assemblies. The presiding bishop is the ELCA's chief pastor and the executive officer of the churchwide organization. Both the presiding bishop and secretary are elected by the Churchwide Assembly. Their terms of office are six years and incumbents are eligible for reelection. The treasurer is elected by the Church Council to six-year renewable terms. A lay vice president, who is elected to the volunteer position by the Churchwide Assembly, chairs the Church Council.

Units within the churchwide organization include: congregational ministries, rostered ministries, outreach, higher education and schools, church in society, and global mission. Ecumenical relations are coordinated through the presiding bishop's office and include ecumenical, inter-Lutheran, and inter-religious activities as well as administration of relationships with the Lutheran World Federation,

World Council of Churches, and National Council of the Churches of Christ in the U.S.A. The publishing unit, located in Minneapolis, is known as Augsburg Fortress, Publishers. The pension board also is based in Minneapolis and provides pension and other benefit programs for clergy, other church workers, and congregations. The main periodical of the ELCA is *The Lutheran,* published monthly.

A formal relationship of full communion was established in 1997 between the ELCA and the Presbyterian Church (U.S.A.),* Reformed Church in America,* and the United Church of Christ.* In 1999 relationships of full communion were formed with the Episcopal Church* and with the Moravian Church.* As a member of the Lutheran World Federation, the ELCA affirmed in 1999 the "Joint Declaration on the Doctrine of Justification" with the Roman Catholic Church.*

The ELCA promotes the Lutheran theological and liturgical tradition while allowing greater freedom for laity and clergy to address contemporary social and intellectual concerns than most of the other Lutheran denominations. It also engages in extensive ministries to promote both greater social justice and mercy in the world.

For more information: www.elca.org

Headquarters: 8765 West Higgins Rd., Chicago, IL 60631

EVANGELICAL LUTHERAN SYNOD

Founded: 1918
Membership: 21,442 in 138 churches (2002)

This synod traces its roots to the formation of a synod for Norwegian immigration in the middle of the nineteenth century. The ELS was organized in 1918 by a minority group that declined to join the other Norwegian groups when they united in the Norwegian Lutheran Church (later, the Evangelical Lutheran Church) in 1917. The jurisdiction of the synod is entirely advisory. The officers and boards of the synod, however, direct work of common interest insofar as they do not interfere with congregational rights or prerogatives. The ELS is in fellowship with the Wisconsin Synod and has maintained Bethany Lutheran College and Bethany Theological Seminary at Mankato, Minn.

For more information: www.evluthsyn.org

Headquarters: 6 Browns Court, Mankato, MN 56001

121

LATVIAN EVANGELICAL LUTHERAN CHURCH IN AMERICA

Founded: 1975, 1955
Membership: 13,584 in 68 churches (2002)

This body grew out of the Federation of Latvian Evangelical Lutheran Churches and is part of the international network of Latvian Lutherans around the world as well as a member of the Lutheran World Federation. It holds to the traditional doctrinal statements of Western Christianity (the Apostles,' Nicene, and Athanasian Creeds) and the statements of traditional Lutheranism (the unaltered Augsburg Confession, the smaller and larger catechisms, and the *Book of Concord*). In addition to promoting Lutheran worship, spirituality, and theology, the LELCA preserves the customs and traditions of Latvian Protestantism. The church has its headquarters in Minnesota.

For more information: www.dcdraudze.org

LUTHERAN CHURCH—MISSOURI SYNOD

Founded: 1847
Membership: 2,512,714 in 6,142 churches (2002)

This second-largest Lutheran denomination in the U.S. was founded in Missouri by German immigrants in 1847. Many of these immigrants had rejected the planned merger of the Lutheran and Reformed churches in Prussia, and from the beginning this synod has been devoted to the maintenance of confessional Lutheranism, coupled with a strong sense of mission outreach. It stresses the authority of the classic Lutheran confessional statements and the inerrancy of Scripture.

The synod has long been considered a leader in the field of communications. It operates the world's oldest religious radio station, KFUO in St. Louis, Missouri, and produces the 75-year old "Lutheran Hour," heard in more than one hundred countries. It also operates Concordia Publishing House, one of the largest religious publishers in the U.S. In addition, the church has given great attention to ministry to deaf and blind persons, producing literature in Braille and supporting nearly sixty congregations for the hearing impaired.

Because of differences in doctrine and practice, the Missouri Synod was not a part of the 1988 merger that united three other Lutheran denominations. However, it continues to cooperate with those churches in a variety of ministries, particularly in areas of social work, such as world hunger relief and the resettlement of refugees.

The church's headquarters are in the International Center, in suburban St. Louis. Directors for the church body are set by a triennial convention of pastors and laypeople, whose members represent the congregations of the synod. Christian education for members of all ages has always been stressed. The synod operates twelve universities and seminaries in North America, with an enrollment of more than 17,000. Its elementary and secondary system of more than 1,500 schools is the largest of any Protestant denomination in the U.S. Mission work is conducted in more than 40 foreign countries.

For more information: www.lcms.org

Headquarters: 1333 S. Kirkwood Road, St. Louis, MO 63122-7295

WISCONSIN EVANGELICAL LUTHERAN SYNOD

> Founded: 1850
> Membership: 403,345 in 1,936 congregations (2003)

Organized in Milwaukee as the German Evangelical Lutheran Synod of Wisconsin, this church merged with the Minnesota and Michigan synods in 1917 to become the Evangelical Lutheran Joint Synod of Wisconsin and other states. Today it is known as the Wisconsin Evangelical Lutheran Synod, or WELS. This synod subscribes to confessional Lutheranism and is committed without reservation to the inspiration and infallibility of Holy Scripture. It seeks fellowship with those who believe that full agreement in doctrine and practice is necessary for Biblical fellowship.

Divided into twelve districts, it maintains its national headquarters in Milwaukee. Mission churches are supported in Malawi, Zambia, Cameroon, Nigeria, Albania, Bulgaria, Japan, Russia, Sweden, Norway, Finland, Hong Kong, Indonesia, Taiwan, Thailand, India, Brazil, Colombia, the Dominican Republic, Mexico, Puerto Rico, and among Native Americans in Arizona. For the education of its pastors, teachers and staff ministers, it maintains a college in New Ulm, Minn., a seminary at Mequon, Wisc., and two preparatory schools at Watertown, Wisc. and Saginaw, Mich. Associations of congregations support twenty-three Lutheran high schools.

For more information: www.wels.net

Headquarters: 2929 North Mayfair Road, Milwaukee, WI 53222

REFORMED, CONGREGATIONALIST AND PRESBYTERIAN CHURCHES

The most influential religious tradition in colonial America was the Reformed tradition. The Puritans (Congregationalists) in New England were representatives of the Reformed tradition, as were the Scots-Irish Presbyterians who immigrated to the middle colonies and southward. Many of the institutions of higher education in colonial America were founded by Reformed churches, and those schools produced some of America's best theologians, such as Jonathan Edwards (1703–58). Reformed thought and practice influenced American literature, law, education, and government during the formative period of the country.

The Reformed family of churches originated in the Swiss Reformation, whose greatest theologian was John Calvin (1509–64). Because of this, these churches are sometimes called "Calvinist." Calvin viewed himself primarily as an interpreter of Scripture rather than a priest or even a theologian, and he bequeathed a strong Biblicism to the Reformed tradition. Basic to Calvin's thought was God's sovereignty over the world and people's lives; humans are completely dependent upon God for their lives and salvation. The most controversial Calvinist proposition was "double predestination," which means that eternal salvation and damnation are predetermined by God. Calvin also taught that the natural world as well as human history work according to God's rational law and providential will.

Doctrine in Reformed Churches is based primarily on the Belgic Confession (1561), the Heidelberg Catechism (1563), and the Canons of the Synod of Dort (1618). Presbyterian churches also use the Westminster Confession of Faith (1648). These confessions emphasize salvation through Christ and the primacy of God's power

124

in human life. More cerebral and verbal than emotional and aesthetic, Reformed theology places more value on understanding, learning, and doctrinal unity than most branches of Christianity. Reformed worship also tends to focus on biblical exposition and preaching rather than music and the sacraments.

The Reformed churches in Europe developed along national lines. Particularly strong were the Reformed churches in the Netherlands (Holland), Germany, England, Scotland, Hungary, Bohemia, and Poland. Presbyterian Churches are in the Reformed tradition, but the Scottish reformer John Knox (ca. 1513–72) played as great a role in their formation as John Calvin. Though they were often tolerated or even supported by local governments, the Reformed churches were officially outlawed throughout Europe until the Peace of Westphalia in 1648. Their theology and church structure were thus formed in the midst of persecution and a struggle for religious and political independence. It was the Reformed churches that rejected the idea of "divine right" for monarchs.

The Reformed tradition was dominant in the English Puritan movement in the 1600s. The Westminster Assembly (1643–48) met in an effort to resolve the struggle over the compulsory use of the Anglican *Book of Common Prayer* in the Church of England (see EPISCOPAL and ANGLICAN CHURCHES). That assembly produced a Larger and a Shorter Catechism; a directory for the public worship of God; a form of government; and the Westminster Confession of Faith, which became the doctrinal standard of Scottish, British, and American Presbyterianism.

Types of Reformed Churches: Many of the divisions among Reformed churches can be traced to different interpretations of Calvin's teaching and the authority of the basic confessions. Over time, many pastors and congregations in the Reformed tradition turned away from Calvin's strict teaching on predestination and adopted a more covenantal understanding of God's relationship to the world and to believers.

Other divisions within the Reformed family of churches involve church order. The Reformed rejected episcopacy (rule by bishops) and attempted to follow the structure of the New Testament church. But there were disagreements over the details of that structure. Calvin promoted a presbyterial system in which a council of clergy (presbyters) exercised authority within a geographical region. Reformed and Presbyterian churches follow Calvin's approach. The governing body in the local church is called a consistory, session, or council depending on the denomination. Typically, it is made up of elders, deacons, and ministers, who undertake the administrative duties common to congregational life. Churches in a geographical area are then organized into a presbytery or classis that supervises congregations and clergy within its bounds. This body is generally comprised of elder delegates from each congregation and the ministers in the area. The presbytery or classis is in turn under the authority of regional synods that supervise planning and programming. The highest legislative and judicial body of most Reformed and Presbyterian churches is a representative body called General Synod or General Assembly, which meets once a year,

Congregationalist churches adopted a different polity. In Congregationalism, the assembled body of believers on the local level has final authority. Local and national assemblies may provide programming and assist in cooperative ministries, but they have little direct power over congregations and pastors. Many other denominations influenced by the Reformed tradition, such as the Baptists* and churches in the Stone-Campbellite tradition (see CHRISTIAN CHURCHES) also hold to congregational polity.

Because of their deep commitment to local authority, whether through congregations or presbyteries, Reformed churches developed along ethnic lines. Language, culture, and national heritage were closely connected to theological and liturgical concerns. Several Reformed denominations in the United States continue to reflect their European national origins.

Congregationalists in America: In 1609 John Robinson (1575–1625) fled persecution in England and settled at Leiden in the Netherlands. There he met William Ames (1576–1633), Congregationalism's first theologian, who was also a fugitive from the ecclesiastical courts of England. Robinson and his congregation enjoyed peace and freedom under the Dutch but wanted to remain English. A large company sailed for the American colonies in 1620 aboard the historic *Mayflower,* earning the name "Pilgrims." Between 1630 and 1640, twenty thousand more Puritans, mostly Congregationalists, arrived at Massachusetts Bay. There they established a "theocratic" government based on biblical law and Calvin's theology. Contrary to popular belief, it was not a stern and rigid regime of the saints, but it was strict and intolerant of religious dissent. When four Quakers (see FRIENDS), including a woman, were

126

hanged on Boston Common in the 1660s, there was a public outcry in England. New England was forced to accept the Act of Toleration in 1689.

Congregationalists in New England were leaders in the American Revolution, and during the next century Congregationalism played a major role in developing American institutional and religious life. In the field of education, Congregationalists founded Harvard in 1636, Yale in 1707, and Dartmouth in 1769. Dartmouth developed from Eleazer Wheelock's (1711–79) school for Native Americans.

Interest in missions among Congregationalists began the day the Pilgrims landed at Plymouth. John Eliot (1604–90) spent seven years mastering Algonquian and translated the Bible. He also published a catechism in 1653, which was the first book to be printed in a Native American language. By 1674 there were about four thousand "praying Indians" in New England and twenty-four native preachers.

The American Board of Commissioners for Foreign Missions, organized in 1810, was concerned at first with both home and foreign missionary work. It included representatives from Congregationalist, Presbyterian, Dutch Reformed, and Associate Reformed churches. Missionaries were sent to more than thirty foreign countries and American territories. In 1826 the American Home Missionary Society was founded, and in 1846 the American Missionary Association, which was active in the South before the Civil War, was founded.

Meanwhile, differences of opinion between theological liberals and conservatives developed during the nineteenth century. A famous sermon by the Unitarian* William Ellery Channing (1780–1842) at Baltimore in 1819 made a division inevitable. In spite of the Unitarian separation, Congregationalism continued to grow until a national supervisory body became necessary. A council held at Boston in 1865 proved so effective that a regular system of councils was established.

Unity and cooperation across denominational lines have been outstanding characteristics of Congregationalism. Christian Endeavor, at one time the largest young people's organization in Protestantism, was founded in 1881 by a Congregationalist, Francis E. Clark (1851–1921). By 1885 it had become interdenominational.

Dutch and German Reformed Churches in America: The Reformed Church came to America along with the first Dutch colonists. As early as 1614 there was informal Reformed worship along the upper reaches of the Hudson River near modern Albany,

127

New York. The Reformed were numerous enough to require the services of lay ministers, two of whom came from Holland in 1623 as "comforters of the sick." By 1628 the Dutch in New Amsterdam had a pastor of their own, Jonas Michaelius (b. 1577) who organized the first church in the middle colonies.

When the English took possession of New Amsterdam in 1664, perhaps eight thousand Dutch church people were holding services in their own language. It was difficult and expensive to send native-born ministerial candidates to Holland for education and ordination, so a college and seminary were established at New Brunswick, New Jersey. This institution later became New Brunswick Theological Seminary and Rutgers University. Michael Schlatter (1718–90), was sent to the middle colonies by the Reformed Synod of South and North Holland. He worked tirelessly to bring organization to the Reformed churches and improve the quality of the ministry.

A large majority of the clergy and laypeople of the Reformed Church supported the American Revolution. As the Dutch became Americanized, the English language gradually became accepted in churches, but not without a struggle. A second emigration from the Netherlands began in the middle of the nineteenth century, bringing entire congregations with their pastors. One group, led by Albertus van Raalte (1811–76), established a community called Holland in western Michigan. Van Raalte and his group became part of the Reformed Church in America in 1850.

German Reformed churches in America originated in the flood tide of German immigrants to Pennsylvania in the eighteenth century. More than half the Germans there in 1730 were Reformed, but the congregations often lacked ministers and employed school teachers to lead the services. Johann Philip Boehm (1683–1749), a schoolmaster, lead worship services and in 1725 he assumed the pastoral office for German Reformed settlers in southeastern Pennsylvania. He worked closely with the Dutch Reformed minister Michael Schlatter in expanding and organizing Reformed congregations.

The American synod declared its independence in 1793, taking the name German Reformed Church. In that year it reported 178 congregations and fifteen thousand communicants. The word German was dropped from the name in 1869, and thereafter the denomination was called the Reformed Church in the United States. Difficulties arose in the early years of the nineteenth century. Older Germans preferred the use of the German language; second-generation members demanded English. Some churches withdrew to form a separate synod, but returned in 1837 when compromises were made. District synods of both German-speaking and English-speaking congregations were created, and two Hungarian classes from the Old Hungarian Reformed Church were added in 1924.

The Evangelical and Reformed Church was the product of a union of the Evangelical Synod of North America and the Reformed Church in the United States in 1934. Few difficulties were encountered in reconciling the doctrines of the two bodies. Both churches were German in ethnicity and Calvinistic in doctrine.

Presbyterians in America: After Oliver Cromwell's death in 1658 and the ending of Puritan rule in England, British Presbyterians fled to North America with the Congregationalists. An attempt to establish episcopacy in Scotland after 1662 sent many Presbyterians out of Scotland into Ireland, where economic difficulties and religious inequalities then drove them on to the U.S. From 1710 until the middle of the eighteenth century, between three thousand and six thousand Scottish immigrants arrived annually, settling at first in New England and the middle colonies.

The first American presbytery or association of local churches was founded in Philadelphia in 1706. In 1729 Presbyterians adopted the Westminster Confession of Faith, together with the Larger and the Shorter Catechism. The same synod denied civil magistrates any power over the church and banned the persecution of anyone for religious faith.

In the 1720s William Tennent, Sr. (1673–1746), organized a "log college" in a cabin at Neshaminy, Pennsylvania to train Presbyterian ministers and evangelists. Eventually it became the College of New Jersey (later Princeton University), and it produced a stream of revivalistic Presbyterian preachers who played leading roles in the Great Awakening of the 1740s. Such preachers, especially Gilbert Tennent (1703–64), promoted an emotional "new birth" revivalism, which conflicted with the old creedal Calvinism. The camp-meeting revival, born as a Presbyterian institution, grew out of that Great Awakening enthusiasm; however, it split the denomination. Preachers on the "old side" opposed revivalism, while those of the "new side" endorsed it, claiming that less attention should be paid to college training of ministers and more to recruiting regenerated common men. The two sides quarreled until they reunited in 1757.

The next year, in the first united synod, there were ninety-four ministers in the colonial Presbyterian Church with two hundred congregations and ten thousand members. One of the ablest of the new-side preachers was John Witherspoon (1723–94), president of Princeton, who was the only clergyperson to sign the Declaration of Independence. The Scots-Irish accepted the Revolution with relish; their persecution in England and Northern Ireland had made them solid anti-British dissenters. Their old cry, "No bishop and no king," was heard back in England.

After the Revolution, Presbyterian and Congregational preachers and laypeople moving into the new western territory worked together. Ministers of the two groups preached in one another's pulpits, and members held the right of representation in both the congregational association and the presbytery. The plan worked well on the whole, absorbing the fruits of the national revivals and giving real impetus to missionary work at home and abroad.

This co-operation with the congregations, though, contributed to the split between "Old School" and "New School" Presbyterians over matters of discipline and the expenditure of missionary money. The General Assembly of 1837 expelled four New School synods, which promptly met in their own convention to form a new General Assembly.

More tragic was the division between the southern and northern Presbyterians over the issue of slavery. In 1846 the Old School assembly regarded slavery as no bar to Christian communion, but in that same year, the New School condemned the practice strongly. By 1857 several Southern New School synods had withdrawn to form the United Synod of the Presbyterian Church. The greater schism came in 1861, following the outbreak of the Civil War, when forty-seven Southern presbyteries of the Old School formed the Presbyterian Church in the Confederate States of America. In 1867, following the war, they merged to form the Presbyterian Church in the United States (PCUS).

The Old School and New School bodies of the northern Presbyterian Church were united in 1870 on the basis of the Westminster Confession. Most of the Cumberland Presbyterian churches joined them in 1907; the Welsh Calvinist Methodists joined in 1920. In the decades from 1920 until 1950, an emphasis on theology was evident in a liberal/conservative struggle. Old divisions were healed when the Presbyterian Church (U.S.A.) was founded in 1983.

Suggestions for further reading:

Bercovitch, Sacvan. *The Puritan Origins of the American Self.* New Haven: Yale University Press, 1975.

Bozeman, Dwight. *To Live Ancient Lives: The Primitivist Dimension in Puritanism*. Chapel Hill, NC: University of North Carolina Press, 1988.

Bratt, James D. *Dutch Calvinism in Modern America*. Grand Rapids, Mich.: Eerdmans, 1984.

Dunn, David, et. al. *A History of the Evangelical & Reformed Church*. Philadelphia: Westminster, 1961.

Gunnemann, Louis H. *The Shaping of the United Church of Christ: An Essay in the History of American Christianity*. New York: United Church Press, 1977.

Hart, D. G., and Mark A. Noll, eds. *Dictionary of the Presbyterian and Reformed Tradition in America*. Downers Grove, Ill.: InterVarsity, 1999.

Horton, Douglas. *The United Church of Christ: Its Origins, Organization, and Role in the World Today*. New York: Thomas Nelson, 1962.

Hutchinson, William R. *Between the Times: The Travail of the Protestant Establishment in America, 1900-1960*. New York: Cambridge University Press, 1989.

Miller, Perry. *The New England Mind*, 2 vols. Boston: Beacon, 1961.

Porterfield, Amanda. *Female Piety in Puritan New England: The Emergence of Religious Humanism*. New York: Oxford University Press, 1992.

Smylie, James H. *A Brief History of the Presbyterians*. Louisville: Geneva, 1996.

Thompson, Ernest T. *Presbyterians in the South*, 3 vols. Richmond, Va.: John Knox Press, 1963-73.

VandenBerge, Peter M., ed. *Historical Directory of the Reformed Church in America: 1628–1978*. Grand Rapids, MI: Eerdmans, 1978.

ASSOCIATE REFORMED PRESBYTERIAN CHURCH

Founded: 1782
Membership: 35,566 in 260 congregations (2004)

The Associate Reformed Presbyterian Church traces its origin to controversies in the national Presbyterian Church in Scotland in the eighteenth century, when a group of presbyters seceded from the national church in protest over a number of issues of polity and worship. The controversy over the "Seceders" and "Covenanters" was carried to Northern Ireland with the Scottish migration there. The Scots-Irish immigrants to North America established congregations along the lines followed in the British Isles, but in 1782 two of the seceding branches united to form the Associate Reformed Synod in Philadelphia.

Eight years later, the Associate Reformed Presbytery of the Carolinas and Georgia was formed in Abbeville County, South Carolina, followed in 1803 by the division of the entire church into four Synods and one General Synod. In 1822 the Synod of the South was granted separate status and by the end of the nineteenth century was the sole remaining body of the Associate Reformed Presbyterian Church, as several mergers over the years had absorbed the rest of the denomination into the old United Presbyterian Church. There are now nine presbyteries in North America, primarily in the east.

The doctrinal standards of the Apostles' Creed and the Westminster Confession are followed. For some years the only music in this church was the singing of psalms. This was modified in 1946 to permit the use of hymns.

The General Synod of the church meets annually to elect officers and conduct business. The chief officers are the Moderator (one-year term), who presides over the General Synod and is the spokesperson for the church during the year, and the Principal Clerk (four-year term), who establishes and maintains the official records for the General Synod. These and other officers serve as the Executive Board of the General Synod.

Associate Reformed Presbyterian Church foreign mission fields are located in Germany, Mexico, Pakistan, Turkey, Asia, and the Middle East. The *Associate Reformed Presbyterian* is published monthly in Greenville, South Carolina; Erskine College and Erskine Theological Seminary are in Due West, South Carolina. The church supports an assembly ground, Bonclarken, in Flat Rock, North Carolina, and three retirement centers.

For more information: www.arpsynod.org

Headquarters: 3132 Grace Hill Rd., Columbia, SC 29204

BIBLE PRESBYTERIAN CHURCH

Founded: 1938
Membership: est. 10,000 in 32 congregations (2000)

On June 11, 1936, during the fundamentalist/modernist controversy, a group of about three hundred people, led by J. Gresham Machen (1881–1937) formed a new Presbyterian church based on their belief "that the great battle in the world today is the faith of our fathers versus modernism, compromise, indifferentism, and worldliness. With all our hearts we throw our strength into the great task of winning lost souls to Jesus Christ by the Gospel of the Grace of God." It soon became apparent that the new church was actually composed of two groups with divergent views; therefore, on September 6, 1938, one group formed the Bible Presbyterian Church; the other subsequently took the name Orthodox Presbyterian Church.*

The BPC is fundamentalist,* but subscribes to the Westminster Confession of Faith and the Shorter and Larger Westminster Catechisms. Local congregations may call their pastors "without interference" from presbyteries or synods. Among its approved agencies are Western Reformed Seminary, Cohen Theological Seminary, Faith College of the Bible, and two Independent Boards for Presbyterian Missions. Its greatest strength is in the Midwest.

For more information: www.bpc.org

Headquarters: P.O. Box 26164, Charlotte, NC 28221-6164.

CHRISTIAN REFORMED CHURCH IN NORTH AMERICA

Founded: 1857
Membership: 194,868, in 755 congregations (2004)

This Reformed group originated with Dutch immigrants in Michigan in 1847 during the great wave of Dutch immigration to the Midwest in the mid-nineteenth century. It was affiliated with the Reformed Church in America from 1850 until 1857, when it found itself in disagreement on matters of doctrine and discipline. A conference held in Holland, Michigan, effected the separation of the True Holland Reformed Church, which, after a series of name changes, became the present Christian Reformed Church in North America. Emigration from Holland brought several other groups into the new organization, rapidly increasing its membership.

The Christian Reformed Church (CRC) today is largely English-speaking, although the Dutch, Spanish, French, Navajo, Zuni, Korean, Chinese, and Vietnamese languages are used in some of the churches. Conservative theologically, the CRC holds to the three historic Reformed statements as the basis of union: the Belgic Confession (1561), the Canons of Dort (1618), and the Heidelberg Catechism (1563). Organization bears the usual Reformed characteristics. There are forty-seven classes (thirty-five in the U.S., twelve in Canada) that meet every four months (in some cases every six months) but no intermediate or regional synods between the classes.

A general synod made up of two clergy and two elders from each classis meet annually. The general synod makes decisions regarding theological, liturgical, and ethical matters. It also oversees the ministries shared by CRC churches generally. To this end, the synod has created eight boards and agencies to oversee its ministries, including general church administration, radio and TV ministry, Calvin Theological Seminary, Calvin College, home missions, world relief, publications, and world missions.

Christian Reformed Home Missions provides guidance and financial assistance to some two hundred new and established churches that maintain ministries in many North American communities, including Navajos, Zunis, African-Americans, Asian Americans, Hispanic Americans, and on many university campuses. Almost three hundred foreign missionaries are stationed in Latin America, the Caribbean, Africa, Eastern Europe, and Asia. The Christian Reformed World Relief Committee carries on a relief program serving in twenty-seven countries.

The "Back to God Hour" radio program, broadcast from a chain of stations in the U.S. and abroad, reaches Europe, Africa, and Asia as well as South America; a television ministry also broadcasts in the U.S. and Canada. The church sponsors a publishing house in Grand Rapids that provides literature for the church and its agencies, as well as educational material for many other churches.

For more information: www.crcna.org

Headquarters: 2850 Kalamazoo Ave. SE, Grand Rapids, MI 49560

CONSERVATIVE CONGREGATIONAL CHRISTIAN CONFERENCE

Founded: 1948
Membership: 40,414 in 242 churches (1999)

The origins of this group go back to 1935 and the work of H. B. Sandine, a pastor in Hancock, Minnesota. He was convinced that the Congregational Christian churches (see UNITED CHURCH OF CHRIST) had departed from the beliefs, policies, and practices of historic Congregationalism. He carried on an educational effort through mimeographed documents until 1939, when his efforts were consummated in a monthly publication. A Conservative Congregational Christian Fellowship was organized in Chicago in 1945. The ongoing process of merger among Congregational bodies precipitated the Fellowship's reorganization into the Conservative Congregational Christian Conference in 1948.

The Conference's statement of faith is conservative and evangelical. It includes belief in: the infallibility and authority of the Scriptures; the Trinity; the deity, virgin birth, sinlessness, atoning death, resurrection, ascension, and promised return of Jesus Christ; regeneration by the Holy Spirit; the resurrection of both the saved and the lost; and the spiritual unity of all believers in Christ. Local churches are completely autonomous. An annual meeting of clergy and lay representatives from member churches elects a board of directors and a set of officers for the Conference. Work is largely in the areas of missions, church planting, and Christian education, carried on through recognized evangelical home and foreign mission agencies, Bible institutions, colleges, seminaries, and Sunday school publishing houses. The conference is especially active in the fields of church extension, pastoral placement, and regional activities.

For more information: www.ccccusa.org

Headquarters: 7582 Currell Blvd., Suite 108, St. Paul, MN 55125

CUMBERLAND PRESBYTERIAN CHURCH

Founded: 1810
Membership: 86,049 in 775 congregations (1999)

135

This church was a product of the great revival known as the Second Great Awakening that swept across the new nation around 1800. On February 4, 1810, in Dickson County, Tennessee, three Presbyterian ministers, Finis Ewing (1773–1841), Samuel King (1775–1842), and Samuel McAdow (1760–1844), constituted a new presbytery. They objected to the doctrine of predestination in the Westminster Confession of Faith and insisted that educational standards for ordination of the clergy be more flexible in view of the extraordinary circumstances that then existed on the American frontier. The General Assembly of the church was organized in 1829.

A confession of faith was formulated in 1814, drawing on the Westminster Confession, but affirming key points made by the founders of the church: (1) There are no eternal reprobates; (2) Christ died for all humankind, not for the elect alone; (3) there is no infant damnation; and (4) the Spirit of God operates in the world coextensively with Christ's atonement, so "as to leave all men inexcusable." This confession was revised in 1883 and again in 1984. The 1984 document expresses a clear recognition of God's action in the salvation of human beings, noting that repentance is a necessary condition of salvation but not a sufficient one, as God's grace is the fundamental element.

An attempted union with the Presbyterian Church (U.S.A.) in 1906 was only partially successful. A considerable segment of the Cumberland Presbyterian membership, to whom the terms of merger were unsatisfactory, perpetuated the church as a separate denomination. Congregations are located for the most part in southern and border states. The church sponsors missionaries in Colombia, Japan, Hong Kong, and Liberia in West Africa. It supports Bethel College in McKenzie, Tennessee; Memphis Theological Seminary; and a children's home in Denton, Texas.

For more information: www.cumberland.org

Headquarters: 1978 Union Ave., Memphis, TN 38104

CUMBERLAND PRESBYTERIAN
CHURCH IN AMERICA

Founded: 1874
Membership: 15,142 in 152 congregations (1996)

This church developed after the Civil War, when African-American pastors and lay members of the Cumberland Presbyterian Church* sought to establish their own organization. It has been estimated that some twenty thousand African-Americans were associated with the parent church at the time. Led by Moses T. Weir, a former slave, black ministers formed the Synod of Colored Cumberland Presbyterians in 1869. In 1874 the first General Assembly of the Colored Cumberland Presbyterian Church was held. The parent church offered some financial support in the early years of the denomination and has continued to work with the African-American body on various issues, including theological formulations.

The Colored Cumberland Presbyterian Church eventually became known as the Second Cumberland Presbyterian Church and, late in the twentieth century, as the Cumberland Presbyterian Church in America. The church's doctrinal position is similar to that of the Cumberland Presbyterian Church. Members of the two bodies worked together on the 1984 Confession of Faith. This document gives contemporary expression to the historic Presbyterian witness, with particular emphasis on God's saving grace.

The Cumberland Presbyterian Church in America now has four synods, primarily in the Midwest and the South. The church's ministers are trained at the Cumberland Presbyterian Church College in McKenzie, Tennessee, and at its seminary in Memphis. Serious conversation continues concerning unification with the Cumberland Presbyterian Church.

For more information: www.cumberland.org
Headquarters: 226 Church St., Huntsville, AL 35801

EVANGELICAL PRESBYTERIAN CHURCH

Founded: 1981
Membership: 69,610 in 190 congregations (2002)

The Evangelical Presbyterian Church (EPC) grew out of a series of meetings of conservative Presbyterian pastors and church elders held in St. Louis, Missouri in 1980–1981. They wished to form a church informed by Scripture and the historic confessions of the Christian faith and committed to evangelism. The EPC is a conservative denomination composed of eight presbyteries in the U.S. with

137

churches in twenty-nine states. It identifies itself as, "Reformed in doctrine, Presbyterian in polity, and evangelical in spirit." The EPC places high priority on church planting in the U.S. and world missions. About eighty world outreach missionaries serve the church's mission at home and abroad. High priority is also placed on developing its women's ministries and youth ministries.

The Westminster Confession and its catechisms are the church's doctrinal standards. Unlike other conservative Presbyterian bodies, it includes chapter 34, "Of the Holy Spirit," and chapter 35, "Of the Love of God and Missions" in the Confession. The historic motto, "In essentials, unity; in nonessentials, liberty; in all things, charity," expresses the irenic spirit of the EPC. To the broader world, the General Assembly bears witness on particular issues through position papers.

For more information: www.epc.org

Headquarters: 29140 Buckingham Ave., Suite 5, Livonia, MI 48154

KOREAN-AMERICAN PRESBYTERIAN CHURCH

Founded: 1976
Membership: 55,100 in about 250 churches (2002)

The Korean-American Presbyterian Church (KAPC) was established to serve Korean immigrants in North America. The Presbyterian Church is the largest Christian body in Korea, a country in which many Christian denominations are represented. The KAPC is theologically conservative. In addition to the Westminster Confession and the Larger and Shorter Catechisms, pastors ascribe to a creed that emphasizes biblical inerrancy, the absoluteness of God, the sin of Adam and Eve, and the necessity of faith. Works and obedience to the law of God result from saving faith. The church is headquartered in Phoenix, Arizona.

NATIONAL ASSOCIATION
OF CONGREGATIONAL CHRISTIAN CHURCHES

Founded: 1955
Membership: 70,000 in 432 churches (2004)

This association was organized in order to "preserve historical Congregational forms of freedom and fellowship (the Congregational Way)." It is the largest of Congregational bodies that did not participate when the General Council of Congregational Churches and the Evangelical and Reformed Church merged to form the United Church of Christ* in 1957. The National Association brings local churches together for counsel, inspiration, and fellowship, but preserves the independence and autonomy of the local churches. It describes its mission as encouraging and assisting local churches "in their development of vibrant and effective witnesses to Christ in congregational ways."

There is no binding ecclesiastical authority and no required creed or program. Members are "bound together not by uniformity of belief but by the acceptance of a covenant purpose to be 'the people of God.'" The association leaves to each church any decision to participate in social and political questions and action. A moderator presides over an annual meeting of representatives of all the member churches; an executive committee of twelve acts for the association between meetings. There is widespread missionary work in the U.S. and around the world, in the Philippines, Mexico, Bulgaria, Kenya, Nigeria, Ghana, India, and Honduras.

For more information: www.naccc.org

Headquarters: P.O. Box 1620, Oak Creek, WI 53154

NETHERLANDS REFORMED CONGREGATIONS IN NORTH AMERICA

Founded: 1907
Membership: 9,500 in 27 congregations (2002)

The Netherlands Reformed Congregations in North America broke away from the Christian Reformed Church* over doctrinal differences. This body stresses the classic doctrines of the Reformed tradition as expressed in the Belgic Confession of Faith (1561), the Heidelberg Catechism (1563), and the Canons of Dort (1618). It supports several home and foreign missions and eleven schools. A seminary was established in Grand Rapids, Michigan in 1996.

Headquarters: 2281 Mapleleaf Terrace, Grand Rapids, MI 49505

139

ORTHODOX PRESBYTERIAN CHURCH

Founded: 1936
Membership: 26,448 in 237 congregations (2002)

This church originated in protest against what were believed to be modernistic practices by the Presbyterian Church in the U.S.A. The dissenters, led by Princeton professor J. Gresham Machen (1881–1937), were suspended from the Presbyterian Church in the U.S.A. and organized the Presbyterian Church of America. However, an injunction was brought against the use of that name by the parent body, and in 1938 the name was changed to Orthodox Presbyterian Church.

Orthodox Presbyterians lay strong emphasis on the infallibility and inerrancy of the Bible. They believe that the writers of the books of the Bible were "so guided by [God] that their original manuscripts were without error in fact or doctrine." Fundamental doctrines include original sin; the virgin birth, the deity and substitutionary atonement of Christ; his resurrection and ascension; his role as judge at the end of the world and the consummation of the kingdom; the sovereignty of God; and salvation through the sacrifice and power of Christ for those "the Father purposes to save." Salvation is "not because of good works [but] in order to do good works." The Westminster Confession and the Larger and the Shorter Catechisms are accepted as subordinate doctrinal standards or creedal statements.

The Orthodox Presbyterian Church has published *Trinity Hymnal,* probably the only hymnal designed as a worship supplement to the Westminster Confession of Faith. Membership is concentrated in eastern Pennsylvania, New Jersey, and southern California.

For more information: www.opc.org

Headquarters: Box P, Willow Grove, PA 19090-0920

PRESBYTERIAN CHURCH IN AMERICA

Founded: 1973, with roots in the colonial period
Membership: 310,750 in 1,499 congregations (2002)

This denomination was formed in 1973 when delegates from 260 conservative congregations that had withdrawn from the southern

Presbyterian Church, U.S. (PCUS) convened a general assembly. These congregations opposed the PCUS's ecumenical involvements in the National Council of the Churches of Christ, the World Council of Churches, and the Consultation on Church Union. They also opposed the impending merger with the more liberal United Presbyterian Church in the U.S.A. The Presbyterian Church in America (PCA) also rejected the ordination of women. At first known as the National Presbyterian Church, the present name was adopted in 1974.

The Westminster Confession of Faith is the Presbyterian Church in America's primary doctrinal standard. The church teaches that the Holy Spirit guided the writers of the Scriptures so that the writings are free of error of fact, doctrine, and judgment. They also emphasize the doctrines human depravity, salvation by grace, Christ's death for the elect only, and the perseverance of the saints.

The PCA maintains the historic polity of Presbyterian governance: rule by presbyters (or elders) and the graded courts, the session governing the local church; the presbytery for regional matters; and the general assembly at the national level. It makes a distinction between the two classes of elders: teaching elders (ministers) and ruling elders (laymen).

In 1982 the Reformed Presbyterian Church, Evangelical Synod (RPCES), joined the PCA, bringing with it Covenant College on Lookout Mountain, Georgia, and Covenant Theological Seminary in St. Louis, Missouri. The PCA headquarters is in Atlanta, where work by three program committees is coordinated: Mission to the World, Mission to North America, and Christian Education and Publications.

For more information: www.pcanet.org

Headquarters: 1852 Century Pl., Atlanta, GA 30345-4305

PRESBYTERIAN CHURCH (U.S.A.)

Founded: 1983, with roots in the colonial period
Membership: 3,400,329 in 11,097 congregations (2002)

Following formal separation that began during the Civil War and lasted for 122 years, the two largest American Presbyterian churches (PCUS and UPCUSA) were reunited on June 10, 1983. Over the next fifteen years, great effort was expended to work out the administrative details of combining the two denominations and their numerous presbyteries and ministry groups.

The southern denomination had been established as the PCUS at the time of the Civil War, and its church government developed parallel to that of the northern churches. Offices were gradually centralized in Atlanta under the General Assembly Mission Board; mission work was always undertaken on a worldwide scale, a special source of pride to southern Presbyterians.

The northern body (PCUSA) merged with the United Presbyterian Church of North America (UPCNA) in 1958. The UPCNA had been formed exactly a century earlier by a merger of the Associate Presbyterian Church with the Associate Reformed Presbyterian Church. Their doctrines, traditions, and institutions were preserved in the new church's presbyterial style of government by local sessions, presbyteries, synods, and general assembly.

There were no insurmountable differences when the UPCNA and the PCUSA merged in 1958, but conservatives and liberals in each denomination carried their disagreements over to the new church. On the whole, all found agreement in the Westminster Confession, their accepted doctrinal statement. The UPCUSA eventually reorganized its offices into three agencies based in New York City. In 1982 on the eve of reunion with the southern churches, the UPCUSA had 2,351,119 members nationwide and 15,178 ordained ministers. Its 8,975 churches were grouped in 151 presbyteries and 15 synods; 17 of the presbyteries were joint "union" bodies with similar units in PCUS.

The Westminster Confession (1647) had been the basic doctrinal statement of American Presbyterians since colonial times, but when the UPCUSA was formed in 1958 it was noted that the Westminster Confession was more than three hundred years old. In 1967 the first new major Presbyterian doctrinal statement since 1647 was ratified by the General Assembly. The 4,200 word confession is Christ-centered and avoids what many saw as the confusing terminology of the Westminster Confession. Instead, it stressed the concepts of love, sin, eternal life, and the work of reconciliation in God, Christ, and the church.

Some felt that the new document watered down the Westminster Confession, but most United Presbyterians accepted the document as reflecting true Presbyterianism and as offering a wide theological basis on which all Presbyterians could stand together. With the acceptance of the new creed, the UPCUSA has a *Book of Confessions* with nine creeds: the Nicene Creed, the Apostles' Creed, the Scots Confession of 1560, the Heidelberg Confession of 1563, the Westminster Confession of 1647, the Larger Catechism of 1647, the Shorter Catechism of 1647, the 1934 Theological Declaration of Barmen, and the Confession of 1967. This *Book of Confessions* was adopted by the Presbyterian Church (U.S.A.) with the reunification of 1983.

The PCUSA follows typical Presbyterian polity. The yearly General Assembly is the final authority, but it cannot amend the church's constitution without ratification from the presbyteries. There are two officers of the General Assembly: a stated clerk (the chief executive officer of the church) is elected for a four-year term and may be reelected; a moderator is chosen each year to preside over the meetings and often speaks for the church during the year.

In 1988 the national headquarters of the new denomination was dedicated in Louisville, Kentucky, representing the marriage of the old national church's offices from New York and the southern church's offices from Atlanta. The church has operated two publishing companies, now united in Louisville as Westminster John Knox Press. There are sixty-eight Presbyterian-related colleges, eleven seminaries, and six secondary schools in the U.S.

For more information: www.pcusa.org

Headquarters: 100 Witherspoon Street, Louisville, KY 40202-1396

PROTESTANT REFORMED CHURCHES IN AMERICA

Founded: 1926
Membership: 7,085 in 28 congregations (2004)

In 1924 three consistories and the pastors of the Classis Grand Rapids East and Grand Rapids West of the Christian Reformed Church in North America* were deposed from that denomination as the result of a disagreement over the doctrine of common grace. This doctrine states that grace is extended in some measure to those who are not part of God's elect. Herman Hoeksema (1886–1965) was foremost among those who taught that grace for the elect alone is an essential aspect of Reformed faith.Those who objected to the doctrine and were forced out of the church formally organized as the Protestant Reformed Churches in America in 1926.

The PRC holds to the three basic Reformed confessions (the Heidelberg Catechism of 1563, the Belgic Confession of 1561, and the Canons of Dort of 1618) as the basis of their belief in the infallible Word of God. In government they are Presbyterian. There are two classes organized geographically; a general synod meets annually in June. Membership is found mainly in the upper Midwest. The church maintains a theological seminary at Grand Rapids, Michigan.

For more information: www.prca.org

Headquarters: 4949 Ivanrest Ave., Grandville, MI 49418

REFORMED CHURCH IN AMERICA

Founded: 1792
Membership: 281,475 in 901 congregations (2002)

The Reformed Church in America was established in North America 150 years before the Revolutionary War. Marble Collegiate Church in New York City, once served by Norman Vincent Peale, traces its history to 1628, when the Dutch Reformed Church established its first congregation in New Amsterdam. By the time the English took possession in 1664, Dutch Reformed congregations had been organized in several boroughs. Gradually the churches became Americanized, serving ties with the Netherlands and adopting the English language. In order to provide an educated pastorate, the church established Queen's College (now Rutgers University) and New Brunswick Theological Seminary in New Jersey.

The Reformed Church remained largely an eastern church until the mid-1800s, when a second wave of Dutch immigrants came to the new world. One group, led by Albertus van Raalte, established a community called Holland in western Michigan. Another was established in Iowa. Beginning in the 1920s the church spread westward. A substantial number of Reformed churches organized or revitalized during recent decades have been African-American, Asian-American, and Hispanic. The Reformed Church has been a mission-minded denomination from the beginning. RCA personnel were among the first Christian missionaries in Arabia, China, Japan, and

India. The church continues to support more than one hundred missionaries on five continents.

The church holds to the traditional Reformed doctrinal statements, especially the Belgic Confession (1561), the Heidelberg Catechism (1563), and the Canons of Dort (1618); but it interprets them more flexibly than do many Reformed groups. The church also affirms the Apostles' Creed, the Athanasian Creed, and the Nicene Creed. A contemporary statement of faith, "Our Song of Hope," was approved in 1978.

The church follows typical Reformed polity. The highest representative body is the General Synod, which meets once a year. The services and ministries of the denomination are overseen by a representative body called the General Council. Today the greatest numerical strength is in New York, Michigan, New Jersey, Iowa, Illinois, and California. Its best-known congregation is the Crystal Cathedral in Garden Grove, California, pastured by Robert H. Schuller. In 1998 the church entered into full communion with Evangelical Lutheran Church in America,* the Presbyterian Church (U.S.A.),* and the United Church of Christ.*

For more information: www.rca.org

Headquarters: 475 Riverside Dr., 18th Fl., New York, NY 10115

REFORMED PRESBYTERIAN CHURCH OF NORTH AMERICA

Founded: 1809
Membership: 6,105 in 86 congregations (1997)

This church traces its roots to the Covenanter Presbyterians of Scotland in the eighteenth century who resisted the king's attempts to impose religious beliefs and practices on them. A synod was constituted at Philadelphia in 1809, only to split into Old Light and New Light groups in 1833. This dispute concerned citizenship and the right of members to vote or participate in public affairs. However, restriction was finally removed in 1964, and members are free to participate in civil government and to vote on issues and for political candidates committed to Christian principles of civil government. The church places special emphasis on the inerrancy of Scripture, the sovereignty of God, and the Lordship of Christ over every area of

145

human life. Church government is thoroughly Presbyterian, except that there is no general assembly. Members use only the psalms in their worship services; no instrumental music is permitted. Members cannot join secret societies. Home missionaries work in seven states; foreign missionaries are stationed in Japan, Cyprus, and Taiwan. Geneva College is located at Beaver Falls, Pennsylvania, and the Reformed Presbyterian Theological Seminary is at Pittsburgh.

For more information: www.rpcna.org

Headquarters: 7408 Penn Ave., Pittsburg, PA 15208

UNITED CHURCH OF CHRIST

Founded: 1957, with roots to the colonial period
Membership: 1,330,985 in 5,850 congregations (2002)

The UCC traces its origins to the Congregationalists of New England, but it also represents one of the most significant products of the ecumenical movement. In 1957 four major American denominations united to constitute the United Church of Christ: the Congregational churches, the Christian Church, the Evangelical Synod, and the Reformed Church in the U.S. The first two bodies had merged in 1931 to become Congregational Christian Churches. The Evangelical Synod of North America and the Reformed Church in the United States united in 1934. Within the new denomination, local congregations for the most continued to observe the liturgy and theological positions they had before the merger. In essence, the UCC remains a federation of four denominations with related but distinct identities.

On July 8, 1959, at Oberlin, Ohio, representatives of the Congregational Christian Churches and the Evangelical and Reformed Church, upon merging into the United Church of Christ, adopted a statement, understood as a "testimony rather than a test of faith." It affirms belief in God the creator who "in Jesus Christ, the man of Nazareth, our crucified and risen Lord, ... has come to us and shared our common lot, conquering sin and death and reconciling the world to himself." The statement also identifies the church as a "covenant faithful people of all ages, tongues, and races," which is called to "the service of men." Although this statement was not intended to set forth doctrinal positions or to stand as a substitute for

146

the historic creeds, confessions, and covenants of the churches involved, it served as a witness to the faith, charity, and understanding of the merging groups.

The United Church of Christ represents a union of Congregationalism and Presbyterianism. The church establishes Congregationalism as the rule for the local congregation and Presbyterianism as the basis of organization of the member churches' connectional life. The constitution is explicit: "The autonomy of the local church is inherent and modifiable only by its own action. Nothing . . . shall destroy or limit the right of each local church to continue to operate in the way customary to it."

Local churches in a geographical area are grouped into an association, which assists needy churches; receives new churches into the United Church of Christ; licenses, ordains, and installs clergy; adopts its own constitution, bylaws, and rules of procedure; and is made up of the ordained ministers and elected lay delegates of the area. Associations are grouped into conferences, again by geographical area, with the exception of the Calvin Synod, which consists of churches from the Hungarian Reformed tradition. A conference acts on requests and references from the local churches, associations, general synod, and other bodies. Its main function is to coordinate the work and witness of its local churches and associations, to render counsel and advisory service, and to establish conference offices, centers, institutions, and other agencies.

The General Synod is the highest representative body. It meets biennially and is composed of conference delegates and voting members of boards of directors of the Covenanted Ministries of the church. An Executive Council is elected by the General Synod to act for the synod between its meetings. It recommends salaries for officers of the church as part of a national budget, has responsibility for the church's publications, and appoints committees not otherwise provided. It also submits to the General Synod "any recommendation it may deem useful" for the work of the church. General church offices are located in Cleveland, Ohio, as is the church's publishing arm, Pilgrim Press.

Since 1985 the United Church of Christ has enjoyed an ecumenical partnership with the Christian Church (Disciples of Christ).* Both denominations are active in the Consultation on Church Union; and they join in common witness through Global Ministries, which operates teaching and service ministries throughout the world.

147

Twenty-nine colleges and universities are related to the UCC, six of which are historically African-American. The UCC makes social justice a high priority in its Christian witness.

For more information: www.ucc.org

Headquarters: 700 Prospect Ave., Cleveland, OH 44115

MENNONITE AND ANABAPTIST CHURCHES

Dating from the 1520s in Central Europe, these Protestants take their name from Menno Simons (ca. 1496–1561), an early Dutch leader of the "Radical Reformation." These reformers rejected the "magisterial Reformation" of Martin Luther (1483–1546) and John Calvin (1509–64) whom they believed compromised Jesus' teachings. The first Anabaptist congregation of historical record was organized at Zurich, Switzerland, in 1525 by those who disagreed with Ulrich Zwingli (1484–1531) in his readiness to forge a union of church and state. They also denied the scriptural validity of infant baptism and hence were labeled Anabaptist, or Rebaptizers.

They were treated as outsiders, heretics, and even outlaws by Catholics and Protestants alike. Their primary concerns were not with proper theology, the sacraments, or liturgy. Rather, they believed themselves called to exemplify godly living based on the Sermon on the Mount (Matt. 5:1–7:29). Until recently, most of those quietly dedicated Christians frowned on involvement in secular activity, refusing to take oaths, bear arms, vote, or hold public office. They are a called-out (from the state, from conventional society) fellowship of believers. Always emphasizing the local congregation, some groups insist on living in "intentional communities."

Menno Simons, a former Roman Catholic priest who was baptized by an Anabaptist preacher in Holland, organized so many congregations that his name became identified with the movement. Simons was a strict pacifist, and his writings continue to influence the Mennonites. Mennonite beliefs are based on a confession of faith signed at Dordrecht, Holland, in 1632. In eighteen articles, the following doctrines were laid down: faith in God as Creator; humanity's fall and restoration at the coming of Christ; Christ as the Son of God, who redeemed humankind on the cross; obedience to Christ's law in

148

the gospel; the necessity of repentance and conversion for salvation; baptism as a public testimony of faith; the Lord's Supper as an expression of common union and fellowship; matrimony only among the "spiritually kindred"; obedience to and respect for civil government, except in the use of armed force; exclusion from the church and social ostracism of those who sin willfully; and future reward for the faithful and punishment for the wicked.

Their pacifism and rejection of the state religion brought severe persecution, and the number of martyrs might have been much greater had it not been for the haven offered by William Penn (1644–1718) in the American colonies. Several families settled in Germantown near Philadelphia in 1683, and eventually a Mennonite congregation was established there. Mennonite immigrants from Germany and Switzerland spread over Pennsylvania, Ohio, Virginia, Indiana, Illinois, and into the far western U.S. and Canada; these were later joined by others from Russia, Prussia, and Poland.

The Lord's Supper is served twice a year in almost all Mennonite congregations; in most, baptism is by pouring. Most also observe foot-washing as an ordinance in connection with the Lord's Supper, after which they salute one another with the "kiss of peace." The sexes are separated in the last two ceremonies. Mennonites baptize only on confession of faith, refuse to take oaths before magistrates, oppose secret societies, and strictly follow the teachings of the New Testament. They have a strong intra-church program of mutual aid and provide world-wide relief through the Mennonite Central Committee.

The local congregation is more or less autonomous and authoritative, although in some instances appeals are taken to district or state conferences. The officers of the church are bishops (often called elders), ministers, and deacons (almoners). Many ministers are self-supporting, working in secular employment when not occupied with the work of the church. Other officers are appointed for Sunday school, young people's work, and other duties.

The Amish are the most conservative branch of the Mennonite movement. Jacob Amman (ca. 1656 – ca. 1730), a Swiss Mennonite bishop, insisted on strict adherence to the confession of faith, especially in the matter of shunning excommunicated members. This literalism brought about a separation in Switzerland in 1693. Early Amish immigrants to the U.S. concentrated in Pennsylvania and spread into Ohio, Indiana, Illinois, Nebraska, and other western states and into Canada.

Many Amish, distinguished by their severely plain clothing, are found in the Conservative Amish Mennonite Church and the Old Order Amish Mennonite Church. They are still the literalists of the movement, clinging tenaciously to the Pennsylvania Dutch language and seventeenth-century culture of their Swiss-German forebears. Most Amish oppose the use of automobiles, telephones, and higher education and are recognized as extremely efficient farmers.

Suggestions for further reading:

Dyck, Cornelius J. *An Introduction to Mennonite History: A Popular History of the Anabaptists and the Mennonites.* Scottdale, PA: Herald Press, 1993.

Hostetler, Beulah Stauffer. *American Mennonites and Protestant Movements: A Community Paradigm.* Scottdale, PA: Herald Press, 1987.

Hostetler, John A. *Hutterite Society.* Baltimore: Johns Hopkins University Press, 1974.

Hostetler, John A. *Amish Society,* 4th ed. Baltimore: Johns Hopkins University Press, 1993.

Kraybill, Donald B. and Mark A. Olshan. *The Amish Struggle with Modernity.* Hanover, NH: University Press of New England, 1994.

MacMaster, Richard K. *Land, Piety, Peoplehood: The Establishment of Mennonite Communities in America 1683-1790.* Scottdale, PA: Herald Press, 1990.

Williams, George Huntson. *The Radical Reformation.* Philadelphia: Westminster, 1962.

BEACHY AMISH MENNONITE CHURCHES

Founded: 1927
Membership: 9,205 in 153 churches (2000)

These churches are made up mostly of Amish Mennonites who separated from the more conservative Old Order Amish* over a period of years, beginning in 1927. They were led by Bishop Moses M. Beachy, and they are now found principally in Pennsylvania and Ohio. They believe in the Trinity and that the Bible is the infallible

Word by which all people will be judged. To some degree, they resemble the Old Order Amish in garb and general attitude, but their discipline is milder. These Mennonites worship in church buildings, have Sunday schools, and are active in supporting missionary work. Nearly all of the churches sponsor Christian day schools. They sponsor a monthly publication, *Calvary Messenger,* and an annual twelve-week Calvary Bible School. The Mission Interests Committee sponsors homes for the aged and handicapped as well as missions in the U.S. and Europe.

For more information: www.mhsc.ca (Mennonite Historical Society of Canada)

Headquarters: 3015 Partridge Rd., Partridge, KS 67566

BRÜDERHOF COMMUNITIES

Founded: 1920, came to U.S. in 1954
Membership: 2,000 worldwide (2004)

Though small in terms of actual membership, the Brüderhof represent one of the newer manifestations of the Anabaptist communal witness. The movement began in Germany following the economic and social devastation of the First World War. Founded by Eberhard Arnold (1883–1935), a theologian and writer, it gained attention in North America during the 1960s, and has now grown to thirteen communities in the U.S. (five in New York, two in Penn., one in New Jersey), England, and Australia, where about 2,000 men, women, and children live in common in accordance with the witness of the early Christians as described in the book of Acts (chaps. 2 and 4). They live together in full community, share their property, work and worship together, and in all things seek unity. Several thousand people are associated with the movement without being members.

Theologically the Brüderhof affirm the Apostles' Creed but place their emphasis on the expectation of God's kingdom coming to this earth. They hold that followers of Jesus are empowered by the Spirit to live now in accordance with God's rule and reign as expressed in the Sermon on the Mount (Matt. 5:1–7:29). The mission of the Brüderhof is to witness to the good news that in Christ it is possible to live a new life and to share this life together with others in brotherhood, community, and justice: "We acknowledge God's working in

151

all who strive for justice and peace, no matter their religion or creed. All the same, we take Christ's commands seriously."

Because of Jesus' teachings, the Brüderhof affirm the sanctity of every life; thus they oppose every form of violence and killing, including abortion, capital punishment, war, and physician-assisted suicide. They also believe in the sanctity of marriage (between one man and one woman) and the sanctity of sex (sexual intimacy within marriage only). They do not proselytize, but instead seek to work together with others, whatever their belief and wherever possible, in the spirit of Christian unity and common concern.

For more information: www.bruderhof.org

CHURCH OF GOD IN CHRIST, MENNONITE

Founded: 1859
Membership: 12,984 in 115 churches (2002)

This church grew out of the preaching and labors of John Holeman (1832–1900), a member of the Mennonite church in Ohio, who became convinced that the church had moved from the doctrines and practices of its forebears. He preached ardently on the necessity of the new birth, Holy Ghost baptism, more adequate training of children in the fundamentals of the faith, disciplining of unfaithful members, avoidance of apostates, and condemnation of worldly-minded churches. He separated from the Mennonite Church and in 1859 began to hold meetings with a small group of followers.

The church holds that the same confession of faith must be believed and practiced by all churches, "from the time of the apostles to the end of the world," and that the Bible, as the inspired, infallible Word of God, must govern all doctrine and teaching. It accepts the Eighteen Articles of Faith drawn up at Dordrecht, Holland, in 1632. Women are required to cover their heads and men to wear beards. Non-involvement in the military and in secular government is enforced. The church teaches nonconformity to the world in dress, bodily adornment, sports, and amusements.

Most congregations in the church maintain a Christian school for the education of their children. Around the world members are found in Belize, Brazil, Burkina Faso, Canada, the Dominican Republic, Ethiopia, Ghana, Guatemala, Haiti, India, Jamaica, Kenya, Latvia, Malawi, Mexico, Mozambique, Nicaragua, Nigeria, the Philippines, Romania, Uganda, Ukraine, and Zimbabawe. In the U.S., Kansas is the state of heaviest concentration.

For more information: www.cogicm.org

Contact: Information and Gospel Publishers, CGIC, Mennonite, P.O. Box 230, Moundridge, KS 67107

CONSERVATIVE MENNONITE CONFERENCE

Founded: 1910
Membership: 11,100 in 112 churches (2004)

The Conservative Mennonite Conference (CMC) is an autonomous affiliation of congregations within the Mennonite church that was formed in 1910 in a meeting of concerned Amish Mennonite church leaders who were reluctant to adopt the Old Order Amish Mennonite conservatism toward cultural expressions but who were also more conservative than the prevailing Mennonite approach of that time. The present name of the association was adopted in 1954.

The CMC subscribes to the Mennonite Confession of Faith (1963), the Conservative Mennonite Statement of Theology (1991), and the Danver's Statement. These documents affirm the full humanity and full divinity of Jesus Christ, the full inspiration and autographical inerrancy of the Scriptures, believers' baptism, and nonviolence. Members are expected to refrain from gambling, alcohol, tobacco, immodest attire, swearing oaths, and premarital and extramarital sexual activity.

The highest decision-making body is the semi-annual Minister's Business Meeting, which elects an executive board and a general secretary to oversee the day-to-day operations of the conference. Internationally affiliated church bodies are found in Costa Rica, Nicaragua, Ecuador, Haiti, India, Germany, and Kenya. Rosedale Bible College in Irwin, Ohio offers an associate's degree in various Christian studies.

Headquarters: 9910 Rosedale Milford Ctr. Rd., Irwin, OH 43029

153

FELLOWSHIP OF EVANGELICAL CHURCHES

Founded: 1865
Attendance: 11,584 in 38 churches (2003)

Formerly the Defenseless Mennonite Church and Evangelical Mennonite Church,* this body was founded as a result of a spiritual awakening among the Amish in Indiana under the leadership of Henry Egly, who stressed the need for repentance and regeneration before baptism. Egly's practice of rebaptizing Amish who experienced conversion led to conflict within the Amish community, leading to the formation of the evangelical church. It continues to emphasize regeneration, separation and nonconformity to the world, and nonresistance.

Today the Fellowship of Evangelical Churches' program is largely one of missions and church-extension evangelism. A children's home in Flanagan, Illinois, and a camp near Kalamazoo, Michigan, are maintained. The name Evangelical Mennonite Church was adopted in 1949; however, representatives voted on August 2, 2003, to change the name to the Fellowship of Evangelical Churches because of the changing constituency of the church. In so doing, the Fellowship of Evangelical Churches (FEC) affirmed its core values anchored in Evangelical theology and Anabaptist identity, and its mission to help the local church accomplish the Great Commandment and the Great Commission.

For more information: www.fecministries.org

Headquarters: 1420 Kerrway Court, Fort Wayne, IN 46805

GENERAL CONFERENCE OF
MENNONITE BRETHREN CHURCHES

Founded: 1860
Membership: 82,130 in 368 churches (1996)

Dutch and German in background, this church was organized in the Ukraine by a small group of Mennonites seeking greater attention to prayer and Bible study than they found in their native Mennonite church. Its founders were heavily influenced by German

154

Pietism,* but they retained the congregational polity common to Mennonite churches.

A general conference meets biennially as the chief administrative body, gathering delegates from its two areas (Canada and the U.S.). Each area has a number of districts. The area conferences supervise work in home missions, education, and publications. General offices are maintained in Fresno, California. The Krimmer Mennonite Brethren merged with this church in 1960, and General Conference Mennonites continue to work closely with other Mennonites in mission. Foreign missions are found in Africa, Asia, Europe, South America, and Mexico; a radio ministry broadcasts worldwide in English, German, and Russian; and a French-language Bible Institute was established in Quebec in 1976.

For more information: www.mhsc.ca

HUTTERIAN BRETHREN

Founded: ca. 1530 (came to the U.S. in 1870s)
Membership: est. 43,000 in 444 colonies
in the U.S. and Canada (2000)

This is one of the few American bodies to stem directly from the Anabaptist movement without being connected to the Mennonites. Like others in the Radical Reformation, the Hutterian Brethren reject infant baptism and insist on separation of church and state. The New Testament, particularly the Sermon on the Mount (Matt. 5:1–7:29), is taken as the literal authority for true Christians; therefore, they embraced nonviolence. They got their name from their founder Jacob Hutter, a sixteenth-century Tyrolean Anabaptist who advocated communal ownership of property. The community thrived in the under-populated areas of Central Europe, particularly Moravia, but always lived under the threat of persecution. Hutter himself was martyred in Austria in 1536. Over time, they migrated to Russia, where the need for hard-working and peaceful farmers was evident. As persecution there increased in the nineteenth century, many Hutterites left Russia for Canada and the U.S.

Most Hutterites are of German ancestry and use that language in their homes and churches. Aside from the idea of common property, they are quite similar to the Old Order Amish. They seek to express their Bible-centered faith in brotherly love and aim at the recovery of New Testament spirit and fellowship. They feel this requires non-conformity to the world; accordingly, they practice nonresistance, refuse to participate in local politics, and dress in traditional attire. Choral singing plays a major role in Hutterite worship and daily life. They maintain their own schools in which the Bible is paramount. There are different branches of Hutterites in America, including the Schmiedeleut, Lehrerleut, and Dariusleu. Some are more open to modern technology, such as computers, than others.

For more information: www.hutterites.org

MENNONITE CHURCH U.S.A.

Founded: 1525 (organized in the U.S. in 1725)
Membership: 112,688 in 964 churches (2002)

This is the major Mennonite body, and it was brought to Germantown, Pennsylvania in 1683 by Dutch and German immigrants. In 2001 this church merged with the General Conference Mennonite Church (founded in 1860). In 1995 General Conference Mennonites and members of the Mennonite Church adopted a new "Confession of Faith in a Mennonite Perspective." The confession is the most recent in a series of historical Anabaptist faith statements, beginning with the Schleitheim Articles written in 1527. The new confession of faith includes twenty-four articles that interpret Mennonite beliefs about God, Jesus Christ, the Holy Spirit, Scripture, creation, sin, salvation, the church, Christian life and mission, peace and justice, and the reign of God.

It is similar to the older confession adopted in 1963 which sought to set forth the major doctrines of Scripture as understood in the Anabaptist-Mennonite tradition. The confession stresses faith in Christ, the saved status of children, the importance of proclaiming God's Word and "making disciples," baptism of believers, absolute love, nonresistance rather than retaliation as one's personal response to injustice and maltreatment, and the church as a non-hierarchical community. Because of their insistence on freedom from the traditional Mennonite regulations on attire, this group has been regarded as "liberal in conduct" by some other Mennonites, but it still represents the Radical Reformation.

156

The General Assembly meets every two years. It brings together representatives from all area conferences and from many congregations throughout North America. Discussion is open to all; however, only elected delegates (women and men, ordained and lay) may vote. Church-wide program boards are in charge of mission, congregational ministries, education, publishing, and mutual aid work; all are under the supervision of the church's general board. Home missions stress evangelism, and missions are found in Asia, Africa, Europe, and Central and South America. The church sponsors hospitals, retirement homes, and child-welfare services. Membership is strongest in Pennsylvania and the Midwest states. Associated Mennonite Biblical Seminary in Elkhart, Indiana, trains General Conference and Mennonite Church pastors, missionaries, pastoral counselors, peace workers, and lay leaders.

For more information: www.mennonites.org

Headquarters: 421 South Second St., Suite 600, Elkhart, IN 46516

MISSIONARY CHURCH

Founded: 1969
Membership: 46,015 in 383 churches (2002)

The Missionary Church is made up of two groups that merged in March 1969, the Missionary Church Association and the United Missionary Church. Both former denominations had a Mennonite heritage and came into existence through the holiness revivals of the late 1800s. The Missionary Church is conservative and evangelical in theology and practice. Local churches are free to manage their own affairs, but recognize and adhere to the authority of a general conference made up of clergy, missionaries, and laity, held biennially. Working under the general conference is a general board that oversees a variety of agencies and missions activities. The president, vice president, and secretary are elected for terms of four years.

The international ministry of the Missionary Church is done under the name of World Partners U.S.A. Primary activities include evangelism, discipleship, church planting, Bible translation, theological education, leadership development and community development. There are over 120 staff members serving in over twenty countries in the world. Presently there are fifteen national Missionary Churches

157

whose leaders meet together for inspiration, vision casting and formation of cooperative ministries under the name of the Fellowship of Missionary Churches. The church is affiliated with one educational institution in the U.S.: Bethel College in Mishawaka, Indiana.

For more information: www.mcusa.org

Headquarters: P.O. Box 9127, Fort Wayne, IN 46899

OLD ORDER AMISH CHURCHES

Founded: 1720s
Membership: est. over 100,000 in about 900 districts (2000)

The Old Order (*Ordnung*) Amish hold to the old traditions of the Amish movement more strictly than do the so-called Church Amish. For example, their "plain dress" requires the use of hooks and eyes instead of buttons or zippers, and members do not own automobiles. They are strict pacifists and seek to remain separate from all secular governments and the influence of secular culture.

It is impossible to give precise membership statistics since the Old Order is not a denomination in the usual sense of the word. There are no church buildings because believers worship in private homes. Moreover, there are no conferences. Members do not believe in missions, benevolent institutions, or centralized schools; some, however, do contribute to the missions and charities of the Mennonite Church. There are nearly nine hundred Old Order Amish districts, each averaging one hundred to 150 members, with approximately half that number baptized. The church continues to grow rapidly due to the birth rate in Amish families.

For more information: www.mhsc.ca

OLD ORDER (WISLER) MENNONITE CHURCH

Founded: 1872
Membership: est. 17,000 adults in 150 churches (2002)

This church was named for Jacob Wisler, the first Mennonite* bishop in Indiana, who led a separation from that church in 1872 to protest the use of English in the services and the introduction of Sunday schools. Similar to Old Order (Ordnung) Amish, these

158

Mennonites maintain the old style of clothing, make only limited use of modern technology, and keep separate from the world. Joined in 1886, 1893, and 1901 by groups with similar ideas from Canada, Pennsylvania, and Virginia, the church is still maintained on the basis of those protests. Each section of the church has its own district conference, and there are conferences twice each year in each community. All churches take part in relief work, especially for the needy at home and in foreign lands, and some contribute to the work of the Mennonite Church.

For more information: www.mhsc.ca

Headquarters: 376 N. Muddy Creek Rd., Denver, PA 17517

FRIENDS (QUAKER)

Dating from the 1650s in England, the Society of Friends is an unconventional but esteemed Protestant body. Because they affirm the "Inner Light," the spiritual nerve center that God has placed in every person, classical Friends deny the validity of clergy, liturgy, and sacraments. Friends believe that the practice of inward listening and obedience to God results in lives that begin to reflect the character of Jesus. From this arises the Friends' testimonies to peace, simplicity, equality, moral purity, and integrity. The fact that every person has this inward spiritual endowment has prompted Friends to stand for the equality of all people and thus to oppose slavery and to be exceptionally service-minded.

Despite their small numbers, Friends have had a deep and lasting influence on Western society. Contributions in both religious and humanitarian spheres have won them universal respect and admiration, and their loyalty to their quiet faith offers a challenge and inspiration to all churches. Friends take seriously the prophetic vision of the world at peace and cooperate with the historic peace churches in the context of the wider ecumenical movement. In the United States, seven colleges and three seminaries reflect Friends' long-standing emphasis on the importance of education.

History. The Society of Friends began with the vision of George Fox (1624–91), a seeker after spiritual truth and peace during the turmoil of the English Civil War and its aftermath. After failing to find satisfactory truth or peace in the churches of his time, Fox discov-

159

ered what he sought in a direct personal relationship with Christ: "When all my hopes in [churches] were gone . . . I heard a voice which said, 'That is the Inner Voice, or Inner Light, based upon the description of John 1:9: "the true Light, which lighteth every man that cometh into the world. (KJV)" ' " This voice, Fox maintained, is available to all and has nothing to do with the ceremonies, rituals, or creeds over which Christians have fought. Every heart is God's altar and shrine.

Fox and his early followers not only refused to attend the state church, they also insisted on freedom of speech, assembly, and worship. They would not take oaths in court and would not go to war. They condemned slavery and England's treatment of prisoners and the mentally ill. The names they adopted—Children of Truth, Children of Light, and Friends of Truth—aroused ridicule and fierce opposition. When Fox, hauled into court, advised one judge to "tremble at the Word of the Lord," the judge call him "a quaker," thus coining a term that became a name for the movement. Fox spent six years in jail. From 1650 until 1689, more than three thousand suffered for conscience's sake, and three hundred to four hundred died in prison. In spite of persecution, the group grew, and the Religious Society of Friends was founded in 1652. When Fox died in 1691, Quakers numbered fifty thousand.

Friends soon brought their message to the American colonies. Ann Austin (d. 1665) and Mary Fisher (ca. 1623–98) arrived in Massachusetts from Barbados in 1656. They were promptly accused of being witches and were deported. Eventually, four Friends were hanged in Boston, but the passage of the Act of Toleration of 1689 ended most persecution. William Penn (1644–1718) was granted the colony of Pennsylvania by the British Crown and made it a refuge for his fellow Quakers. Penn's "Holy Experiment" allowed complete religious toleration in the colony of Pennsylvania, removing the government from the business of religion. This was a milestone on the path to full religious freedom in the American Constitution.

As persecution waned and Friends settled down to business and farming in the eighteenth century, many grew prosperous. Meetings and community life became well organized; it was a time of creativity and mystical inwardness, and closely knit family life was emphasized. Quaker philanthropy increased and became widely admired. Their ideas on prison reform began to take effect, and their schools increased in number and attendance. The Quakers lost control of the

Pennsylvania legislature in 1756 over the issue of taxation to pay for a war against the Shawnee and the Delaware peoples.

Quaker leaders, now looking within rather than without, began to enforce such strict discipline upon their members that they became, in fact, a "peculiar people." Members were disowned or dismissed for even minor infractions; thousands were cut off for "marrying out of Meeting." Pleasure, music, and art were taboo; sobriety, punctuality, and honesty were demanded in all matters; dress was plain; and speech was biblical. They were "different" and dour; they gained few new converts and lost many old members during this period. A number of separate groups were formed as a result: the Hicksites in 1827, the Wilburites in 1845, and the Primitives in 1861.

Influenced by revival movements of the nineteenth century, most Friends in the United States abandoned the quietism of an earlier generation and many engaged with other Christians in evangelism and the world missionary movement. Independently, various "Orthodox" yearly meetings started missions in Mexico, Cuba, Jamaica, and Palestine that combined emphases on evangelism, education, and economic development. In 1887 these yearly meetings gathered to issue a Declaration of Faith which reacted against two trends in American Quakerism. They opposed, on the left, a mysticism that seemed to disconnect the "inner Light" from the cross of Christ; and, on the right, they opposed use of outward rituals to celebrate baptism and communion. Friends traditionally view baptism and communion as purely inward and spiritual.

Service and Peace Work. Even during the quietistic phase of Quaker life, Friends continued to work for peace, public education, temperance, democracy, and the abolition of slavery. In 1688 the Friends of Germantown, Pennsylvania, announced that slavery violated the Golden Rule. It took nearly a century for Quakers to rid their own society of slavery, but they did so years in advance of any other religious body in the U.S. The writings of Friends John Woolman (1720–72) and John Greenleaf Whittier (1807–92) helped to further the abolition movement in American society.

During World War I, Friends from all branches of society were at work in the American Friends Service Committee (A.F.S.C.) in relief and reconstruction efforts abroad. The A.F.S.C. remains today one of the most effective of such agencies in the world. The A.F.S.C. and its British counterpart were jointly awarded the Nobel Peace Prize in 1947. Friends who enter military service are no longer disowned from membership, but many leave the society and join a church that does not profess pacifism. Conversely, pacifists brought up in other traditions often join the Friends in young adulthood. Peace conferences have had a prominent place in Friends' ministries.

Worship and Polity. The Inner Light is the heart of Quaker theology and practice. Friends believe that grace, the power from God to help humankind pursue good and resist evil, is universal among all people. They seek not holiness but perfection—a higher, more spiritual standard of life for both society and the individual—and they believe that truth is unfolding and continuing. They value the Bible but prefer to rely on fresh individual guidance from the Spirit of God, which produced the Bible, rather than follow only what has been revealed to others.

Worship and business in the society are conducted in monthly, quarterly, and yearly meetings. The monthly meeting is the basic unit, made up of one or more meetings (groups) in a neighborhood. It convenes each week for worship and once a month for business. It keeps records of membership, births, deaths, and marriages; appoints committees; considers queries on spiritual welfare; and transacts all business. Monthly meetings join four times a year in a quarterly meeting to stimulate spiritual life and decide on any business that should be brought to the attention of the yearly meeting. The yearly meeting corresponds to a diocese in an episcopal system. In Friends' business meetings at every level, there often is frank inquiry into members' conduct of business and treatment of others.

Group decisions await the "sense of the meeting." Lacking unity of opinion, the meeting may have a "quiet time" until unity is found, or it may postpone consideration of the matter or refer it to a committee for study. Minority opinion is not outvoted, but convinced. Every man, woman, and child is free to speak in any meeting; delegates are appointed at quarterly and yearly meetings to ensure adequate representation but enjoy no unusual position or prerogatives. Church officers, elders, and ministers are chosen for recognized ability in spiritual leadership, but they too stand on equal footing with the rest of the membership. A few full-time workers are paid a modest salary, and "recorded" ministers who serve as pastors in meetings that have programmed worship also receive salaries.

Worship may be either programmed or unprogrammed, but the two are not always distinct. The former more nearly resembles an ordinary Protestant service, although there are no rites or outward sacraments. While Friends believe in spiritual communion, partaking of the elements is thought unnecessary. In unprogrammed meetings there is no choir, collection, singing, or pulpit; the service is devoted to quiet meditation, prayer, and communion with God. Any vocal contributions are prompted by the Spirit.

Friends World Committee for Consultation (F.W.C.C.), organized at Swarthmore, Pennsylvania, following the Second World Conference of Friends in 1937, functions as an agent, or clearing-house, for interchange of Quaker aspirations and experiences through regional, national, and international inter-visitation, person-to-person consultations, conferences, correspondence, and a variety of publications. The F.W.C.C. maintains a world office in London, England, and is a nongovernmental organization (NGO) that helps to operate a program at U.N. headquarters to forward world peace and human unity. Something of a world community has been set up in the Wider Quaker Fellowship, in which non-Friends in sympathy with the spirit and program of Quakerism may participate in the work without coming into full membership.

Suggestions for further reading:

Bacon, Margaret Hope. *Mothers of Feminism.* San Francisco: HarperSanFrancisco, 1986.

Barbour, Hugh and J. William Frost. *The Quakers.* New York: Greenwood, 1989.

Bowden, James. *The History of the Society of Friends in America,* 2 vols. New York: Arno, 1972.

Brock, Peter. *Pioneers of a Peaceable Kingdom: The Quaker Peace Testimony from the Colonial Era to the First World War.* Princeton, NJ: Princeton University Press, 1972.

Hall, Francis. *Friends in the Americas.* Philadelphia: Friends World Committee, 1976.

Hamm, Thomas D. *The Transformation of American Quakerism: Orthodox Friends: 1800–1907.* Bloomington: University of Indiana Press, 1988.

Stoneburner, Carol and John, eds. *The Influence of Quaker Women on American History: Biographical Sketches.* Lewiston, NY: Mellen, 1986.

Weeks, Stephen B. *Southern Quakers and Slavery.* Baltimore: Johns Hopkins University Press, 1986.

EVANGELICAL FRIENDS INTERNATIONAL

Founded: 1990
Attendance: 39,913 in 288 meetings (2004)

This is the newest and one of the largest organizations of Friends meetings in the U.S. It grew out of the Evangelical Friends Alliance, which was formed in 1965 to encourage evangelical emphases and denominational unity. The Evangelical Friends represent one part of the general evangelical renewal that profoundly shaped American Christianity in the latter part of the twentieth century.

The Evangelical Friends are organized into six regions of the U.S., with commissions devoted to missions, education, youth ministry, and communication. Worship is programmed and includes Scripture readings, congregational singing, and a sermon by the pastor. The theology is generally conservative, and Evangelical Friends cooperate with other evangelical bodies. Of primary concern is the Great Commission (Matt. 28:19) to make disciples of all nations. Worldwide EFI has nearly 1,100 churches with over 150,000 regular attenders.

For more information: www.evangelical-friends.org

Headquarters: 5350 Broadmoor Cir, NW, Canton, OH 44709

FRIENDS GENERAL CONFERENCE

Founded: 1900
Membership: est. 34,000 in 650 meetings (2002)

Friends General Conference is an association of fourteen yearly meetings and regional associations and seven monthly meetings of Friends (Quakers) in the United States and Canada. It is less a denomination than a service organization that provides resources for yearly and monthly meetings. Most of these meetings are "unprogrammed," meaning that worshipers meet in silence, expecting that one or more Friends may be moved by the Spirit to speak. No pastors are employed; the responsibilities handled by pastors in other denominations are shared among the members of the meeting. This group of Friends emphasizes the Quaker belief that faith is based on direct experience of God and that God is found in every individual.

164

Friends General Conference serves the members of affiliated meetings by preparing and distributing educational and spiritual materials, providing opportunities for Friends to share experiences and strengthen the Quaker community, and helping monthly and yearly meetings to nurture and support the spiritual and community life of Friends in North America. It is best known for the annual "Gathering of Friends," which attracts between 1,500 and 2,000 Friends from all over North America. Friends General Conference offices are in Philadelphia, Pennsylvania. The Conference publishes various books and religious education materials and supports *Friends Journal,* a magazine for Friends and other seekers.

For more information: www.fgcquaker.org

Headquarters: 1216 Arch St #2B, Philadelphia, PA 19107

FRIENDS UNITED MEETING

Founded: 1902
Membership: 41,184 in 472 meetings (2002)

Friends United Meeting was formed in 1902 as the umbrella for Friends mission activities and the communications arm for a broadly Christian understanding of the Quaker movement. Friends United Meeting is an international association of twenty-six yearly meetings (regional bodies of Quaker meetings) the purpose of which is "to energize and equip Friends through the power of the Holy Spirit to gather people into fellowships where Jesus Christ is known, loved and obeyed as Teacher and Lord." Friends United Meeting includes Friends meetings with both pastor-led services and those that practice traditional unprogrammed silent waiting on God.

The international work of Friends United Meeting includes medical, educational, and children services in Kenya, Palestine, and the Caribbean as well as pastoral leadership training through the Friends Theological College in Kaimosi, Kenya. Of the 172,000 members of Friends United, 128,000 are in East Africa. The headquarters in Richmond, Indiana, houses departments of Global Ministries and Communications, which includes a bookstore, press, denominational magazine and Internet outreach.

For more information: www.fum.org

Headquarters: 101 Quaker Hill Drive, Richmond IN 47374

165

BRETHREN AND PIETIST CHURCHES

An international religious revival began in Germany in the late 1600s with the writings of Philipp Jakob Spener (1635–1705). Spener decried the barren intellectualism, theological factionalism, and general ineffectiveness of the Protestant churches of his day. He called for a new type of Reformation that would complete the promise of Luther's Reformation. Luther had reformed the church doctrinally and liturgically; Spener wanted to reform it morally and spiritually. He called for pastors to find ways to make the doctrine of the priesthood of all believers effective in the hearts and souls of the people.

To do this, Spener proposed that pastors form small groups of believers to meet for study, prayer, and mutual encouragement. The staples of modern church life, such as Sunday school, youth fellowship, and women's circle meetings, grew out of this idea. Also, Spener urged pastors to leave polemics aside and concentrate on edifying preaching that could transform individuals from sinners to laborers for God. This "religion of the heart" spread throughout Protestant Germany and profoundly influenced John Wesley's (1703–91) early Methodist* movement. When Pietism, as it was called in Germany, came to the U.S. in the 1740s, it helped to fuel the First Great Awakening.

In the 1750s Philip Otterbein (1726–1813), a German Reformed pastor of Pietist leanings, began his career as an evangelist in Pennsylvania and Maryland. His activities led to the formation of the United Brethren Church, later called the Evangelical United Brethren (EUB). This body was one of the groups that eventually formed The United Methodist Church* in 1968. Although there are only a few, relatively small denominations in the U.S. that emerged out of German Pietism, American Christianity in all its varieties has been influenced by this spiritual movement.

Many Pietist bodies use the name "Brethren" in various forms. For them, the church is primarily a company of brothers and sisters in Christ joined together by the Holy Spirit for mutual edification. The inner spiritual life, piety, is cultivated in prayer and study of Scripture and through association with fellow believers. For most Brethren, the local church is central, but they are often bound in close-knit national communities. The church claims their primary loyalty and is understood more as a community of people who love God and one another than as part of an organization or a body that formulates doctrine.

166

Brethren do not emphasize rigid doctrinal standards; rather, the Spirit of God within each person, which binds them together in love, takes precedence for them. Some place emphasis on prophecy and direct inspiration from the Holy Spirit. They usually live a simple, unadorned life. In their early decades in Europe and the United States, most Brethren were separatists from the state and conventional churches. While not manifesting a judgmental attitude, they devoted themselves to a moral purity that set them apart from other Christians as well as from general society.

Many Pietist groups took the New Testament literally and endeavored to put its teachings into practice, even in the minute details of their daily living. At the heart of their religious ritual was the love feast, or agape, and the serving of the Lord's Supper, preceded by a ceremony of foot washing. They saluted one another with a kiss of peace, dressed in the plainest of clothing, covered women's heads at services, anointed their sick with oil for healing and consecration, refrained from worldly amusements, and refused to take oaths, go to war, or engage in lawsuits. Those Pietist groups that were not Brethren tended to be more embracing of the secular world.

Many of the Brethren churches stem from the work of Alexander Mack, Sr. (1679–1735) in Schwarzenau in Wittgenstein, Germany. After his experience of conversion, Mack was convinced of the need for those who had experienced regeneration to form separate communities modeled on the early church's practice of sharing goods in common. Exiled from the Palatinate for preaching separatism, Mack gathered a company of fellow refugees and in 1708 took the bold, and at that time illegal, step of rebaptizing adult believers. Eventually persecution in Germany led these German Baptists (see NORTH AMERICAN BAPTIST CONFERENCE) to emigrate to the U.S.

They were known for years simply as the German Baptist Brethren, but that title has largely disappeared, except in the case of the Old German Baptist Brethren, who were also known as "Dunkers." The terms "Brethren" and "Dunker" have been the cause of much confusion. Dunker is a direct derivation of the German tunken, "to dip or immerse," and is identified with the peculiar method of immersion employed by this group of churches in which the new believer is immersed three times, face forward, in the name of the Father, the Son, and the Holy Ghost.

Several communal societies in American history were established by Pietist groups. Such communes were an intense expression of the

Pietist ideal of brotherhood and sisterhood, and in many cases were inspired by the vision of the New Jerusalem in the book of Revelation. Among the most important were Ephrata Cloister and Bethlehem in Pennsylvania, Salem in North Carolina, and Amana in New York (and later Iowa). Amana survived as a commune until 1932. At that time the organization was divided between the Amana Business Society and the Amana Church Society. The latter continues as a small denomination in Iowa that does not have an ordained ministry.

Suggestions for further reading:

Atwood, Craig D. *Community of the Cross: Moravian Piety in Colonial Bethlehem.* University Park, Pa.: Pennsylvania State University Press, 2004.

Bach, Jeff. *Voices of the Turtledove: The Sacred World of Ephrata.* University Park, Pa.: Pennsylvania State University Press, 2003.

Brown, Dale. *Understanding Pietism.* Grand Rapids, Mich.: Eerdmans, 1978,

Durnbaugh, Donald F., ed. *The Brethren Encyclopedia.* 3 vols. Philadelphia: Brethren, 1983–84.

Durnbaugh, Donald F. *The Church of the Brethren Past and Present.* Elgin, Ill.: Brethren, 1971.

Hoestetler, John A. *Hutterite Society.* Baltimore: Johns Hopkins University Press, 1974.

Longenecker, Steve. *Piety and Tolerance: Pennsylvania German Religion, 1700-1850.* Metuchen, N.J.: Scarecrow, 1994.

Stoeffler, Ernst, ed. *Continental Pietism and Early American Christianity.* Grand Rapids, Mich.: Eerdmans, 1976.

Wittlinger, Carlton O. *Quest for Piety and Obedience: The Story of the Brethren in Christ.* Nappanee, Ind.: Evangel, 1978.

BRETHREN CHURCH (ASHLAND)

Founded: 1882
Membership: 10,287 in 117 congregations (2002)

In 1882 the Church of the Brethren* voted to expel a member for advocating Sunday schools, missions, a paid clergy, congregational polity, and more freedom in dress and worship. The supporters of such changes withdrew and formed the Progressive Convention of the Tunker Church in Ashland, Ohio. The following year it was officially organized as the Brethren Church. Most Brethren churches are still found in Ohio, Pennsylvania, and Indiana. The church's college and a seminary in Ashland, Ohio, have historically been at the center of its ministry.

Theologically, the Brethren Church tries to seek a balance between the Calvinist and Arminian perspectives on salvation; however, for the Brethren, style of life is more important than doctrine. The believing community of faith leads believers into the path proposed in the Sermon on the Mount. Nonetheless, the church suffered a schism during the fundamentalist*/modernist controversy that gripped American Christianity in the 1920s and 1930s. The more conservative ministers formed the Fellowship of Grace Brethren Church.* The church has a missionary board and cooperates with the Church of the Brethren in relief activities around the world. It also works with the Mennonites* in the area of evangelism.

For more information: www.brethrenchurch.org

Headquarters: 524 College Avenue, Ashland, OH 44805

BRETHREN IN CHRIST CHURCH

Founded: 1778
Membership: 20,739 in 232 congregations (2002)

The church began as a result of a spiritual awakening that took place in Lancaster, Pennsylvania, in the 1760s, inspired by the preaching of Philip Otterbein (1726–1813) and Martin Boehm (1725–1812). The group that gathered along the Susquehanna River was called simply the River Brethren until the Civil War. Primarily of Mennonite* descent, the River Brethren separated from the Mennonites over the issue of triple immersion in baptism. The River Brethren were pacifists, and with the outbreak of the Civil War and the institution of a national military draft, it became necessary for the Brethren to obtain legal recognition as an established religious organization in order to protect the objectors. A council meeting in Lancaster County, Pennsylvania, in 1863 adopted the name Brethren in Christ Church, but the group was not legally incorporated until 1904.

169

The Brethren in Christ Church pledges loyalty to the following doctrines: the inspiration of the Holy Scriptures; the self-existent, Triune God; the deity and virgin birth of Christ; Christ's death as atonement for our sins and his resurrection from the dead; the Holy Spirit, who convicts the sinner, regenerates the penitent, and empowers the believer; justification as forgiveness for committed sins and sanctification as heart cleansing and empowerment by the Holy Spirit; observance of the ordinances of God's house; temperance and modesty of apparel as taught in the scriptures; the personal, visible, and imminent return of Christ; the resurrection of the dead, with punishment for the unbeliever and reward for the believer; and worldwide evangelism as the supreme duty of the church. The Brethren in Christ remains a "peace church," however. Members are not excluded from membership if they serve in the military.

While the government of this church is largely in the hands of the local congregations, there are eight regional conferences and a general conference, which is the ultimate authoritative body. Its publishing arm, Evangel Publishing House, is in Nappanee, Indiana. The church has two institutions of learning: Messiah College at Grantham, Pennsylvania, and Niagara Christian College at Fort Erie, Ontario. Missionaries are at work in Africa, India, Japan, London, Colombia, Nicaragua, Venezuela, and Cuba and are engaged in Mennonite Central Committee work around the world.

For more information: www.bic-church.org

Headquarters: P.O. Box A, Grantham, PA 17027-0901

CHURCH OF THE BRETHREN

Founded: 1708
Membership: 134,844 in 1,069 churches (2002)

The Church of the Brethren, the largest of the Brethren churches, was formed in 1708 in Schwarzenau, Germany with the work of Alexander Mack. The early Brethren were influenced by the Anabaptists as well as by Pietism, and they covenanted to be a people shaped by personal faith in Christ, prayer, and study of Scripture. They stressed daily discipleship and service to neighbor. Severe persecution and economic conditions prompted virtually the entire movement to migrate to North America between 1719 and 1729.

Commonly known as German Baptist Brethren, or even Dunkers or Dunkards, in its bicentennial year, 1908, the group adopted "Church of the Brethren" as its official name. "Brethren" was seen as a New Testament term that conveyed the kinship and warmth of Jesus' early followers.

The Brethren emphasize right living more than right doctrine, and their current website invites those "fed up with doctrine and still hungry" to try the Brethren way, which includes "open-minded consideration of Jesus, the scriptures, and our own hearts." True to Pietist principles, the Brethren develop their understanding through community discussion and study, using Jesus' own teaching as a guide for modern living. Although non-creedal, the Church of the Brethren has held firmly to basic tenets of the Free Church, or Believers Church, tradition. Among the most distinctive Brethren practices are the baptism of confessing believers by threefold immersion and the anointing of the ill for spiritual and bodily health. The Last Supper is observed with a service of foot washing that symbolizes servanthood, a fellowship meal that symbolizes family, and the commemorative Eucharist that symbolizes Saviorhood.

Brethren have long held an official peace witness, expressed often in conscientious objection to military service. During World War II, Civilian Public Health camps were maintained for religious objectors who performed work in the national interest. During and after the war, many of the programs were continued under the alternative service provisions of Selective Service, and voluntary service abroad, a forerunner of the Peace Corps, was introduced. Also growing out of the peace concern was a worldwide program of relief, reconstruction, and welfare, conducted by the Brethren Service Commission and later by the World Ministries Commission, as a service of love to those suffering from war, natural disasters, or social disadvantage. Since 1948 Brethren Volunteer Service has enlisted nearly five thousand men and women for one or two years of social service at home and abroad. Work with migrant laborers, inner-city dwellers, prison inmates, refugees, and victims of abuse exemplify the types of activity undertaken. Increasingly, older volunteers have enrolled in the program, quite often after they have reached retirement age.

Numerous projects initiated by the group have become full-scale ecumenical enterprises. Among them are the Heifer Project International, Christian Youth Exchange, Christian Rural Overseas

Program (CROP), Sales Exchange for Refugee Rehabilitation Vocation (SERRV; handcraft sales for Third World producers), and International Voluntary Service. Other pioneering ventures were agricultural exchanges begun with Poland in the 1950s and with China in the 1980s and ecumenical exchanges with the Russian Orthodox Church in the 1960s.

In polity, the Brethren combine both congregational and presbyterian practices, with final authority vested in an Annual Conference of elected delegates. The General Board of elected and ex officio members is the administrative arm of the church. Congregations are organized into twenty-three districts in thirty-six states, usually with one or more full-time executives in each district. The heaviest concentration of churches is in Pennsylvania, Virginia, Maryland, Ohio, Indiana, and Illinois.

The Brethren are related to six accredited liberal arts colleges: Bridgewater College in Virginia; Elizabethtown and Juniata Colleges in Pennsylvania; University of LaVerne in California; Manchester College in Indiana; and McPherson College in Kansas. The church sponsors one graduate school, Bethany Theological Seminary, in Richmond, Indiana. General offices are in Elgin, Illinois, also the home of Brethren Press, which produces the monthly publication *Messenger* and various books and curriculum resources.

For more information: www.brethren.org

Headquarters: 1451 Dundee Ave., Elgin, IL 60120

CHURCH OF THE UNITED BRETHREN IN CHRIST

Founded: 1800, with roots to 1767
Membership: 22,740 in 217 congregations (2002)

This group had its origins in the Pennsylvania awakening led by Philip Otterbein (1726–1813) and Martin Boehm (1725–1812) in the 1760s. In 1800 the ministers of the Brethren officially adopted the name United Brethren in Christ and elected Otterbein and Boehm as the first bishops. In 1815 they adopted a confession of faith based on one that Otterbein had written in 1789. The United Brethren took a strong stand against slave holding in the 1820s; thus they did not spread in the South but did make the western U.S. a mission area. In 1841 a constitution was adopted. When the constitution was changed in 1889, some members viewed the changes as unconstitutional and separated from the main body. The main body of United Brethren eventually merged with the United Methodists*, leaving the name "United Brethren" to the smaller group.

United Brethren believe in the Trinity and in the deity, humanity, and atonement of Christ. Observance of "scriptural living" is required of all members, who are forbidden use of alcoholic beverages and membership in secret societies. Baptism and the Lord's Supper are observed as ordinances.

Local, annual, and general conferences are held. The highest governing body, the General Conference, meets quadrennially. General church offices are located in Huntington, Indiana; the majority of local churches are found in Pennsylvania, Ohio, northern Indiana, and Michigan. Both men and women are eligible for the ministry and are ordained only once as elders. Missionary societies administer evangelism and church aid in the U.S. and in Costa Rica, El Salvador, Honduras, Hong Kong, India, Jamaica, Macau, Mexico, Myanmar, Nicaragua, Sierra Leone, and Thailand. Worldwide membership numbers over thirty-six thousand. The United Brethren Church maintains a college and a graduate school of Christian ministries at Huntington, Indiana, with secondary schools in Sierra Leone.

For more information: www.ub.org

Headquarters: 302 Lake St., Huntington, IN 46750

EVANGELICAL CONGREGATIONAL CHURCH

Founded: 1894 and 1928, with roots to 1800
Membership: 20,743 in 154 congregations (2003)

This denomination traces its origin to the work of Jacob Albright (1759–1808), a Pietist and Methodist* evangelist among the Germans of Pennsylvania in the early 1800s. Albright helped to organize the Evangelical Association that later became the Evangelical Church, which eventually merged with the United Brethren Church to form the Evangelical United Brethren Church. A division within the church 1891 was healed by a merger in 1922, but some congregations in the Ohio River valley region objected and continued their separate existence. They chose the name Evangelical Congregational Church in 1928. This church, like its parent

173

Evangelical Church, is "Methodist in polity, Arminian in doctrine." Emphasis is on the inspiration and integrity of the Bible and "fellowship of all followers of Christ."

Each congregation owns its property, determines its membership, manages its affairs, and chooses its ecclesiastical affiliation. There is a National Conference that supervises conference ministers. The stationing committee, composed of the bishop and congerence ministers, assigns pastors to churches. The Global Ministries Commission supervises the missionary programs. Church headquarters, the Evangelical School of Theology, and the Evangelical Congregational Church Retirement Village are located at Myerstown, Pennsylvania.

For more information: www.eccenter.com

Headquarters: 100 West Park Ave., Myerstown, PA 17067

EVANGELICAL COVENANT CHURCH

Founded: 1885
Membership: 107,379 in 689 congregations (2003)

The Evangelical Covenant Church is not a Brethren church but grew out of Pietism in Sweden. It traces its roots from the Protestant Reformation through the biblical instruction of the Lutheran state church of Sweden to the great spiritual awakenings of the nineteenth century. The Covenant Church was founded by Swedish immigrants in the Midwest and adheres to the affirmations of the Reformation regarding the Holy Scriptures as the Word of God and the only perfect rule for faith, doctrine, and conduct. It has traditionally valued the historic confessions of the Christian church, particularly the Apostles' Creed, but emphasizes the sovereignty of the Word over all creedal interpretations.

The Covenant Church's evangelical emphasis includes the necessity of the new birth, the ministry of the Holy Spirit, and the reality of freedom in Christ. It values the New Testament emphasis on personal faith in Jesus Christ as Savior and Lord and the church as a fellowship of believers that recognizes but transcends theological differences. Baptism and the Lord's Supper are seen as divinely ordained sacraments. While the denomination has traditionally practiced the baptism of infants, it has also recognized the practice of believer baptism.

The local church is administered by a board elected by the membership; its ministers, ordained by the denomination, are called, generally with the aid and guidance of the denominational Department of the Ordered Ministry and the conference superintendent. Each of the ten regional conferences elects its own superintendent. The highest authority is vested in an annual meeting composed of ministers and laypeople elected by the constituent churches. An administrative board, elected by the annual meeting, implements its decisions.

The Covenant Church sponsors churches in Burkina Faso, Cameroon, the Central African Republic, Central Asia, Colombia, the Czech Republic, the Democratic Republic of Congo, Ecuador, Equitorial Guinea, France, Germany, Japan, Laos, Mexico, Spain, Taiwan, and Thailand. Educational institutions include North Park University and North Park Theological Seminary in Chicago, Illinois. The church maintains fifteen retirement communities and nursing homes in seven states, two hospitals, three homes for adults with developmental disabilities, a children's home, a ministry for victims of domestic violence, and several camps and conference centers across North America.

For more information: www.covchurch.org

Headquarters: 5101 N. Francisco Ave., Chicago, IL 60625

EVANGELICAL FREE CHURCH OF AMERICA

Founded: 1950, with roots to 19th century
Membership: est. 336,000 in 1,273 congregations (2004)

The Evangelical Free Church traces its origin to the Pietist revivals in Scandanavia in the late nineteenth century. Immigration brought members of various "free" churches to the U.S. A number of Swedish-speaking evangelical congregations, centered in Iowa, formed a fellowship of "free" congregations to be known as the Swedish Evangelical Free Mission in 1884. In that same year, two Norwegian-Danish groups began fellowshiping, one on the East coast and one on the West. In 1912, these merged to form the Norwegian-Danish Evangelical Free Church Association. In 1950 the Swedish denomination merged with the other Scandinavian bodies to form the present Evangelical Free Church, with headquarters in Minneapolis, Minnesota.

Doctrinally, the church endorses a variation on the popular Pietist statement: "In essentials, unity. In non-essentials, charity. In all things, Jesus Christ." In 1950 the merged denominations adopted a twelve-point doctrinal statement, which is now incorporated into the constitution of most local congregations. The constitution stresses faithfulness to evangelical beliefs while avoiding disputes over minor matters. Affirming both the rational and the relational dimensions of Christian faith, the church maintains that sound Christian doctrine must be coupled with dynamic Christian experience, facilitating a ministry of love and reconciliation. It includes belief in the premillennial return of Jesus and biblical inerrancy.

Local congregations are autonomous, but the church maintains administrative offices in Minneapolis, Minnesota. The president works with various boards and leadership teams to guide the several ministries of the denomination. Some six hundred missionaries serve stations in over forty countries around the world. The church sponsors Trinity International University, which includes Trinity Evangelical Divinity School, with the main campus located in Deerfield, Illinois; other campuses of the university are maintained in Chicago, Illinois; Miami, Florida; and Santa Ana, California.

For more information: www.efca.org

Headquarters: 902 East 78th St., Minneapolis, MN 55420-1300

FELLOWSHIP OF GRACE BRETHREN CHURCHES

Founded: 1939
Membership: 30,371 in 260 congregations (1997)

This body was part of the Brethren Church (Ashland) that separated from the main Church of the Brethren* in the early 1880s. In part, as a result of the fundamentalist*/modernist controversy of the 1920s and 1930s, that church further divided. In 1939 the Ashland group and the Grace group went their separate ways. In 1969 the Grace group adopted its own statement of faith that expressed the church's beliefs which include the primacy of the Bible; the Trinity; the church as made up of believers; the Christian life as a way of righteousness; the ordinances of baptism and the threefold Communion service (including foot washing and the love feast); the reality of Satan; the Second Coming of Jesus; and the future life. The

176

group was separately incorporated in 1987 as the Fellowship of Grace Brethren Churches and a new constitution was adopted in 1997.

Grace Brethren churches are grouped geographically into districts, which hold annual conferences. The entire church holds an annual conference, often at Winona Lake, Indiana, where the group's headquarters are located. This conference, made up of delegates from Fellowship churches, elects a board of directors, known as the Fellowship Council, and general church officers. The church supports both international and North American missionary and relief efforts, and it maintains Grace College and Seminary in Winona Lake.

For more information: www.fgbc.org

Headquarters: P.O. Box 386, Winona Lake, IN 46590

MORAVIAN CHURCH (UNITAS FRATRUM)

Founded: 1458 (came to the U.S. in 1735)
Membership: 51,618 in 188 congregations (2002)

The Moravian Church is one of the few pre-Reformation Protestant churches (the Waldensians are another). Its roots go back to John Hus (ca. 1372–1415), a Czech reformer who was burned at the stake at the Council of Constance in 1415. In 1458, dissatisfied with the lifestyle and worship of the major Hussite church, Brother Gregory organized a community dedicated to living according to the Sermon on the Mount and the example of the early church. They called their pacifist, communitarian body *Jednota Bratrska,* "the Unity of the Brethren." At times they used the Latin form, *Unitas Fratrum,* which remains the official name of the church. In 1467 the group established an independent episcopacy and clergy.

Persecution under the Hapsburgs almost exterminated the church, but in 1722 refugees settled on the estate of Count Nicholas Ludwig von Zinzendorf (1700–60), one of the leaders of German Pietism, in Saxony. There they built the town of Herrnhut, a highly structured religious community that would be the model for similar communities in the U.S. Under the direction of Zinzendorf, the Moravians carried out an extensive mission enterprise beginning with work among the slaves on St. Thomas in the Virgin Islands. The Moravian evan-

177

gelist David Zeisberger (1721–1808) had great success among the native tribes of the northern United States, but that effort was virtually destroyed by the massacre of Moravian Indians at Gnaddenhutten, Ohio, in 1777 by an American militia.

The Moravians attempted to establish a settlement in Georgia in the 1730s, but the only lasting result of that work was the conversion of John Wesley (1703–91) to "heart religion." Permanent work was established in Pennsylvania and North Carolina. In the nineteenth century the church supported work among German and Scandanavian immigrants in the upper Midwest. Recent growth in the United States comes mainly from immigration from Central America and the Caribbean, where the Moravians have long had a strong presence.

It is sometimes said that the Moravians never developed a unified system of doctrine. That may be an overstatement, but it certainly is true that no doctrine is peculiar to them. The major doctrinal statement is *The Ground of the Unity,* which emphasizes the love of God manifested in the life and death of Jesus, the teachings of Christ, the inner testimony of the Spirit, ecumenism, and Christian conduct in everyday affairs, including the pursuit of social justice. There has not been a schism in the church since 1495. In addition to infant baptism and Holy Communion, the Moravians observe the practice of the love feast, a simple meal taken communally.

There is only one Moravian Church worldwide, but it is divided into twenty governing units called provinces. The provinces in North America are the Northern (including Canada), Southern, and Alaska provinces. The highest administrative body in each is the provincial synod, which meets every four years to direct missionary, educational, and publishing work and to elect a Provincial Elders' Conference, which functions between synod meetings. Bishops, elected by provincial and general synods, are the spiritual, not the administrative, leaders of the church.

Missionary work has always been a primary concern. There are nearly 800,000 Moravians worldwide, more than half in Tanzania and South Africa. Always committed to education, the church founded Moravian College and Theological Seminary in Bethlehem, Pennsylvania, and Salem College in Winston-Salem, North Carolina. The church is also known for its distinctive musical heritage.

For more information: www.moravian.org

Headquarters: P.O. Box 1245, Bethlehem, PA 18016-1245

OLD GERMAN BAPTIST BRETHREN

Reorganized: 1881
Membership: 6,285 in 55 churches (2004)

While the Brethren Church left the Church of the Brethren because the latter body seemed too conservative in the early 1880s, the Old German Baptist Brethren left because they considered the Church of the Brethren not conservative enough. The dissenters stood for the old order and traditions. The salient point in their opposition lay in their suspicion of Sunday schools, salaried ministers, missions, higher education, and church societies.

The basic objections still hold but with certain modifications. Children are not enrolled in Sunday schools, but are encouraged to attend the regular services of the church and to join the church by baptism during their teens; however, the decision is left entirely to the individual. Many congregations list a majority of members between fifteen and fifty years of age. The church today is not completely opposed even to higher education; most of the youth enter high school, and some take training in college or professional schools.

The church stands for a literal interpretation of the Scriptures in regard to the Lord's Supper and practices closed Communion, which excludes all but its own members. While it advocates compliance with the ordinary demands of government, it opposes cooperation in war. Any member who enters into military service will fall under the judgment of the church. Non-cooperation in political and secret societies is required; dress is plain, and all amusements deemed worldly are frowned upon. The group has no salaried ministers and enforces complete abstinence from alcoholic beverages; the members refuse to take oaths or engage in lawsuits; the sick are anointed with oil; the heads of the sisters are veiled, and wedding ceremonies are not performed for previously divorced persons while their former spouses are living.

There are no missions, except the witness portrayed in their daily life. An annual conference that rules on matters on which the Scriptures are silent is held each year at Pentecost; a brotherhood council is vital to their church body. Most of the members live in Ohio, Indiana, California, Virginia, Pennsylvania, and Kansas.

179

SCHWENKFELDER CHURCH

Founded: 1782, with roots to 1519
Membership: est. 2,800 in 6 congregations (2000)

This church predates the Pietist movement but shares so many Pietist features that it is included in this section as a "forerunner" of the movement. Though small in size, it represents such a unique branch of the Protestant Reformation that it merits inclusion in this *Handbook*.

The church is named for Caspar Schwenkfeld von Ossig (1489–1561), a Silesian nobleman who experienced a spiritual awakening in 1518. Disappointed in his hope to help reform the Roman Catholic Church from within, he played a leading role in the Reformation, advocating wider reading of the Bible by laypeople, urging the need for the power, guidance, and leading of the Holy Spirit, and preaching that the sacramental consumption of the Lord's Supper is a mystical partaking of Christ as food for the soul—but that the food is really bread.

This interpretation of the Lord's Supper, together with his insistence on complete separation of church and state, led Schwenkfelder into disagreement with Lutheranism.* Espousing a "Reformation of the Middle Way," Schwenkfelder and his followers emphasized the supremacy of the Spirit over literalistic interpretations of scriptural faith and practice. By the end of the sixteenth century the movement numbered several thousand, gathered basically by Schwenkfelder's writings and sermons. He organized no church; but the group was persecuted by other religious bodies and remained small and rather dispersed.

Schwenkfelders arrived in Philadelphia in six migrations between 1731 and 1737. Unable to find land for common purchase, the immigrants spread out and settled in the region between Philadelphia and Allentown, Pennsylvania. The Society of Schwenkfelders was formed in 1782, and the Schwenkfelder Church was incorporated in 1909. Although descendants of the original settlers live in all regions of the U.S., the remaining Schwenkfelder churches are found within a fifty-mile radius of Philadelphia.

All theology, the members hold, should be constructed from the Bible, but Scripture is considered dead without the indwelling Word. They believe that Christ's divinity was progressive, his human nature becoming more and more divine without "losing its identity." Faith, regeneration, and subsequent spiritual growth change human nature, but justification by faith must not obscure the positive regeneration imparted by Christ; thus the theology is Christocentric.

For more information: www.schwenkfelder.com

Headquarters: 105 Seminary St., Pennsburg, PA 18073

BAPTIST CHURCHES

The Baptists comprise one of the largest and most diverse groupings of Christians in the United States. Technically, there are no such things as Baptist denominations, because Baptists are strongly congregational in polity: Each local congregation is independent of the others. However, Baptist churches are commonly grouped into larger associations for purposes of fellowship. National conventions have been established to carry on educational and missionary work and to administer pension plans. For the purposes of this *Handbook,* these national conventions will be considered denominations.

Most state and regional conventions meet annually with delegates from all Baptist churches in a given area. These conventions receive reports, make recommendations, and help to raise national mission budgets; but they have no authority to enforce their decisions. Baptists have insisted on freedom of thought and expression in pulpit and pew. They have insisted, too, on the absolute autonomy of the local congregation; each church arranges its own worship and examines and baptizes its own members. There is no age requirement for membership, but the candidate is usually of an age to understand and accept the teachings of Christ. Candidates for the ministry are licensed by local churches and are ordained upon recommendation of a group of sister churches.

Doctrine and Polity. Despite their emphasis on independence and individualism, Baptists are bound together by an amazingly strong "rope of sand" in allegiance to certain principles and doctrines based generally on the competency of each individual in matters of faith. While they differ in certain minor details, Baptists generally agree on the following principles of faith: the inspiration and trustworthiness of the Bible as the sole rule of life; the lordship of Jesus Christ; the inherent freedom of persons to approach God for themselves; the granting of salvation through faith by way of grace and contact with the Holy Spirit; two ordinances (rather than sacraments), the Lord's Supper and the baptism of believers by immersion; the independence of the local church; the church as a group of regenerated believers who are baptized upon confession of faith; infant baptism as unscriptural and not to be practiced; complete separation of church and state; life after death; the unity of humankind; the royal law of God; the need of redemption from sin; and the ultimate triumph of God's kingdom.

These overall doctrines have never been written into any official Baptist creed for all the churches, but they have been incorporated into two important confessions of faith. The Baptist churches of London wrote a Philadelphia Confession in the year 1689 that was enlarged by the Philadelphia Association in 1742. The New Hampshire State Baptist Convention drew up another confession in 1832. The Philadelphia Confession is strongly Calvinist, the New Hampshire Confession only moderately so.

Baptists in the United States. The Baptist movement in the United States grew out of English Puritanism in the early seventeenth century. Convinced that Puritanism needed further reform, Separatists began to teach that only self-professed believers were eligible for membership in the church. That is, the church is properly made up of only regenerated people. Fleeing persecution under James I, some of the English Separatists settled in Holland, where they encountered the Mennonites.* Many of the Mennonites' principles agreed with their own convictions, including the beliefs that the Scriptures are the sole authority for faith and practice, that church and state should be completely and forever separated, and that church discipline should be rigidly enforced in business, family, and personal affairs. Before long the congregation of John Smyth (ca. 1570–1612) accepted another bedrock Mennonite principle and adopted the practice of "believer's baptism"—that is, baptism only of adults who make a profession of faith. Smyth rebaptized himself and his followers in 1609. When he tried to make Mennonites of his people; however, he was rejected by his own congregation. Baptist they would be, but not Mennonite because that meant a threat to their British heritage. Smyth's people eventually moved back across the channel and established a Baptist church in London.

The first churches were General Baptist churches, which means that they believed in a general atonement for all persons. In the course of time there arose a Particular Baptist Church, which held to the doctrine of predestination associated with the teachings of John Calvin (1509–64). The first British Particular Baptist churches dates back to 1638.

In 1631, Roger Williams (ca. 1603–83) came to America and soon became the first great champion of freedom for faith and conscience in North America. Williams was not a Baptist but a Separatist minister when he arrived. Preaching new opinions against the authority of the Puritan magistrates, Williams organized a Baptist church at Providence, Rhode Island. John Clarke (1609–76) established another Baptist church at Newport at about the same time. Many scholars date the Providence church to 1638, and the Newport church to 1644. The Baptist movement grew rapidly during the First Great Awakening (a revival of religious interest) of the 1740s, but a dispute soon arose among Baptists over the question of emotionalism. The Old Lights, or Regulars, distrusted revivals, while the New Lights insisted on an experience of rebirth as a condition for membership in their churches. Despite internal disagreements Baptists continued to agitate for religious freedom in the new land and played a significant role in the adoption of the First Amendment.

Landmark Baptists. Many Baptists hold to the belief that the Baptist Church has existed since the days of John the Baptist. Of particular interest in this regard are the Landmark Baptists. The name originated with the writings of James Madison Pendleton (1811–91) and James Robinson Graves (1820–93) in Kentucky and Tennessee in the latter part of the nineteenth century. The four distinguishing tenets of Landmarkism are the following:

(1) The church is always local and visible. While members of Protestant churches may be saved, they are not members of true churches.

(2) The commission was given to the church; consequently, all matters covered by it must be administered under church authority. Clergy of other denominations are not accepted in Landmark Baptist pulpits.

(3) Baptism, to be valid, must be administered by the authority of a New Testament (Baptist) church. Baptisms administered by any other authority are not accepted.

183

(4) There is a direct historic succession of Baptist churches from New Testament times. Baptist churches have existed in practice, though not in name, in every century.

These principles are held primarily by the churches of the American Baptist Association and Baptist Missionary Association, though an estimated one and a half million members of different Baptist churches hold to the Landmark position and doctrine, the largest concentration being in the South and the Southwest. More than fifteen Bible institutes and seminaries are supported by these churches.

Black Baptists. Baptist preachers had been particularly effective in converting African-Americans to Christianity before emancipation. The great majority of blacks in pre-Civil War days were either Baptist or Methodist. In 1793 there were 73,471 Baptists in the U.S., one-fourth of them black. When the Battle of Bull Run was fought in 1861, there were 200,000 black members of the Methodist Episcopal Church, South, and 150,000 black Baptists. Usually, slaves sat in the galleries of white churches, identifying with the faith of their owners. White preachers, sometimes assisted by black helpers, moved from one plantation to another, holding services more or less regularly. Occasionally a black preacher was liberated to give full time to religious work among blacks, and these ministers had great influence. The first black Baptist church was organized at Silver Bluff, across the Savannah River, near Augusta, Georgia, in 1773. Other churches followed in Petersburg, Virginia, 1776; Richmond, Virginia, 1780; Williamsburg, Virginia, 1785; Savannah, Georgia, 1785; and Lexington, Kentucky, 1790.

The slave rebellion led by Nat Turner (ca. 1800–31) in 1831 appears to have been fueled by Christian rhetoric of freedom and divine justice. Whites were so frightened that laws were passed in some sections of the South that made it illegal to teach blacks to read. Almost everywhere slave meetings were monitored by owners, lest unrest be fomented. However, slaves continued to conduct their own meetings hidden from sight and sound of the masters in "the invisible institution." After the Civil War, numerous black Baptist congregations emerged and organized their own conventions. Aided by the Freedman's Aid Society and various Baptist organizations, nearly one million black Baptists were worshiping in their own churches by 1880.

Baptist Missions. Strongly evangelical in theology, the Baptists were early participants in foreign missions, following the lead of English Baptist William Carey (1761–1834), who went to India in 1793. In 1814 Baptists in the U.S. organized their own General Missionary Convention of the Baptist Denomination in the United States of America for Foreign Missions. This convention, representing a national Baptist fellowship, marked the first real denominational consciousness. It was followed eventually by other organizations that welded them firmly together: general Baptist conventions; a general tract society, later called the American Baptist Publication Society; various missionary societies for work at home and abroad; an education society; and the Baptist Young People's Union. These organizations were on a national scale. Their unity was disrupted first by a feeling that home-missions agencies within the body had failed to evangelize Southern territory and later by arguments over slavery. The great division occurred in 1845, when Southerners formed their own Southern Baptist Convention. From that point forward there were both Northern and Southern conventions.

The Baptist Joint Committee on Public Affairs, supported by the American Baptist Churches in the U.S.A., some Southern Baptist churches, and some other bodies, is housed in Washington, D.C. This committee serves mainly to spread Baptist convictions on public morals and to safeguard the principle of separation of church and state. The Baptist World Alliance, organized in 1905, now includes more than forty million Baptists in 170 member bodies. The Alliance meets every five years to discuss common themes and problems and is purely an advisory body. Its headquarters are located in Falls Church, Virginia.

Suggestions for further reading:

Ammerman, Nancy T. *Baptist Battles: Social Change and Religious Conflict in the Southern Baptist Convention.* New Brunswick, NJ: Rutgers University Press, 1990.

Balmer, Randall. *Mine Eyes Have Seen the Glory: A Journey into the Evangelical Subculture of America.* New York: Oxford University Press, 1989.

Brackney, William H. *The Baptists.* New York: Greenwood, 1988.

Dayton, Donald W., and Robert K. Johnston, eds. *The Variety of*

185

American Evangelicalism. Downer's Grove, IL: InterVarsity, 1991.

Fitts, Leroy. *A History of Black Baptists.* Nashville: Broadman, 1985.

Lincoln, C. Eric, and Lawrence H. Mamiya. *The Black Church in the African-American Experience.* Durham, NC: Duke University Press, 1990.

Gardner, Robert. *Baptists of Early America: A Statistical History, 1639-1790.* Atlanta: Georgia Baptist Historical Society, 1983.

Hill, Samuel and Robert G. Torbet. *Baptists: North and South.* Valley Forge, PA: Judson, 1964.

Hill, Samuel S, ed. *Encyclopedia of Religion in the South.* Macon, Ga.: Mercer University Press, 1984.

Leonard, Bill J., ed. *Dictionary of Baptists in America.* Downers Grove, IL: InterVarsity, 1994.

Leonard, Bill J. *God's Last and Only Hope: The Fragmentation of the Southern Baptist Convention.* Grand Rapids, MI: Eerdmans, 1990.

MacBeth, Leon. *Baptist Heritage.* Nashville: Broadman Press, 1987.

Matthews, Donald G. *Religion in the Old South.* Chicago: University of Chicago Press, 1977.

McLoughlin, William G. *Soul Liberty: The Baptists' Struggle in New England, 1630-1833.* Hanover, NH: University Press of New England, 1991.

Pelt, O. D. and R. L. Smith. *The Story of the National Baptists.* New York: Vantage, 1960.

Sernett, Milton C., ed. *Afro-American Religious History: A Documentary* Witness. Durham, NC: Duke University Press, 1985.

Wardin, Albert W. *Baptists Around the World: A Comprehensive Handbook.* Nashville: Broadman & Holman, 1995.

ALLIANCE OF BAPTIST CHURCHES

Founded: 1987
Membership: est. 62,000 in 122 churches (2003)

The Alliance of Baptists is a confederation of Baptist congregations, and individuals that separated from the Southern Baptist

Convention during the conservative/moderate conflict of the 1980s. The Alliance churches stress the historic Baptist principles of individual and congregational autonomy, particularly in regard to biblical interpretation and missions. The Alliance churches encourage the use of modern methods of biblical study, theological education, and free inquiry into the history of Christianity. Most important, the Alliance has dedicated itself to social and economic justice and equity. Women are encouraged to seek ordination and assume leadership roles in the Alliance and in congregations. Leadership of the Alliance is composed of three elected officers who serve no more than two years and a thirty-four-member Board of Directors. The annual meeting of the Alliance is held each spring and reviews all decisions of the Board. There are nine standing committees that supervise such areas as women in ministry and interfaith dialogue.

For more information: www.allianceofbaptists.org

Headquarters: 1328 16th NW, Washington, DC 20036

AMERICAN BAPTIST ASSOCIATION

Founded: 1905
Membership: est. 275,000 in 1,680 churches (2004)

Organized in 1905 as the Baptist General Association, the group adopted its present name in 1924. Teaching that the Great Commission of Christ (Matt. 28:18-20) was given only to a local congregation, members believe that the local church is the only unit authorized to administer the ordinances (baptism and communion) and that the congregation is an independent and autonomous body responsible only to Christ. Because of their belief that no universal church or ecclesiastical authority is higher than a local congregation, members of the American Baptist Association claim that those Baptists organized in conventions are not faithful to Bible mission methods.

Maintaining that their own way is the true New Testament form, they hold themselves separate from all other religious groups. They strongly protest the trend of many Baptist groups to identify themselves with Protestantism, since they believe that their faith preceded the Protestant Reformation, and indeed has a continued succession from Christ and the apostles. They do not accept as valid baptisms performed in other churches, and they serve communion only to members of the local congregation.

The Association's doctrine is strictly fundamentalist* and includes the verbal inspiration of the Bible, the Triune God, the virgin birth and deity of Christ, the suffering and death of Christ as substitutionary, and the bodily resurrection of Christ and all his saints. The Second Coming of Jesus, physical and personal, is to be the crowning event of the gospel age and will be pre-millennial. There is eternal punishment for the wicked; salvation is solely by grace through faith, not by law or works. There must be absolute separation of church and state and absolute religious freedom. Members denounce abortion on demand, homosexuality, and premarital sex as being contrary to biblical teachings.

Government of both the local congregation and the annual meeting of the association is congregational in nature. Missionary work is conducted on county, state, interstate, and international levels, the program originating in the local church; and missionaries are supported by the cooperating churches. Educational work is pursued through the Sunday schools, five seminaries, three colleges, and twenty-seven Bible institutes. The greater strength of this group is found in the South, Southeast, Southwest, and West, but much new work has begun in recent years in the East and the North.

A comprehensive publishing program includes fourteen monthly and semimonthly periodicals, Sunday school literature designed to cover the entire Bible in a ten-year period, and literature for young people and vacation Bible schools. National and state youth camps are held annually, as are pastors' and missionaries' conferences on regional and national levels.

For more information: www.abaptist.org

Headquarters: 4605 N. State Line, Texarkana, TN 75503

AMERICAN BAPTIST CHURCHES IN THE U.S.A.

Founded: 1814 or 1845
Membership: 1,484,291 in 5,836 churches (2002)

This body has had several changes in name over the decades. It traces its origins to May 1814, when representatives from various Baptist associations and churches met in Philadelphia to organize the

General Missionary Convention of the Baptist Denomination in the United States of America for Foreign Missions. This body quickly became known as the Triennial Convention and was the first national Baptist organization in the United States. The American Baptist Publication Society and the American Baptist Home Mission Society were established in 1824 and 1832 respectively. By 1841 sectional and theological differences centered around the issue of slavery began to erode the unity of the foreign mission board. In 1845, one year after the final meeting of the Triennial Convention, the Northern and Southern groups met and reorganized separately. The northern group became the American Baptist Missionary Union and the southern group became the Southern Baptist Convention.* The women of the Northern churches formed their own home and foreign missionary societies in the 1870s.

Separate appeals for funds to support these competing societies created confusion and dissatisfaction, leading eventually to the formation of the Northern Baptist Convention in 1907. This convention was actually a corporation with restricted powers in conducting religious work, receiving and expending money, and affiliating itself with other bodies. The Convention reorganized in 1950, changing its name to the American Baptist Convention. In 1955 the two women's missionary societies joined administratively with their counterparts, the older foreign- and home-mission societies. In 1950 the first general secretary was elected.

In 1972 the convention adopted its third and present name and restructured to strengthen the representational principle and to integrate more fully the national program bodies into the larger organization. A larger (200 member) general board composed of election-district representatives and at-large representatives makes up the policymaking body. A general council of chief executives and staff of national program boards, chief executives of regions, and other American Baptist bodies serves to coordinate the corporate affairs of the denomination under the leadership of the general secretary.

The denomination is at work in twenty children's homes and special services, seventy-seven retirement homes and communities, twenty-seven hospitals and nursing homes, nine theological seminaries, and sixteen senior colleges and universities. Judson Press is its publishing arm. The Board of National Ministries has workers in thirty-six states. This board supports Bacone College for Native

Americans in Oklahoma and carries on widespread work among African-Americans, Native Americans, and Asians in the U.S. The Board of International Ministries currently supports missionaries in six countries in Asia (Hong Kong, India, Japan, the Philippines, Singapore, and Thailand), two countries in Africa (South Africa and Zaire), and seven countries in Latin America and the Caribbean (Bolivia, Costa Rica, the Dominican Republic, El Salvador, Haiti, Mexico, and Nicaragua).

In matters of faith, American Baptist Churches hold to typical Baptist doctrines described above. They have historically taken a stand on such controversial issues as abolition, temperance, racial and social justice, and the ordination of women. They have traditionally been a denomination with diversity of race, ethnicity, culture, class, and theology. The ordinances of baptism and the Lord's Supper are considered aids more than necessities for salvation. Generally it may be said that Baptists represented in the American Baptist Churches in the U.S.A. are less conservative in thought and theology than those in the Southern Baptist Convention. American Baptists are represented in the National Council of the Churches of Christ in the U.S.A. and the World Council of Churches; Southern Baptists are represented in neither. American Baptists have made gestures toward union with General Baptists, Southern Baptists, the National Baptist Convention, Seventh-Day Baptists, Disciples of Christ, Church of the Brethren, and the Alliance of Baptists and have welcomed Free Baptists into full fellowship.

For more information: www.abc-usa.org

Headquarters: P.O. Box 851, Valley Forge, PA 19482-0851

BAPTIST BIBLE FELLOWSHIP INTERNATIONAL

Founded: 1950
Membership: est. 525,165 in 3,294 churches (2000)

Baptist Bible Fellowship was founded by some one hundred Baptist ministers and missionaries to promote fellowship among independent Baptists in three main areas of church life: evangelism, education of church workers, and the founding of churches. Many of the founders had been part of the World Fundamental Baptist Missionary Fellowship (today known as the World Baptist

Fellowship),* which had roots in the Baptist Bible Union, founded in 1921. The Baptist Bible Fellowship's statement of faith was based on that of the Baptist Bible Union. It is strongly fundamentalist* in character, emphasizing the inerrancy of Scripture, the virgin birth, the deity of Christ, the substitutionary atonement, the resurrection of the body of Christ, biblical miracles, and the literal millennial kingdom on earth. Ministers and members of the fellowship use only the King James Version of the Bible in English-speaking churches.

The Baptist Bible Fellowship also teaches that Jesus was a Baptist in his thinking and work. They recognize baptism by immersion only, participate in Communion only with members of their own church, and are adamantly opposed to dancing, drinking, smoking, movies, gambling, and sex outside of marriage. No formal membership statistics are kept, and the above figures are estimates based on attendance figures. In 2000 there were 768 missionaries at work on every continent. There are churches in every state, but the greatest concentration is in the Great Lakes region and the South. Almost one third of the congregations have dual affiliation with other fundamentalist* bodies.

Baptist Bible College in Springfield, Missouri, and Baptist Bible College East in Boston, Massachusetts, are owned and supported by these independent Baptists. Recently the Baptist Bible Graduate School of Theology was founded in Springfield, Missouri. Other schools supported by the fellowship are Pacific Coast Baptist Bible College and Spanish Baptist Bible Institute in Miami, Florida.

For more information: www.bbfi.org

Headquarters: P.O. Box 191, Springfield, MO 65801

BAPTIST GENERAL CONFERENCE

Founded: 1852
Membership: 145,148 in 902 churches (2002)

The history of what is now known as the Baptist General Conference began at Rock Island, Illinois, in 1852. Gustaf Palmquist, a middle-aged schoolteacher and lay preacher, had arrived from Sweden the previous year to become the spiritual leader of a group of Swedish immigrants who had been influenced by the Pietist* movement within the (Lutheran) state church of Sweden. At

191

Galesburg, Illinois, he came in contact with Baptists, and early in 1852 he was baptized and ordained a Baptist minister. Visiting the Swedish people at Rock Island, Palmquist won his first converts to the Baptist faith and baptized three in the Mississippi River on August 18, 1852. There were sixty-five churches when the national conference of the Swedish Baptist General Conference of America was organized in 1879.

For several decades the American Baptist Home Mission Society and the American Baptist Publication Society of the American (then Northern) Baptist Convention* aided the new work among the Swedish immigrants, but gradually the church became self-supporting. A theological seminary was founded in Chicago in 1871, and the first denominational paper was launched the same year. From 1888 until 1944, foreign missionary activities were channeled through the American Baptist Foreign Mission Society. The Swedish Conference set up its own foreign-mission board in 1944 and today has more than 135 regular and 55 short-term missionaries in India, Japan, the Philippines, Ethiopia, Mexico, Argentina, Brazil, the Ivory Coast, Cameroon, and France.

Following World War I, with its intensified nationalistic conflicts, the transition from Swedish- to English-language church services was greatly accelerated and was practically completed in three decades. In 1945, Swedish was dropped from the name of the conference. With the language barrier removed, the growth of the conference has been rapid and far-reaching. Although its greatest strength lies in the North Central and Pacific Northwest sections of the U.S., home missionaries are at work in all the northern states and some of the southern states. Less than half of the pastors are of Swedish descent, and a large number of churches contain few members of that descent.

The conference owns and controls Bethel College and Seminary in St. Paul, Minnesota, a four-year college and a three-year theological school with 2,300 students; the seminary also has a campus in San Diego, California. Also affiliated with the conference are three children's homes, seven homes for the aged, and *The Standard,* the official denominational organ issued by the Board of Overseers. Harvest Publications offers Bibles, books, and Sunday school materials.

Basically, the church's doctrine is theologically conservative, with unqualified acceptance of the Word of God, and holds the usual

Baptist tenets. It is a strong fellowship of churches, insistent upon the major beliefs of conservative Christianity but with respect for individual differences on minor points.

For more information: www.bgcworld.org

Headquarters: 2002 South Arlington Heights Rd., Arlington Heights, IL 60005

BAPTIST MISSIONARY ASSOCIATION OF AMERICA

Founded: 1950
Membership: 234,110 in 1,384 churches (2004)

Organized at Little Rock, Arkansas, as the North American Baptist Association, this group changed its name to Baptist Missionary Association of America in 1968. It concentrates on fostering and encouraging missionary cooperation. There are workers in home missions and missionary work abroad in Mexico, Japan, Brazil, Taiwan, Portugal, Cape Verde Islands, Uruguay, Guatemala, Costa Rica, Nicaragua, Australia, Italy, France, Africa, India, Bolivia, Honduras, Korea, and the Philippines. A strong publications department issues literature for Sunday school and training classes, pamphlets, books, tracts, and magazines in both English and Spanish. The association also owns and operates a printing business in Brazil, where literature is printed in Portuguese for use in Africa and Europe. A worldwide radio ministry is also maintained.

The members are thoroughly fundamentalist* in conviction, placing strong emphasis on the verbal inspiration and accuracy of Scripture, direct creation, the virgin birth and deity of Jesus, his blood atonement, justification by faith, salvation by grace alone, and the imminent personal return of Christ to earth. The Lord's Supper and baptism are accepted as ordinances, and baptism is considered "alien" unless administered to believers by the divine authority as given to the Missionary Baptist churches. With its roots in the American Baptist Association, this body carries on the Landmark Baptist movement (see BAPTIST CHURCHES), holding to the historic succession of independent Baptist churches from the time of Christ.

Churches are completely autonomous in the Baptist tradition and, regardless of size, have an equal voice in the cooperative missionary, publication, evangelical, and educational efforts of the association. Member churches must, however, conform to the doctrinal standards of the association. Three junior colleges and several orphans' homes are maintained on a state level, and a theological seminary is located in Jacksonville, Texas.

For more information: www.bmaam.org

Headquarters: P. O. Box 30910 - Little Rock, AR 72260

CONSERVATIVE BAPTIST ASSOCIATION OF AMERICA (CBAMERICA)

Founded 1947
Membership: est. 210,000 in 1200 churches (2004)

The Conservative Baptist Association is described as a "voluntary fellowship of sovereign, autonomous, independent, "Bible-believing" Baptist churches." The founders of this association of churches were active in the Fundamentalist* Fellowship that was started within the Northern Baptist Convention in 1920 (See AMERICAN BAPTIST CHURCHES). Doctrinal disagreement, which grew out of different views of the reliability and credibility of the Scriptures, was aggravated by the "inclusive policy" by which both theologically liberal and conservative missionaries were sent to foreign and home fields.

The Conservative Baptist Foreign Mission (now CBInternational) was founded in 1943 for the purpose of sending only Bible-believing missionaries to the mission field. In 1947 the Conservative Baptist Association of America (now CBAmerica) was formed. Churches were free to belong to both this new association and the Northern Baptist Convention. The Conservative Baptist Home Mission Society (now Mission to the Americas) and the Conservative Baptist Theological Seminary (now Denver Seminary) were begun by the leaders of this new church association. Western Seminary of Portland, Oregon, Bethel Seminary of the East, Philadelphia, Pennsylvania, Southwestern College, Phoenix, Arizona, New England Bible College, Portland, Maine and International College and Graduate School, Honolulu, Hawaii are associated with Conservative Baptist churches.

The ministry of CBAmerica through regional offices and the

194

national office includes providing resources and counsel in the areas of Christian Education, church planting, women's ministry, pastoral placement and church administration. Administering one benevolent fund for pastors, leaders and their families and another for churches in crisis are responsibilities of the Association. Endorsing and administrating thirty-five active military chaplains, plus hospital, prison and law enforcement chaplains is a major focus of ministry.

The name "Conservative" was chosen to indicate the desire to conserve the basic doctrines of historic, biblical Christianity. These include the infallibility of the Scriptures; God as Father, perfect in holiness, infinite in wisdom, measureless in power; Christ as the eternal and only begotten Son of God—his sinlessness, virgin birth, atonement, bodily resurrection, ascension and return to earth; the Holy Spirit as coming forth from God to convince the world of sin, of righteousness, and of judgment; the sinfulness of all people and the possibility of their regeneration, sanctification and comfort through Christ and the Holy Spirit; the church as the living body of Christ, with Christ as the head; the local church as free from interference from any ecclesiastical or political authority; the responsibility of every human being to God alone; that human betterment is a direct result of the gospel; and the ordinances of believer's baptism by immersion and the Lord's supper.

Members for the CBAmerica Board are elected through the eight regional offices. The offices of the Association of Churches are located in Littleton, Colorado.

For more information: www.CBAmerica.org

Headquarters: 3686 Stagecoach Rd., Unit F, Longmont, CO 80504

COOPERATIVE BAPTIST FELLOWSHIP

Founded: 1991
Membership: statistics not available; 1,800 churches (2000)

As with many Baptist groups, the Cooperative Baptist Fellowship (CBF) cannot quite be termed a denomination. It is a recently created and vital fellowship of Baptist churches, primarily in the South. The CBF was formed during the years of struggle within the Southern Baptist Convention* (SBC) between conservatives and moderates.

195

Some of the moderates disapproved of the tactics of the conservatives and believed that the Convention itself was in danger of violating the historic Baptist affirmation of individual freedom. In 1991 the new CBF was formed as an alternative body to the SBC, although congregations are free to hold joint membership.

The mission of the Cooperative Baptist Fellowship focuses on ministry rather than theology, as indicated by their mission statement adopted in July, 2000: "We are a fellowship of Baptist Christians and churches who share a passion for the Great Commission of Jesus Christ and a commitment to Baptist principles of faith and practice. Our mission is to serve Baptist Christians and churches as they discover and fulfill their God-given mission."

With an annual budget of almost seventeen million dollars, the CBF focuses its work on global missions to the world's most neglected (the impoverished, homeless, victims of HIV/AIDS, and other marginalized peoples) and the least evangelized. It also fosters advocacy of historic Baptist values, such as local church autonomy, the priesthood of all believers, and religious liberty. The CBF has partnerships with a dozen seminaries and theological schools and has helped found new schools of theology in historical Baptist colleges in the South.

For more information: www.thefellowship.info

Headquarters: P.O. Box 450329, Atlanta, GA 31145-0329

DUCK RIVER (AND KINDRED) ASSOCIATIONS OF BAPTISTS

Founded: 1826
Membership: 10,888; 99 churches (2000)

The Duck River Baptists originated in Tennessee as part of a protest within the old Elk River Association, which was strongly Calvinist. Duck River Baptists are liberally Calvinist in that they believe that Christ died for all rather than for the elect. In addition they believe that God will save those who come to him through Christ; that sinners are justified by faith; and that the saints will persevere in grace. In addition to the Lord's Supper and believers' baptism (by immersion), they view foot washing as a biblical ordinance. An 1843 dispute over missions divided the Duck River Baptists into two groups, which were formerly known as Missionary Baptists and Separate Baptists. They are congregational in polity and hold annual association meetings. In 1939 they and kindred associations formed the General Association of Baptists. They are found in mainly in Tennessee, Alabama, Mississippi, and Georgia.

For more information: www.duckriverbaptistassociation.org

Headquarters: P .O. Box 820, Tullahoma, TN 37388,

GENERAL ASSOCIATION OF GENERAL BAPTIST CHURCHES

Founded: 1870
Membership: 75,368 in 1,086 churches (2002)

The General Association of General Baptist Churches traces its origin to the work of John Smyth (ca. 1570–1612) and Thomas Helwys (ca. 1550–ca. 1616) who organized Baptist congregations in England and Holland. Roger Williams (ca. 1603–83) is considered the first minister in the American colonies. General Baptists have always been Arminian, and at first they were overwhelmed by the influence of Calvinism (see REFORMED and PRESBYTERIAN CHURCHES) in the American colonies. Their work was reopened by Benoni Stinson (ca. 1798–ca. 1870) in 1823 with the establishment of Liberty Baptist Church in what is now Evansville, Indiana. They spread into Illinois and Kentucky, and a general association was organized in 1870. Since that time the group has grown steadily, especially throughout the Midwest.

The General Baptist confession of faith is basically Arminian: Christ died for all; failure to achieve salvation lies completely with the individual; humankind is depraved and fallen and unable to save itself; regeneration is necessary for salvation; salvation comes by repentance and faith in Christ; Christians who persevere to the end are saved; the wicked are punished eternally; and the dead, both the just and the unjust, will be raised at the judgment. The Lord's Supper and believer's baptism by immersion are the only authorized ordinances, but some General Baptist churches practice foot washing.

Their polity is similar to that found in most Baptist groups, but a peculiar feature of the General Baptist church lies in the use of a presbytery into which the ordained members of local associations are grouped. They examine candidates for the ministry and for the diaconate. Ministers and deacons are responsible to this presbytery, which exists only on the local level.

The church maintains a liberal arts university in Indiana, Oakland City University, and Chapman Seminary for theological study. A publishing house, Stinson Press, is operated at Poplar Bluff, Missouri, where the monthly paper is issued. Foreign missionary work is supported in Guam, Saipan, Jamaica, Honduras, China, Mexico, and the Philippines, and home missionary work is actively carried out in various states.

For more information: www.generalbaptist.com

Headquarters: 100 Stinson Dr., Poplar Bluff, MO 63901

GENERAL ASSOCIATION OF REGULAR BAPTIST CHURCHES

Founded: 1932
Membership: 129,407 in 1,415 churches (2002)

Twenty-two Baptist churches of the American Baptist Convention* left that organization in May 1932 to found the General Association of Regular Baptist Churches. Their protest was against what they considered the Convention's modernist tendencies and teachings, the denial of the historic Baptist principle of independence and autonomy of the local congregation, the inequality of representation in the assemblies of the convention, and the control of missionary work by convention assessment and budget.

Basically fundamentalist* in outlook, the GARBC understands its mission "to champion the Biblical truth, impact the world for Christ, perpetuate a Baptist heritage, and advance the Association churches." The association subscribes to the New Hampshire Confession of Faith (1832) with a premillennial interpretation of the final article of that confession. It holds to the infallibility of the Bible, the Trinity, the personality of Satan as the author of all evil, humankind as the creation of God, and humankind born in sin. Doctrines deal with the virgin birth, the deity of Jesus, and faith in Christ as the way of salvation through grace. The saved are in everlasting felicity; the lost are consigned to endless punishment. Civil government is by divine appointment. There are only two approved ordinances: baptism by immersion and the Lord's Supper.

198

Any Baptist church coming into the General Association is required to withdraw all fellowship and cooperation from any convention or group that permits modernists or modernism within its ranks. Dual fellowship or membership is not permitted. Church government is strictly congregational. Associated churches have the privilege of sending six voting messengers to an annual convention. A Council of Eighteen is elected (six each year) to serve for three years. The Council makes recommendations to the association for the furtherance of its work and puts into operation all actions and policies of the association. The Council's authority depends completely on the will and direction of the association, but it does appoint a National Representative to oversee the denominational office in Schaumburg, Illinois and to represent the Association to its churches and constituencies. The Regular Baptist Press publishes *The Baptist Bulletin*, a monthly magazine.

For more information: www.garbc.org

Headquarters: 1300 North Meacham Road, Schaumburg, IL 60173

INTERSTATE AND FOREIGN LANDMARK MISSIONARY BAPTIST ASSOCIATION

Founded: 1951, with roots to mid-19th century
Membership: 14,225 in 135 churches (2000)

This association traces its origins to the Landmarkian controversy among Southern Baptists* in the middle of the nineteenth century when James Robinson Graves, James Madison Pendleton, and Amos Cooper Dayton challenged the accepted understanding of church history. They argued that the Baptist Church was begun during the time of Jesus and has had an unbroken history through the century. The Baptist Church is the only true church; therefore baptism and the Lord's Supper are only valid in the Baptist Church. Moreover, they argued that the only church is the visible, local congregation, and thus the great commission was given only to the local church

Landmark ideas had a strong impact on many Baptist groups in the South, especially the American Baptist Association and the Baptist Missionary Association. The Interstate and Landmark group developed from a split within the ABA. It seeks to promote cooper-

199

ation among Landmark Baptists who support their ministries only through free-will offerings rather than regular salaries. Doctrinally, they follow typical Baptist teachings, but they do practice foot washing as an ordinance. They are strongest in the southern Mississippi River region but support missions in Mexico and the Philiphines.

NATIONAL ASSOCIATION OF FREE WILL BAPTISTS

> Founded: 1935, with roots to Colonial days
> Membership: 198,796 in 2,458 churches (2002)

The rise of Free Will Baptists can be traced to the influence of Arminian-minded Baptists who migrated to the American Colonies from England. The southern line, or Palmer movement, began in 1727 when Paul Palmer (d. 1750) established a church in Chowan, North Carolina. The northern line, or Randall movement, began with a congregation organized by Benjamin Randall in 1780 in New Durham, New Hampshire. Both groups taught the doctrines of free grace, free salvation, and free will. There were gestures toward uniting the northern and southern groups until the outbreak of the Civil War.

The northern body extended more rapidly into the West and the Southwest, and in 1910 this line of Free Will Baptists merged with the Northern Baptist denomination, taking along 857 of its 1,100 churches, all of its denominational property, and several colleges. In 1916 representatives of remnant churches from the Randall movement organized the Cooperative General Association of Free Will Baptists. By 1921 the southern churches had organized into new associations and conferences, and finally into a General Conference. The division continued until November 5, 1935, when the two groups merged into the National Association of Free Will Baptists in Nashville, Tennessee.

Doctrinally, the church holds that Christ gave himself as a ransom for all, not just for the elect; that God calls all persons to repentance; and that whosoever will, may be saved. Baptism is by immersion. One of the few Baptist groups that practice open communion, the Free Will Baptists also practice foot washing. Government is strictly congregational. There are two Bible colleges and two liberal arts colleges. The church's greatest strength is in the South.

For more information: www.nafwb.org

Headquarters: P.O. Box 5002, Antioch, TN 37011-5002

NATIONAL BAPTIST CONVENTION OF AMERICA, INC.

Founded: 1895
Membership: statistics not available, but
est. 1,700,000 in 6,716 churches (2000)

"National Baptist" has been the name of some aspect of organized black Baptist life since at least 1886. By 1876 all of the southern states except Florida had a state missionary convention, but smaller bodies had existed since the 1830s in the Midwest; organized missionary efforts date back to that same period in the North.

The first black Baptist group, the Providence Baptist Association of Ohio, was formed in 1836, and the first attempt at national organization occurred in 1880 with the creation of the Foreign Mission Baptist Convention at Montgomery, Alabama. In 1886 the American National Baptist Convention was organized at St. Louis, and in 1893 the Baptist National Educational Convention was begun in the District of Columbia. All three conventions merged into the National Baptist Convention of America in 1895 in Atlanta. For the next twenty years a single National Baptist body functioned through a variety of activities, the publication of Sunday school material being a major one. It sponsored foreign mission enterprises, especially to African and Caribbean countries; and it founded some colleges and provided support for others, several of them the result of dedication to providing education for the emancipated people on the part of Northern Baptist and other churches.

In 1915 a division arose over the adoption of a charter and the ownership of the National Baptist Publishing Board. The group that rejected the charter continued to function as the National Baptist Convention of America. The group that accepted the charter became known as the National Baptist Convention, U.S.A., Inc.* The former is frequently referred to as "the unincorporated" (although it did eventually incorporate in 1986) and the latter as "the incorporated," but both trace their beginnings to the Foreign Mission Baptist Convention. In 1988 the NBCA broke its ties to the Board. Churches that wished to continue a relationship to the publishing house formed the National Missionary Baptist Convention.

The NBCA adopted a mission statement in 1991 that focuses on education, evangelism, benevolence, stewardship, publication, social and economic justice, and commitment to religious liberty and Baptist doctrine. Much of the denominational activity revolves around the annual meeting in September, which is followed by additional meetings in February and June. The June convention meeting lasts four days and focuses on instruction from an approved curriculum with qualified teachers.

The National Baptist Convention of America, Inc, has its greatest strength in Mississippi, Texas, and Louisiana, with large numbers of members also in Florida and California. It holds an annual convention, and officers are elected each year. Since 1985, the headquarters has been located in Shreveport, LA

For more information: www.nbcamerica.net.

Headquarters: 1320 Pierre Avenue, Shreveport, LA 71103.

NATIONAL BAPTIST CONVENTION, U.S.A., INC.

Founded: 1895
Membership: statistics not available but
est. at 6,000,000 in 18,513 churches

The largest body of black Baptists in the U.S. shared a common history with the "of America" denomination throughout the formative years of the two groups. Its formal origins date from 1895, with many roots and predecessors stretching back to the period around 1840. Until the disagreement that arose over control of the publishing house of the denomination in 1915, there was a single National Baptist* body. Once the "of America" convention was created, the Foreign Mission Board became the "U.S.A." body's center of operations.

In 1990 the Baptist World Center was opened in Nashville, Tennessee, where the Sunday School Publishing Board is also located. Nashville is also the home of the American Baptist College, which was opened in 1924 with the assistance of the Southern Baptist Convention.* The school is now entirely under the authority of the National Convention. The convention meets annually, and a Board of Directors directs the convention's business between its annual sessions.

If publishing control has been the most conspicuous fact in the "of America" body, presidential influence has been the "U.S.A." body's most visible feature. That was particularly true during the tenure of Joseph H. Jackson (1953–82). A powerful and effective leader, Jackson promoted the theory and practice of racial uplift in the tradition of Booker T. Washington (1856–1915). "From protest to production" was Jackson's motto. He led the body to steer clear of political and social involvements on any large scale. That policy placed this group mostly outside the civil rights movement of the period 1954–72, in which many black Baptist pastors and lay leaders worked for racial justice. As a result, another National Baptist schism occurred, out of which the Progressive National Baptist Convention* was formed in 1961. Since that period, however, this once less publicly involved body has shifted its practice and has been active in civil rights causes and voter registration drives.

This denomination, too, has been active in missionary, educational, and publication ministries. Recently it has established a ministerial pension plan. It has shown a particularly high degree of commitment to the support of colleges and seminaries, among them Morehouse School of Religion in Atlanta, Georgia, and Virginia Seminary in Lynchburg. The educational institutions are typically supported by Baptist churches and individuals rather than being affiliated officially with the Convention. The body supports missionary stations in the Bahamas, Jamaica, Panama, and Africa.

For more information: www.nationalbaptist.com

Headquarters: 1700 Baptist World Center Drive, Nashville, TN 37207

NATIONAL MISSIONARY BAPTIST CONVENTION OF AMERICA

Founded: 1988
Membership; statistics not kept, but may be as high as 2,000,000

The recent origin of this body of black Baptists (which came into being in 1988) accurately suggests the degree of historical heritage it shares with the two older National Baptist bodies. Once again the issue of control over denominational publication ventures led to a rupture. When the National Baptist Convention of America* broke its ties to the National Baptist Publishing Board, this new fellowship maintained the old relationship. It was not opposed to the private control of the publishing board and the Sunday school congress.

The convention meets in September annually, and the governing boards hold two additional meetings. The National Missionary Baptist Convention is headquartered in Los Angeles, California, and its greatest strength lies in the population of the Pacific Coast states.

For more information: www.nmbca.com

Headquarters: 4269 South Figueroa Street, Los Angeles, CA 90037

NATIONAL PRIMITIVE BAPTIST CONVENTION, U.S.A.

Founded: 1907
Membership: est. 53,630 in 547 churches (2000)

The black population of the South, throughout the years of slavery and civil war, generally worshiped with the white population in their various churches. The members attended white Primitive Baptist churches until the time of emancipation, when their white co-worshipers helped them establish their own churches by granting letters of fellowship and character, ordaining deacons and ministers, and assisting in other ways.

The doctrine and polity are similar to that of the Primitive Baptists,* though earlier the members were opposed to all forms of church organization. There are local associations and a national convention, organized in 1907. Each congregation is independent, receiving and controlling its membership. Unlike the Primitive Baptists, since 1900 this group has been establishing aid societies, conventions, and Sunday schools, over the opposition of some older and more traditional members. As with other Primitive Baptists, they call their pastors "elders" and practice footwashing as an ordinance.

NORTH AMERICAN BAPTIST CONFERENCE

Founded: 1865
Membership: 47,692 in 270 churches (2002)

German Baptists first settled in New Jersey and Pennsylvania, where Quakers offered the religious freedom they sought. Few congregations continue to use the German language in worship. The scattered churches later became the North American Baptist Conference. The first local organizations were in the 1840s, and the local conference idea was enlarged as German immigration spread westward, and today is strongest in the upper Midwest and California. In 1865 delegates from the eastern and western conferences met in a General Conference in Wilmot, Ontario.

Theologically, there is little variance from the basic Baptist position. In general, North American Baptists' 1982 statement of faith follows the New Hampshire Confession (1832), stressing the authority of Scripture, the revelation of God in Christ, regeneration, immersion, separation of church and state, and the congregational form of government. Membership is based on a personal experience of saving grace. The church teaches "soul liberty," which means that individuals do not need a mediator with God, and the church promotes separation of church and state.

The Triennial Conference is now the chief administrative unit. Twenty associations meet annually. The Triennial Conference is made up of clergy and lay representatives from all the churches and superintends the work of publication, education, international missions, and church planting. A general council acts for the conference between sessions. German Baptists were a part of what is now Colgate-Rochester Divinity School, but in 1935 they established a seminary of their own, the North American Baptist Seminary, which relocated from Rochester to Sioux Falls, South Dakota in 1949. The church supports ten homes for the aged and efforts at church planting in Japan, Brazil, Nigeria, Cameroon, West Africa, Russia, the Philippines, and Mexico.

For more information: www.nabconference.org

Headquarters: 1 So. 210 Summit Avenue, Oakbrook Terrace, IL 60181

OLD MISSIONARY BAPTIST ASSOCIATIONS

> Founded: 19th century
> Membership: 48,200 in 358 churches

There is no central body for Old Missionary Baptists, but they do have several local associations concentrated in Tennessee and surrounding states. Their roots go back to the nineteenth-century debates about missions. The Old Missionary Baptists distinguish themselves from Landmark Baptists and Primitive Baptists, but they also place greater emphasis on a preacher's abilities than formal education. Most of the preachers (or elders) are bi-vocational. Preaching is extemporaneous and revivalistic. A personal conversion experience is required for baptism, and they generally practice closed communion. Congregations support missionaries directly rather than through an association.

OLD REGULAR BAPTISTS

> Founded: 1825, 1892
> Membership: 15,218 in 326 churches (1995)

Old Regular Baptists trace their roots to the Second Great Awakening in eastern Kentucky in the early nineteenth century. Eight churches united and formed the New Salem Association in 1825; in 1892 they adopted the name Old Regular to distinguish them from the strictly Calvinist Primitive Baptists and the Arminian Free Will Baptists. They follow a strict patriarchal moral and social code based on New Testament teachings about men and women. Women have no formal voice in the church, but they do join in "shouting" during services. Women are forbidden to wear men's clothing (slacks, jeans, and so forth). Men are expected to own a home if they are married and to be master of the house. Formal education is not expected of ministers. There are sixteen regional associations and an annual convention which includes extended preaching. Old Regular Baptists are particularly known for their distinctive "lined-out" style of hymnody that preserves early American musical practice.

206

ORIGINAL FREE WILL BAPTIST CONVENTION

Founded: 1912, 1961
Membership: 37,198 in 237 churches (2000)

This body shares much in common with other Free Will Baptists* and it traces its history back to the work of evangelist Paul Palmer (d. 1750) in the 1720s in North Carolina. In the early twentieth century, Free Will Baptists in North Carolina organized a state convention and in 1935 joined the National Association. However, the North Carolina churches followed a slightly different ecclesiology than the other Free Will congregations. In particular, they believed that the annual conference should have greater authority to discipline local congregations. They also established their own liberal arts school, Mt. Olive College (established 1920), rather than send students to the Association's Bible college in Nashville. The North Carolina group also wanted to establish a separate publishing house to produce Sunday school curriculum. In 1961, most of the North Carolina Free Will Baptists formed a separate denomination with headquarters in Ayden, North Carolina. In addition to the college and press, the Convention sponsors a children's home and supports missions in Bulgaria, India, Mexico, Nepal, and the Philippines.

For more information: www.fwbpress.com

Headquarters: P.O. Box 159, Ayden, NC 28513-0159

PRIMITIVE BAPTISTS

Founded: 1827
Membership: est. 49,227 in 1,643 churches (2000)

Primitive Baptists have the reputation of being the strictest and most exclusive of all Baptist churches. Certainly they have held to the Baptist belief in local autonomy to an unusual degree. In fact, they have never been organized as a denomination and have no administrative body of any kind beyond the local church and local association. The movement originated in a nineteenth-century protest against money-based mission and benevolent societies. The Primitive Baptists maintained that there were no missionary societies in the days of the Apostles and none directed by the Scripture; there-

207

fore, there should be none now. Spearheading this protest against new measures, in 1827 the Kehukee Association in North Carolina condemned all money-based and centralized societies as being contrary to Christ's teachings. Within a decade, several other Baptist associations across the country made similar statements and withdrew from other Baptist churches.

The various associations adopted the custom of printing in their annual minutes their articles of faith, constitutions, and rules of order. These statements were examined by the other associations, and, if they were approved, there was fellowship and an exchange of messengers and correspondence. Any association not so approved was dropped from the fellowship. Calvinism (see REFORMED AND PRESBYTERIAN CHURCHES) runs strongly through the Primitive Baptist doctrine. In general, the members believe that through Adam's fall, all humankind became sinners; human nature is completely corrupt, and humans cannot by their own efforts regain favor with God; God elected God's own people in Christ before the world began, and none of these saints will be finally lost; Christ will come a second time to raise the dead, judge all people, punish the wicked forever, and reward the righteous forever; and the Old and New Testaments are verbally and infallibly inspired. The authorized ordinances are the Lord's Supper, baptism of believers by immersion, and footwashing.

Pastors are to be called by God, come under the laying on of hands, and be in fellowship with the local church of which they are members in order to administer the ordinances. No theological training is demanded of ministers. In spite of their opposition to missionary societies, their preachers travel widely and serve without charge, except when hearers wish to contribute to their support. The movement is concentrated in the South.

There are three traditional Primitive Baptist groups. The largest is the Old-Line Primitive Baptists (46,954 members) who teach that Christians are responsible for the salvation given by God. The Predestinarian Primitive Baptists or Absoluters stress God's predestination of all things, not just salvation. The Universalist Primitive Baptists (No-Hellers) believe that God predestines all people to salvation. The latter two groups are small and declining, with only about 2,000 members between them.

For more information: www.primitivebaptist.org

PROGRESSIVE NATIONAL BAPTIST CONVENTION, INC.

Founded: 1961
Membership: 2,500,000 in 1800 churches, but not verifiable (2004)

This group of Baptists came into being in 1961, after several years of tension and discussion, breaking away from the National Baptist Convention, U.S.A., Inc. In that year, Martin Luther King, Jr. (1929–68) nominated Gardner C. Taylor as president of the convention against longtime president Joseph Jackson, who was opposed to the protest movement of King. The National Baptist Convention, U.S.A.* followed a policy of disengagement from the civil rights movement and other social justice struggles during the revolutionary years following the 1954 Supreme Court decision concerning desegregation of public facilities.

Following the defeat of Taylor, who called for unity within the National Baptist Convention, U.S.A., the Rev. L. Venchael Booth, chairman of the Volunteer Committee for the Formation of a New National Baptist Convention, issued a call for a meeting at his church in Cincinnati, Ohio. One of the central objectives of the new convention was support for the "freedom fighters" in the civil rights movement. The first president was Dr. T. M. Chambers, who served until 1967, at which point Gardner Taylor was elected to that office. Once the convention was established, it became a focal point of the civil rights movement, and many leaders of that movement assumed significant positions in the new convention. In addition to King and Gardner, this included the famous preachers Ralph David Abernathy (1926–90) and Benjamin Mays (1895–1984). From its inception, the Progressive body has taken a highly active role in civil rights, social justice, and political causes. It also took a strong stand against apartheid in South Africa. Recently it has focused on the HIV/AIDS crisis in Africa and the U.S.

Headquartered in Washington, DC, the Progressive National Baptists are organized into four national regions. Eight departments include women, laymen, young adult women, young adult men, ushers, youth, moderator's council, and Christian education. From its beginning, the convention has been ecumenical in spirit, seeking to work harmoniously with other Christian denominations.

For more information: www.pnbc.org
Headquarters: 601 50th Street, N. E., Washington, DC 20019

PROGRESSIVE PRIMITIVE BAPTISTS

Founded: 20th century
Membership: est. 17,885, 221 churches in three associations

There are three major bodies that can be termed Progressive Primitive Baptists since they come out of the Primitive Baptist* heritage while modifying some of the stricter tenants. The largest body (7,739 members) is the Progressive Primitive Baptist church. They maintain strict Calvinist teaching regarding predestination, but they have adopted such practices as Sunday School, musical instruments in worship, a mission to the Ukraine, and even support for institutions such as summer camps, conferences, nursing facilities, and a school for pastors. It is found mainly in Georgia.

Slightly smaller is the Eastern District Association of Primitive Baptists (6,468 members), which was organized in 1848, and which is still found mainly in the Appalachian Mountains of Tennessee and Virginia. Though it allows musical instruments in worship and has a modified view of predestination, it holds to traditional Primitive Baptist attitudes toward camps, benevolent institutions, foreign mission programs, and similar extra-congregation activities.

In 1956 the Central Baptist Association separated from the Eastern District Association because of its acceptance of Arminianism and greater organization beyond the congregation. It teaches eternal security of the believer and practices footwashing, but it also has musical instrumentals in worship and supports a youth camp in Jasper, Virginia. In addition, the Association assists "churches in a Sunday School program for all ages, weekly prayer meetings, worship services, a monthly business meeting, an active youth program, Bible teaching, evangelistic and missionary work, visitation program, aiding established churches in organizing new churches and related projects; also support a home for adults and a children's home, youth camp, and Bible camp for all ages."

For more information: www.freewebs.com/association/home.html

REFORMED BAPTISTS

Founded: 1950s; 1996
Membership: statistics not kept;
perhaps 90,000 in 200-400 churches

The Reformed Baptists represent a theological movement more than a denominational structure; thus it is impossible to give accurate membership statistics. Modern Reformed Baptists have their origin in the Particular Baptists of the seventeenth century and have been heavily influenced by the nineteenth-century Baptist theologian and popular preacher Charles Haddon Spurgeon (1834-92). During the mid-twentieth century the works of another Baptist theologian and writer, A.W. Pink, were the catalyst for the resurgence of "five-point Calvinism" that gave rise to the modern Reformed Baptists.

"Reformed" in their name refers to the doctrines of the Protestant Reformation, especially Calvinism. They agree almost completely with the doctrines of the Synod and Canons of Dort (1618-19) and the Westminster Assembly, which produced the Westminster Confession of Faith (1646); except in the areas of church government and infant baptism. They profess belief in total human depravity, unconditional election, limited and definite atonement, irresistible (or effectual and invincible) calling, and the final perseverance of all true saints.

In 1996 a number of these confessional Reformed Baptist churches formed the Association of Reformed Baptist Churches of America (ARBCA), which has its office and headquarters in Carlisle, Pennsylvania. This national association has a General Assembly each year, a Coordinator who represents the churches and enlists membership into the Association, an Administrative Council of twelve men, a foreign missions arm, a home missions branch, a publishing house, and the Institute of Reformed Baptist Studies (IRBS) for pastoral training.

Reformed Baptists differ from most Baptists in their stress on theology rather than revivalism, but they also differ from other Calvinistic Baptists who deny the preaching of the gospel to all or who hold a Landmark concept of the church (see BAPTIST CHURCHES). Though their original membership was concentrated in the northeastern and southern states, they have now expanded into almost all the fifty states and Puerto Rico. In addition to U.S. con-

211

gregations, there are Reformed Baptists in Canada; the United Kingdom, France, Germany, Russia and the former eastern bloc communist countries, English-speaking and Francophone Africa, South America, Japan, Malaysia, Singapore, Myanmar and China.

For more information: www.reformedbaptist.com

Headquarters: P.O. Box 289, Carlise, PA 17013

SEPARATE BAPTISTS IN CHRIST

Founded: ca. 1877 and 1912, with roots to the colonial period
Membership: 8,716 in 94 churches (2000)

The Separate Baptists emerged during the First Great Awakening in the mid-eighteenth century. By the end of the century most Separate Baptist churches had merged with Regular Baptists.* Some churches rejected the merger of Separate and Regular Baptists in Kentucky in 1803 and in 1806 formed their own association. Other local associations followed, and the first General Association was formed in 1877. It dissolved but was re-established in 1912. By 1991 there were seven regional associations within the General Association, but then a split occurred over the issue of the millennium after Christ's return.

Along with many other Baptist groups, Separate Baptists do not claim to be Protestants: "We have never protested against what we hold to be the faith once delivered to the saints." Though officially non-creedal, Separate Baptists do have statements of faith in the infallibility of the Scriptures and in the Trinity; regeneration, justification, and sanctification through faith in Christ; and the appearance of Christ on judgment day to deal with the just and the unjust. The election, reprobation, and fatality of Calvinism are rejected. These churches observe foot washing as well as baptism of believers by immersion only and the Lord's Supper as ordinances.

The General Association of Separate Baptists has incorporated a mission program called Separate Baptist Missions, Inc. Through this program, support is given to various mission fields and efforts, both in the U.S. and abroad.

For more information: www.separatebaptist.org

Headquarters: 787 Kitchen Rd., Mooresville, IN 46158

SEVENTH DAY BAPTIST GENERAL CONFERENCE

Founded: 1802, with roots to 1671
Membership: est. 4,940 in 81 churches (2002)

Differing from other groups of Baptists in its adherence to the seventh day (Saturday) as the Sabbath (see ADVENTIST AND SABBATARIAN CHURCHES), the Seventh Day Baptists first appeared as a separate religious body in North America in the Colonial period. Stephen and Ann Mumford came from England in 1664 and entered into a covenant relationship with those who withdrew from John Clarke's (1609–76) Baptist Church in order to observe the Sabbath. In 1671 they officially organized a congregation. Other churches were organized in Philadelphia and New Jersey. Other than the Sabbath observance, their beliefs are similar to other Baptists.

Local churches enjoy complete independence, although all support the united benevolence of the denominational budget. The highest administrative body is the General Conference, which meets annually and delegates interim responsibilities to its president, executive secretary, and general council. The denomination participates in the ecumenical movement at local, regional, national, and world levels. The Seventh Day Baptist conferences include those in Australia, Brazil, England, Germany, Guyana, India, Jamaica, Malawi, Mexico, Myanmar, the Netherlands, New Zealand, Nigeria, the Philippines, Poland, and South Africa as well as in the U.S. and Canada.

For more information: www.seventhdaybaptist.org
Headquarters: P.O. Box 1678, Janesville, WI 53547-1678

SOUTHERN BAPTIST CONVENTION

Founded: 1845
Membership: 16,247,736 in 42,775 churches (2002)

The largest non-Catholic denomination in the United States is the Southern Baptist Convention (SBC), whose membership, as its name suggests, is most numerous in the South. In recent years, however, the SBC has been expanding in all regions of the country. The name "Southern" has, therefore, become something of a misnomer.

The SBC came into being during the years leading up to the Civil War. Although there were significant disagreements between Baptists in the two regions over the question of centralized organization (the South favored one organization to control the various cooperative ministries), it was the issue of slavery that led directly to the formation of a separate Southern Baptist Convention. Specifically, the issue was whether slaveholders could be accepted as foreign missionaries. The mission board, located in Boston, refused to send slaveholders into the fields, and in May 1845 the Southern Baptist Convention (SBC) was organized in order to establish boards for foreign and home missions.

Along with the rest of the South, the Southern Baptist churches suffered great losses during the war. Homes, schools, churches, the livelihood of citizens, indeed the very pattern of southern society, were destroyed with devastating effect on religious bodies. An anti-missionary movement further decimated Baptist ranks. Membership continued to decline when former slaves withdrew to form their own societies and conventions. The recovery of the Southern Baptist Convention was impressive, however. In 1845 there were 351,951 members, of whom 130,000 were black; by 1890, there were 1,235,908 members, predominantly white.

On June 20, 1995, the SBC adopted a resolution to renounce its racist origins and to apologize for its founders' defense of slavery. In its apology to African-Americans, the resolution declared that members of the church must "unwaveringly denounce racism, in all its forms, as deplorable sin" and repent of "racism of which we have been guilty whether consciously or unconsciously." As of 2000 more than 1,900 SBC congregations were predominantly African-American

In 1997 the Convention was reorganized. Twelve denominational agencies work with thirty-nine state conventions and two fellowships. The North American Mission Board operates throughout the U.S. and its territories, with nearly five thousand missionaries active in the field. The International Mission Board sponsors more than 4,500 missionaries in 127 nations, and in 1998 it operated 43 hospitals and 295 clinics, with a staff of 38 physicians, 72 nurses, 9 dentists, and 45 other personnel. Over $10 million was spent on 423 hunger and relief projects in 57 countries. LifeWay Christian Resources (formerly the Sunday School Board) is the world's largest publisher of religious materials. It provides the literature for some thirty-seven thousand SBC churches. The SBC maintains six theological seminaries.

The SBC grew rapidly in the last quarter of the twentieth century, but it also grew more factional. Since 1978, conservatives have exerted control over the seminaries, agencies, and boards that belong to the Convention. Conservatives distinguish their position as a commitment to biblical inerrancy. Others in the convention take their stand on what may be termed the infallibility of biblical authority and a commitment to the traditional Baptist principle of independence.

In the late 1990s controversy arose over the issue of women's ordination. At the SBC annual convention in June 2000 delegates voted to amend the "Baptist Faith and Message" confession of faith first formulated in the 1920s; the convention stipulated that "while both men and women are gifted and called for ministry, the office of pastor is limited to men as qualified by Scripture." The 2000 gathering also put the convention on record as supporting the death penalty in cases of murder and treason.

Earlier in 2000 a group of Southern Baptists opposed to "fundamentalist domination" of churches and state Baptist conventions met in Atlanta, Georgia, and formed the Network of Mainstream Baptists. Over one hundred representatives from fifteen states adopted the label "mainstream" to express their adherence to what they called traditional Baptist beliefs and practices. The tensions within the SBC and between the SBC and other Baptist churches increased in 2004 when the SBC voted to withdraw from the forty-six million-member Baptist World Alliance. The SBC accused the Alliance of promoting the idea of women preachers, liberal theology, and anti-American attitudes.

For more information: www.sbc.net

Headquarters: 901 Commerce St., Suite 750, Nashville, TN 37203

SOVEREIGN GRACE BAPTISTS

Founded 1954
Membership: est. 5,000 in 200 churches

The first "Sovereign Grace Bible Conference" was led by Rolfe P. Barnard in 1954 in Ashland, Kentucky. They maintain a loose fellowship of congregations and do not keep membership statistics, but they are held together by a common commitment to the First London

Confession of 1646. Like the Reformed Baptists,* these congregations were strongly influenced by the neo-Calvinist movement of the mid-20th century. By the 1980s doctrinal differences led to a separation of the Sovereign Grace churches from the Reformed Baptists. The Sovereign Grace churches tend to place greater emphasis on the New Covenant than the Old Covenant and do not hold as strictly to observation of Sunday as a Sabbath day.

For more information: www.sovgrace.net

UNITED AMERICAN FREE WILL BAPTISTS

Founded: 1901, with roots to early 19th century
Membership: est. 50,000 in 816 churches (1995)

This African-American denomination was organized as a separate institution in 1901, but its roots lie in the Free Will Baptist* tradition. Doctrinally, the two bodies are nearly indistinguishable, but the UAFWB does limit local church autonomy. Quarterly, Annual, and General Conferences exercise authority over local churches and may exclude congregations from membership. The church's statement of faith is an interesting variation on the Apostle's Creed that clarifies the church's own doctrine: "We believe in the Holy Ghost, the Free Will Baptist Church, the Communion of Saints, the forgiveness of sins, the resurrection of the body, and eternal life for all true believers who persevere in holiness to the end."

Robert Taft was the first African-American to be ordained as a minister in the church (1827). Although many members moved north in the 20th century, the church is strongest in the South.

For more information: www.uafwbc.org

Headquarters: 207 West Bella Vista Street, Lakeland, FL 33805

UNITED BAPTISTS

Founded: late 18th century
Membership: 54,248 in 436 churches (1990)

In the late 18th century many Regular and Separate Baptists in the South united and thus became the United Baptists. They are opposed to national conventions but do maintain local associations. Some congregations are Arminian; others Calvinist. Some have Sunday schools and use musical instruments; others do not. The practice of foot-washing is dying out. Most of the pastors lack formal education and are unsalaried. Most of the United Baptists are in Kentucky but they are also found in the surrounding states.

METHODIST CHURCHES

With the possible exception of the Reformed Churches,* the Methodists have been the most influential Protestant family of churches in the U.S. Hundreds of American denominations, service organizations, and educational institutions have their roots in the Methodist movement. Until it was eclipsed by the Catholic Church, the Methodist Church was the largest religious organization in the United States, and it still has the greatest geographical scope in the U.S. of any religious body, being represented in virtually every county of the nation. Methodist hymnody is heard in Protestant and Catholic congregations throughout the English-speaking world.

Beginning as a Pietist* movement within the Church of England in the 1730s, Methodism expanded greatly during the eighteenth century under the leadership of the Wesley brothers, John (1703–91) and Charles (1707–88), who preached and wrote hymns on the need for a personal experience of salvation and change of life. Methodism has been more concerned with ministry to the poor and disadvantaged than other forms of Protestantism, and Methodists often express their faith more in compassion for the suffering than in creedal statements. In a variety of ways, the witness of the Spirit among Methodists has been an impelling force for worship, love of neighbor, personal piety, and evangelization.

History. The origins of the Methodist Church can be traced to a small group of serious-minded students and fellows at Oxford University who were dubbed "Methodists" because of their strict regimen of prayer, fasting, Bible reading, and charitable works inspired by William Law's (1686–1761) *A Serious Call to a Devout and Holy Life and A Treatise on Christian Perfection.* Among the members of the group were the Wesleys and the future evangelist George Whitefield (1714–70), all three of whom would be ordained in the Church of England.

217

After John and Charles Wesley left Oxford, they traveled to the colonies, arriving in Georgia in 1735. It was an unsuccessful and unhappy two years for John, but while aboard ship, he met a group of Moravians* and was deeply impressed by their piety and humble Christian way of life. After his return to London, he went to the meeting of a Moravian religious society on Aldersgate Street. There he felt his heart "strangely warmed" as the meaning of Luther's doctrine of "justification by faith" sank into his soul.

The Wesleys gradually separated from the Moravians, and they followed George Whitefield's example of preaching for conversion and holiness of life. When the Church of England closed its pulpits to them, they took to the open air and sought audiences among the large and ignored working class of the new industrial revolution. Converts came thick and fast, and they were soon organized into "societies." Between 1739 and 1744 the organizational elements of Methodism were instituted: a circuit system and itinerant ministry, class meetings and class leaders, lay preachers, and annual conferences. As early as 1739 John Wesley drew up a set of general rules that are still held by modern Methodists as an ideal delineation of biblical rules of conduct.

Methodism was primarily a lay movement, and Wesley did his best to keep it within the Church of England. An evangelical party grew within that church that included such luminaries as hymn writer Isaac Watts (1674–1748) and the social reformer and abolitionist William Wilberforce (1759–1833). But it became evident that a separate Methodist organization was needed to deal with the large numbers recruited from among the unchurched. A Deed of Declaration in 1784 gave legal status to the yearly Methodist conference.

Methodists in the United States. By 1769 New York Methodists had built Wesley Chapel, now known as John Street Methodist Church. Captain Thomas Webb (ca. 1726–96) established societies in Philadelphia. Devereux Jarratt (1733–1801), an Anglican minister, led a revival in Virginia that won thousands. Wesley sent Francis Asbury (1745–1816) and Thomas Rankin (1738–1810) to supervise work of Methodism in America. Rankin presided over the first conference in the colonies called at Philadelphia in 1773.

Since Wesley's pro-British attitude aroused resentment in the colonies, it is surprising that the work of Asbury actually prospered during the Revolution. By the end of the war, membership had grown to fourteen thousand, and there were nearly eighty preachers.

218

It was now an American church, free of both England and the Church of England. Wesley accepted the inevitable; he ordained ministers for the colonies and appointed Asbury and Thomas Coke (1747–1814) as superintendents.

The Christmas Conference, held at Baltimore in December 1784, organized the Methodist Episcopal Church and elected Coke and Asbury as superintendents (later called bishops). *The Sunday Service* (an abridgment of *The Book of Common Prayer*) and Articles of Religion were adopted as written by John Wesley with the addition of an article that the Methodists should vow allegiance to the United States government.

Under Asbury's energetic direction, Methodism was adapted to the American rural setting. Circuit riders, preachers on horseback who traveled the expanding frontier, went to mountain cabins, prairie churches, schoolhouses, and camp meetings, preaching the need for conversion and regeneration. The Methodist Book Concern was established in 1789, putting into the saddlebags of the circuit riders religious literature that followed the march of the American empire south and west. The revivalistic flavor of the camp meeting, born among the Presbyterians,* was adopted by the Methodists. By the middle of the nineteenth century there were some 1.3 million Methodists in the U.S.

All was not peaceful among the Methodists. Objecting to the episcopal system, several bodies broke away: the Republican Methodists, later the Christian Church, withdrew in Virginia; Methodist Protestants seceded in 1830. Between 1813 and 1917, large groups of African-Americans formed independent churches: the African Methodist Episcopal Church;* the Union Church of Africans, now the Union American Methodist Episcopal Church;* and the African Methodist Episcopal Zion Church.*

In 1844 came the most devastating split of all, the bisecting of the Methodist Episcopal Church into the Methodist Episcopal Church and the Methodist Episcopal Church, South, organized in 1845. The cause of this major split was slavery. Bishop J. O. Andrew (1794–1871), a Georgian, owned slaves through inheritance, and his wife also was a slaveholder. The General Conference of 1844 requested that the bishop desist from the exercise of his office while he remained a slaveholder. Incensed, the Southern delegates rebelled. A provisional plan of separation was formulated, and the Southerners organized their own church. The split was not healed until 1939, when the Methodist Episcopal Church, the Methodist Episcopal Church, South, and the Methodist Protestant Church were reunited at Kansas City, Missouri, to form the Methodist Church.

The uniting conference of that year adopted a new constitution in three sections: an abridgment of the Articles of Religion drawn up by John Wesley; the General Rules, covering the conduct of church members and the duties of church officials; and the Articles of Organization and Government, outlining the organization and conduct of conferences and local churches.

Another Methodist body with a distinct history was the Evangelical United Brethren Church, which had arisen from a series of mergers of two groups: United Brethren in Christ and the Evangelical Church. The Evangelical Church, originally Evangelical Association, began as a result of the labors of Jacob Albright (1759–1808) among the German people of Pennsylvania. Preaching first as a Lutheran Pietist* and then as a Methodist exhorter, Albright was made a bishop at the first annual conference of the Evangelical Association in 1807. The name "Evangelical Church" was adopted in 1922.

Another group, Church of the United Brethren in Christ, developed in a parallel manner through the preaching of the Pietists* Philip William Otterbein (1726–1813) and Martin Boehm (1725–1812) among the Germans in Pennsylvania, Maryland, and Virginia. They were elected bishops at a conference in September 1800. That conference created the Church of the United Brethren in Christ, which also was strongly Methodist in polity, doctrine, and practice. Each group had a *Discipline* modeled on that of the Methodists. The Church of the United Brethren in Christ and the Evangelical Church were merged into the Evangelical United Brethren Church (E.U.B.) at Johnstown, Pennsylvania, in 1946.

In April of 1968 the Methodist Church merged with the Evangelical United Brethren (E.U.B.) to form the United Methodist Church. In this union no significant changes were made in either doctrine or polity. Representatives from the African Methodist Episcopal Church, the African Methodist Episcopal Zion Church, the Christian Methodist Episcopal Church, and The United Methodist Church have met since the mid-1980s as the Commission on Pan-Methodist Cooperation. A newer body, the Commission on Union, was formed in 1996, again with representatives from the four churches. Members of the two bodies have recommended that the commissions be merged; the recommendation must be approved by the general conferences of each of the four churches before it can be adopted.

Beliefs and Practices. Historically, Methodists have stressed the foundational beliefs of Protestantism and have offered theological common ground. The theology is Arminian, stressing the free will of the individual and the death of Jesus Christ as atonement for all human beings, as interpreted by Wesley. The church preaches and teaches the doctrines of the Trinity; the natural sinfulness of humankind, its fall and the need of conversion and repentance; freedom of the will; justification by faith; sanctification and holiness; future rewards and punishments; the sufficiency of the Scriptures for salvation; and the enabling grace of God. Two sacraments, baptism and communion, are observed; baptism is administered to both infants and adults, usually by sprinkling. Membership is based on confession of faith or by letter of transfer from another church; admission of children to membership is usually limited to those thirteen years of age or older, but in the South the age may be a few years younger.

There is wide freedom in the interpretation and practice of all doctrines, with some congregations more liberal and others more conservative. Methodists played major roles in many significant American religious movements, especially the Temperance Movement, the Social Gospel, the Holiness Movement, and the Ecumenical Movement. Some of these movements produced new denominations.

Worship and liturgy are based on the English prayer book with widespread modifications. The language of the prayer book is much in evidence in the sacraments of Methodist churches. In many forms of worship, however, each congregation is free to use or change the accepted pattern as it sees fit.

Polity. The local churches of Methodism are called charges. Clergy are appointed by the bishop at the Annual Conference, and each church elects its own administrative board that initiates planning and sets goals and policies on the local level. It is composed of staff members, chairs of various committees, those representing various program interests, and members at large. Charge, Annual, and General Conferences prevail in most Methodist bodies. While the government is popularly called episcopal, it is largely governmental

221

through this series of conferences. The Charge Conference meets at the local church or on the circuit with the district superintendent presiding. It fixes the salary of the pastor, elects the church officers, and sends delegates to the Annual Conference.

Some areas have a district conference between the Charge and the Annual Conference, but it is not a universal arrangement. Annual Conferences cover defined geographical areas; they ordain and admit ministers, vote on constitutional questions, supervise pensions and relief, and exchange pastors with other Annual Conferences through acts of the bishop; and, every fourth year, elect lay and ministerial delegates to the General Conference. The General Conference is the lawmaking body of the church, meeting quadrennially; the bishops preside, and the work of the conference is done largely in committees, whose reports then may be adopted by the General Conference.

Suggestions for further reading:

Bucke, Emory S., ed. *History of American Methodism.* Nashville: Abingdon, 1964.

Campbell, James T. *Songs of Zion: The African Methodist Episcopal Church in the United States and South Africa.* New York: Oxford University Press, 1995.

Heitzenrater, Richard P. *Wesley and the People Called Methodist.* Nashville: Abingdon, 1995.

Lincoln, C. Eric, and Lawrence H. Mamiya. *The Black Church in the African-American Experience.* Durham, NC: Duke University Press, 1990.

Langford, Thomas A., ed. *Doctrine and Theology in The United Methodist Church.* Nashville: Kingswood Books, 1991.

Matthews, Donald G. *Slavery and Methodism: A Chapter in American Morality, 1780-1845.* Princeton, NJ: Princeton University Press, 1965.

Marty, Martin E. *Protestantism in the United States: Righteous Empire.* 2nd ed. New York: Scribner, 1986.

McEllhenney, John G. *United Methodism in America: A Compact History.* Nashville: Abingdon, 1992.

McKinley, Edward H. *Marching to Glory: The History of the Salvation Army in the United States, 1880-1992,* rev. ed. Grand Rapids, MI: Eerdmans, 1995.

Richardson, Harry V. *Dark Salvation: The Story of Methodism as It Developed Among Blacks in America.* Garden City, NY: Anchor, 1976.

Smith, Timothy L. *Revivalism and Social Reform: American Protestantism on the Eve of the Civil War.* Baltimore, MD: Johns Hopkins University Press, 1980

Walls, William J. *The African Methodist Episcopal Zion Church: Reality of the Black Church.* Charlotte, NC: A.M.E. Publishing House, 1974.

AFRICAN METHODIST EPISCOPAL CHURCH

Founded: 1814
Membership: 1,857,186 adults in 6,200 congregations (1999)

The African Methodist Episcopal Church (AME) is one of the oldest and largest Methodist bodies in the world. It was founded by Richard Allen (1760–1831), a former slave from Delaware who had bought his freedom. Allen had been converted while still a slave, and he began preaching to freed African-Americans in Philadelphia up to five times a day. He regularly attended St. George's Methodist Church, where African-Americans were generally welcomed but were segregated from whites. In 1787 Absalom Jones (1746–1818), who later became the first African-American Episcopal priest, was kneeling in prayer when white trustees physically removed him to the back of the church. When the congregational leadership supported this discrimination, Allen and Jones led the black members out of the congregation. In 1793 Allen established the Bethel Church for Negro Methodists in Philadelphia.

Although Francis Asbury dedicated the chapel in Philadelphia and ordained Richard Allen as its minister, Bethel Church was a center of controversy within the Methodist system. The whites in the denomination tried to keep Allen and his congregation from controlling their own property, but in 1816 the Pennsylvania Supreme Court ruled in favor of Allen, setting an important legal precedent for black persons in the U.S. It was during the course of this struggle that the Bethel Congregation and five other predominantly black Methodist churches left the Methodist Church and formed the AMEC in 1814. Allen was consecrated by Asbury as the first bishop in 1816.

223

Other African-American churches throughout the urban North followed suit. Bishop Allen held strongly to the connectional system of the Methodists and tried to bring the new Zion Church* under his umbrella after 1816, but the members of Zion responded by forming their own denomination. In the years preceding the Civil War, the AME Church was largely confined to the Northern states; following the war its membership increased rapidly in the South. Today it is found all across the nation.

There are nineteen bishops (including the first woman bishop, elected in 2000), twelve general officers, and eighteen connectional officers in thirteen districts; a General Conference is held quadrennially. Foreign missions are supported in South Africa; West Africa; India; London, England; the Caribbean; and South America. The church supports six colleges and two theological schools. Journalism has been a central part of the church's work from its early years; the AME Book Concern dates to 1816, and the weekly *Christian Reader* has been published since 1848.

For more information: www.amecnet.org

Headquarters: 1134 11th St. NW, Washington, DC 20001

AFRICAN METHODIST EPISCOPAL ZION CHURCH

Founded: 1821
Membership: 1,430,795 in 3,226 churches (2002)

This church dates from 1796, when it was organized by a group of people protesting racial discrimination in the John Street Methodist Church in New York City. Their first church, named Zion, was built in 1800, and that word was later made part of the denominational name. The first annual conference was held in 1821, with nineteen preachers from six black Methodist churches in New Haven, Connecticut; Philadelphia, Pennsylvania; and Newark, New Jersey. James Varick (ca. 1750–1827), who had led the John Street dissension, was elected the first bishop. The present name was approved in 1848. The church spread quickly over the northern states, and by 1880 there were fifteen annual conferences in the South.

Livingstone College in Salisbury, North Carolina, the largest educational institution of the church, was established in 1879. Departments of missions, education, and publications were created in 1892. Later administrative boards were established to direct work in church extension, evangelism, finance, ministerial relief, and so on. Home missions are supported in Louisiana, Mississippi, and several western states, principally Oklahoma. Missionaries are found also in Liberia, Ghana, Nigeria, South America, and the West Indies. The church maintains five secondary schools and two colleges.

For more information: www.amezionchurch.com

Headquarters: P.O. Box 32843, Charlotte, NC 28232

CHRISTIAN METHODIST EPISCOPAL CHURCH

Founded: 1870
Membership: 784,114 in 3,069 churches (1999)

This body was established in 1870 in an amicable agreement between white and black members of the Methodist Episcopal Church, South. At the time of Emancipation there were at least 225,000 slave members of the Southern church, but following the Civil War, all but eighty thousand joined one of the two independent black bodies, the African Methodist Episcopal Church or the African Methodist Episcopal Zion Church. When the general conference of the Methodist Episcopal Church, South, met at New Orleans in 1866, a commission from the black membership asked to separate into a church of its own. The request was granted, and the Colored Methodist Episcopal Church was organized. In 1954 the name was changed to Christian Methodist Episcopal Church.

The doctrine of the CME is Methodist, but this denomination adds a quarterly conference to the district, annual, and quadrennial conferences usual in Methodism. There are ten episcopal districts, each supervised by a presiding bishop, who together form the College of Bishops. Ten departments oversee the national work, each chaired by a bishop assigned by the College of Bishops. The general secretaries of the various departments are elected every four years by the General Conference, and the president of the Women's Missionary Council is elected every four years by the quadrennial assembly of the Missionary Council. The church issues two periodicals and supports five colleges, a seminary, a hospital, and several low-rent and senior-citizen housing complexes. In the latter decades of the twentieth century, the church encouraged economic growth for African-

225

Americans as part of its ministry. The church sponsors four colleges and a school of theology.

For more information: www.c-m-e.org

Headquarters: 4466 Elvis Presley Blvd, Memphis, TN 38186-1212

CONGREGATIONAL METHODIST CHURCH

Founded: 1852
Membership: 14,738 in 187 churches (1995)

This church was established in Georgia in protest against certain features of the episcopacy and itinerancy of the Methodist Episcopal Church, South. In the late 1880s more than half of this body in turn withdrew to join the Congregational Church (see REFORMED and PRESBYTERIAN CHURCHES). The church grew in the twentieth century, and sent out its first missionary in 1947. In 1972 the headquarters moved to its current location in Florence, Mississippi. It continues to be located primarily in the South. Theologically, it is close to both the Fundamentalist* and Holiness* traditions.

Local pastors are called by the local churches; annual conferences grant licenses, ordain ministers, and review local reports. Annual and general conferences are recognized as church courts, empowered to rule on violations of church law and to coordinate, plan, and promote general church activities. There is a missionary program among the Navajo in New Mexico and Mexico. The church founded Wesley College, which was accredited in 1976 and is located near the denominational headquarters in Florence, Mississippi.

For more information: http://congregationalmethodist.net/

Headquarters: P.O. Box 9, Florence, MS 39073

EVANGELICAL CHURCH OF NORTH AMERICA

Founded: 1968
Membership: 15,011 in 135 congregations (2004)

When the Methodist Church merged with the Evangelical United Brethren to form the United Methodist Church* in 1968, a number of churches in the Brethren body withdrew to form the Evangelical

Church of North America. The new church was organized at Portland, Oregon, and eventually came to include congregations across the country. In 1969 union occurred with the Holiness Methodist Church. From 1982 to 1990 the Northwest Canada Conference was part of the Evangelical Church. In 1990 the Northwest Canada Conference united with the Missionary Church of Canada to form the Evangelical Missionary Church of Canada. The major mission fields are Bolivia, Brazil, and Navajo churches in New Mexico with cooperative ministries with national churches in Japan, Germany, Eastern Europe, and Russia.

The doctrinal position of the Evangelical Church is Wesleyan-Armenian. In polity the local church owns its own property while the clergy are assigned by the conference superintendent. Conference superintendents oversee each annual conference (six); the general administration is carried on by annual conference sessions and program committees. Every four years a general conference is held, at which the general superintendent is elected and oversees the denomination.

For more information: www.theevangelicalchurch.com

Headquarters: 9421 West River Rd., Minneapolis, MN 55444

KOREAN METHODIST CHURCH

Est. 1930
Membership: est. 500,000 (statistics not available)

The Korean Methodist Church is headquartered in Seoul Korea, but it has a strong and growing presence in the United States. It represents one of the important trends in American religion: "reverse missions" whereby former mission churches send evangelists and organizers to America and Europe. The Korean Methodist Church has historical and theological connections to the United Methodist Church, but it is a separate denomination with its own publishing house and administration. Most of the work of the Korean Methodist Church in the U.S. focuses on the Korean-American population, and the American branch maintains close ties to the homeland. Worship services are in Korean or a blend of Korean and English, and education programs often include information on adjusting to American life. As with other immigrant churches, the

227

Korean Methodist Church helps Korean-Americans maintain their cultural heritage while growing in faith. The official website of the church states that the purpose of the denomination is to serve "the human person and all creatures" through evangelism and social welfare programs. The goal of "right relationship" is foundational.

For more information: http://kmc.or.kr/eng/main.htm

Address: General Secretary, 119 N. Belmont Ave. 2nd Floor, Los Angeles, CA 90026

PRIMITIVE METHODIST CHURCH, U.S.A.

Founded: 1840
Membership: 4,399 in 79 churches (2002)

This church came into being as a result of camp meetings in England inspired by the American evangelist Lorenzo Dow (1777–1834). At an all-day meeting held at Mow Cop, Staffordshire, on May 31, 1807, two local preachers, Hugh Bourne and William Clowes, were dismissed from the Wesleyan Church and subsequently organized their followers as the Society of the Primitive Methodists. Four missionaries were sent to the U.S. in 1829 to work with Primitive Methodists who had settled mainly in the East and the Midwest. The American Primitive Methodist Church was established in 1840 to promote "primitive" or original Wesleyan practices, such as open-air preaching.

Doctrinally, the Primitive Methodists embrace a Wesleyan form of fundamentalism* that emphasizes the Bible as the inspired Word of God, the deity of Christ, the fall of Adam and Eve, the necessity of repentance and regeneration for all believers, the return of Christ, and eternal rewards and punishments for all people. The denomination has an annual conference that is both administrative and legislative, the churches being divided into six districts. The general offices are located in Hatboro, Pennsylvania. Mission work is carried out in Guatemala and the Dominican Republic.

For more information: www.primitivemethodistchurch.org

Headquarters: 723 Preston Lane, Hatboro, PA 19040-2321

SALVATION ARMY

Founded: 1880
Membership: 454,982 in 1,369 corps (2001)

The Salvation Army and its related organizations grew out of the Methodist Church's concern for outreach to the impoverished peoples of the growing metropolises in England. In order to bring the gospel to these neglected souls, a new type of religious organization was created. It is neither a traditional denomination nor a traditional service organization but a creative union of both.

William Booth (1829–1912), an ordained minister in the Methodist New Connexion in England, left that church in 1861 to become a freelance evangelist. In 1865 he dedicated his life to the poverty-stricken unchurched masses in the slum areas of London's East End. He first planned to supplement the work of the churches, but this proved impractical because many converts did not want to go where they were sent, and often when they did go, they were not accepted. Moreover, Booth soon found that he needed the converts to help handle the great crowds that came to his meetings.

He began his work under the name "Christian Mission," and in 1878 the name was changed to the Salvation Army. Booth first organized his movement along lines of Methodist polity, with annual conferences at which reports were made and programs planned. But when the name was changed, the whole organization became dominated by the new title. Articles of War (a declaration of faith) were drawn up, and soon the mission stations became corps, members became soldiers, evangelists became officers, and converts were called seekers. Booth was designated as general, and his organization was gradually set up on a military pattern, which provided a direct line of authority and a practical system of training personnel for effective action. He reasoned that it was "just as valid to build an army of crusaders to save souls as it has been to send armies to recover a sepulchre."

While the Salvation Army has a dual function of church and social agency, its first purpose is salvation "by the power of the Holy Spirit combined with the influence of human ingenuity and love." Its social services are a means of meeting the needs of the "whole person," putting the socially disinherited—the needy, both physically and spiritually—into a condition to be uplifted. The fundamental doctrines of the organization are stated in the eleven cardinal affirmations of its

Foundation Deed of 1878. These statements include the Army's recognition of the Bible as the only rule of Christian faith and practice; God as the Creator and Father of all humankind; the Trinity of Father, Son, and Holy Ghost; Jesus Christ as Son of God and Son of man; sin as the great destroyer of soul and society; salvation as God's remedy for human sin and the ultimate and eternal hope made available through Christ; sanctification as the individual's present and maturing experience of a life set apart for the holy purposes of the kingdom of God; and an eternal destiny that may triumph over sin and death.

Administratively, the Army is under the command of a General. The primary unit of the Army is the corps, of which there may be several in a city. Each corps is commanded by an officer, ranging in rank from Lieutenant to Major, who is responsible to divisional headquarters. A number of corps make up each of the forty divisions in the U.S., with the work of each division under the direct supervision of a divisional commander. Divisions are grouped into four territories—Eastern, Central, Southern, and Western—with headquarters in West Nyack, New York; Des Plaines, Illinois; Atlanta, Georgia; and Long Beach, California, respectively. Territorial commanders are in charge of each territory, and the four territorial headquarters are composed of departments to facilitate all phases of Army work.

Basic training for each officer is a two-year, in-residence course at one of the Army's four schools in Suffern, New York; Chicago; Atlanta; and Rancho Palos Verdes. The chief source of officer candidates is the Salvation Army corps. A soldier who has served actively for at least six months may make application and, if accepted, may enter the School for Officers' Training, where the curriculum, in addition to formal study, includes field experience as well as orientation in all possible areas of Salvation Army service. The officer graduates from the school as a lieutenant and, following additional study, is eligible to attain the rank of Captain, Major, Lieutenant Colonel, Colonel, or Commissioner. Today there are 5,481 officers assisted by 62,104 employees and about three million volunteers.

Today the Salvation Army works in over 109 countries with over one million active members. The Army preaches the gospel in some 140 languages at over 14,000 evangelical centers; and operates more than 5,000 social institutions, hospitals, schools, and agencies. The work of the Army in the U.S. includes 162 rehabilitation centers, aiding over 174,000 annually. Over 176,000 people are served each year in 53 medical facilities; 51 camps provide camping facilities for more than 177,000 children, mothers, and senior citizens. The Army maintains more than 300 boys' and girls' clubs with more than 113,000 members; some 28,000,000 meals are served annually; and basic social services are offered to almost 18,000,000. About 150,000 persons make life-changing spiritual decisions under the Army's ministry each year. There are also hotels and lodges for men and women, missing person bureaus, day-care centers, alcoholic care facilities, correctional service bureaus for prisoners and their families, programs for homeless persons, and other allied services. These services are given without respect to race, color, creed, or condition; the whole work is financed largely through voluntary subscriptions, federal funds, and annual appeals.

The national headquarters in Alexandria, Virginia, is the coordinating office for the entire country. The national commander is the chief administrative officer, official spokesperson, and president of all Salvation Army corporations in the U.S. Property and revenues are in the custody of a board of trustees, or directors, and citizen advisory boards assist in interpreting the work of the Army to the general public.

For more information: www.sarmy.org

Headquarters: 615 Slaters Lane, Alexandria, VA 22313

SOUTHERN METHODIST CHURCH

Founded: 1939
Membership: 6,493 in 108 churches (2002)

The Southern Methodist Church was formed by Southern Methodists who opposed the merger with the northern Methodist Episcopal Church in 1939 on grounds of the "alarming infidelity and apostasy found therein." There are no bishops, but there are the usual Methodist Annual and General Conferences; a president is elected every four years from the elders of the clergy. Laypeople and clergy have equal voice and voting privileges in the conferences. Local churches own and control their own property and buildings and call their own pastors, who must be approved by their Annual Conferences. There is one college and a publishing house, Foundry Press, both located at Orangeburg, South Carolina.

For more information: www.southernmethodist.org

Headquarters: P.O. Box 39, Orangeburg, SC 29116-0039

UNITED METHODIST CHURCH

Founded: 1968, with roots to 1784
Membership: 8,251,042 in 35,102 churches (2002)

Two mergers of major importance produced the United Methodist Church. The first merger was the reuniting of three separated Methodist groups in 1939, when the Methodist Episcopal Church, the Methodist Episcopal Church, South, and the Methodist Protestant Church were joined under a new name, the Methodist Church. In 1968, this body merged with the Evangelical United Brethren (E.U.B.) to form the United Methodist Church.

Both the Methodist and the E.U.B. churches, across the years, had been deeply conscious of their common historical and spiritual heritage. Their doctrines were similar. Both were episcopal in government and traced their origins to John Wesley. They had similar books of discipline. Their preachers often exchanged pulpits and congregations, worked together, and shared the same buildings. The only major difference was that of language: German among the Brethren, English among the Methodists, but in time this barrier began to mean less and less. Conversations concerning a merger began as early as 1803; but the long-considered merger was not consummated until the two churches became the United Methodist Church at Dallas, Texas, on April 23, 1968.

There was some dissent at Dallas; fifty-one congregations and nearly eighty ministers of the Evangelical United Brethren withdrew from the Pacific Northwest Conference to establish the Evangelical Church of North America;* eighteen E.U.B. congregations in Montana left to establish the Evangelical Church of North America in Montana. However, roughly 750,000 Brethren accepted the union, and their strength gave the new United Methodist Church a membership of nearly eleven million at its inception. In this union no significant changes were made in either doctrine or polity. The Confession of Faith of the Evangelical United Brethren Church, adopted in 1962, was placed beside the Methodist Articles of Religion. Similar systems of bishops and conferences were in use in both denominations, and the format is still maintained.

Above the sixty-four Annual Conferences are five jurisdictional conferences established for geographical convenience in administrative matters. These meet quadrennially, at times determined by the Council of Bishops, to elect new bishops and to name the members of the larger boards and commissions. Outside the continental U.S., central conferences correspond to jurisdictional conferences; they meet quadrennially and, when authorized to do so, may elect their own bishops. All bishops are elected for life (except in some overseas conferences, where the term is four years), and a Council of Bishops meets at least once a year "for the general oversight and promotion of the temporal and spiritual affairs of the entire church."

The General Conference consists of 1,000 delegates, half laity and half clergy, elected on a proportional basis by the Annual Conferences. The Judicial Council determines the constitutionality of any act of the General Conference that may be appealed, and it hears and determines any appeal from a bishop's decision on a question of law, in any district or annual, central, or jurisdictional conference.

In social ministries and education, the church operates or supports 225 retirement homes and long-term care facilities, 70 hospital and health-care facilities, 50 child-care facilities, 30 ministries for persons with disabilities, 8 two-year colleges, 82 four-year colleges, 10 universities, and 13 theological schools. United Methodists give more than $3.65 billion annually for clergy support and benevolences, local church building and debt retirement, and operating expenses. The church also gives considerable financial support to the National Council of the Churches of Christ in the U.S.A. The World Methodist Council was organized in 1881. Headquartered at Lake Junaluska, North Carolina, the council is designed to draw the whole Wesleyan movement closer together in fellowship and devotion to the Wesleyan heritage.

The 1972 General Conference broadened the basis of doctrine in the church in the first restatement since the eighteenth century. The classic documents of the merging Methodist and Evangelical United Brethren churches were maintained, but the doctrinal door was left open to theological change and revision. A revised statement was adopted in 1988: "In theological reflection, the resources of tradition, experience, and reason are integral to our study of Scripture without displacing Scripture's primacy for faith and practice."

Unusual among churches, The United Methodist Church has adopted a Social Creed that stresses human rights and ecological concerns. The church has considered the question of homosexuality at several General Conferences. At the 2000 conference, a substantial majority of lay and clergy delegates affirmed by vote that the practice of homosexuality is incompatible with Christian teaching and that no self-avowed practicing homosexual can be ordained as clergy or be given a pastoral appointment. This position was challenged several times after 2000 and remains controversial in the church.

For more information: www.umc.org

Headquarters: Council of Bishops, 100 Maryland Ave., NE, Suite 320, Washington, DC 20002

VOLUNTEERS OF AMERICA, INC.

Founded: 1896
Membership: 14,000 employees, 70,000 volunteers, 1.8 million served (2003)

Volunteers of America (VOA) is a Christian church and human-service organization founded in 1896 by Ballington (1857–1940) and Maud (1865–1948) Booth, son and daughter-in-law of William Booth, founder of the Salvation Army.* The mission of VOA is to reach and uplift all people, bringing them to the immediate knowledge and active service of God.

VOA is one of the largest and most financially efficient service organizations in the world. Over 85% of its $770,000,000 budget in 2003 went directly to those whom it serves. It is present in communities across the U.S., providing over 160 different human-service programs and opportunities for individual and community involvement. From rural areas to inner-city neighborhoods, VOA engages tens of thousands of professional staff and volunteers in operating programs that deal with today's most pressing social needs. It responds to individual community needs to help abused and neglected children, youth at risk, the frail elderly, the disabled, homeless individuals and families, and many others. Each year it helps more than 1.8 million people in need.

Volunteers of America adheres to a defined set of beliefs, or Cardinal Doctrines, that conform to biblical teaching and traditional Christian thought and practice. Individuals who are commissioned as VOA ministers (having met all requirements for religious study and spiritual formation) become fully accredited clergy and may perform sacramental and evangelical functions.

Volunteers of America is governed by both a religious body, the Grand Field Council, and a corporate body, the National Board of Directors. The Council is made up of all VOA clergy and represents the membership of the organization. The Council is responsible for framing the articles of incorporation, constitution, bylaws, and regulations and for electing its president. The National Board of Directors consists of thirty-one volunteer members and is responsible for the direction and effective functioning of the organization. The National Ecclesiastical Board is a smaller body of VOA clergy charged with ministerial affairs.

The chief officer of Volunteers of America, Inc., elected for a five-year term, is president of the corporation as well as head of the church. The national office, in Alexandria, Virginia, provides technical and administrative support to local VOA programs and directs other strategic initiatives to address the organization's mission.

For more information: www.voa.org

Headquarters: 110 South Union St., Alexandria, VA 22314-3324

WINDSOR VILLAGE UNITED METHODIST CHURCH

Founded: 1963 as Southmont Methodist Church of Houston
Renamed Windsor Village in 1986
Membership: 15,000

Kirbyjon Caldwell earned an MBA at the Wharton School of Business, and was working as a stockbroker when he followed a different calling and enrolled in seminary at Southern Methodist University. When Kirbyjon Caldwell was appointed Senior Pastor of Windsor Village United Methodist Church in 1982, the Houston congregation numbered 25. Windsor Village is now the largest United Methodist Church in the USA, with an estimated 15,000 adherents who are predominantly African American.

The effectiveness of this congregation is attributed on their Web site to the conviction that the "church must embrace theology, identify societal problems, and deliver solutions holistically. In other words, the church must take the 'sanctuary' to the streets." Through the use of innovative 503c corporations, nine of Windsor Villages' ministries are independent non-profit organizations, including a Christian school, an AIDs ministry, an emergency shelter for abused children, an urban housing ministry that built over 400 homes for economically disadvantaged families, and a girl's empowerment program.

Windsor Villages' ability to blend innovative acts of mercy with an evangelical message is derived from John Wesley's practices, but the development of independent corporations is a new paradigm that other large churches are considering. The effectiveness of this congregation, in renewing urban communities in Houston, was noticed by George W. Bush, who asked Pastor Caldwell to bless the presidential inauguration in 2000 and 2004.

Headquarters: 6000 Heatherbrook Drive, Houston, Texas 77085

HOLINESS CHURCHES

The Holiness movement grew out of the Methodist* Church beginning in the mid-nineteenth century. Early Methodist ministry in the U.S. focused primarily on conversion and church extension, at times neglecting John Wesley's (1703–91) emphasis on sanctification and perfection. As Methodism became more established in the nineteenth century, there was renewed interest in the doctrine of perfection. One of the key figures in this revival of holiness teaching was the traveling evangelist and writer Phoebe Palmer (1807–74), who experienced sanctification by the Holy Spirit in 1837. She worked tirelessly to bring others to a similar experience of holiness.

Toward the end of the nineteenth century, the Holiness movement had spread throughout the country, becoming a source of controversy in local Methodist churches. Congregations divided; holiness-minded preachers left the Methodist Church in order to work independently; and a wide-variety of small, often "store-front," churches sprang up in virtually every U.S. community. Over time, many of these independent congregations formed denominations.

Holiness teaching generally rejects various forms of popular entertainment, such as dancing, movies, popular music, makeup, ornate clothing, gambling, drinking, and smoking. In many ways, the Holiness movement represents a countercultural movement in the U.S., but its adherents continue to live and work in the midst of the wider society.

Many Holiness churches use the word Apostolic in their names to emphasize their aim of returning to the life of the New Testament church, when the Holy Spirit was perceived to be particularly active. After 1900 many in the Holiness movement embraced further works of

the Holy Spirit such as speaking in tongues and physical healing (see PENTECOSTAL CHURCHES). Since the Holiness movement is focused more on lifestyle and an experience of conversion followed by sanctification, it is to be distinguished from the more doctrinally oriented fundamentalist* movement. However, there has been much cross-fertilization between these two forms of conservative Protestantism.
Suggestions for further reading:

Dieter, Melvin Easterday. *The Holiness Revival of the Nineteenth Century.* Metuchen, N.J.: Scarecrow, 1996.

Dupree, Sherry Sherrod. *African-American Pentecostal Holiness Movement: An Annotated Bibliography.* New York: Garland, 1996.

Jones, Charles Edwin. *Perfectionist Persuasion: The Holiness Movement and American Methodism, 1867-1936.* Metuchen, N.J.: Scarecrow, 1974.

Kostlevy, William C. and Gari-Ann Patzwald, *Historical Dictionary of the Holiness Movement.* Lanham, Md.: Scarecrow, 2001.

Niebuhr, H. Richard. *The Social Sources of Denominationalism.* New York: Meridian Books, 1957.

Sanders, Cheryl J. *Saints in Exile: The Holiness-Pentecostal Experience in African American Religion and Culture.* New York: Oxford University Press, 1996.

Smith, Timothy L. *Called unto Holiness: The Story of the Nazarenes: The Formative Years.* Kansas City, MO: Nazarene Publishing House, 1962.

Stanley, Susan C. *Holy Boldness: Women Preachers' Autobiography and the Sanctified Self.* Knoxville, TN: University of Tennessee Press, 2002.

Synan, Vinson. *The Holiness-Pentecostal Movement in the United States.* Grand Rapids, MI: Eerdmans, 1971.

APOSTOLIC CHRISTIAN CHURCHES OF AMERICA

Founded: 1830s (came to the U.S. in 1847)
Membership: 12,930 in 86 churches (2002)

This is the only Holiness group that originated in Europe. It began in Switzerland when S. H. Froehlich had a dramatic conversion experience that he felt marked the New Testament pattern of Christian experience. Froehlich's church first took the name Evangelical Baptist, but adopted the Apostolic title as it embraced the doctrine of holiness. Froehlich himself came to the U.S. in the 1850s and ministered to Swiss and German immigrants in the Midwest. By that time, another Swiss pastor named Benedict Weyeneth, already had organized the first congregation in the U.S. in upstate New York. The theology of the church reflects some of the concerns of German Pietism.*

The church consists of members who are "reborn" and baptized, and who strive for sanctification, and of such friends of the truth who sincerely and earnestly strive to attain adoption by God in Christ. Members are noted for a life of simplicity, separation from worldliness, and obedience to the Bible, which is embraced as the infallible Word of God. Members may serve in the military, but do not bear arms since that violates the commandment to love one's enemies. Though they strive to be good citizens, they do not swear oaths. There are no educational institutions for clergy, and they are not paid. A very close-knit fellowship and strong sense of community exist throughout the denomination, evidenced in the observance of the kiss of peace. A smaller, related body is called the Apostolic Christian Church (Nazarene).

For more information: www.apostolicchristian.org

Headquarters: 3420 North Sheridan Rd., Peoria, IL 61604

APOSTOLIC FAITH MISSION OF PORTLAND, OREGON

Founded: 1907
Membership: est. 4,500 in 50 churches (2000)

This body was organized in Portland, Oregon, by the Rev. Florence L. Crawford in order to "reestablish, maintain, and teach all the doctrines as taught by Christ and his apostles in the days of the early church." Thus it is one of the few denominations founded by a woman. The church stresses justification by faith, entire sanctification, and the baptism of the Holy Spirit as evidenced at Pentecost. Branches exist in several foreign countries, with more members in Africa than in the U.S. The publishing house circulates evangelical literature in more than sixty languages, and dialects are located in Portland.

Although the church keeps baptismal records, there are no membership reports. A born-again experience and subscription to the doctrines of the group are required for membership. It is a church without a collection plate, with no offering being taken during services. True to the Holiness tradition, worldly amusements (dancing, theater, card playing, drinking, smoking) are banned. Members are required to dress conservatively, and marriage with unbelievers is not permitted.

For more information: www.apostolicfaith.org

Headquarters: 6615 SE 52nd Ave., Portland, OR 97206

APOSTOLIC OVERCOMING HOLY CHURCH OF GOD

Founded: 1916
Membership: 10,714 in 129 churches (2000)

Bishop W. T. Phillips (1893–1973), a former member of the Methodist Church,* became deeply concerned with the teaching of the doctrine of holiness and, after four years of study and preaching on the topic, organized the Ethiopian Overcoming Holy Church of God in 1916 in Mobile, Alabama. It is claimed that this church existed even from the days of Enos, when Christianity was known to be in existence in Abyssinia. "Ethiopian" was later changed to "Apostolic." Active in twenty-two states, the West Indies, Haiti, and Africa, the church's clergy, both men and women, are supported by tithes. Worship includes foot washing and divine healing. Services generally are emotionally expressive, with participants speaking in tongues and engaging in ecstatic dances. Marriage to the unsaved, the use of tobacco, foolish talking, jesting, and use of slang are forbidden.

In doctrine, sanctification and holiness are stressed, along with the deity of Christ, the final resurrection of the dead, and the punishment of evil at the time of the last judgment at the Second Coming of Christ. A publishing facility is located in the headquarters building in Birmingham, Alabama.

For more information: www.tittusvilleaohchurch.org

Headquarters:1120 North 24th St., Birmingham, AL 35234

THE CHRISTIAN AND MISSIONARY ALLIANCE

Founded: 1887
Membership: 389,232 in 1,963 churches (2002)

A. B. Simpson (1843–1919), a Presbyterian* minister in New York City, left that church to carry on independent evangelistic

239

work in 1882. This led to the formation of two societies: the Christian Alliance, for home missions work, and the Evangelical Missionary Alliance, for work abroad. These merged in 1897, forming the Christian and Missionary Alliance. When the charismatic Assemblies of God* was founded, about one-tenth of that constituency resulted from the departure of people from the Christian and Missionary Alliance. The two groups have a close-knit history, are doctrinally similar, and maintain ties of fellowship. The Alliance remained a confederation for over seventy-five years, but it formalized its status with bylaws and a constitution in 1974.

Strongly evangelical, the Alliance believes in the inspiration and inerrancy of the Bible, the atoning work of Christ, the reality of supernatural religious experience, sanctification, and the premillennial return of Jesus Christ. It stresses the centrality of Christ as Savior, sanctifier, healer, and coming king. True to its original purpose, the Alliance sponsors foreign missions work in eighty-one countries in Latin America, Africa, Asia, the Pacific Islands, the Middle East, and Europe. There are over one thousand Alliance missionaries and some fifteen thousand national pastors and workers ministering to nearly two million persons. Ethnic groups within the alliance include Cambodian, Dega, Haitian, Hmong, Jewish, Korean, Laotian, Native American, Hispanic, and Vietnamese. Each member church or group is engaged in missionary and evangelistic activities. An overall conference of delegates, the General Council, meets annually. The CMA in Canada became autonomous in 1980 but continues to support missions jointly with the U.S. Alliance.

For more information: www.cmalliance.org

Headquarters: P.O. Box 35000, Colorado Springs, CO 80935

CHURCH OF CHRIST (HOLINESS) U.S.A.

Founded: 1894
Membership: 10,321 in 191 churches (2002)

A Baptist preacher in Alabama and Mississippi, C. P. Jones, seeking a new church and faith that would make him "one of wisdom's true sons . . . like Abraham, a friend of God," founded this church. The body retained its Holiness emphasis when other early black churches moved into

Pentecostalism.* The Church of Christ (Holiness) seeks to spread the gospel around the world, to reclaim those who have fallen away from the faith, to encourage believers to experience sanctification, and to support divine healing. The church has a strong eschatological focus as well.

Doctrinally, the church emphasizes original sin, the Holy Spirit as an indispensable gift to every believer, and Christ's atonement and Second Coming. There are two sacraments: baptism and the Lord's Supper. Foot washing and divine healing are employed as aids to the growth of spiritual life. The church has bishops, who speak for the church, but its government is representative, with final authority vested in a biennial convention made up of elders, clergy, and local lay leaders. There are seven dioceses, each under a bishop's charge. Missionary work is conducted in the U.S. and in Liberia and Nigeria.

For more information: www.cochusa.com

Headquarters: P.O. Box 3622, Jackson, MS 39207

CHURCH OF GOD (ANDERSON, INDIANA)

Founded: 1881
Membership: 246,316 in 2,229 churches (2004)

The Church of God, with general headquarters in Anderson, Indiana, grew out of the nineteenth-century American Holiness Movement, but it was a radical expression of the Holiness Movement in that it was convinced that holiness was to be understood in terms of the doctrine of the church as a spiritual fellowship of Christians. Both Anabaptist* and Pietistic* emphases also influenced the Church of God. Daniel S. Warner (1842-1925) and several associates rejected denominational hierarchies and formal creeds. They understood unity as being a natural outgrowth of personal holiness, and holiness to be the basis of biblical unity.

The Church of God's generally accepted doctrines include the divine inspiration of the Scriptures; forgiveness of sin through the atonement of Christ and repentance of the believer; the experience of holiness; the personal (amillennial) return of Christ; the kingdom of God as the reign and rule of God in the human heart; resurrection of the dead; and a final judgment in which the righteous are rewarded and the wicked punished. Baptism by immersion is viewed as a witness to the new believer's regeneration by Christ and inclusion in the family of God. The Lord's Supper reminds participants of the grace experienced in the life of the believer. Foot washing is practiced in acknowledgement and acceptance of the servant ministry of Christians to each other and to the world. These New Testament practices are understood as divine ordinances of the church.

Local churches are responsible for their own way of functioning. As a result, one finds a wide variety of organizational structures among congregations. Ministers and lay leaders meet in voluntary state and regional assemblies for inspiration and instruction as well as to conduct business. The General Assembly meets in connection with the annual international convention held in Anderson. In 1996 and 1997 the assembly initiated a restructuring of the church's work in the U.S. The result was the formation of Church of God Ministries, Inc. The church's ministries emphasize outreach, congregational ministry, and service to pastors and others. Warner Press serves as the church's publisher of curriculum and other materials. There is no formal membership in the Church of God (Anderson), but persons are assumed to be members on the basis of conversion and holiness of life. Congregations are found mainly in the Midwest and Pacific Coast regions. It supports Anderson University and its School of Theology along with Mid-American Christian University, Warner Southern College and Warner Pacific College. It carries on work in ninety countries, involving 767,830 worshipers.

For more information: www.chog.org

Headquarters: P.O. Box 2420, Anderson, IN 46018-2420

CHURCH OF GOD (HOLINESS)

Founded: 1886
Membership: est. 8,000 in approx. 140 churches (2000)

The Church of God (Holiness) is an association of autonomous congregations that was founded by former Methodists* who were active in the Southwest Holiness Association. They believed that entire sanctification was a biblical doctrine that described the teaching as a second definite work of God's grace in the heart and life of the believer subsequent to regeneration, at which time the believer is cleansed of the effects of original sin and is completely submitted to the controlling hand of the Holy Spirit.

The church today is concentrated in Missouri and Kansas, and has a rapidly expanding work among Hispanics in the U.S. The Home Missions Department also works with Haitian immigrants in New York City and sponsors a Navajo mission in the Southwest. Missions are concentrated in the Caribbean basin, Nigeria, Mexico, and the Ukraine. In addition to Kansas City College and Bible School, the church operates a printing house which produces Sunday School literature for all ages, devotional books, and a periodical. A General Convention is held annually.

For more information: www.cogh.net (unofficial)

Contact: Kansas City College and Bible School, 7401 Metcalf, Overland Park, KS 66204

CHURCH OF THE NAZARENE

Founded: 1908
Membership: 639,330 in 4,983 churches (2002)

The Church of the Nazarene is one of the largest and most influential of the Holiness bodies, and it is one that has self-consciously held to its Wesleyan roots. The church resulted from the merger of three independent Holiness groups in the U.S. In 1907, an eastern Holiness body, the Association of Pentecostal Churches of America joined with a California body, the Church of the Nazarene. Then in 1908, this body merged with a Southern group known as the Holiness Church of Christ. The current name was adopted in 1916. While many were involved in the founding of the church, the principal figure was Phineas F. Bresee (1838–1916), who became its first general superintendent.

The church's theological background is Wesleyan. Four of the first five general superintendents of the Church of the Nazarene, including Bresee, were former Methodist* ministers, and the church's *Manual* is similar to the Methodist *Book of Discipline*. The doctrine of the church is built around the justification and the sanctification of believers by faith. This includes a believer's entire sanctification as a second work of grace subsequent to regeneration. All clergy, both men and women, and local church officials must profess this experience of entire sanctification. Other doctrines include belief in the plenary inspiration of the Scriptures; the atonement of Christ for the whole human race (i.e., Arminianism); the justification, regeneration,

243

and adoption of all penitent believers in Christ; the Second Coming of Christ; the resurrection of the dead; and the final judgment.

Members believe in divine healing, but never to the exclusion of medical agencies. The use of tobacco and alcoholic beverages is denounced. Two sacraments, baptism by sprinkling, pouring, or (most often) immersion and communion are accepted as "instituted by Christ." Baptism of young children is allowed, but believer's baptism predominates. The General Assembly, the highest body of the church, elects six general superintendents whose terms last until the next General Assembly, and the General Board, consisting of an equal number of lay and clergy members. The General Board meets annually and oversees the five administrative divisions of the church: World Mission, Church Growth, Sunday School Ministries, Communications, and Finance. The church is organized in 109 world areas and supports some six hundred missionaries. There is strong emphasis on evangelism. The church's International Center is located in Kansas City, Missouri.

Worldwide, the church supports ten liberal arts colleges, two graduate theological seminaries, forty-three Bible colleges, two hospitals, thirty-eight medical clinics, three nurse training colleges, one teacher training college, one junior college, and 430 primary and secondary schools that serve over 51,000 children. The books, periodicals, and curriculum of the church are produced at the Nazarene Publishing House in Kansas City.

For more information: www.nazarene.org

Headquarters: 6401 The Paseo, Kansas City, MO 64131

CHURCHES OF CHRIST IN CHRISTIAN UNION

Founded: 1909
Membership: 11,504 in 235 churches (2003)

This church began when five ministers and several lay persons withdrew from Christian Union* churches in 1909. The Christian Union had been founded in 1864 in Ohio "to promote fellowship among God's people, to put forth every effort to proclaim God's saving grace to the lost . . . and to declare the whole counsel of God for the edification of believers." Some of the clergy in the Christian Union felt that key doctrines were being neglected, and so the Churches of Christ in Christian Union was organized "to allow a

244

complete freedom in the preaching of full salvation as stated doctrinally by John Wesley." The first council was held that year at Jeffersonville, Ohio. The Reformed Methodist Church merged with the Churches of Christ in Christian Union in September 1952.

Churches in this body are generally evangelistic in faith and work; camp meetings, revivals, and soul-winning campaigns are held regularly throughout the denomination. Worship follows simple forms, with little prescribed ritual. Emphasis is placed "on the blessing of God rather than on the ingenuity of man." A general council meets every two years at Circleville, Ohio, the body's headquarters. Circleville Bible College, established in 1948, trains clergy and lay workers.

For more information: www.cccuhq.org

Headquarters: 1426 Lancaster Pike, Circleville, OH 43113

FREE METHODIST CHURCH OF NORTH AMERICA

Founded: 1860
Membership: 72,711 in 999 congregations (2003)

The Free Methodist Church was formed as part of the abolitionist movement prior to the Civil War. Its founder was the Reverend B. T. Roberts (1823–93) who objected to "new school" Methodism, which he and his associates believed compromised the Wesleyan standards of the church. They called for a return to stricter doctrine and lifestyle in the Methodist Church,* which included the abolition of slavery, abolishing the practice of pew rentals, opposition to secret societies, and more freedom in worship. They were "read out" of their churches and organized the Free Methodist Church in Pekin, New York.

Doctrinally, the Free Methodists stress the virgin birth, the deity of Jesus, and his vicarious atonement and resurrection. No one may be received into membership without undergoing confession and forgiveness of sin, and the experience of entire sanctification is sought in all members.

The church is connectional, in a basic Methodist pattern, with a board of four bishops who supervise the four basic geographic areas of the church, a General Conference that meets every four years, Annual Conferences, and districts. Headquarters are in Indianapolis, Indiana. The publishing arm of the church is Light and Life Communications. The church operates six four-year colleges and a seminary and maintains a seminary foundation in cooperation with Asbury Theological Seminary and George Fox Evangelical Seminary. Social services include a hospital, a home for unwed mothers, five retirement and nursing facilities for the elderly, and many day-care centers for children.

The Free Methodist Church has become a world fellowship, consisting of thirteen general conferences (Brazil, Burundi, Canada, Congo, Dominican Republic, Egypt, Japan, Mozambique, the Philippines, Rwanda, South Africa, Zimbabwe and the U.S.) with a common constitution. Free Methodist churches are found in sixty-nine countries; membership outside the U.S. is over six hundred thousand.

For more information: www.fmcna.org

Headquarters: P.O. Box 535002, Indianopolis, IN 46253

NEW APOSTOLIC CHURCH OF NORTH AMERICA

Founded: 1862
Membership: 37,382 in 348 churches (2002)

The New Apostolic Church of North America is a variant of the Catholic Apostolic Church movement in England, a movement that originated with Edward Irving (1792–1834), a Presbyterian pastor in London. It is difficult to place this body into a category because it emerged from the evangelical movement in the Anglican Church, adopted some Pentecostal practices, and over the years moved closer to Roman Catholic practice and piety.

The founders of the church believed in the imminent return of Christ. In preparation for the expected eschaton, they attempted to recreate the apostolic offices of the church. Thus there were apostles, prophets, evangelists, pastors, and so on. The twelve apostles held their first conference in 1835. In a dispute over the appointment of new apostles to fill vacancies left by attrition, Bishop Schwarz of Hamburg was excommunicated from the Catholic Apostolic Church in 1862. To lead the dissenting body, a priest named Preuss was elected to the office of apostle "through the spirit of prophecy," and Bishop Schwarz served under him until his own elevation to the apostolic office.

Under Preuss and Schwarz, the New Apostolic Church spread from Europe to North America, where today it is organized into districts under apostles, bishops, and elders. This church teaches that only the Apostles

246

have received from Christ the commission and power to forgive sin. All clergy and other "office-bearers" are selected by the apostleship. The American church is a constituent of the international organization supervised by Chief Apostle Richard Fehr in Zurich, Switzerland.

The New Apostolic Church of North America accepts the Apostles' Creed, but adds a number of articles that stress the authority and inspiration of the living apostles as well as the Bible, the apostolic ordinances of the laying-on of hands, the necessity of gifts of the Holy Spirit, freewill offerings, and the speedy, personal, pre-millennial return of Christ. Three means of grace are found in three sacraments: baptism (including children), Holy Communion, and Holy Sealing (the dispensing and reception of the Holy Spirit). Work "along broader interior and missionary lines" is conducted in the U.S., Canada, Mexico, and Puerto Rico.

For more information: www.nak.org

Public Relations, c/o Verlag Friedrich Bischoff GmbH, Gutleutstrasse 298, D-60327, Frankfurt am Main, Germany.

WESLEYAN CHURCH

Founded: 1843
Membership: 123,160 in 1,628 churches (2002)

The Wesleyan Church was formed in 1968 through the merger of the Pilgrim Holiness Church and the Wesleyan Methodist Church. Many beliefs of the Wesleyan Church are based on doctrines set forth by the Dutch theologian, Jacobus Arminius, and John Wesley.

The Wesleyan Methodist Church was the first Holiness denomination founded in the U.S. as a protest against slavery. Orange Scott (1800–1847) was a leader of abolitionist Methodist preachers, and when Methodist bishops urged silence on the subject of slavery as the country was moving towards Civil War, Orange and his associates organized a separate Wesleyan Methodist Connection. Many of the Wesleyan Methodists of that day were activists in what came to be known historically as the underground railway before the Civil War.

Following the Civil War and emancipation, the Wesleyan Methodist Connection embraced the Holiness movement, which promoted the doctrine of sanctification as taught by John Wesley, with an uncompromising commitment to a temperate lifestyle. In 1947 the word "Connection" was change to "Church". By the late nineteenth century several Holiness groups had formed into functioning, autonomous, ecclesiastical bodies as a result of the Holiness revival that spread through much of Protestantism in the late nineteenth century. In 1897 a process was begun and resulted in one organized church in 1922 which adopted the name the Pilgrim Holiness Church. In 1966 the decision was made by the respective General Conferences to merge the Pilgrim Holiness Church and the Wesleyan Methodist Church as their doctrine and church polity was so similar. This merger was accomplished in June of 1968 and took place on the campus of Anderson University in Anderson, Indiana.

Today, the Wesleyan Church has a presence in 76 countries including the United States and Canada. A worldwide membership of 306,000 meets in 4,055 churches each week. There are over eleven thousand men and women involved in ministry either as ordained ministers or credentialed laymen.

For more information: www.wesleyan.org

Headquarters: P.O. Box 50434, Indianapolis, IN 46250

CHRISTIAN AND RESTORATIONIST CHURCHES (STONE-CAMPBELLITE TRADITION)

Protestantism, with its emphasis on the Bible alone as the basis of faith and practice, has always sought to remain true to the church of the Apostles in the New Testament. Most Protestants have been willing to accept some historical development of the church and its doctrine in the post-biblical period, accepting the Apostles' Creed, for example. There have been others, though, who have seen the history of Christianity as the story of a decline from New Testament purity. These Christians have attempted to "restore" original or "primitive" Christianity by purging the church of all non-biblical elements, including creeds and confessions of faith. During the Second Great Awakening of the early nineteenth century, this restorationist impulse grew particularly strong. In politics, the U.S. had "restored" Greek democracy; many thought Americans could also restore the structure and doctrine of the original church in the new land. By returning to the New Testament alone, without recourse to creeds or rituals, the restorationists also hoped to end fraternal strife among churches.

248

Thomas Campbell (1763–1854) was a Scottish Presbyterian who left his church in Ireland to come to western Pennsylvania in 1807. Campbell was convinced that the historical creeds and confessions of the church were a source of Christian division rather than union, and he preached that all Christians should share in the Lord's Supper together. When his views led to a censure from the Presbyterians* in 1809, he formed the Christian Association of Washington County, Pennsylvania, and published the Declaration and Address, which was to become the Magna Carta of the restorationist movement. In that document he argued that "schism, or uncharitable divisions" in the church were "anti-Christian, anti-Scriptural, and anti-natural" and "productive of confusion and every evil work."

God has spoken clearly, Campbell declared, and laid down the rules for church practices in the New Testament. "We will speak when the scriptures speak, and remain silent when they are silent." With that phrase, Campbell abolished many traditional church practices, including the use of musical instruments in worship. Soon the Campbells adopted believer's baptism. Campbell's son, Alexander (1788–1866), was less scholarly than his father, but more dynamic and consistent in his application of his father's principles. He fought many public battles against atheism, Mormonism, Unitarianism, creedalism, sectarianism, emotionalism, and even slavery; but he was singularly unsuccessful in bringing about church unity. His non-creedal church became one of the first independent denominations to be born in the United States.

The other major branch of the nineteenth-century restorationist movement had its origins in the convictions of James O'Kelly (1757–1826), a Methodist minister; Abner Jones (1772–1841), a Baptist; and Barton Stone (1772–1844), a Presbyterian. When the Second Great Awakening swept through Tennessee and Kentucky in the early 1800s, preaching focused on the need for conversion rather than denominational or doctrinal distinctions. Barton Stone was instrumental in the famous Cane Ridge, Kentucky, revival, which began on August 7, 1801. Somewhere between ten thousand and twenty-five thousand people appeared during the weeklong revival in which preachers from a variety of churches took part. The revival convinced Stone that salvation has little to do with church affiliation and that "deeds are more important than creeds." The egalitarian promise of the American Revolution was being felt in Cane Ridge and other Western "camp meeting" revivals, but the controversy over them led to a schism in the Presbyterian Church.

The groups led by O'Kelly, Jones, and Stone engaged in a long series of conferences that resulted in agreement on six basic Christian principles: (1) Christ, the only head of the church; (2) the Bible, sufficient rule of faith and practice; (3) Christian character, the measure of membership; (4) a right, individual interpretation of the Scripture, as a way of life; (5) "Christian," the name taken as worthy of the followers of Christ; (6) unity, Christians working together to save the world. By 1832 the "Stoneites" and the "Campbellites" had come together for a meeting in Lexington, Kentucky. Stone used the word *Christian* to designate his group, feeling that all of God's children should be known as such. Alexander Campbell used the phrase "Disciples of Christ." After 1832, some of the Christians and the Disciples of Christ merged; both names are still used, but commonly and officially the body is known today as the Christian Church (Disciples of Christ). Very soon thereafter, however, differences arose among the restorationists, and, over time, distinct fellowships emerged, most of which go by the name "Christian Churches."

Suggestions for further reading:

Garrison, W. E., and A. T. DeGroot. *The Disciples of Christ: A History.* St. Louis: Bethany, 1958.

Harrell, David E., Jr. *A Quest for Christian America, 1800-1865: A Social History of the Disciples of Christ,* 2 vols. Tuscaloosa, Ala.: University of Alabama Press, 2003.

Harrell, David E., Jr., ed. *The Churches of Christ in the 20th Century: Homer Hailey's Personal Journey of Faith.* Tuscaloosa, Ala.: University of Alabama Press, 2000.

Hughes, Richard T. *Reviving the Ancient Faith: The Story of Churches of Christ in America.* Grand Rapids, MI: Eerdmans, 1996.

McAllister, Lester G. and William E. Tucker, *Journey in Faith: A History of the Christian Church (Disciples of Christ).* St. Louis: Bethany, 1975.

Williams, D. Newell. *A Case Study of Mainstream Protestantism: The Disciple's Relation to American Culture, 1880-1989.* Grand Rapids, MI: Eerdmans, 1991.

CHRISTIAN CHURCH (DISCIPLES OF CHRIST)

> Founded: 1832 or 1812
> Membership: 786,334 in 3,691 congregations (2002)

The Disciples of Christ were organized primarily by Alexander Campbell and preserve the original ecumenical aim of Campbell more fully than other restorationist bodies. The first national convention of the Disciples of Christ and the first missionary society (American Christian Missionary Society) were organized in 1849, but state conventions and societies had begun to meet in 1839. The group grew rapidly in the nineteenth century in the Midwest. Differences between conservatives and progressives over such matters as the organization of missionary societies and instrumental music in the churches led to the separation of the Churches of Christ* and Disciples by the end of the century.

In matters of belief, the church allows for freedom in interpretation, stemming from the conviction that there is no creed but Christ and no saving doctrines save those of the New Testament. Faith is a matter of personal conviction, but there are areas of general agreement and acceptance. The Lord's Supper is served at every Sunday service, and baptism is by immersion for adult believers. The Disciples are firm in their belief in immortality. They do not accept the doctrine of original sin, but they do teach that all people are of a sinful nature until redeemed by the sacrifice of Christ. They are not concerned with speculation about the Trinity and the nature of a triune God. They have no catechism and no set orders of worship. Faith in Christ as Lord is the only requirement.

For more than a century Disciples of Christ were strictly congregational in polity, but in the twentieth century it was felt that such an arrangement needed restructuring in the interests of efficiency and economy. A new organization was adopted at Kansas City in 1968: the whole church works under a representative government referred to as "three manifestations"—local, regional, and general. The local church is still the basic unit, and each congregation manages its own affairs, but the congregations are grouped in thirty-five regions, organized to provide help, counsel, and pastoral care to members, ministers, and congregations. The General Asembly of the church meets every two years, and the Administrative Committee, with forty-four voting members, meets twice annually. The Office of Communication is located in Indianapolis, Indiana; the church's publishing arm, the Christian Board of Publication, is in St. Louis, Missouri.

The changes adopted in 1968 completed a long process of separation between moderates and conservatives in the Campbellite tradition. Those pastors who held to the original congregational polity and who had reservations about the liberalism of the Disciples formed a loose confederation of independent congregations known as the Christian Churches and Churches of Christ.* All three major branches of the old denomination (the Churches of Christ split in 1906) saw a severe decline in membership after the split.

There are now twenty-one colleges and seminaries in covenant relation with the Disciples, the largest of which is Texas Christian University, in Fort Worth, Texas. The church's National Benevolent Association operates eighty-three facilities and programs in twenty-two states, serving over thirty thousand a year in residential facilities and community-based programs. True to their founding principles, the Disciples emphasize the importance of community, reconciliation, and laboring to make the kingdom of God visible in the world. Alexander Campbell was an early opponent of slavery and modern Disciples continue to oppose discrimination in its many forms.

For more information: www.disciples.org

Headquarters: P.O. Box 1986, Indianapolis, IN 46206-1986

CHRISTIAN CHURCHES AND CHURCHES OF CHRIST

Founded: 1830s
Membership: est. 1,100,000 in 5,600 churches (2000)

Even more so than most Baptist* groups, these independent churches reject the designation as a denomination, and they do not keep denominational statistics. Until 1968, these congregations were listed as part of the Christian Church (Disciples of Christ),* but the reorganization of that denomination resulted in a formal separation. The Christian Churches and Churches of Christ are more of a fellowship of independent congregations with roots in the Restorationist movement, especially the Barton Stone tradition, than a denomination. However, they do distinguish themselves from the other Churches of Christ* that separated in 1906 over the issue of instrumental music.

Though the final straw for separation was the move toward centralization in the 1960s, there were theological issues involved as well. During the fundamentalist*/modernist controversy in the 1920s, many

252

Christian Churches and Churches of Christ tended toward fundamentalism and believed that the Disciples were too liberal in theology. The more evangelical pastors formed the North American Christian Convention* in 1927, and this gathering served as the organizing unit of the later Christian Churches and Churches of Christ.

Key doctrines include the divinity of Christ, the authority of the Bible, the indwelling of the Holy Spirit for the believer, future reward or punishment, and God as a loving, prayer-answering deity. They baptize by immersion and observe the Lord's Supper in open Communion every Sunday. Many Christian Churches and Churches of Christ still maintain the nineteenth-century practice of the extended revival, known as the "camp meeting."

The various congregations support over twenty related colleges, most of which are preacher-training schools insulated from liberal influences. Standard Publishing, in Cincinnati, Ohio, is identified with this group as well. The North American Christian Convention, an annual preaching and teaching assembly, draws as many as twenty thousand attendees to an annual gathering each July. Active in foreign missions, with a missionary presence in about a dozen foreign countries and a domestic missionary presence as well, these churches sponsor a National Missionary Convention that meets each fall, with an attendance of between three thousand and five thousand. The Christian Churches and Churches of Christ remains strongest in the Midwest, but grew on the West Coast towards the end of the twentieth century.

For more information: www.christian-church.org; www.naccthe-connectingplace.org

CHRISTIAN CONGREGATION, INC.

Founded: 1887
Membership: 120,563 in 1,465 churches (2003)

The philosophy and work of the Christian Congregation, formed in Indiana in 1887, revolve around the "new commandment" of John 13:34-35. Unlike many other descendents of the Restorationist movement, the Christian Congregation is pacifistic and opposes all war and sectarian strife. The origins of the group go back to Barton Stone, but in 1887 a number of ministers desired greater coordination of activities and formally organized a church. Inspired by the preaching of

253

John Chapman and John L. Puckett, the church insists that "the household of faith is not founded upon doctrinal agreement, creeds, church claims, names, or rites," but solely on the relationship of the individual to God. Because of its teachings concerning the sanctity of life, the church condemns abortion, capital punishment, and all warfare. They believe that the ethical demands of the Scripture transcend all national and racial barriers and should unite all persons in activism for peace.

The church remains strongest in the areas where Barton Stone preached and the original Christian Congregation groups were located: Kentucky, the Carolinas, Virginia, Pennsylvania, Ohio, Indiana, Tennessee, and Texas. The greater part of the group's work is carried on in rural and mountain areas. Polity is congregational. Headquarters: 812 W. Hemlock St., La Follette, TN 37666.

CHURCHES OF CHRIST

Founded: 1906, with roots to the 1820s
Membership: est. 1,200,000 in over 10,000 churches (2000)

The Churches of Christ represent the most conservative branch of the Restorationist movement. They are located throughout the nation but are concentrated in the South and the Southwest. They reject the idea of denominationalism and have no central headquarters; therefore, accurate statistics are impossible to attain, but they appear to have declined since 1970. This group has no governing bodies, but it does cooperate voluntarily in international radio programs sponsored by any congregation.

Like other Restorationist groups, the Churches of Christ are anti-creedal and look for a Christian union based on the Bible alone. In the nineteenth century, their leaders followed the more conservative Stone tradition rather than the leading of Campbell. Stressing a strict adherence to the New Testament pattern of worship and church organization, they refused to join any inter-congregational organization, such as a missionary society. Worship was simple, and they opposed the addition of instrumental music on the grounds that the New Testament did not authorize it and that the early church did not use it. Around the beginning of the twentieth century, the differences between the conservative and the more liberal wings of the Restoration movements became evident, and in the 1906 census of religious bodies, Churches of Christ were listed separately for the first time.

Key doctrines of Churches of Christ include belief in the Father, the Son, and the Holy Ghost as members of one Godhead; in the incarnation, virgin birth, and bodily resurrection of Christ; and in the universality of sin after the age of accountability, its only remedy the vicarious atonement of the Lord Jesus Christ. Also strong emphasis is laid on the church as the body and bride of Christ. A figurative, rather than literal, view is prevalent with reference to the book of Revelation. Church membership is contingent upon an individual's faith in Jesus Christ as the only begotten Son of God, repentance, confession of faith, and baptism by immersion for the remission of sins. Church attendance is stressed. Churches of Christ maintain that the final judgment of all religious groups is reserved for the Lord. This view, however, still allows for a vigorous evangelism that finds unacceptable the "doctrines, practices, names, titles, and creeds that have been grafted onto the original practice of Christianity."

The most conservative congregations reject instrumental music and use only a capella singing in worship, but that practice appears to be declining. There are some pastors who espouse premillennial theology, but only about twelve thousand persons are members of those congregations. Increasingly Churches of Christ congregations are adopting the style of other American evangelical denominations.

Clergy are ordained rather than licensed, and they hold tenure in their pulpits under mutual agreement with the elders of the churches in which they preach. Ministerial authority is essentially moral; the actual governance of the church is vested in its elders. A vigorous missionary program is carried on in ninety-two nations outside the U.S. Churches of Christ support twenty-four Bible colleges, liberal arts colleges, and universities, and twenty-seven high schools and/or elementary schools in the U.S. They also sponsor numerous facilities for care of the aged. The church publishes over one hundred periodicals, newspapers, and magazines.

For more information: www.church-of-christ.org

INTERNATIONAL CHURCHES OF CHRIST

Founded: 1979
Membership: est. 140,000 in 230 churches (worldwide)

The International Churches of Christ is the most controversial body to emerge from the Restorationist movement, and many of its former members describe it in negative terms. It was founded by Kip McKean (1955–) while serving as pastor of the Lexington Church of Christ in Massachusetts. McKean was an evangelist in the Crossroads movement which Charles Lucas began in Gainesville, Florida, in the 1960s, and the ICC utilizes many of the principles of Crossroads evangelism. This includes intensive recruitment of members, especially among college students and other young adults, without a church community. They call their evangelical method "discipling," which means that members of the church commit themselves as disciples and to bringing new disciples into the fold. Discipling is based on a strict obedience to the "discipler." All personal decisions, including dating and marriage, are subject to the approval of the discipler. Members are expected to confess all of their sins, which may be recorded for future reference.

Members are carefully instructed in Scripture according to the interpretation provided by McKean, who serves as the top of a pyramid structure of authority and obedience. The ICC, unlike the other Restorationist churches is not congregational in polity. All congregations are linked in a pyramid structure with McKean's Los Angeles congregation at the top. The ICC teaches that believer's baptism by immersion is necessary for salvation. Those not baptized into the International Churches of Christ are considered damned, and members are urged to sever ties with those not baptized. All members are expected to devote their personal time to evangelism and discipling of new members.

For more information: www.icoc.org

Headquarters: 530 Wilshire Blvd., Ste. 1750, Los Angeles, CA 9001

ADVENTIST AND SABBATARIAN (HEBRAIC) CHURCHES

Throughout the history of Christianity there have been communities and individuals who have awaited the return of Jesus Christ with eager anticipation. From the evidence of the New Testament, it appears that the expectation of the imminent return of the resurrected Christ was widespread among the first generation of Christians. As the apostolic age passed without the Second Coming, hope in the immediate return of Christ waned and the church adjusted to the delay of the return of Christ. In place of the earlier fervent hope in

256

the end of history and the consummation of the messianic mission, the church placed its faith in the ongoing presence of the risen Christ through Scripture, sacrament, and faith.

However, when the New Testament canon was sealed in the fourth century, it included many writings about the end time, the most famous of which is the book of Revelation, also known as the Apocalypse. The symbolic language of the Apocalypse, combined with the speculations of Paul in the letters to the Thessalonians, apocalyptic statements by Jesus in the Gospels, and the Old Testament book of Daniel gave ample scope for the imagination of the faithful for centuries.

The hope that Christ would soon return to rule the world in justice and peace was particularly strong in the United States following the American Revolution. Even the phrase "the New World" conjured up images of the millennial kingdom long awaited. Ordinary farmers and merchants had defeated the world's greatest military power, had thrown off the rule of the king, and were creating a new nation. It seemed to many, even men like John Adams, that the millennial age was dawning and that Christ would soon appear to take up his rightful throne. The Second Great Awakening, a series of revivals that swept across the western frontier in the early decades of the nineteenth century, added fuel to this fire as reports about the phenomenal activity of the Holy Spirit in converting lost souls circulated around the nation.

The Adventist family of churches in the United States was born in this era of new possibilities and great hopes. Today regarded as conservative Protestants, the Adventists were originally seen as dangerous radicals because of their intense focus on the theme of the return, or Second Advent (coming to our world), of Jesus Christ. By 1844, Adventist groups could be recognized as a distinct religious body separated from the traditional Protestant churches.

Modern Adventism began as an interchurch movement whose most vocal proponent was William Miller (1782–1849) of New York, a veteran of the War of 1812. Miller had experienced conversion from skeptical Deism to evangelical Christianity in 1816 during the Second Great Awakening. He became an ardent student of Scripture. Using a Bible that contained the famous chronology of Archbishop Ussher, Miller concentrated his attention on the prophecies of the end time in Daniel and Revelation.

Accepting the usual interpretation that the symbolic day of Bible prophecy represents one year, Miller concluded that the 2,300 days of Daniel 8:14 started concurrently with the seventy weeks of years of Daniel 9—that is, from 457 B.C.E., the year of the command to rebuild and restore Jerusalem. He believed that the longer of the two periods would end in or about the year 1843, as calculated by Jewish reckoning. Miller thought that the sanctuary mentioned in Daniel 8:14 was the earth (or the church), which would be cleansed by fire at the Second Advent and that this cleansing would occur sometime between March 21, 1843, and March 21, 1844.

Miller was not the only person fascinated with such apocalyptic reckoning, and his writings struck a chord in the popular culture of the 1830s. Under the direct influence of Miller, a New England pastor published an entire hymnal, *The Millennial Harp,* devoted to the theme of the imminent return of Christ and the restoration of paradise on earth. Miller himself made speaking tours in which he used elaborate charts and chronologies to support his reading of end-time prophecies. All of his research supported his central claim that the Advent would occur in the spring of 1844. Between fifty thousand and one hundred thousand people in the United States believed in Miller's calculations and looked forward to the great day when the world would be cleansed and the righteous would meet Christ.

When March and April passed, and this expectation failed to materialize, some devotees left the movement and returned to their former churches. However, Miller's associates, on the basis of the study of Old Testament typology, arrived at a second date, October 22, 1844. This was to be the great Day of Atonement, prefigured in the Mosaic law. When October 22 also passed with no second coming, vast numbers faced what has been termed "the Great Disappointment." Many gave up on Adventism; some gave up on the Christian faith itself; others simply gave up the desire to fix a date for the Advent. Out of the ashes of the disappointment, new Adventist bodies arose.

Those persons who continued to hold Adventist beliefs formed several smaller bodies, divided over the relevance of Miller's original interpretations. The majority group abandoned its earlier belief and concluded that the 2,300 years in the prophecy of Daniel 8 would end sometime in the future. They formed a loosely knit organization in Albany, New York, in 1845, and they held generally to Miller's teaching. This included the personal and premillennial character of the Second Advent, which means that Christ will return in person, not in spirit, before the millennial kingdom comes into being.

They also taught that the resurrection of the dead happens in two stages. The faithful are to be raised at Christ's coming, but the rest of humanity will rise a thousand years later. Furthermore, the earth will be redeemed and restored as an eternal abode of the faithful. Known at first as the American Millennial Association, a portion later came to be called the Evangelical Adventist Church. That church has now dwindled to the point of obscurity. The churches discussed in this section grew from the minority bodies that formed after the Disappointment.

Despite the differences between the various groups, Adventism as a whole is based on the conviction that the Second Advent of Christ is the sole hope of the world. The present age is evil and irredeemable, except through the direct action of God. Adventism holds that humanity's nature is fallen because of sin and that those who rebel against the government of God will be ultimately destroyed, while believers, by God's grace, will be saved. After that cataclysmic event, Jesus Christ will reign in triumph through the thousand-year period, or millennium, of Revelation 20:1-6.

Thus Adventists are pessimistic about the present but are filled with confidence and hope for God's future. In the meantime, they teach that God's people must be righteous, devout, and disciplined. Those who would be saved should practice a wholesome personal and family life, as well as a life of obedience to God. They should also work diligently toward the evangelization of the whole world in preparation for the return of Christ.

In other areas there have been differing viewpoints among Adventists. Are the dead conscious or unconscious as they await the resurrection? Who are to arise: both the righteous and the wicked or only the righteous? Is there to be eternal punishment or ultimate annihilation for the wicked? What is the nature of immortality? Does the cleansing of the sanctuary in Daniel 8 refer to a sanctuary in heaven or to one on earth? Answers to these questions have served to divide various Adventist groups.

Though Adventism looks to the future, it has encouraged people to examine the Old Testament. In general, the different Adventist groups have viewed the Old Testament as prefiguring the coming millennial kingdom. Therefore it gives a reliable guide to God's will for the church. As a result, many of those influenced by Adventist teaching in the nineteenth century adopted many features of the Mosaic law; some observe the Jewish Sabbath; others use the name "Jehovah" for God.

Suggestions for further reading:

Beckford, James A. *The Trumpet of Prophecy: A Sociological Study of Jehovah's Witnesses*. Oxford: Basil Blackwell, 1975.

Bull, Malcolm and Keith Lockhart. *Seeking a Sanctuary: Seventh Day Adventism and the American Dream*. San Francisco: Harper & Row, 1989.

Davidson, James West. *The Logic of Millennial Thought: Eighteenth Century New England*. New Haven: Yale University Press, 1977.

Dick, Everett N. *William Miller and the Advent Crisis, 1831-1844*. Berrien Springs, Mich.: Andrews University Press, 1994.

Doan, Ruth A. *The Miller Heresy, Millennialism, and American Culture*. Philadelphia: Temple University Press, 1987.

Gausad, Edwin, ed. *The Rise of Adventism: Religion and Society in Mid-Nineteenth Century America*. New York: Harper & Row, 1974.

Neufeld, Don. F., ed. *Seventh-Day Adventist Encyclopedia*. Rev. ed. Washington, DC: Review and Herald Publishing, 1961.

Penton, James. *Apocalypse Delayed: The Story of Jehovah's Witnesses*. Toronto: University of Toronto Press, 1985.

ADVENT CHRISTIAN CHURCH
GENERAL CONFERENCE

Founded: 1860
Membership: 25,277 in 302 churches (2002)

The Advent Christian Church grew out of the main body of Adventists* who reorganized in 1845 following the Great Disappointment. While William Miller was not directly involved in the founding of this church, his preaching and teachings concerning the Second Coming of Christ formed the basis for Advent Christian theological, biblical, and organizational thought. They reject the prophecies of Ellen Harmon White (see SEVENTH-DAY ADVEN-TIST) and accept the Bible as the only source of authoritative teaching. The denomination maintains no formal creedal statement but does have a declaration of principles. Two sacraments are observed: baptism (of adults by immersion) and the Lord's Supper. Worship is held on the first day of the week rather than on the Sabbath.

Like several Adventist groups, it teaches the doctrine of conditional immortality, which states that only the redeemed receive ever-lasting life. The dead await the resurrection in an unconscious state; when Christ returns, all will rise and face the final judgment. The righteous will be given immortality, but the wicked will suffer eternal extinction as opposed to eternal torment. After the final judgment and destruction of the wicked, Christ will restore the earth and make it the eternal home for the just.

The first Advent Christian General Conference in 1860 was followed closely by the founding of publications, missions societies, and Aurora University. In 1964 Advent Christian Church merged with Life and Advent Union. Congregational in polity, the church is grouped in five regional districts in the U.S. and Canada. The General Conference meets every three years and maintains denominational offices in Charlotte, North Carolina, which oversee work in missions, urban ministries, church growth, Christian education, publications, administration, women's ministries, and public relations. The denomination also maintains missions in Japan, Mexico, India, Nigeria, Ghana, South Africa, Honduras, the Philippines, and Malaysia.

For more information: www.adventchristian.org

Headquarters: P.O. Box 23152, Charlotte, NC 28227

BRANCH DAVIDIANS

Founded: 20th century
Membership: statistics not available

Largely unknown before 1993, the Branch Davidians became world famous through their fifty-one-day standoff against federal authorities. Relatively unimportant in the current scope of American Christianity, the Davidians remain of historical and social interest. The events of April 19, 1993, which ended in the fiery deaths of over eighty members, including children, is one of the most tragic and spectacular episodes in American religious history. The members who lived at Mt. Carmel Center, a compound near Waco, Texas, followed their self-proclaimed messiah, David Koresh (1959–1993). Koresh commanded resistance against government officials whom he saw as the armies of the Antichrist inaugurating the final apocalyptic battle. It is generally accepted that it was Koresh himself who ignited the fire that took the lives of almost all Davidians still living there.

This group of radical sectarians is a subset of one offshoot of the Adventist movement. They trace a lineage to 1930, when Victor T. Houteff, a Seventh-day Adventist church member in Los Angeles, expounded his new and, he claimed, divinely inspired message in a book, *The Shepherd's Rod*. Houteff found that his prophecies were not acceptable to the Seventh-day Adventist leadership, and in 1935 he took his followers to central Texas. The group believed that the redeemed 144,000 mentioned in the biblical book of Revelation would gather temporarily while directing the establishment of the Davidic kingdom. Living in Texas under theocratic rule, they would await the Second Coming of Christ, who would assume the leadership of the Davidic kingdom on earth.

Houteff and his group broke completely with the Seventh-day Adventists in 1942, and Houteff named his group the Davidian Seventh-day Adventists. In the decades following, various power struggles and disappointments over failed prophecies led to further divisions among the Davidians. Houteff died in 1955; and eventually the group in Waco became known as the Branch Davidians, apparently from one leader's statement that members should "Get off the dead [Shepherd's] Rod and move onto a living Branch."

David Koresh assumed the mantle of leadership over the Waco group in 1986, and the community became ever more isolated and defensive. His sermons and radio broadcasts were filled with imagery of the Apocalypse taken from the book of Revelation. He associated the events of the twentieth century with the prophecies of Revelation and urged his followers to prepare for the coming cataclysm, which would destroy and purify the earth as part of the final judgment. Influenced by the "survivalist" literature that proliferated during the Cold War era and that fueled militia movements, Koresh and his followers began stockpiling food and arms as they prepared to fight for the "Lamb of God" (Koresh).

Reports of the acquisition of a large cache of weapons and of the sexual abuse of children sparked the interest of the U.S. Attorney General. Four agents of the Bureau of Alcohol, Tobacco, and Firearms were killed and over twenty were wounded when they attempted an ill-advised raid on the Branch Davidian compound. After a lengthy siege, during which Koresh proclaimed his messianic rule, the compound was consumed by fire. The details of the disaster continue to be investigated and debated. The anniversary of the conflagration on April 19 has become an important date to a wide variety of anti-government extremist groups unrelated to the Davidians. It figured in the terrorist attack on a government building in Oklahoma City that killed over two hundred persons, including dozens of children in a day-care center.

Two other Davidian Adventist groups remain, one near Exeter, Missouri, the other near Salem, South Carolina. They, too, stand in the heritage of Houteff and his vision of the restoration of the King David-like theocracy in anticipation of Christ's return. No reliable membership information on these groups, or on the remnant that still believes in the messianic status of Koresh, is available. Branch Davidian theology and biblical interpretation is promoted by New Light Publications in Eastanollee, Georgia.

For more information: www.sevenseals.com.

CHRISTADELPHIANS

Founded: 1844
Membership: est. 15,000 in 170 ecclesias (2000)

Though Adventist and unitarian in theology, the Christadelphians actually have their roots in the Disciples of Christ.* When John Thomas (1805–71) came to the United States from England in 1832, he soon joined the Disciples, but decided that they neglected many important biblical doctrines. In 1844, he founded a number of societies that preached the need for a return to primitive Christianity. Loosely organized, those various societies bore no name until the outbreak of the Civil War, when their members' doctrine of nonresistance forced them to adopt a name in order to avoid the draft. They chose the term *Christadelphians*, or Brothers of Christ.

Christadelphians reject belief in the devil and maintain that the Scriptures teach that Christ was not pre-existent, but was born of Mary by the Holy Spirit, that is, by the power of God. Humankind is mortal by nature, and Christ is the only means of salvation. Eternal life comes only to the righteous. In the U.S., some Christadelphians, called Unamended, believe Christ will raise only those who died in the faith; all other persons will simply remain dead, without consciousness. Other Christadelphians, known as Amended, believe that Christ will raise all responsible persons, rewarding the righteous and annihilating the wicked. Both groups believe the faithful will be gathered together, and the world will be ruled from Jerusalem for a thousand years. They hold the Bible to be the inspired Word of God, inerrant in its original text.

263

The church is congregational in policy; local organizations are known as ecclesias. Membership is by profession of faith, and baptism is by immersion. There are no paid or ordained ministers in the usual sense. Women take no part in public speech or prayer, though all vote equally in the affairs of the ecclesia. Christadelphians do not vote in civil elections or participate in war, and they refuse to accept public office. There are no associations or conventions, but there are fraternal gatherings for spiritual inspiration. Many meetings are held in rented halls, schools, or private homes, though a number of ecclesias have their own buildings. Foreign missions and ecclesias are found in sixty countries.

For more information: www.christadelphia.org

Headquarters: 1000 Mohawk Dr., Elgin, IL 60120-3148

CHURCH OF GOD GENERAL CONFERENCE

Founded: 1921, with roots to the 1840s
Membership: 7,634 in 162 churches (2004)

This church is the outgrowth of several independent local groups of similar faith, some in existence as early as 1800; others date their beginnings from the arrival of British immigrants to this country around 1847. These diverse groups shared in general Adventist theology. A national organization was instituted at Philadelphia in 1888 and 1889; however, because of strong convictions relating to congregational rights and authority, the national body ceased to function until 1921, when the present general conference was formed at Waterloo, Iowa. The corporate name today is Church of God General Conference, Morrow, Georgia.

Members of the Church of God General Conference accept the Bible as the supreme and literal standard of faith. They teach that when Christ returns, he will establish a literal kingdom of God on earth. The Church of God is Arian, teaching the absolute oneness of God and that Christ as the Son of God did not exist prior to the birth of Jesus. The Holy Ghost is the power and influence of God on earth until the return of Christ. The church also promotes the belief in the restoration of Israel as a kingdom at the time of restitution. As with many other Adventist groups, the Church of God General Conference denies the immortality of the soul. The righteous will then receive their reward on earth, but the wicked will be completely destroyed in a second death.

Due to the congregational nature of the church's government, the general conference exists primarily as a means of mutual cooperation and development of yearly projects and enterprises. The general conference supports Atlanta Bible College for the training of pastors, a Publishing Department; and an Outreach and Church Development Department, which promotes youth work, mission, and evangelism in preparation for the return of Christ on earth. Mission stations are located in India, Mexico, the Philippines, Malawi, Mozambique, Great Britain, and Peru.

For more information: www.abc-coggc.org

Headquarters: P.O. Box 100,000, Morrow, GA 30260-7000

CHURCH OF GOD (SEVENTH DAY)

Founded: 1863
Membership: est. 11,000 in 185 churches (1999)

The Church of God (Seventh Day) grew out of the Adventist movement that developed in the first half of the nineteenth century. Like the larger Seventh-day Adventist Church, the founders of the Church of God believed that Christians should observe the Sabbath; however, under the leadership of Gilbert Cranmer in Michigan, this body rejected Ellen Harmon White's visions (see SEVENTH-DAY ADVENTIST) and separated in 1858 from other Sabbath-keeping Adventists. A similar group of anti-White Sabbatarians who had organized themselves in Iowa in 1860 joined the Michigan branch in 1863. Several denominational designations were used in its early history, including Church of Christ and Church of Jesus Christ. The present name was chosen in 1884, and the words "Seventh Day" were added in 1923.

In 1933, owing in part to disparate views on polity and administration, the church divided into two groups. An attempted merger in 1949 led to some realignment of membership and the relocation of the headquarters to Denver, Colorado. Those who did not join the merger maintained their headquarters at Salem, West Virginia, and use "7th Day" rather than "Seventh Day" in its name. The Salem body claims a membership of one thousand in seven churches. Both groups follow basic Adventist teaching on the reign of Christ and the extermination of the wicked. In addition to baptism and the Lord's Supper, this body practices footwashing. The Salem body also

265

claims a "Biblical organization," which means that the numbers 7, 12, and 70 have particular relevance in church organization. They also teach that the physical Church of God (7th Day) is the "true church." The national organization headquartered in Denver supports Spring Vale Academy, a residential high school in Michigan, and the Summit School of Theology in Denver.

For more information: www.cog7.org

CHURCH OF GOD AND SAINTS OF CHRIST

Founded: 1896
Membership: est. 40,000 in approx. 200 congregations (1999)

The Church of God and Saints of Christ is a Christian body that tries to live according to a literal understanding of Old Testament law. As such, they are sometimes called "Christian Israelites" or "Black Jews"; however, they have no direct relationship to historical Judaism.* Though not properly Adventist, they do share similarities with Adventists groups that emphasize the Mosaic law and continuing revelance of prophecy.

The church was begun by William Saunders Crowdy (1847–1908), who was born to slave parents in Maryland. After serving in the Union Army, Crowdy bought a farm near Guthrie, Oklahoma. Active in the Baptist church, in 1893 Crowdy began having disturbing visions and hearing voices. He dreamed of tables covered in filth, each of which had the name of a denomination. Then he saw a clean table that came down from heaven; on it was the name "Church of God and Saints of Christ." Crowdy began preaching on the streets in towns and villages in the Midwest and in November of 1896 he formally organized his church in Lawrence, Kansas. Arrested numerous times because of his ministry, he made converts in prison as well.

In a vision, he received "The Seven Keys," which form the core set of doctrines: repentance of sin; baptism by burial into water upon confession of faith; unleavened bread and water for Christ's body and blood; foot washing by elders; obedience to the commandments; the holy kiss; and the Lord's Prayer. In Philadelphia he founded a church and also several businesses; the Church of God and Saints of Christ continues to stress the importance of individual enterprise and business acumen as marks of religious life.

266

Crowdy taught that his followers should celebrate a number of Jewish holy and feast days. Of particular importance are the observance of the Sabbath, Passover, the Day of Atonement, and the Jewish new year. Members believe their church is built on the patriarchs and prophets of the Jewish tradition, and "Jesus the Anointed" is their chief cornerstone. They differentiate between prophetic Judaism, "which seeks to follow the living insight into the spiritual idea to its fullest implication," from "legalistic" Judaism. They accept the Decalogue as the standard of conduct for all humankind. Men and women are instructed to wear particular clothing on the Sabbath according to the season of the year, and men are expected to wear the yarmulke and a tallith.

An executive bishop stands at the head of the church and of the bishops' council; the church maintains headquarters in Cleveland, Ohio. *The Newsletter* (Church of God and Saints of Christ), published every two weeks, serves to inform members through sermons, lectures, and announcements. An a cappella choir formed of members of the church has released recordings of gospel music to critical acclaim.

For more information: www.churchofgod1896.org

Headquarters: 3825 Central Avenue, Cleveland, OH 44115

JEHOVAH'S WITNESSES

Founded: ca. 1870
Membership: 1,029,652 in 11,930 congregations (2003)

The Jehovah's Witnesses are among the most zealous religious bodies in terms of promotion of their beliefs. Meeting in Kingdom Halls (not in churches), members witness and publish their faith in testimony and in a remarkably comprehensive missionary effort. They do not believe in separation into clergy and laity, since "Christ Jesus did not make such a separation," and they never use titles like "Reverend." All members are expected to give generously of their time in proclaiming their faith and teaching in private homes. Called "publishers of the Kingdom," they preach only from the Bible. Pioneers, or full-time preachers, are required to give at least seventy hours per month; special pioneers and missionaries donate a minimum of 140 hours per month and are sent to isolated areas and foreign lands where new congregations can be formed. All pioneers provide for their own support, but the society gives a small allowance to some in view of their special needs. This missionary activity has made Jehovah's Witnesses one of the most widely known (although not widely understood) churches in the U.S.A.

It was Charles Taze Russell (1852–1916) who established the Witnesses, and until 1931 they were known as Russellites, Millennial Dawn People, or International Bible Students. Russell, the first president, is acknowledged not as founder (there is no human founder), but as general organizer. Witnesses claim to have been on earth as an organization for more than five thousand years (based on Isa. 43:10-12; Hebrews 11; John 18:37).

Russell was deeply influenced by Adventist thought, which captivated American attention around the middle of the nineteenth century. He developed his own Adventist ideas based on personal study of the Bible, and his lectures attracted huge crowds. To date, some thirteen million copies of his books have been circulated, and they have profoundly influenced the Witnesses. The first formal Russellite group was organized in Pittsburgh, Pennsylvania, in 1870, and soon after a board of directors was elected by vote of all members who subscribed ten dollars or more to support the work (a practice discontinued in 1944). In 1884 Zion's Watch Tower Tract Society was incorporated. In 1939 the name of this corporation was changed to Watch Tower Bible and Tract Society of Pennsylvania, and it remains one of the world's largest publishers.

When Russell died in 1916, Joseph F. Rutherford (1869–1942), known widely as Judge Rutherford, became president. He had been a lawyer and occasionally sat as a circuit court judge in Missouri. His numerous books, pamphlets, and tracts supplanted those of Russell, but his neglect of some aspects of Russell's teaching brought dissension.

The vast literature of the Witnesses (all circulated without bylines or signatures) quotes extensively from the Bible and relates the eschatological teachings of the church. Witness theology is based on the idea of theocracy, or rule of God. It teaches that there is only one God, Jehovah; Jesus is not God. In the beginning, the world was under the theocratic rule of the Almighty. At that time all was "happiness, peace, and blessedness." But Satan rebelled and became the ruler of the world, and from that moment, humankind has followed his evil leading. Then, as the prophets had predicted, Jesus, the first creation of Jehovah, came to earth as a human being, "the beginning of the creation of God" (Rev. 3:14, KJV) to end Satan's rule.

Witnesses maintain that Jesus's heavenly rule, after he paid the ransom sacrifice of his death on earth, began in 1914. Russell had seen World War I as the final apocalyptic struggle that would usher in the return of Christ. When that did not happen, Rutherford reorganized the movement and announced in 1918 that Christ then "came to the temple of Jehovah." With Jesus now enthroned in the temple of Jehovah, the rule of Satan was nearly over, so Rutherford began to send out his followers to preach the good news in the final days.

God, according to Witness belief, will take vengeance on wicked human beings in our time. God is now showing great love by "gathering out" multitudes of people of goodwill, to whom God will give life in the new world that is to come after the battle of Armageddon. This is to be a universal battle; Christ will lead the army of the righteous, composed of the "host of heaven, the holy angels," and they will completely annihilate the army of Satan. The righteous of the earth will watch the battle and the suffering of God's enemies, but they will not participate.

After the battle, Witnesses teach, the believers in God and God's servants will remain on the earth. Those who have proven their integrity in the old world will multiply and populate the new earth with righteous people. A resurrection of the righteous will also take place as an additional means of filling the cleansed earth with better inhabitants. After the Great Tribulation, "righteous princes" will rule the earth under Christ, "King of the Great Theocracy." One special group—the 144,000 Christians mentioned in Revelation 7 and 14—will become the "bride of Christ" and rule with him in heaven.

Administration of the group changed during Rutherford's presidency. The governing body today is in the hands of older and more "spiritually qualified" men who base their judgments on the authority of Scripture. This is not considered a governing hierarchy, but an imitation of early apostolic Christian organization. Under direction of the leaders at headquarters, local congregations of Witnesses (always called congregations, never churches) are arranged in circuits, with a traveling minister who spends a week with each congregation. Approximately twenty congregations are included in each circuit, and circuits are grouped into districts, with more than forty in the U.S.; circuit organizations are now found in 235 countries and islands around the world.

The headquarters is located at Bethel Home in Brooklyn, New York. Staff engage primarily in editorial and printing work and receive an allowance of $45.00 a month, in addition to room and board. They write, print, and distribute literature in almost astronomical proportions. The official journal, *The Watchtower,* has a circulation of 25,600,000. More than one billion Bibles, books, and leaflets have been distributed since 1920; they are made available in more than 290 languages.

Although predictions of Armageddon have repeatedly been disappointed, Witnesses maintain their belief in its imminence. They have been especially active in opposing what they consider the three allies of Satan: false teachings of the churches, tyranny of human governments, and oppression by big business. This "triple alliance" of ecclesiastical, political, and commercial powers has misled humankind, the Witnesses claim, and must be destroyed at Armageddon before the new world can be born. They refuse to salute the flag, bear arms in war, or participate in the political affairs of government, not because of pacifist convictions, but because they desire to remain apart from what they consider expressions of Satan's power over humankind.

This attitude has brought them into conflict with law enforcement agencies; they have also endured whippings, assaults by mobs, stonings, being tarred and feathered, the burning of their homes, imprisonment, and detention in concentration camps. All of this they have accepted in a submissive spirit. Their position is that they will obey the laws of the earth when those laws are not in conflict with the laws of God.

For more information: www.jw.org

Headquarters: Watch Tower Society, Brooklyn, NY 11201

SEVENTH-DAY ADVENTISTS

Founded: 1845; 1863
Membership: 974,271 in 4,958 churches (2002)

Today the largest Adventist church is the Seventh-day Adventist Church. It arose in the aftermath of the Great Disappointment, the failure of the Millerites' prediction that Christ would return on October 22, 1844. The Seventh-day group came from one of the smaller Adventist groups that advocated a radical reinterpretation of William Miller's predictions. They concluded that a significant event had, indeed, occurred in October 1844, but not quite in the way Miller had foreseen. It was not an earthly event that took place on that prophesied day, but an event in heaven itself. Christ's ministry in heaven moved from the Holy to the Most Holy Place.

As these Adventists explored the meaning of this transferal to the Most Holy Place, which they understood as Christ's ministry of judgment according to Revelation 14:7 "the hour of His judgment has come" (the first of the Three Angels' Messages), the group focused on the commandments of God and the faith of Jesus, seeking to show the interrelationship of the Old Testament law and the New Testament gospel. The faithful, they taught, must observe the Ten Commandments literally and faithfully, including the fourth commandment to honor the seventh day as the biblical Sabbath.

As early as 1844, a small group of Adventists near Washington, New Hampshire, had begun to observe the Sabbath on the seventh day. A pamphlet written by Joseph Bates in 1846 gave the question wide publicity and created great interest. Shortly thereafter, Bates, together with James White, Ellen Harmon (later Mrs. James White), Hiram Edson, Frederick Wheeler, and S. W. Rhodes, with the aid of regular publications, set out to champion the seventh-day Sabbath, along with the imminence of the Second Advent. The observation of the Sabbath was to be a way to await the Advent of the Lord; hence the name, Seventh-day Adventist. The growth of the group around these leaders was slow at first, owing to the general derision in which Adventists were held after the Great Disappointment. By 1855, however, that group was prosperous and numerically strong enough to set up headquarters at Battle Creek, Michigan, and publish a weekly magazine called *Review and Herald*. In 1860 the name Seventh-day Adventist was officially adopted, and in 1903 the headquarters was moved to Washington, D.C. Its present location is in Silver Spring, Maryland.

Ellen Harmon White (1827-1915) was the key figure in this rejuvenation of Adventism. When she was only in her teens, she began having visions and receiving messages from heaven. Her visions contributed to the development of the new Seventh-day Adventist Church, doctrinally and structurally. White's followers believed that she was granted insight into "the great controversy between Christ and Satan," making this cosmic conflict central to Adventist theology. Ellen White's visions were also instrumental in introducing principles of healthful living to the fledgling church that were later promulgated by figures such as the vegetarian John Harvey Kellogg (1852-1943). Because of their holistic understanding of human nature, Seventh-day Adventists consider the human body to be the temple of the Holy Spirit; in consequence, they rigidly abstain from the use of alcoholic beverages, tobacco, and drugs. They advocate

271

sound principles of healthful living through diet, exercise, and philanthropic outlook. Medically, they encourage evidence-based treatments and therapies and operate many allopathic health institutions.

Doctrinally, Seventh-day Adventists today are considered evangelical conservatives, holding to the authoritative nature of the revelation of God through the inspired writings of the entire Bible. The church holds that the great principles of God's law are embodied in the Ten Commandments and exemplified in the life of Jesus Christ. They proclaim a belief in the transcendent, personal, communicating God as revealed in the Father, the Son, and the Holy Spirit, each equally and uniquely divine, personal, and eternal. The gift of prophecy, as exemplified by Ellen White, continues in the church.

Seventh-day Adventists also believe in creation by divine fiat and recognize the fall of the human race through the sin of Adam. Unlike most Christian churches, however, they teach that humans are by nature mortal, but may receive immortality through divine grace and the redemption effected through the atoning work of Jesus Christ. According to Adventist teaching, the dead await the resurrection in an unconscious state until the whole person (body, mind, and soul) is resurrected on the last day when Christ will return in person. The righteous will then receive immortality, while the wicked are destroyed by fire.

The visible return of Christ will occur at a time unknown, but it is close at hand. When Christ returns a new earth will be created out of the ruins of the old, and this will be the final abode of the redeemed. Among the distinctive practices, in addition to observing the Sabbath as a day of rest and worship, are baptism of adults by immersion and the practice of foot washing in preparation for Holy Communion.

Seventh-day Adventists are particularly noteworthy for their long tradition of promoting religious liberty and the complete separation of church and state, which at times has led to conflict over issues of conscience, such as being required to say the Pledge of Allegiance, serve in the military, or salute the American flag. Their evangelistic, publishing, educational, and health activities have been highly successful. They consider themselves a movement established in the fulfillment of Bible prophecy to prepare humankind for the Second Advent and to revive and restore neglected teachings of the Reformation and the apostolic church.

Seventh-day Adventists operate over fifty publishing houses around the world, four in the U.S. and Canada. The church's message is carried around the world in over 850 languages and dialects, with publications in nearly

350 languages. Included in this message of redemption and preparation for the return of Christ is a message of bodily health and personal responsibility that has had an impact far beyond the boundaries of the church. The Adventist Development and Relief Agency (ADRA) is famous for its work with victims of both natural and human-made disasters. In the U.S. and abroad, the church supports approximately 720 medical units, more than 90 universities and colleges, over 1,000 secondary schools, and more than 4,800 elementary schools. There are about 7,000 weekly radio and television broadcasts reaching nearly every country, and approximately 1,500,000 students are enrolled in Bible correspondence schools.

The entire support of the ministry of the church consists of the tithe. Beyond their tithes, Seventh-day Adventists give generously to missions, local church expenses, and other church enterprises. One of the few Protestant churches that is a worldwide community, the overall administrative body of the church is the executive committee of the General Conference, chosen by delegates from the various church groups in the quinquennial sessions. Working under the General Conference are lesser governmental units. The North American Division is one of thirteen divisions that administer church affairs on different continents. It is composed of nine union conferences that make up the divisional organizations, which in turn comprise fifty-eight local conferences. Each unit has a large degree of autonomy in a highly representative form of government. Local congregations elect lay elders, deacons, and other officers; the local conference office supervises all local pastoral and evangelistic work and pays all pastors and other workers in its territory from a central fund. Since the Seventh-day Adventists practice adult (age of accountability) baptism, no infants or children are reported in their world membership, which now exceeds thirteen million persons in over 53,500 congregations.

For more information: www.adventist.org

Headquarters: 12501 Old Columbia Pike, Silver Spring, MD 20904-6600

WORLDWIDE CHURCH OF GOD

Founded: 1933
Membership: est. 63,000 worldwide (2004)

The Worldwide Church of God has one of the most distinctive histories in American Christianity. The original WCG divided into sev-

273

eral bodies in the last decades of the twentieth century. The largest group, which retains the name Worldwide Church of God, has become a typical evangelical church that is very similar to many Baptist denominations, but it was originally characterized by its adoption of many Sabbatarian and Mosaic practices. The smaller groups retain their original Mosaic orientation.

Originally known as the Radio Church of God, the WCG began its work in 1933 under the leadership of Herbert W. Armstrong (1892–1986). The mission statement of the church was to proclaim the gospel of Jesus Christ around the world and to help members grow spiritually. The church grew rapidly from 1964 to 1974, but controversy erupted in the 1970s. Garner Ted Armstrong, the founder's son, was "disfellowshiped" on four occasions for adultery, and in 1977 took part of the membership with him when he founded the rival Church of God International. That body appears to have never numbered more than five thousand, and with the death of the founder in 2003, it is struggling for existence.

The original church weathered another bitter legal battle over control of the finances, and its situation became more unstable in the 1980s. After Herbert Armstrong's death in 1986, Joseph W. Tkach became Pastor General. Tkach and his son, Joseph W. Tkach, Jr., led the church through an experience nothing short of religious conversion in the late 1980s and 1990s. The church officially repudiated many of Armstrong's most distinctive teachings.

The elder Armstrong saw himself as the apostle-messenger of the Last Days and so assumed absolute authority in the organization. His church was to be the Philadelphian church described in Revelation. Congregations generally worshiped in rented facilities or private homes rather than building separate structures. At the time of his death, he left a church with some 120,000 members, a budget of $2,000,000, and a publication, *Plain Truth,* with a circulation of eight million copies a month. His organization was a worldwide ministry, with churches in one hundred countries and territories, carried out from a headquarters in Pasadena, California.

The Worldwide Church of God held to some traditional Christian teachings, but it maintained several distinctive theological ideas. Herbert Armstrong taught that there is one God, who is the Father. Jesus was accepted as divine, constituting with the Father a divine family. Armstrong did not, however, believe the Holy Spirit was a distinct person. Concerning human nature, the inspiration of the

Scriptures, Christ's bodily resurrection, and baptism, the church held traditional positions. Like many Adventist* groups, they took a strong stand against bearing arms and the taking of human life, and they rejected the concept of everlasting conscious torment in hell for the unsaved.

Accepting a number of Jewish (see JUDAISM) observances as scripturally mandated, the church observed the Lord's Supper, or Passover of Jesus Christ, annually as a memorial of the death of Jesus. The Sabbath (Friday sunset to Saturday sunset) was honored as a day of worship. Seven annual holy days were kept, and certain "unclean" meats were avoided. Holidays, such as Halloween, Easter, and Christmas, were condemned as pagan. The three ordinances of baptism, the Lord's Supper, and foot washing were practiced. Such was Armstrong's theological conviction that he did not acknowledge as Christian those who failed to keep the Sabbath.

However, under the leadership of the Tkaches, the Worldwide Church of God made a dramatic theological turn, essentially moving to an evangelical position. Key changes included an affirmation of the Trinity (1993) and renunciation of Old Testament covenant laws (1994). The church issued formal apologies for error to the wider Christian community, and in 1997 it was accepted as a member of the National Association of Evangelicals. The wholesale conversion of the entire movement, from "an unorthodox church on the fringes of Christianity, into an evangelical church that believes and teaches orthodox doctrines," is one of the singular events in American religious history. The church practices adult baptism by immersion and does not promote Pentecostal practices.

Many adherents were disillusioned by the changes following Armstrong's death, and thousands left the church. Hundreds of staff were laid off, finances and programs were depleted, radio and television ministries were cut back, and the church's educational institution, Ambassador University, was closed. A number of splinter groups formed to promote Armstrong's teaching. The most important are the Philadelphia Church of God, Global Church of God, United Church of God, and Restored Church of God.

Only the Philadelphia Church appears to have more than five thousand members. It was founded in 1989 in Edmond, Oklahoma, by Gerald Flurry and John Amos and now has about one hundred churches. It holds strictly to Armstrong's teaching, especially as out-

275

lined in his book *Mystery of the Ages.* The church is named after the church of Philadelphia in Revelation 3:7-13 and its members believe that only their church will survive when Christ returns. Unlike the Worldwide Church of God, the Philadelphia Church holds to Armstrong's rejection of medical treatment.

The Worldwide Church of God under Tkaches founded Plain Truth Ministries (PTM) in 1996 as a separate non-profit, interdenominational media ministry. It publishes *The Plain Truth* and various booklets, hosts a website, and airs daily and weekly radio programs. Worldwide, over 850 congregations remain affiliated, and the Ambassador Center at Azusa Pacific University helps provide church members with Christian education in a liberal arts setting. The church also sponsors the online Ambassador College of Christian Ministry.

For more information: www.wcg.org; www.pcog.org; www.ptm.org; www.ucg.org

Headquarters: Worldwide Church of God, 300 West Green St., Pasadena, CA 91120

PENTECOSTAL CHURCHES

Pentecostalism is a modern American Christian movement that emerged out of the Holiness* movement around the turn of the twentieth century. Two key figures in the genesis of Pentecostalism were Charles Fox Parham (1873–1929), the founder of Bethel Bible College in Topeka, Kansas, and William J. Seymour (1870–1922), an African-American Holiness evangelist from Louisiana. Through his study of Paul's letters, Parham became convinced that the gifts of the Holy Spirit that were evident in apostolic times are available to Christians in modern times as well. Of particular interest was speaking in tongues, the first incidence of which occurred at Bethel Bible College in 1901. Five years later, Seymour, who had studied at Bethel with Parham, led a revival on Azusa Street in Los Angeles that lasted for several months. Participants experienced a "baptism in the Holy Ghost." Some were healed of illnesses, while others spoke in tongues. Thousands from across the U.S. traveled to Azusa Street and carried the message back to their home states.

The movement eventually became known as "Pentecostal" because of its similarity to the first Pentecost, fifty days after Christ's resurrection, when the Spirit came upon the early Christians and enabled them to speak in unfamiliar languages. There are a great variety of Pentecostal churches, most of which are theologically and socially conservative. In general, Pentecostals are in the evangelical tradition and teach that the Holy Spirit continues to act as it did at the first Pentecost. Teaching that contemporary Christians can receive the same spiritual gifts that the apostles did, many Pentecostal churches use the word *apostolic* in their names.

Seeking and receiving the gift of tongues is regarded as a sign of the baptism of the Holy Spirit, and in many Pentecostal churches this is a requirement for full discipleship. Other spiritual gifts, such as healing, love, joy, prophecy, and answers to prayer, also make up Pentecostals' experience of God. Pentecostals are generally less bound to traditional forms of worship than are other churches, and many have adapted contemporary music for evangelistic purposes. Like the Baptists, many Pentecostal churches refer to rites such as baptism as "ordinances" rather than as "sacraments." The term "Neo-Pentecostalism" is often used to describe churches that embrace charismatic worship practices, such as speaking in tongues, but not the Holiness tradition of the older Pentecostal bodies. In the 1960s Pentecostal beliefs and practices made inroads in many liturgical churches, including the Roman Catholic and Episcopal churches, but the term "charismatic" is used in mainline churches rather than Pentecostal. Charismatics tend to be less sectarian in orientation than Pentecostals, and they generally restrict overt displays of the gifts to private gatherings rather than public worship.

In general, Pentecostal denominations are Protestant and evangelical, but many were influenced by the fundamentalist* movement. They commonly hold to beliefs in original sin, salvation through the atoning blood of Christ, the virgin birth and deity of Jesus, the divine inspiration and literal infallibility of the Scriptures, pre-millennialism (the return of Jesus Christ prior to his thousand-year reign on earth), and future rewards and punishments. Two sacraments are found in most groups: baptism, usually by immersion, and the Lord's Supper. Some of the smaller bodies also observe foot washing. Pentecostals are generally trinitarian; but they place greater emphasis on the direct action of the Holy Spirit, which is manifested in a "baptism in the Spirit" accompanied by spiritual gifts, than on creation.

Originally strongest among the rural peoples of the South and the Midwest, early Pentecostalism also found a home among the urban poor in the 1930s. Now the movement has spread to all fifty states and represents a cross-section of American society. For the most part, Pentecostal bodies do not have educational requirements for clergy. More important for them is evidence of the Spirit in a preacher's life and ministry. Many Pentecostal associations serve primarily as accrediting bodies for freelance ministers, and they tend to have far more clergy than congregations listed, since many clergy do not have churches. In the 1980s and 1990s many Pentecostals grew prosperous, and several members of Pentecostal churches, such as Attorney General John Ashcroft, rose to positions of prominence in national government.

Suggestions for further reading:

Anderson, Robert Mapes. *Vision of the Disinherited: The Making of American Penecostalism.* New York: Oxford University Press, 1979.

Blumhofer, Edith. *Aimee Semple McPherson: Everybody's Sister.* Grand Rapids, MI: Eerdmans, 1993.

———. *Restoring the Faith: The Assemblies of God, Pentecostalism, and American Culture.* Urbana, IL: InterVarsity, 1993.

Cox, Harvey. *Fire From Heaven: The Rise of Pentecostal Spirituality and the Shaping of Religion in the 21st Century.* Reading, MS: Addison-Wesley, 1994.

Dayton, Donald. *Theological Roots of Pentecostalism.* Grand Rapids, MI: Francis Asbury, 1987.

Faupel, David W. *The American Pentecostal Movement.* Wilmore, KY: B. L. Fisher Library, 1972.

Harrell, David E. *All Things Are Possible: The Healing and Charismatic Revivals in Modern America.* Bloomington: IN University Press, 1975.

Synan, Vinson. *The Holiness-Pentecostal Movement in the United States.* Grand Rapids, MI: Eerdmans, 1971.

APOSTOLIC FAITH MISSION CHURCH OF GOD

Founded: 1906
Membership: 10,426 in 23 churches (2002)

This mission was a fruit of the Azuza Street Revival in Los Angeles and the preaching of William Seymour. F. W. Williams experienced the outpouring of the Holy Spirit during that revival and founded the Apostolic Faith Mission in Mobile, Alabama to spread the revival. Bishop Williams incorporated the church in 1915 under the present name. The church spread to Georgia and Florida. Pastors are called bishops in this church. The headquarters is called Ward's Temple in Cantonment, Florida.

Headquarters: National Sunday School Supt., 3298 Toney Dr., Decatur, GA 30032.

APOSTOLIC WORLD CHRISTIAN FELLOWSHIP

Founded 1970
Membership: statistics unavailable, but est. 135 churches

W. G. Rowe founded the AWCF as a way to heal the divisions among the various Pentecostal churches in the U.S. and the world. It is not a denomination, but a fellowship of black and white Pentecostal churches and organizations that work cooperatively. In addition to typical evangelical and Pentecostal teachings, the AWCF places great emphasis on Jesus' high priestly prayer (John 17) in which he prays that the world will be one. For the AWCF, this unity comes through the Holy Spirit, whose gifts are still evident. In 1991 leadership passed to Samuel Smith and the headquarters moved to Evansville, Ind. Its most unusual feature is that two white bishops and two black bishops serve as the principle officers of the church.

For more information: www.awcf.org

Headquarters: 11 West Iowa St., Evansville, IN 47710

ASSEMBLIES OF GOD, GENERAL COUNCIL OF

Founded: 1914
Membership: 2,687,366 in 12,133 churches (2002)

The General Council of the Assemblies of God is actually a group of churches and assemblies that joined together at Hot Springs, Arkansas, in 1914. The founders were former pastors of evangelical persuasion who wished to unite in the interest of doctrinal unity, more effective preaching, and an enlarged missionary crusade.

Theologically, the Assemblies of God is Arminian (after Jacobus

279

Arminius, 1560-1609), stressing Christ's atoning death for all persons, the freedom of human will, and the need for conversion. There is also a strong belief in the infallibility and inspiration of the Bible, the fall and redemption of the human race, baptism in the Holy Spirit, a life of holiness and separation from the world, divine healing, the second advent of Jesus and his millennial reign, eternal punishment for the wicked, and eternal bliss for believers. Two ordinances, baptism, and the Lord's Supper are practiced. Assemblies of God members are especially insistent that baptism in the Holy Spirit be evidenced by speaking in tongues. They hold that all the gifts of the Spirit should be evident in a church modeled after that of the New Testament.

The government of the assemblies is an unusual mixture of Presbyterian and congregational systems. Local churches are independent in polity and in the conduct of local affairs. District officers have a pastoral ministry to all the churches and are responsible for the promotion of home missions. Work is divided into fifty-eight districts in the U.S. and Puerto Rico, including eleven foreign-language districts, each with a district presbytery that examines and recommends credentialing of ministers. The General Council consists of all ordained ministers and lay representatives from local churches. The biennial General Council (business meeting) elects general officers, sets doctrinal standards, and provides for church expansion and development. The General Superintendent and other general church officers serve at the national headquarters in Springfield, Missouri.

The denomination's publishing arm, the Gospel Publishing House, produces curriculum, other resources, and several periodicals, including the weekly *The Pentecostal Evangel,* which has a circulation of approximately 230,000. In the U.S. there are eighteen colleges and a seminary in Springfield. Missionary work is conducted under the guidance of a central missionary committee; there are over 1,880 foreign missionaries at work in 198 nations. The church sponsors 831 Bible schools abroad.

For more information: www.ag.org

Headquarters: 1445 Boonville Ave., Springfield, MO 65802

ASSEMBLIES OF THE LORD JESUS CHRIST

Founded: 1952
Membership: statistics unavailable; 413 churches (2001)

Three Pentecostal groups, known as the Assemblies of the Church of Jesus Christ, Jesus Only Apostolic Church of God, and the Church of the Lord Jesus Christ, formulated a merger in 1952, adopting the name "Assemblies of the Lord Jesus Christ." The Assemblies promotes many basic Pentecostal doctrines, including the infallibility and direct divine inspiration of Scripture, the fall of humankind, salvation by grace, a pre-millennial tribulation, water baptism and baptism by the Holy Spirit, holy communion, the service of foot washing, divine healing, and holiness in life.

The church teaches that the "one True God manifested Himself in the Old Testament in diverse ways, in the Son while he walked among men, as the Holy Ghost after the ascension." Baptism is in the name of Jesus only. Members are forbidden to attend dances or theatrical events, even in public schools; thus private Bible schools are preferred. Another distinctive teaching of the church is that Christians are to obey the government in all matters except for the bearing of arms. Members are thus conscientious objectors.

The Assemblies of the Lord Jesus Christ has churches in thirty-five states, with particular strength in the Midwest and the South. It maintains offices in Memphis, Tennessee. Administration includes a general superintendent and three assistant superintendents. The church maintains Parkersburg Bible College in West Virginia and the Memphis School of Ministries in Tennessee; it supports missions in eight countries outside the U.S.; and it carries out prison ministry, ministry to Native Americans, and church building programs throughout the U.S.

For more information: www.aljc.org

Headquarters: 875 N. White Station Rd., Memphis, TN 38122

BIBLE WAY CHURCH OF OUR LORD JESUS CHRIST, WORLD WIDE, INC.

Founded: 1957
Membership: est. 300,000 in 350 churches worldwide (1995)

The Bible Way Church is an organization of primarily African American Pentecostal churches formed in 1957 when Apostle Smallwood Edmond Williams led some seventy churches out of the Church of Our Lord Jesus Christ of the Apostolic Faith* to form the Bible Way Church, World Wide. The vision of the founder was to promote evangelistic goals. The church's basic beliefs include Christ's resurrection and pre-millennial Second Coming, the resurrection and translation of the saints, the priesthood of all believers, and the final judgment of humankind. Baptism is by immersion, and baptism of the Holy Spirit is necessary for second birth. Foot washing is also practiced.

Phenomenal growth has been reported by the church, but precise numbers are difficult to obtain. The Bible Way Church has twenty-seven dioceses, six of which lie outside the U.S. A board of bishops directs the church, and individual bishops preside over the various dioceses. A general conference is held annually in July, and the church sponsors various convocations. A publishing house at Washington, D.C., circulates periodicals, religious pamphlets, and recordings.

For more information: www.biblewaychurch.org

Headquarters: 261 Rochester Ave. Brooklyn, NY 11213

CHRISTIAN CHURCH OF NORTH AMERICA, GENERAL COUNCIL

Founded: 1948
Membership: 7,200 in 96 churches (1999)

Originally known as the Italian Christian Church, this body originated in a gathering of Italian Pentecostal ministers held in 1927 at Niagara Falls, New York. The leader was Luigi Francescon (1866–1964) who had left the Roman Catholic Church in 1892, joining the First Italian Presbyterian Church in Chicago. He embraced believer's baptism in 1903 and established the first Italian American Pentecostal congregation in 1907 in Chicago. When the church was incorporated in 1948 at Pittsburgh, it took the name "Missionary Society of the Christian Church of North America." The present name was adopted in 1963 when the body was reorganized as a denomination.

The Christian Church of North America, General Council holds to basic Pentecostal beliefs, emphasizing the infallibility of Scripture, the Trinity, and salvation through faith in Jesus Christ. Although affirming the experiences of salvation and spirit baptism, the body does not teach the doctrine of entire sanctification. Headquarters are in Transfer, Pennsylvania.

For more information: www.ccna.org

Headquarters: 1294 Rutledge Rd., Transfer, PA 16154-9005

282

CHURCH OF GOD (CLEVELAND, TENNESSEE)

Founded: 1886; 1907
Membership: 944,857 in 6,623 churches (2002)

The Church of God (Cleveland, Tennessee) claims the distinction of the being the oldest Pentecostal body. It traces its founding to 1886 in Monroe County, Tennessee, when the Christian Union* was organized by Richard Spurling (1810–91), a Baptist*, and his son, R. G. Spurling (1857–1935). The Spurlings had been led to the Bible to stem the tide of the church's "spiritual indifference, formality, and accommodation to modern culture." In 1892 a second church was formed in Cherokee County, North Carolina, under the leadership of William F. Bryant (1863–1949); four years later, this group experienced speaking in tongues for the first time. R. G. Spurling met with the North Carolina group and others, and two more congregations were added over the next few years. The small organization was renamed the Holiness Church in 1902.

In 1903, Ambrose J. Tomlinson (1865–1943) of the American Bible Society joined the Holiness Church. In January of 1907 the name was changed once more, to Church of God, and headquarters were moved to Cleveland, Tennessee. Tomlinson was elected general overseer in 1909, and the church began publishing *The Church of God Evangel* the following year. The Church of God embraced Pentecostal practices and grew rapidly across the South and Midwest.

A crisis occurred in 1923 that raised concerns over the personal role of Tomlinson (see CHURCH OF GOD OF PROPHECY) and, more important, the nature of the church's government and the leader's authority. The majority, those with whom the Church of God (Cleveland, Tennessee) is continuous, rejected Tomlinson's leadership and selected F. J. Lee as overseer.

The church's major doctrines blend many Protestant themes with those that are specifically Pentecostal: justification by faith, sanctification, baptism of the Holy Spirit, speaking in tongues, the need to be born again, fruitfulness in Christian living, and a strong interest in the pre-millennial Second Coming of Christ (Christ to return before reigning on earth for a thousand years). The Church of God professes reliance on the Bible "as a whole rightly divided rather than upon any written creed." It practices divine healing; condemns the use of alcohol and tobacco; opposes membership in secret societies; and accepts baptism, the Lord's Supper, and foot washing as ordinances. The Church of God elects its officers at a biennial General Assembly. The administration of the church includes a general overseer, three assistant overseers, a secretary general, and an eighteen-member International Executive Council, which is responsible for the day-to-day operations of the church. Administrative divisions include education, world evangelism, church ministries, care ministries, and support services. Pathway Press is the publishing arm of the church, producing resources for Christian education and books for ministers and lay people. The Church of God operates Lee University and the Church of God School of Theology in Cleveland, Tennessee, a school of ministry, and a preparatory school. Its foreign missions enterprise is extensive, serving in Africa, Asia, Europe, Central America, and South America.

For more information: www.churchofgod.org

Headquarters: P.O. Box 100,000, Cleveland, TN 37320

CHURCH OF GOD IN CHRIST

Founded: 1897
Membership: est. 5,500,000 in 15,300 churches (unverifiable)

Generally acknowledged to be the largest African-American Pentecostal body in the U.S., the Church of God in Christ was founded after ministers Charles H. Mason (1866–1961) and Charles P. Jones were expelled by Baptist* groups in Arkansas for what was considered an overemphasis on holiness. Together they founded the Church of Christ (Holiness) U.S.A. in 1895. This church stressed the doctrine of entire sanctification. Mason also organized a congregation in Lexington, Mississippi, in 1897, to which he gave the name Church of God in Christ. In 1907 Mason went to Azusa Street in Los Angeles, California, to observe the Pentecostal revival taking place there. While in attendance, he had his first experience of speaking in tongues.

Subsequently, Mason raised the issue of Pentecostal experience in a gathering of leaders of the Church of Christ (Holiness) U.S.A. Charles P. Jones and others did not share Mason's enthusiasm for the Pentecostal movement and withdrew fellowship from him. Mason

284

then called for a meeting in Memphis, Tennessee, of ministers who endorsed Pentecostal doctrine. With this group, he organized a general assembly of the Church of God in Christ, of which he was named general overseer and chief apostle. Mason remained head of the church until his death in 1961.

The Church of God in Christ is Trinitarian and stresses repentance, regeneration, justification, sanctification, speaking in tongues, and the gift of healing as evidence of the baptism of the Spirit. The sanctifying power of the Holy Spirit is considered a prerequisite to living a holy life, separate from the sin of the present world. Ordinances include baptism by immersion, the Lord's Supper, and foot washing. The Church of God in Christ is governed by executive, legislative and judicial bodies. The executive branch is composed of the General Board, which is chaired by the Presiding Bishop. Executive officers are chosen at a general assembly that meets every four years. Clergy consist of bishops, district superintendents, pastors, evangelists and evangelist missionaries. The denomination has its headquarters in Memphis, Tennessee, which is also the location of the publishing house and All Saints Bible College. Atlanta, Georgia is the location of the church's Charles H. Mason Theological Seminary, which is a founding member of the Interdenominational Theological Center. The church has established ministries in fifty-six countries and all fifty states in the U.S.

For more information: www.cogic.org

Headquarters: P.O. Box 1779, Memphis, TN 38101

CHURCH OF GOD OF PROPHECY

Founded: 1923
Membership: 75,112 in 1,862 churches (1999)

The Church of God of Prophecy is one of the churches that grew out of the work of A. J. Tomlinson (1865–1943). At his death, his son M. A. Tomlinson was named General overseer, a position he held until 1990. He emphasized church unity and fellowship unlimited by social, racial, and political differences. The present general overseer, Billy D. Murray, Sr., has made promoting Christian unity and worldwide evangelism his priorities.

From its beginnings, the church has based its beliefs on "the whole

Bible, rightly divided" and has accepted the Bible as God's Holy Word, inspired, inerrant, and infallible. The church affirms that there is one God eternally existing in three persons. It believes in the deity, virgin birth, sinlessness, miracles, atoning death, bodily resurrection, ascension to the Father, and physical Second Coming of Christ. The church professes that salvation results from grace alone through faith in Christ, that regeneration by the Holy Spirit is essential for the salvation of sinners, and that sanctification by the blood of Christ makes personal holiness possible. The church stresses the ultimate unity of believers, based on John 17, and the sanctity of marriage and family.

Other official teachings include baptism by the Spirit with the speaking of tongues as evidence; divine healing; the pre-millennial Second Coming of Christ; baptism by immersion; abstinence from tobacco, alcohol, and narcotics; and holiness in lifestyle. In addition to the Lord's Supper, the church practices foot washing.

The church is racially integrated on all levels, and women play a prominent role in church affairs, including serving in pastoral roles. The General Oversight Group consists of at least two bishops who, along with the General Overseer, are responsible for setting the vision for the entire church body. Doctrinal and business concerns of the church are addressed at the biennal General Assembly.

For more information: www.cogop.org

Headquarters: P.O. Box 2910, Cleveland, TN 37320-2910

CHURCH OF OUR LORD JESUS CHRIST OF THE APOSTOLIC FAITH, INC.

Founded: 1919
Membership: est. 30,000 in 450 churches (1998)

This church was organized in 1919 at Columbus, Ohio, by Robert C. Lawson as "a continuation of the great revival begun at Jerusalem on the day of Pentecost." Lawson moved to New York City later that year, where he founded Refuge Temple, which he pastored until his death in 1961. He also led the wider organization as chief apostle until his death. He was succeeded as pastor of the church (now Greater Refuge Temple) by William L. Bonner, who later also became chief apostle of the Church of Our Lord Jesus Christ of the Apostolic Faith, Inc.

Church doctrine is held to be "that of the apostles and the prophets," with Christ as the cornerstone. The basic emphases are Christ's resurrection and pre-millennial Second Coming, the resurrection and translation of the saints, the priesthood of all believers, and the final judgment of humankind. The church is non-trinitarian, maintaining belief "in the oneness of God, who was the Father in creation, the Son in redemption, and today, He is the Holy Ghost in The Church." Baptism is by immersion, and baptism of the Holy Spirit is necessary for second birth. Foot washing is practiced, but not as an ordinance.

The Church of Our Lord Jesus Christ of the Apostolic Faith, Inc. has congregations in thirty-two states, the British West Indies, Africa, the Philippines, Haiti, the Dominican Republic, and London, England. It operates a Bible college in New York City, where general offices are maintained, and carries out various ministries of caring in the communities in which it serves. A national convocation meets every year. National officers include a chief apostle, a presiding apostle, a board of apostles, a board of bishops, and a board of presbyters.

For more information: www.cooljc.org

Headquarters: 2801 Adam Clayton Powell Blvd., New York, NY 10029

CHURCH OF THE LIVING GOD, CHRISTIAN WORKERS FOR FELLOWSHIP

Founded: 1889
Membership: est. 20,000 in 120 temples (2002)

This body claims to be the first black church in the U.S. that was not begun by white missionaries. The Church of the Living God, Christian Workers for Fellowship came out of an organization formed in 1889 at Wrightsville, Arkansas, by William Christian (1856–1928), a former slave. At a time when many white Christians treated blacks as less than human, Christian began a group that maintained that many of the prominent people of the Bible, including Jesus and David, were black. Christian held the office of "Chief" in the new church, and was succeeded in the office by his wife and, eventually, by their son.

Christian held to trinitarian doctrine and accepted Pentecostal practices, such as speaking in tongues, without requiring the practices of members; he did, however, hold that inspired speaking must be in recognizable languages. The Church of the Living God, Christian Workers for Fellowship observes three ordinances: water baptism, washing of feet, and the Lord's Supper celebrated with water and unleavened bread.

Christian also was fascinated by Freemasonry, and he developed a church structure that resembled a fraternal organization. He insisted that his "organism" be known as "operative Masonry" and characterized the three ordinances as the "first three corporal degrees." A chief bishop is the presiding officer of the organization. Members tithe their incomes to support their churches, which they call temples. The current head of the denomination is in the process of removing the Masonic aspects of the denomination.

Headquarters: 430 Forest Ave., Cincinnati, OH 45229

CHURCH OF THE LIVING GOD, THE PILLAR AND GROUND OF THE TRUTH, INC.

Founded: 1903
Membership: est. 2,000 in 100 churches (1988)

Though under 5,000 members, this church is significant because it is one of the few denominations founded by a woman. Mary Lena Lewis-Tate (1871–1930), later known as Mary Magdalena Lewis-Tate, was the "First Chief Overseer and Mother in True Holiness" of the Church of the Living God, the Pillar and the Ground of Truth, Inc. at Steele Springs, Tennessee. She chose as her co-laborers her two sons, and two of her sisters also became ministers and bishops in the church. By 1908 Lewis-Tate organized the first general assembly of the church that year at Greenville, Alabama. The church has experienced two major schisms. Doctrinally, the church promotes basic Holiness* and Pentecostal beliefs. One distinctive feature is the use of water rather than wine in Holy Communion. The church maintains offices in Nashville, Tennessee, which is also the home of the church's publishing arm.

For more information: www.cotlg.net

Headquarters: 400 21st. St., McComb, MS 39648

288

CONGREGATIONAL HOLINESS CHURCH

Founded: 1921
Membership: est. 15,000 in 201 churches (2004)

Doctrinally, the Congregational Holiness Church affirms basic evangelical and Pentecostal doctrines along with idea of the imminent rapture of the church and the personal, premillenial second coming of Christ. Speaking in tongues is seen as the initiatory evidence of the experience of baptism in the Holy Spirit. Ordinances include baptism by immersion, the Lord's Supper, and foot washing.

Church government is congregational. Congregational Holiness Church pastors are elected by a majority vote of the congregation to which they are called; both women and men are ordained. In the early days of the denomination, there were no full-time elected leaders. This arrangement continued until 1935, when there was an organizational change. The local churches are now grouped into eight geographical districts in the southeast region of the U.S, along with a Hispanic Conference headquartered in Texas with churches located in several states. Each district has a presbytery of five members, which licenses and ordains ministers. The General Committee, made of district officials, governs the church between the General Biennial Conferences. The General Conference is the highest ruling body of the church. Offices are maintained in Griffin, Georgia. The denomination conducts mission work primarily in South America, and worldwide there are over four thousand churches.

For more information: www.chchurch.com

Headquarters: 3888 Fayettville Highway, Griffin, GA 30223

ELIM FELLOWSHIP

Founded: 1947
Membership: est. 20,000 in 100 churches (2004)

This body is an outgrowth of the missionary-oriented Elim Ministerial Fellowship, formed in 1933, and the work of graduates of the Elim Bible Institute in Lima, New York, founded in 1924 by Ivan and Minnie Spencer. The group was incorporated in 1947 as the Elim Missionary Assemblies; the present name was adopted in 1972.

Members of the Elim Fellowship hold to basic Pentecostal tenets of belief, beginning with affirmation of the Bible as the inspired and infallible Word of God. The fellowship espouses the trinitarian understanding of the Godhead, the atoning death and resurrection of Jesus Christ, salvation, sanctification, water baptism, the celebration of Communion among believers, the baptism of the Holy Spirit as evidenced in charismatic gifts and ministries, divine healing, and resurrection of the saved and unsaved for eternal reward or punishment.

The organizational pattern of Elim Fellowship is congregational, with individual churches autonomous in decision making. An annual assembly meets in Lima, where the General Chairman maintains offices. Over eight hundred ministers have credentials through Elim Fellowship, and over 150 missionaries affiliated with the fellowship are at work in Africa, Asia, Europe, and South America.

For more information: www.elim.edu

Headquarters: 1703 Dalton Rd., P.O. Box 57A, Lima, NY 14485

FIRE BAPTIZED HOLINESS CHURCH OF GOD OF THE AMERICAS

Founded: 1898
Membership: statistics unavailable, est. 170 churches (2004)

The Fire Baptized Holiness Church of God was founded by William Edward Fuller, Sr. It is closely related to the International Pentecostal Holiness Church and shares a common history in southern African American-Pentecostalism. Coming out of the Methodist Holiness tradition, it is an episcopal church, but in addition to baptism and Holy Communion, its members practice foot-washing. The church maintains that there is no distinction between male and female in Christ; therefore it was one of the early churches to ordain women as preachers and pastors. The church holds to basic evangelical, Holiness, and Pentecostal teachings, but it also provides a list of things that it opposes. This includes Unitarianism,* Mormonism,* Islam,* Psychics, Spiritualists,* and the Seventh-day Adventists'* doctrines.

For more information: www.fbhchurch.org

Headquarters: 901 Bishop William Edward Fuller, Sr. Highway, Greenville, SC 29601

FULL GOSPEL FELLOWSHIP OF CHURCHES AND MINISTERS, INTERNATIONAL

Founded: 1962
Membership: 326,900 in 902 churches (2002)

This fellowship was founded in Dallas, Texas, at a meeting called by Gordon Lindsay to support, encourage, and promote apostolic, Pentecostal ministry. As Lindsay and others envisioned it, the organization would give expression to the essential unity of those who believe in Christ and in the active work of the Holy Spirit. It was not to be a denomination as such but a fellowship of ministries. The organization also made it easier for independent churches to have tax-exempt status with the Internal Revenue Service.

Although individual churches or groups of churches affiliated with the Full Gospel Fellowship have doctrinal and ecclesial autonomy, certain core beliefs form the basis for fellowship. Among the suggested tenets of faith are belief in the Bible as the inspired Word of God, in the trinitarian understanding of the Godhead, in the atoning death and resurrection of Jesus Christ, in the need for personal salvation and sanctification, in the return and reign of Jesus Christ, and in heaven and hell. The fellowship strongly advocates baptism by the Holy Spirit, as evidenced by the gift of speaking in tongues.

Regional conventions and an annual international convention are held, and various cooperative ministries, including curriculum development, are facilitated by the organization. The fellowship maintains offices in Irving, Texas.

For more information: www.Fgfemi.org
Headquarters: 4325 W. Ledbetter Dr., Dallas, TX 75233

INDEPENDENT ASSEMBLIES OF GOD, INTERNATIONAL

Founded: 1922
Membership: statistics not available

This group is to be distinguished from the Assemblies of God,* but it shares a common heritage in the early Pentecostal movement. It traces its origins to the Azusa Street revival in Los Angeles in 1906

291

that soon spread across the country and across ethnic lines. In 1918 Scandinavian Pentecostals, who were particularly concerned to pre-serve the principles of Congregationalism,* formed the Scandinavian Assemblies of God in the United States, Canada, and Foreign Lands. This group operated essentially as a fellowship of like-minded churches until 1935, when they merged with the Independent Pentecostal Churches to form the Independent Assemblies of God, International.

Doctrinally, the church's statement of faith includes the common tenets of Pentecostalism, such as belief in the Bible as the inspired and infallible Word of God, in the Trinity, in the reality of Satan, and in the need for baptism by the Holy Spirit as evidenced through speaking in tongues. Ordinances include baptism by immersion and the Lord's Supper.

The churches in this assembly are autonomous but work together on common ministries. The leadership of the Assemblies of God International includes a general overseer, an assistant general over-seer, and an international missions director. The offices are in Santa Ana, California, and the organization supports missionaries and national pastors in Africa, Central America, South America, Mexico, India, and the Philippines.

For more information: www.iaogi.org

Headquarters: P.O. Box 2130, Laguana Hills, CA 92645-2130

INTERNATIONAL CHURCH OF
THE FOURSQUARE GOSPEL

Founded: 1927
Membership: 305,852 in 1,846 congregations (2001)

Founded during the evangelistic work of Aimee Semple McPherson (1890–1944), this church is a tribute to the organizing genius and striking methods of its founder. Born in Ontario in 1890, McPherson was converted under the preaching of her first husband, Robert Semple, an evangelist. Semple died while they were serving as missionaries in China, and Aimee Semple returned to the U.S. in 1911, where she conducted evangelistic crusades throughout North America.

In 1918, after her remarriage, Aimee Semple McPherson and her children, Roberta and Rolf, settled in Los Angeles. With the help of her followers, she built Angelus Temple, which was dedicated on January 1, 1923. She also founded the Echo Park Evangelistic Association, the Lighthouse of International Foursquare Evangelism (L.I.F.E.) Bible College, and the International Church of the Foursquare Gospel.

With her speaking ability and faith in prayer for the sick, McPherson attracted thousands to her meetings. Her critics felt that the meetings were too much like a spectacle, but others appreciated her presentation. Her followers showed great interest in the sick and the poor; "more than a million and a half" are said to have been fed by Angelus Temple during the Depression years. McPherson was president of the church during her lifetime and, together with a board of directors, oversaw the denomination's expansion. Upon her death in 1944, her son, Rolf Kennedy McPherson, became president and led the church until 1988.

The "four-square gospel" refers to four central Pentecostal teachings that pre-date McPherson but that she popularized nationally. They are (1) salvation, (2) baptism by the Spirit, (3) divine physical healing, and (4) the Second Coming of Jesus Christ. The broader teaching of the church is set forth in a twenty-one-paragraph Declaration of Faith written by McPherson. It also stresses the return of Christ prior to his reign on earth, personal holiness,* and the trinitarian conception of God. The Bible is affirmed as "true, immutable, steadfast, unchangeable, as its author, the Lord Jehovah." Baptism with the Holy Spirit, with the initial evidence of speaking in tongues, is subsequent to conversion, and the power to heal is given in answer to believing prayer. The ordinances of baptism and the Lord's Supper are observed in the church.

The official business of the church is conducted by a board of directors, a missionary cabinet, and an executive council made up of corporate officers. The highest seat of authority is the annual Foursquare Convention, which alone has the power to make or amend the bylaws of the church and which elects the president of the church to a four-year term. District supervisors are appointed for ten districts in the United States and are ratified by pastors of the respective districts every four years. Pastors are appointed by the board of directors of the denomination and are assisted by a local church council. Congregations are subordinated units of the denomination and contribute monthly to home and foreign missionary work. The official publication of the church is the *Foursquare World ADVANCE* magazine, published bimonthly.

While membership is highest on the West Coast, there are Foursquare churches in all fifty states. Overseas, the foursquare gospel is preached in 107 countries, with over three million members and adherents in over twenty-six thousand churches and meeting places. In addition to L.I.F.E. Bible College in Los Angeles and L.I.F.E. Bible College East in Christiansburg, Virginia, the church supports numerous Bible colleges and institutes around the world. There is also an extensive youth camping program. The church sponsors radio station KFSG-FM in Los Angeles.

For more information: www.foursquare.org

Headquarters: P.O. Box 26902, Los Angeles, CA 90026-0176

INTERNATIONAL PENTECOSTAL HOLINESS CHURCH

Founded: 1911
Membership: 213,348 in 1,905 churches (2002)

The International Pentecostal Holiness Church traces its origins to an organization founded in 1898 in Anderson, South Carolina, by a number of Holiness* associations. At that time the group was called the Fire-Baptized Holiness Church. In the same year, in Goldsboro, North Carolina, another group was organized as the Pentecostal Holiness Church. In 1907 G. B. Cashwell (1826–1916), a participant in the Azusa Street revival, led a Pentecostal revival in North Carolina and brought these two groups into Pentecostalism. The two bodies united in 1911 as the Pentecostal Holiness Church; and a third body, the Tabernacle Pentecost Church, joined them in 1915. The present name was adopted in 1975.

The theological standards of Methodism* prevail in the International Pentecostal Holiness Church with certain modifications. The denomination accepts the pre-millennial teaching of the Second Coming, holding that Christ's return will precede his thousand-year reign on earth, and believes that provision was made in the atonement for healing of the human body. Divine healing is practiced, but not to the exclusion of medicine. Three distinctive experiences are taught: two works of grace—justification by faith and sanctification—and Spirit baptism attested to by speaking in other tongues. Services are

294

often characterized by "joyous demonstrations." Two ordinances are observed: water baptism and Holy Communion.

The church's general executive board is elected by a quadrennial conference. There is a general superintendent and directors of World Missions, Evangelism, Church Education, Stewardship, and representatives from the different regions. Twenty-nine conferences or regional judicatories cover the U.S. General offices are in Oklahoma City, Oklahoma. IPHC sponsors Emmanuel College in Georgia and Southwestern College of Christian Ministries in Oklahoma, both four-year accredited colleges. The church operates a children's home at Falcon, North Carolina; a children's convalescent center at Bethany, Oklahoma; and a home for the aged. Foreign mission work takes place in ninety-eight countries.

For more information: www.iphc.org

Headquarters: P.O. Box 12609, Oklahoma City, OK 73157

OPEN BIBLE STANDARD CHURCHES, INC.

Founded: 1935
Membership: est. 40,000 in 325 churches (2002)

This association of churches was originally composed of two revival movements rooted in the Azusa Street meetings of 1906: Bible Standard, Inc., founded in Eugene, Oregon, by Fred Hornshuh in 1919 and Open Bible Evangelistic Association, founded in Des Moines, Iowa, by John R. Richey in 1932. The Pacific Coast group, with activities centered in Oregon, spread through Washington, California, and into the Rocky Mountain areas of the West; the Iowa group expanded into Illinois, Missouri, Ohio, Florida, and Pennsylvania. Similar in doctrine and government, the two groups joined on July 26, 1935, taking the combined name Open Bible Standard Churches, Inc., with headquarters in Des Moines. There are now churches in thirty-seven states.

The teachings of the Open Bible Churches are "fundamental in doctrine, evangelical in spirit, missionary in vision, and Pentecostal in testimony." They include emphasis on the infallibility of the Word of God, the blood atonement of Christ, baptism by immersion, personal holiness, baptism of the Holy Spirit, divine healing, and the return of Jesus Christ. Open Bible Churches are grouped into five geographical regions, subdivided into twenty-seven districts. Individual churches are congregationally governed, locally owned, and affiliated by charter with the national organization. The highest governing body is the general convention, which meets biennially. The church has over one thousand credentialed ministers.

Internationally, the association ministers in thirty-eight countries (outside the U.S.), in 1,248 churches, and sponsors ten Bible institutes serving over 1,427 students. Mission emphasis is on the training of nationals for ministry. Institute of Theology by Extension (INSTE), a non-traditional educational program, operates in twenty-nine countries with over twelve thousand students, both in Open Bible and other denominational churches. The program is translated in or being translated into ten languages. In the U.S., Open Bible Churches sponsor Eugene Bible College in Oregon, Master's Commission discipleship and leadership development groups in Iowa and Washington, and many INSTE groups serving over fourteen hundred students studying in Spanish or English.

For more information: www.openbible.org
Headquarters: 2020 Bell Ave., Des Moines, IA 50315

PENTECOSTAL ASSEMBLIES OF THE WORLD, INC.

Founded: 1907
Membership: est. 1,500,000 in 1,750 churches (1998)

Tracing its origin to the Azusa Street revival in 1906, this body is the oldest "oneness" Pentecostal body, meaning that its baptism is in the name of Jesus only. The goal of the Pentecostal Assemblies of the World, Inc., is to spread the message that Jesus Christ is Lord to all people. From its beginning, the group, including its leadership, has been interracial; however, the church is predominantly African-American today. Two of it most influential leaders were G. T. Haywood, who directed the church during a period of consolidation from 1924 until his death in 1931, and Samuel Grimes, a former missionary, who led the church through a period of expansion from 1937 until his death in 1967.

Basic Pentecostal and Holiness* doctrine and practice are followed, except for rejection of the trinitarian understanding of God. The church stresses holiness of life, holding that believers must be wholly sanctified to fully participate in salvation. Strict codes governing dress and leisure pursuits are maintained. Water baptism and the Lord's Supper are practiced, with wine used in the latter. Only the King James Version of the Bible is accepted as the true Word of God. The Pentecostal Assemblies of the World hosts two major conferences annually, to which its constituents come from around the globe to worship God and to fellowship with one another. The church is headed by a presiding bishop who guides its members spiritually. There is also an executive board including an assistant presiding bishop, a general secretary, a general treasurer, and lay directors. The organization's administrator and staff handle its business affairs from general offices in Indianapolis, Indiana. This body is heavily concentrated in urban areas, such as Chicago, Detroit, and Indianapolis, but there are ministers serving in all fifty states.

The Aenon Bible College, located in Indianapolis, Indiana, serves to train Pentecostal Assemblies ministers and lay members. The college has affiliate institutes all over the U.S. and two foreign affiliates in Liberia: the Samuel Grimes Bible Institute and the Haywood Mission.

For more information: www.pawinc.org

Headquarters: 3939 Meadows Dr., Indianapolis, IN 46205

PENTECOSTAL CHURCH OF GOD

Founded: 1919
Membership: 104,000 in 1,197 churches (2002)

This body was organized in Chicago under the name "Pentecostal Assemblies of the U.S.A." in order to better organize early Pentecostalism in the Midwest for evangelism and to preserve congregations from unethical preachers pretending to be Spirit-filled. When the church was reorganized in 1922, the name was changed to "Pentecostal Church of God." For a number of years "of America" was a part of the name, but this was dropped in 1979.

The Pentecostal Church of God is evangelical and Pentecostal in faith and practice. The doctrines of salvation, divine healing, baptism in the Holy Spirit (with the evidence of speaking in tongues), and the Second Coming of Christ are strongly emphasized. Ordinances include water baptism, the Lord's Supper, and foot washing.

A General Convention of the church meets biennially. Executives of the denomination include a general superintendent, a general secretary, a director of world missions, a director of home missions/evangelism, and a director of (American) Indian missions. Headquarters are located in Joplin, Missouri. The church has six regional divisions, each presided over by an assistant general superintendent. Most of the divisions have annual conventions.

The Pentecostal Church of God conducts mission work in forty-nine countries in Europe, Asia, Africa, and the Americas; thirty-seven missionaries serve in the field. Over 4,950 churches have been established outside the U.S., and over 2,500 national ministers have been commissioned. The group sponsors twenty-two Bible schools, fifty-seven training centers, and fifty-one day schools across the globe. Messenger College, Messenger Publishing House, and Messenger Towers, all in Joplin, are supported by the church. *The Pentecostal Herald* is the official publication.

For more information: www.pcg.org

Headquarters: P.O. Box 850, Joplin, MO 64802

PENTECOSTAL FREE WILL BAPTIST CHURCH, INC.

Founded: 1959
Membership: est. 28,000 in 150 churches (1998)

The Pentecostal Free Will Baptist Church came into existence through the merging of four Free Will Baptist conferences in North Carolina in 1959. These various groups traced their origins as Free Will Baptists* to the work of Paul Palmer (d. 1750) in the Carolinas during the first half of the eighteenth century. The Pentecostal aspect of the church's doctrine was developed in response to the preaching of G. W. Cashwell (1826–1916), who had participated in the Azusa Street revival of 1906 in Los Angeles, California. Cashwell launched a series of meetings in North Carolina on New Year's Eve, 1906; in response, many Free Will Baptist individuals and churches adopted Pentecostal doctrine and practice.

The church's doctrine is a mixture of Baptist and Pentecostal beliefs. Central affirmations include the inerrancy of the Bible, regeneration through faith in the shed blood of Christ, sanctification as a second definite work of grace (subsequent to regeneration), Pentecostal baptism of the Holy Spirit as evidenced through speaking in tongues, divine healing, and the pre-millennial Second Coming of Christ. Ordinances include baptism by immersion, the Lord's Super, and foot washing.

A general meeting of the Pentecostal Free Will Baptist Church is held biennially in August; lay and ministerial representatives attend. Church officials include a general superintendent, a general secretary, and a general treasurer. Offices are maintained in Dunn, North Carolina, where Heritage Bible College was established in 1971. Most of the group's churches are in eastern North Carolina; but mission work is carried on in nine foreign countries, and Bible institutes are operated in Mexico, the Philippines, and Venezuela.

For more information: www.pfwb.org

Headquarters: P.O. Box 1568, Dunn, NC 28355

UNITED HOLY CHURCH OF AMERICA, INC.

Founded: 1918; 1886
Membership: statistics not available, but est. 100,000

This is a Pentecostal/Holiness body that was first organized in 1886 in Method, North Carolina as a regional body. Known originally as the Holy Church of North Carolina, it was reorganized in 1918 as the United Holy Church of America, Inc. Its purpose is to establish and maintain holy convocations, assemblies, conventions, conferences, public worship, and missionary and educational efforts. The church's famous logo features a cross in the intersection of three circles in a triangle.

Articles of faith contain statements of belief in the Trinity, the record of the revelation of God in the Bible, redemption through Christ, justification with instantaneous sanctification, baptism of the Holy Spirit, divine healing, and the ultimate reign of Christ over the earth. Baptism by immersion, the Lord's Supper, and foot washing are observed as ordinances. The United Holy Church believes in speaking in tongues and views Spirit baptism as normative, although it shares the position held by many Pentecostal groups that speaking in tongues is not required for full membership, full discipleship, or even spirit baptism.

The church maintains headquarters in North Carolina. The chief officer is the General President. Other officials include two general vice presidents, a general recording secretary, a general financial secretary, and a general treasurer. A board of bishops supervises the work of the church. The United Holy Church's primary publication is *The Holiness Union.*

Headquarters; 312 Umstead Street, Durham, NC 27702

UNITED PENTECOSTAL CHURCH INTERNATIONAL

Founded: 1945
Membership: est. 500,000 in 4,142 churches (2004)

The United Pentecostal Church International (UPCI) was founded in 1945 by the union of the Pentecostal Assemblies of Jesus Christ and the Pentecostal Church, Inc. Each of those bodies was itself the result of mergers of other Pentecostal bodies in the 1930s. All the constituent members were "oneness" ("Jesus only") Pentecostals who withdrew from the Assemblies of God in 1916.

The doctrinal views of the UPCI reflect most of the beliefs of the Holiness-Pentecostal movement, with the exception of the "second work of grace." Holiness of life is understood to be an aspect of God's salvation of an individual, not the result of a subsequent experience.

Theologically, the church is non-trinitarian. The oneness view held by the UPCI asserts that God "revealed Himself in the Old Testament as Jehovah and in the New Testament revealed Himself in His Son, Jesus Christ." Jesus Christ is thus the one true God manifested in flesh and the Holy Ghost is the Spirit of God/the resurrected Christ. Baptism is carried out in Jesus' name only. The church embraces the Pentecostal view that speaking in tongues is the initial sign of receiving the Holy Spirit. For the UPCI, the Bible is the inerrant and infallible Word of God, and the church rejects all extrabiblical revelations and writings, such as church creeds and articles of faith.

UPCI polity is essentially congregational, with autonomous local churches. The General Conference of the church meets annually to elect officials. A general superintendent, two assistants, and a secretary-treasurer are members of a general board that also includes district superintendents, executive presbyters, and division heads. Denominational offices are located at Hazelwood, Missouri, as is

World Aflame Press, the church's publishing house. The press publishes books, Sunday school materials, and a wide variety of religious literature. *The Pentecostal Herald* is the official organ of the UPCI, and there are various divisional publications. The church also sponsors "Harvest Time," an international radio broadcast.

UPCI's foreign missions program sponsors work in 170 countries outside the U.S. and claims an international membership of four million. Within the U.S., the church supports seven Bible colleges and opened a graduate school of theology outside St. Louis, Missouri, in 2001. Other UPCI ministries include children's homes in Tupelo, Mississippi and Hammond, Louisiana; a chaplaincy program for persons in prison; and a chaplaincy program for the armed services.

For more information: www.upci.org

Headquarters: 8855 Dunn Rd., Hazelwood, MO 63402

VINEYARD CHURCHES, ASSOCIATION OF

Founded: 1983
Membership: approx. 100,000 members in 500 churches (2000)

The Vineyard movement began as part of the Calvary Chapel* movement in California in the 1970s and grew rapidly. Kenn and Joanie Gulliksen served in a Calvary Chapel in Los Angeles, and around 1974 they began to emphasize the gifts of the Spirit. In 1982 the congregation changed its name to Vineyard to distinguish it from Calvary Chapel, because the Vineyard congregation promoted public expressions of glossolalia, healing, exorcisms, and prophecy, while Calvary Chapel saw such things as private gifts of the Spirit. Another Calvary Chapel minister, the former rock musician John Wimber (1934-1997), teamed up with Gulliksen to promote charismatic gifts among the younger generation. Wimber was the major public figure of the church until his death in 1997.

Wimber's "Signs and Wonders" course at Fuller Theological Seminary in Pasadena attracted many younger ministers to the movement despite the controversy it evoked. He called his movement the Third Wave of Pentecostalism and urged his followers to adopt Power Evangelism, using miracles to attract people to the faith. Christian rock music was also used effectively in evangelical outreach through recordings and radio broadcasts. The church embraces evangelical and Pentecostal theology regarding the infallibility of Scripture, the fall of the human race, the need for an experience of salvation, and the spiritual gifts of healing and speaking in tongues. The Vineyard also emphasizes informal worship and provides fellowship for disaffected youth.

Contrary to the original anti-establishment character of the movement, Wimber had already begun the process of denominationalization before his death in 1997. His death was a serious blow to a movement that was centered on the idea that prayer produces healing. It has also become evident that Wimber's own personality was an important aspect of the church, and the movement has been struggling with issues of organization, leadership, and future direction. In 2000 Bert Waggoner, a successful Vineyard pastor, was appointed national director.

For more information: www.avc.vineyard.org; www.vineyard.org
Headquarters: P.O. Box 17580, Anaheim, CA 92817

NATIVE AMERICAN CHURCH

Founded: 1918 with roots to 1880s
Membership: 300,000 (est.)

Traditional tribal religions are still practiced throughout the U.S. wherever native peoples have communities. Since tribal religion is based on oral tradition, it is difficult to determine how much it has changed since contact with Europeans, but oral tradition has been one glue that has held tribes together in the face of white hostility. It is impossible here to give a concise statement of the details of the various tribal religions. Suffice it to say that there is more variety than uniformity among traditional native religions in terms of both practice and belief.

Contrary to popular belief, the largest single religion among the native peoples of North America is Christianity in one form or another. As many as 700,000 Native Americans profess Christian beliefs. Early missions were primarily Roman Catholic, particularly in the Southwest. There the Pueblo and Yaqui peoples adapted Christian beliefs and practices to tribal traditions, creating an innovative religious syncretism. The various Protestant denominations were generally more hostile to tribal ritual and insisted on European practices.

Once native peoples were confined on reservations and native children required to attend American schools, Protestant evangelical churches played a greater role in Native American life. The Pentecostal movement was more tolerant of traditional native styles of worship, such as drumming, and Pentecostal evangelists had great success on reservations. Many Native American Christian congregations today are evangelical in orientation, teaching that members must have a personal conversion experience. Cook Christian Training School in Phoenix is an important institution for contemporary Native American missions.

In the twentieth century there was a revival of interest in traditional beliefs and practices among the tribes, and schools have been established to preserve the languages in which the old stories are passed down. The 1978 American Indian Religious Freedom Resolution has made it easier for native peoples to practice traditional tribal religion on federal lands.

Native American spirituality has also become a topic of great interest in the dominant culture primarily through the "New Age" movement. The book *Black Elk Speaks,* which was published in 1932 by John Neihardt, has been a major guide for whites and natives alike who are seeking to connect with a nature-based mysticism in which "Mother Earth" and all her inhabitants live in ecological and spiritual harmony. Shamanism, sweat lodges, vision quests, and other features of some tribal religions have become part of the American religious economy. This Native American spirituality is often an amalgam of many aspects of the different tribal religions.

There have also been attempts to create new types of indigenous religion that unite people across tribes without joining the European churches. Beginning around the turn of the last century, a group of Native Americans formed the Native American Church with principal concentration of membership in the Southwest. Its beliefs and practices are syncretistic, blending elements of Christianity with various traditional tribal practices. It was chartered in 1918 and reports about 300,000 members.

It is popularly, but inaccurately, called the "peyote religion" because its ceremonies frequently make use of the button or crown of the hallucinogenic peyote, a plant in the cactus family. The Native American Church is a uniquely American religion dedicated to the

Peyote spirit. Worshipers hold all-night ceremonies filled with chanting to the rhythms of a water drum while peyote is consumed. The reason for its use is not individual ecstasy but to serve as a communal ritual to foster bonded relationships. Males perform the leadership functions; the central figure is the shaman, who is thought to be endowed with psychic abilities. A 1988 Supreme Court decision severely curtailed use of peyote as a sacrament. Despite its reputation as a "drug" church, the Native American Church is quite conservative and has been effective in dealing with drug and alcohol abuse among Native Americans.

For more information: www.ncai.org

Contact: National Congress of American Indians, 1301 Connecticut Ave. NW, Suite 200, Washington, DC 20036.

Suggestions for further reading:

Bowden, Henry. *American Indians and Christian Missions: Studies in Cultural Conflict*. Chicago: University of Chicago Press, 1981.
Gill, Sam. *Native American Religions*. Belmont, CA: Wadsworth, 1982.
La Barre, Weston. *The Peyote Cult*. Norman, OK: University of Oklahoma Press,1989.
Niehard, John G. *Black Elk Speaks: Being the Life Story of a Holy Man of the Oglala Sioux*. Omaha: University of Nebraska Press, 2000 (reprint), 1932 (original).

FUNDAMENTALIST
AND BIBLE CHURCHES

Representing the most conservative form of Protestantism, socially and theologically, fundamentalism was one of the most potent forces within American Christianity in the twentieth century. Fundamentalism is a form of conservative evangelical Protestantism, but may be distinguished from other types of evangelical churches by its intense opposition to modern scientific theories and popular culture. Doctrinally, fundamentalists place great stress on the literal fulfillment of the apocalyptic prophecies of the books of Daniel and Revelation. According to fundamentalist teaching, the world is divided between the forces of God and Satan. Satan will exert ever greater control over society until the cataclysmic moment when Christ returns.

It is difficult to categorize and study fundamentalist churches because of the variety within fundamentalism and the fact that fundamentalism exerts an influence beyond its membership rolls. Fundamentalist churches tend to be congregationalist and Baptist* in orientation; therefore, structure exists primarily on the local level. Pastors tend to found their own congregations and work to build them into major bodies that are loosely joined to like-minded congregations. Rather than having traditional denominational structures, fundamentalist churches generally establish a variety of cooperative ministry programs, such as radio and television ministries, sponsorship of foreign missions, and educational programs. Bible colleges, often associated with local congregations, are one of the backbones of fundamentalism. Graduates of these Bible colleges often serve in denominations that are not in themselves fundamentalist.

Fundamentalism grew out of nineteenth-century American evangelicalism and revivalism. Dwight L. Moody (1837–99), founder of Moody Bible Institute, was one of the key figures in the formation of fundamentalist organizations, but the roots of the movement go back to the Plymouth Brethren (see CHRISTIAN BRETHREN) in England. The early Brethren dismissed with clergy and encouraged any members with spiritual gifts to preach, evangelize, and offer the sacraments. One of the key preachers was John Nelson Darby (1800–82), who stressed the importance of biblical prophecy, especially that found in the apocalyptic books, for understanding human history. Darby taught that history was divided into seven dispensations, the first six of which ended in a cataclysm, such as the great flood. The seventh dispensation will be the millennial age that Christ will inaugurate. Cyrus Scofield (1843–1921) made Darby's theory the centerpiece of his popular reference Bible early in the twentieth century. According to this scenario, life on earth will grow increasingly violent and sinful, as in the days before the flood.

Fundamentalism thus runs directly counter to modern trends in biblical scholarship and scientific theories about the origin, age, and evolution of the universe. It also rejects the modern idea of social progress in favor of a view of declension. Since biblical truth is under attack, according to fundamentalists, true believers must defend the Bible. *The Fundamentals: A Testimony to the Truth* was a popular pamphlet series designed to defend the Bible from critics. It appeared between 1910 and 1915 and included nearly one hundred articles that sought to defend the deity of Christ, the virgin birth, the historical resurrection, the inerrancy of Scripture as the Word of God, and the reality of sin and Satan.

World War I put the fundamentalist controversy on hold as Christians of all kinds joined in the war effort, but by 1920 the fundamentalist controversy heated up as Baptist* and Presbyterian* fundamentalists fought to preserve their churches from modernism. This early period culminated in the famous Scopes "Monkey Trial" of 1925 over the teaching of evolution in the public schools. Following that celebrated trial, fundamentalists began organizing separate congregations, schools, and inter-church organizations.

By the end of the twentieth century, Protestant fundamentalists had successfully created a significant subculture in American society. World events fueled the growth of fundamentalism. In particular, the formation of the State of Israel in 1948 seemed to confirm the fundamentalist belief that the Jews would return to the Promised Land shortly before the return of Christ; plus the threat of nuclear destruction during the Cold War gave renewed vigor to fundamentalist preaching and writing. Though prone to fractures and doctrinal disputes, fundamentalists since the Second World War have increasingly established cooperative ministries with other evangelicals.

Though some fundamentalist bodies were originally connected to the Holiness* movement, most have roots in the Baptist* and Presbyterian* churches. Some of the major fundamentalist associations are discussed below, but it should be noted that separatism is part of the nature of fundamentalism, and many bodies only keep records of individual pastors who participate. Though hostile to modern science, fundamentalists have made very effective use of modern technology to communicate their message far beyond the membership of fundamentalist churches.

A fairly reliable estimate of total membership in fundamentalist congregations in the U.S. is 700,000, but the influence of fundamentalism extends more broadly in conservative Evangelicalism in the U.S. Pastors in many Evangelical denominations have been trained in fundamentalist educational institutions such as Dallas Theological Seminary, and the Scofield Study Bible and its descendents are widely used. Jerry Falwell, who became famous through his *Old Time Religion* television show, brought fundamentalism into national conservative politics in the 1970s with his Moral Majority. The best-selling *Left Behind* fiction series written by Jerry B. Jenkin has introduced millions to fundamentalist pre-millennial eschatology while making allies in the anti-abortion and anti-gay rights effort.

Suggestions for further reading:

Balmer, Randall. *Mine Eyes Have Seen the Glory: A Journey into the Evangelical Subculture of America.* New York: Oxford University Press, 1989.

LaHaye, Tim. *The Battle for the Family.* Old Tappan, NJ: Revell, 1984.

Lawrence, Bruce B. *Defenders of God: The Fundamentalist Revolt Against the Modern Age.* San Francisco: Harper & Row, 1989.

Lindsey, Hal. *The Late Great Planet Earth.* Grand Rapids, MI: Zondervan, 1970.

Longfield, Bradley J. *The Presbyterian Controversy: Fundamentalists, Modernists, and Moderates.* New York: Oxford University Press, 1991.

Marsden, George M. *Fundamentalism and American Culture: The Shaping of Twentieth-century Evangelicalism, 1870–1925.* New York: Oxford University Press, 1980.

Marty, Martin and R. Scott Appleby. *The Glory and the Power: The Fundamentalist Challenge to the Modern World.* Boston: Beacon, 1992.

Marty, Martin and R. Scott Appleby, eds. *The Fundamentalism Project*, 5 vols. Chicago: University of Chicago Press, 1991-1995.

Sandeen, Ernest. *The Roots of Fundamentalism.* Chicago: University of Chicago Press, 1970.

AMERICAN EVANGELICAL CHRISTIAN CHURCHES

> Founded: 1944
> Membership: 18,412 in 180 churches (2001)

The American Evangelical Christian Churches (AECC) are less a denomination than an inter-church organization that offers credentials for ministers. Congregations associated with the AECC are autonomous but agree to a fundamentalist statement of belief. Clergy credentialed by the AECC serve in a variety of capacities, including

307

prison ministry, military and hospital chaplaincy, as well as outreach to truckers, bikers, and others without a permanent Christian community. Ministerial applicants must subscribe to "Seven Articles of Faith": (1) the Bible as the written Word of God; (2) the virgin birth; (3) the deity of Jesus Christ; (4) salvation through the atonement of Christ; (5) the guidance of life through prayer; (6) the return of Christ; and (7) the establishment of the millennial kingdom. Upon completion of training, ministerial students are granted licenses enabling them to perform all the functions and offices of the ministry, with the exception of officiating at marriages. Full ordination is withheld until the licentiate has become pastor of a regular congregation or is engaged in full-time evangelistic or missionary work. Twelve regional offices in the U.S. and one in Canada supervise the work of the organization.

For more information: www.aeccministries.com

Headquarters: P.O. Box 47312, Indianapolis, IN 46227

BEREAN FUNDAMENTAL CHURCH

Founded: 1947
Membership: est. 8,000 in 51 churches (1997)

In the mid-1930s, Dr. Ivan E. Olsen became the first pastor of the Berean Fundamental Church, an independent congregation in North Platte, Nebraska. Following the principle of evangelism found in Acts 1:8, Olsen assisted in planting sixteen other churches in surrounding communities. In 1947 the churches formed the Berean Fundamental Church Council, Inc. Currently, there are churches in eight states—California, Colorado, Kansas, Minnesota, South Dakota, Oregon, Wyoming, and Nebraska.

The member churches possess a common constitution, stressing the basic doctrines of Christianity and the verbal, plenary inspiration of Scripture (the inerrancy of the Bible in all matters of faith and morals); the virgin birth of Christ; the deity of Christ; the blood atonement; the bodily resurrection of Christ; and the return of Christ to earth, following the rapture and preceding the millennial kingdom. The local assemblies are also Bible centered and evangelistic.

Berean Fundamental churches support a variety of independent faith missions, draw their pastors from various seminaries and Bible institutes, and freely choose their own Sunday school curricula and church

literature. The Berean Fundamental Church Council, Inc., supports its own Maranatha Bible Camp and Conference Grounds near North Platte.
For more information: www.bereanchurchfellowship.org
Headquarters: P.O. Box 1264, Kearney, NE 68848

BIBLE FELLOWSHIP CHURCH

Founded: 1858
Membership: 7,308 in 57 churches (2002)

This body was formed in the 1850s when Mennonite* leaders in Pennsylvania resisted the more evangelical style of some of the younger generation. The evangelical Mennonites formed their own group. Originally it was called the Evangelical Conference, but the name was changed in 1959 when a new confession of faith was adopted. The church now has a more fundamentalist outlook but retains some of its Mennonite heritage.

Bible Fellowship Church's doctrinal emphases include salvation through the death and resurrection of Christ, transformed life through new birth by the Holy Spirit, the authority and trustworthiness of the Bible as the Word of God, the culmination of history in the Second Coming of Jesus (pre-millennialism), and a shared life in the church of believers, with every member's being responsible for the propagation of the gospel through evangelism and missions. Churches are found mainly in Pennsylvania, New Jersey, New York, and Ontario, Canada.

The churches support missions on five continents, the Pinebrook Junior College, the Victory Valley Camp for children and youth, a home for the aging, and Pinebrook-in-the-Pines, a conference and retreat center—all in Pennsylvania.
For more information: www.bfc.org
Headquarters: 693 Church Rd., Graterford, PA 19426

CHRISTIAN BRETHREN (PLYMOUTH BRETHREN)

Founded: 1820s
Membership: est. 86,000 in 1,200 churches (2003)

The Plymouth Brethren is a widely used, but unofficial, designation for a loose grouping of churches with early nineteenth-century roots in

309

the British Isles. Within these churches, the common terminology is simply "Brethren" or "Christian Brethren," but they are to be distinguished from Brethren* churches associated with the Pietist movement. Similar to the Restorationist bodies in the U.S., the early Brethren envisioned a basis for Christian unity by forsaking denominational structures and names in order to meet simply as Christians. The autonomy of the local congregation is another feature of the movement.

The weekly hour-long "remembrance meeting" is probably the surest way to identify a Brethren assembly. In accordance with the meaning of "priesthood of believers," the service is unstructured and participatory. Brethren have consistently refused to restrict the administration of baptism or the Lord's Supper to ordained ministers, thus effectively eliminating a clergy/laity distinction and the traditional concept of ordination. A preacher may serve full-time with a congregation, but will not be identified as clergy or be given control of the congregation.

The Brethren are committed to all the fundamentals of conservative Christianity, including the verbal inspiration of Scripture. They emphasize gospel preaching and the necessity for personal conversion. Except for the weekly breaking of bread and the absence of collections at other meetings, their services are much like those of evangelical Baptist* and Bible churches.

Among American evangelicals, Brethren have had an influence out of proportion to their numbers. Their pre-millennial theology helped to shape evangelicalism, especially in the proliferation of independent churches and mission boards. In recent years, many have responded to the Brethren emphasis on plurality of leadership and participatory worship in the local church. Brethren are also characteristically found in leadership positions in interdenominational evangelistic campaigns and the founding and operation of nondenominational Bible schools, colleges, seminaries, and parachurch organizations. They have only one multiple-year, college-level institution, Emmaus Bible College in Dubuque, Iowa.

As a result of a division in England in 1848, there are two basic types of assemblies, commonly known as exclusive and open. Led in the beginning by John Nelson Darby (1800–82), the exclusive assemblies produced most of the movement's well-known Bible teachers, such as William Kelly, F. W. Grant, and C. H. Macintosh. They operated on the premise that disciplinary action taken by one assembly was binding on all. As a result, once started, a division often spread worldwide, until by the end of the century the exclusive

Brethren were divided into seven or eight main groups. Recent mergers have reduced that number somewhat, and an important American group has merged with the open assemblies.

Open assemblies were led by George Müller (1805–95), well known for his orphanages and life of faith. The Brethrens' strength has always been in evangelism and foreign missions. Lacking the exclusive disciplinary premise, local disputes spread only as far as there was interest and involvement; thus open assemblies have never experienced worldwide division.

Headquarters: 327 W. Prairie Ave., Wheaton, IL 60187-3408

EVANGELICAL METHODIST CHURCH

Founded: 1946
Membership: 8,615 in 123 churches (1997)

The Evangelical Methodist Church is "fundamental in doctrine, evangelistic in program, and congregational in government." It represents a double protest against what was considered an autocratic and undemocratic government, on the one hand, and a tendency toward modernism, on the other hand, in the Methodist Church. The church is Arminian in theology and Wesleyan in doctrine. Members seek to apply the spirit and revivalistic fervor of original Wesleyanism to the needs of society today. Fundamentalist in theology, they oppose the "substituting of social, educational, or other varieties of cultural salvation for the gospel message." Local churches own and control their own property and select their own pastors. The international headquarters are in Indianapolis, Indiana. The church maintains missionary work in Bolivia and in Mexico.

For more information: www.emchurch.org

Headquarters: P.O. Box 17070, Indianapolis, IN 46253

GRACE GOSPEL FELLOWSHIP

Founded: 1945
Membership: est. 60,000 in 128 churches (1992)

Dispensational and premillennial, this fellowship had its beginnings as a pastors' fellowship at a conference of pastors and missionaries at the Berean* Bible Church in Indianapolis, Indiana, in 1943. A year later, at Evansville, Indiana, its purpose was defined in a constitution: "to promote a fellowship among those who believe the truths contained in [our] doctrinal statement and to proclaim the Gospel of the Grace of God in this land, and throughout the world."

That doctrinal statement includes belief in the Bible as infallibly inspired by God; in the total depravity of the human race; in redemption by God's grace through the blood of Christ by means of faith; in eternal security for the saved; in the gifts of the Spirit (as enumerated in Eph. 4:7-16); and that the human nature of sin is never eradicated during this life. Its members believe in baptism by the Holy Spirit but hold that, while water baptism is biblical, it is not relevant to the present dispensation. Any church may vote to become affiliated with Grace Gospel Fellowship, provided it meets the doctrinal standards. The constitution was revised in 1995 and now the church is divided into ten regions.

The church is present in Zaire, Puerto Rico, India, the Philippines, Australia, South Africa, Tanzania, and South America. Grace Bible College and the headquarters of the Fellowship are located in Grand Rapids, Michigan. Closely connected to Grace Gospel Fellowship are Grace Ministries International, Grace Publications, and Grace Youth Camp in Indiana.

For more information: www.ggfusa.org

Headquarters: Fellowship, 2125 Martindale SW Box 9432, Wyoming, MI 49509

IFCA INTERNATIONAL

Founded: 1930
Membership: 61,655 in 659 churches (1999)

Originally known as the Independent Fundamental Churches of America, this body was organized at Cicero, Illinois to safeguard fundamental doctrine. Members must agree with doctrines of the verbal plenary inerrant inspiration of the Bible; the virgin birth, deity, and sinless life of Jesus Christ; the death, burial, and resurrection of Christ to provide salvation for all; the person and work of the Holy Spirit; the reality of Satan and his destructive work today; the personal and bodily return of Jesus Christ; and the bodily resurrection of all people, some to eternal life and some to "everlasting punishment." The name was changed in the 1990s to disassociate the group from "radical fundamentalists," such as snake handlers.

This body is less a traditional denomination than a sponsoring agency for autonomous churches and ministries. It has a strong commitment to various forms of chaplaincy, particularly military and prison ministries, and publishes *Voice* magazine and other materials devoted to evangelical/fundamentalist ministries. There are five Bible camps, seven Bible institutes, and two children's homes.

The president of the body presides over an annual conference in which the members have voting power; an executive committee of twelve serves for three years. The constituent churches are completely independent but are required to subscribe to the statement of faith of the organization. A home office is maintained in Grandville, Michigan.

For more information: www.ifca.org

Headquarters: P.O. Box 810, Grandville, MI 49468

INDEPENDENT BAPTIST FELLOWSHIP INTERNATIONAL

Founded 1984
Membership: statistics not available; 647 churches (1999)

Raymond Barber broke with the World Baptist Fellowship in 1984 after having served as president of that body. Barber was a pastor in Fort Worth, Texas and a professor at Arlington Baptist College, a fundamentalist school. After the split he founded Norris Bible Baptist Institute and began a publication to promote his views. The IBFI is strongest in Texas and Oklahoma, but has a presence in Michigan, Ohio, and Florida; it supports about twenty-five missionaries. Though its directory lists 647 churches, about two-thirds of them have membership in other fundamentalist associations as well.

For more information: www.ibfi-nbbi.org

Headquarters: 724 North Jim Wright Frwy., Ft. Worth, TX 76108

INDEPENDENT FUNDAMENTALIST BAPTIST CHURCHES

Founded: roots to 1920s
Membership: est. over 150,000 in 1,400 churches

It is impossible to give accurate statistics for membership in the many independent fundamentalist churches because so many maintain dual membership in various state and regional associations. Some of the independent churches maintain fellowship in the New Testament Association of Independent Baptist Churches and the Fundamental Fellowship. Many of these bodies separated from the Northern Baptist Convention (see AMERICAN BAPTIST CHURCHES) in the 1920s during the Modernist controversy and formed the Fundamental Fellowship of the Northern Baptist Convention. In the 1940s some of the members created the Conservative Baptist Association* with foreign and homeland mission societies. Some of the more fundamentalist pastors criticized the Conservative Baptists for supporting the Billy Graham crusades and other "neo-evangelical" activities.

A number of organizations were founded, such as the Fundamental Baptist Fellowship (which has 1,376 individuals representing some 800 churches) and the New Testament Association of Independent Baptist Churches (14,300 members in 118 churches). Conservative Baptist state conventions in Minnesota, Illinois, Indiana, and Montana-Wyoming are basically fundamentalist. In a number of states the fundamentalists among the Conservative Baptist formed their own associations.

SOUTHWIDE BAPTIST FELLOWSHIP

Founded: 1956
Membership: at least 100,000 in 500 churches

Lee Robinson, pastor of Highland Park Baptist Church in Chattanooga, Tennessee, withdrew from the Southern Baptist Convention* in 1955 and formed the Southern Baptist Fellowship the following year. In the previous decade he had established Tennessee Temple Schools, which had four campuses and which

314

taught premillennialist theology. In 1948 he founded the Tennessee Pre-millennial Fellowship out of which the SBF developed. In 1960 he helped establish Baptist International Missions which today includes over one thousand missionaries worldwide. The doctrine and practices of the fellowship are similar to other fundamentalist churches, and nearly half of the members are also in other fundamentalist associations.

For more information: www.wayoflife.org

WORLD BAPTIST FELLOWSHIP

Founded: 1932, 1950
Membership: 998 churches (2001)

One of the most famous and controversial leaders of the early fundamentalist movement was J. Frank Norris (1877-1952) who in 1932 founded the Premillennial Baptist Missionary Fellowship, which was renamed World Baptist Fellowship in 1950. Norris was pastor of the First Baptist Church of Fort Worth, Texas, and he led his congregation out of the Southern Baptist Convention* in protest against what he perceived as liberal trends in the convention. He was also a vigorous proponent of dispensationalist theology which is taught at Arlington Baptist College, the WBF's theological institution.

The denomination does not keep statistics of overall membership, but it does list pastors who are in fellowship. About sixty percent of the congregations represented are also counted in other fellowships and associations of fundamentalist and conservative Baptist churches. The WBF officially promotes the primacy of the local church, but Norris's autocratic leadership led to splits in the WBF, the most notable being the formation of the Baptist Bible Fellowship International. The WBF continues to publish *The Fundamentalist,* a paper started by Norris in 1917 to combat modernism and promote premillennial dispensationalism. It also supports some 145 missionaries, primarily in Latin America.

For more information: www.wbfi.net

Headquarters: P. O. Box 13459, Arlington, TX 76094-0459

COMMUNITY
AND NEW PARADIGM CHURCHES

One of the most important trends in American Christianity since 1980 has been the rapid increase in the number and size of congregations with few or no ties to traditional denominations. Some authors have gone so far as to call this a "reinvention of American Protestantism" or a third (or fourth) Great Awakening. These churches report nearly a 90% increase in worship attendance since 1980.

As the population has shifted from rural and urban areas to the suburbs, the residents of new neighborhoods, like their ancestors who settled the frontier, sometimes have taken it on themselves to establish a local church and hire their own minister without consulting with denominational authorities. Increasingly in the 1980s and '90s, energetic and entrepreneurial ministers responded to demographic shifts by establishing congregations that reflected the musical and social tastes of the "baby boomer" generation. Some of these dynamic congregations have become "mega-churches" that are larger than some denominations in this *Handbook*. Most are located in the West and South in cities with populations greater than 250,000. Some of these new-style churches officially have a denominational connection (and their statistics are included in those denominations), but for the most part they are functionally independent. They resemble other New Paradigm or Community Churches more than they do congregations in their own denomination. Doctrine is rarely the defining feature of the churches in this category. In general, the New Paradigm churches stress personal transformation and spiritual growth more than traditional doctrinal themes or social justice.

The Community Church movement actually dates from the mid-1800s, when Midwestern and Western communities took charge of their own church life. The first national organization of community churches was in 1933. Community Churches are a result of the desire to eliminate over-churching in some communities; to replace the restrictiveness and divisiveness of denominationalism with self-determination and Christian unity; to refocus primary loyalty from organizations outside a community to the community itself; and, by addressing specific needs within a community, to make religious expression more immediately relevant.

There are several types of Community Churches; Federated and

United Churches resulted from mergers of congregations previously affiliated with certain denominations. Some have continued alignments with two or more denominations; others have become entirely independent. However, the majority of Community Churches never have had denominational affiliation. Since each church is adjusted to the needs of a different community, there is great variety among Community Churches in worship, work and witness styles, and methods. They are generally more flexible in worship, more casual in dress, and more focused on family issues than denominational churches. Community churches depend heavily on active lay involvement in the work of the congregation, and pastors are expected to be resource persons rather than chaplains.

Even more than the typical community church, New Paradigm or mega-churches depend on the entrepreneurial zeal and organizational skill of the head pastor. A mega-church usually has a large staff that encourages specialization. Thus there are pastors for children, youth, young adults, singles, young married people, families, and so forth. With congregations of two thousand members or more, most of the ministry of mega-churches takes place in small, intense "cell" groups inspired by Wesley's bands in early Methodism.* Researchers estimated that there were over five hundred mega-churches with over 1.5 million worshipers in the U.S. in 2000. Approximately 325 mega-churches are located in just four states: California, Texas, Florida, and Georgia.

New Paradigm and mega-churches may be compared to the shopping malls and warehouse stores that proliferated during the same period of American history. They offer an attractive variety of services under one roof: counseling, worship, private schools, support groups, teen clubs, movie theaters, health centers, sports teams, travel agencies, and business associations. Increasingly they even have food courts with chain restaurants. Deliverance Evangelical Church in Philadelphia, for instance, financed its multi-million-dollar facility in part through its profitable shopping mall, which in turn helped revitalize an economically troubled black community. Windsor Village United Methodist Church in Houston, TX has revitalized its community with business incubators and housing developments.

In some ways mega-churches are an updated organized version of the nineteenth-century camp meetings, where thousands of people traveled from miles around for twenty-four-hour, seven-day-a-week religious services, including evangelistic preaching, baptisms, weddings, Bible studies, and fellowship. The key difference from the past is an effective and creative use of sophisticated communication technologies, and a savvy business sense on the part of the pastors.

The theology and doctrine of community churches and mega-churches vary according to the beliefs of the pastor, but in general they may be termed conservative evangelical. A personal decision of faith is expected and members are encouraged to bring others to faith. Most of the New Paradigm churches have "seeker" services and classes that introduce potential converts to basic Christian doctrine and discipleship. For the most part, they require adult baptism by immersion along with intensive "discipling classes."

Some New Paradigm churches advertise themselves as churches "for people who do not like church." Many community churches and mega-churches adopt some of the attitudes, style, and worship music of the Pentecostal churches, but are less fervent in their promotion of the gifts of tongues, healing, and prophecy. New Paradigm churches focus more on personal transformation and family issues than social justice, but as political clout increases, these churches exercise influence on matters of sexuality and morality. Some of the large churches do operate charitable organizations.

Because of their independent nature, it is difficult to give an adequate account of the number and variety of New Paradigm and Community Churches, but some of the most visible organizations are included below. Many of the pastors of these churches have national and international influence through their book, workshops, tapes, Internet resources, radio and television ministries, and speaking engagements.

Suggestions for further reading:

Miller, Donald E. *Reinventing American Protestantism: Christianity in the New Millennium.* Berkeley: University of California Press, 1997.

Pritchard, G. A. *Willow Creek Seeker Services: Evaluating a New Way of Doing Church.* Grand Rapids, MI: Baker, 1996.

Quebedeaux, Richard. *Worldly Evangelicals: Has Success Spoiled America's Born Again Christians?* San Francisco: Harper & Row: 1978.

Schaller, Lyle E. *The Seven Day a Week Church.* Nashville: Abingdon, 1992.

———. *The Very Large Church.* Nashville: Abingdon, 2000.

Vaughan, John N. *Megachurches & America's Cities: How Churches Grow.* Grand Rapids, MI: Baker, 1993.

Wuthnow, Robert. *The Restructuring of American Religion: Society and Faith Since World War II.* Princeton, NJ: Princeton University Press, 1988.

Thumma, Scott. "Megachurches Today: Summary of Data from the *Faith Communities Today Project,*" http://hirr.hartsem.edu/org/faith_megachurches.html

CONGREGATIONS WITH OVER 6,000 MEMBERS

The data for this list was provided by the Faith Communities Today Project of Hartford Institute. Links to the websites of these congregations are available at (www.hartfordinstitute.org). A star (*) indicates that there is a separate entry on this congregation in the *Handbook.*

*The Potter's House (Pentecostal/non-denominational) Dallas, TX
    28,000 members (cong. claims 28,000); pastor T. D. Jakes
*Calvary Chapel of Costa Mesa (Calvary Chapel) Costa Mesa, CA
    25,000 members; pastor Chuck Smith, Sr.
*Saddleback Community Church (Community) Lake Forest, CA
    20,000 members; pastor Rick Warren
*Willow Creek Community Church (Community) South Barrington, IL
    17,500 members; pastor Bill Hybels
*World Changers Ministries (Baptist/non-denomational) College Park, GA
    20,000 members; pastor Creflo Dollar
*Southeast Christian Church (Christian) Louisville, KY.
    18,000 members; pastor Robert Russell
Crenshaw Christian Center (Church of God) Los Angeles, CA
    16,000 members; pastor Fred Price
Fellowship Church (Southern Baptist) Grapevine, TX
    16,000 members; pastor Ed Young
Windsor Village United Methodist Church (UMC) Houston, TX
    15,000 members; pastor Kirbyjon Caldwell
New Birth Missionary Baptist (Missionary Baptist) Decatur, GA
    15,000 members; pastor Eddie Long
Harvest Christian Fellowship (Calvary Chapel) Riverside, CA
    15,000 members; pastor Greg Laurie

Calvary Chapel (Calvary Chapel) Ft. Lauderdale, FL
    15,000 members; pastor Robert Coy
New Light Christian Center (Pentecostal/non-denominational)
    Houston, TX
    14,000 members; pastor I. V. Hillard
West Angeles Church of God in Christ (COGIC) Los Angeles, CA
    13,000 members; pastor Charles E. Blake
First Baptist Church (Baptist) Hammond, IN
    12,000 members; pastor Jack Schaap
Brooklyn Tabernacle (Pentecostal/non-denominational) Brooklyn,
    NY
    10,000 members; pastor Jim Cymbala
Christian Cultural Center (Non-denominational) Brooklyn, NY
    10,000 members; pastor A. R. Bernard, Sr.
Fellowship of the Woodlands (Baptist/non-denominational) The
    Woodlands, TX
    10,000 members; pastor Kerry Shook
Greater St. Stephen Full Gospel Church (Full Gospel Fellowship)
    New Orleans, LA
    10,000 members; pastor Paul Morton
Mars Hill Bible Church (Bible/Fundamentalist) Grandville, MI
    10,000 members; pastor Rob Bell, Jr.
Grace Community Church (Community) Sun Valley, CA
    10,000 members; pastor John MacArthur
First Baptist Church of Central Florida (Southern Baptist) Orlando,
    FL
    10,000 members; pastor Clayton Cloer
Detroit World Outreach Center (Assemblies of God) Redford, MI
    9,200 members; pastor Jack Wallace
Coral Ridge Presbyterian Church (PCA) Ft. Lauderdale, FL
    9,000 members; pastor James Kennedy
The Dream Center (Assemblies of God) Los Angeles, CA
    8,900 members; pastor Matthew Barnett
Christ's Church of the Valley (Christian) Peoria, AZ
    8,700 members; pastor Donald J. Wilson
Faith Central Missionary Baptist Church (Missionary Baptist)
    Inglewood, CA
    8,000 members; pastor Kenneth Ulmer
The Church on the Way (Four Square Gospel) Van Nuys, CA
    8,000 members; pastors Jack Hayford and Scott Bauer

New Hope Christian Fellowship (Four Square Gospel) Honolulu, HI
    8,000 members; pastor Wayne Cordeiro
The Jericho City of Praise (Baptist) Landover, MD
    8,000 members; pastor Betty Peebles
Brentwood Baptist Church (Southern Baptist) Houston, TX
    8,000 members; pastor Joe Ratlifff
First Baptist Church (Southern Baptist) Houston, TX
    8,000 members; pastor Gregg Matte
Second Baptist Church (Southern Baptist) Houston, TX
    8,000 members; pastor Edwin Young
Calvary Chapel (Calvary Chapel) Capistrano Beach, CA
    8,000 members; pastor Church Smith, Jr.
First Baptist Church (Southern Baptist) Jacksonville, FL
    7,800 members; pastor Jerry Vines
Deliverance Evangelistic Church (Conservative Evangelical) Philadelphia, PA
    7,300 members; pastor Benjamin Smith
Memorial Baptist Church (Southern Baptist) Killeen, TX
    7,200 members; pastor Joe D. Rich
Greater Allen Cathedral of New York (African Methodist Episcopal) Jamaica, NY
    7,000 members; pastor Floyd Flake
High Desert Church (Baptist) Victorville, CA
    7,000 members; pastor Tom Mercer
Calvary Chapel (Calvary Chapel) Downey, CA
    7,000 members; pastor Jeff Johnson
McLean Bible Church (Bible/fundamentalist) Vienna, VA
    7,000 members; pastor Lon Solomon
Times Square Church (Pentecostal/Non-denominational) New York, NY
    7,000 members; pastors David Wilkerson, Carter Conlon
Rhema Bible Church (Bible/Fundamentalist) Tulsa, OK
    7,000 members; pastor Kenneth Hagin
Victory Christian Center (Independent) Oklahoma City, OK
    6,500 members; pastor Mark Crow
Elmbrook Church (Community) Brookfield, WI
    6,500 members; pastor Stuart Briscoe
North Phoenix Baptist Church (Southern Baptist) Phoenix, AR
    6,500 members; pastor Dan Yeary

First Baptist Church (Southern Baptist) Atlanta, GA
    6,155 members; pastor Charles Stanley
Shepherd of the Hills (Christian) Porter Ranch, CA
    6,000 members; pastor Dudley Rutherford
Jubilee Christian Center (Community) San Jose, CA
    6,000 members; pastor Dick Bernal
New Life Church (Community) Colorado Springs, CO
    6,000 members; pastor Ted Haggard
Greater Grace Temple of the Apostolic Faith (Pentecostal Assemblies of the World) Detroit, MI
    6,000 members; pastor Charles Ellis III

CALVARY CHAPELS

> Founded: 1965
> Membership: statistics not available,
> but at least 500,000 in 1,000 churches (2004)

The Calvary Chapels is one of the most successful new denominations in U.S. history. It began as a single Calvary Chapel in Costa Mesa, California, in 1965 and has grown to over seven hundred related congregations, most of them also named Calvary Chapel, across the nation. The founder and head of Calvary Chapels is Church Smith (b. 1927), who began his ministry career in 1946 in the Foursquare Gospel Church.* Frustrated with the restrictions of that and other denominations, Smith went independent in the early sixties with a focus on campus ministry. His focus was on addressing the everyday needs and concerns of his listeners. Two years after taking over the twenty-five-member Calvary Chapel, he had increased attendance to over two thousand. Soon they built a much larger facility which regularly has over twenty-five thousand worshipers (18,000 members). It is the fountainhead for the Calvary Chapel network.

One of the hallmarks of Smith's ministry in the 1960s was reaching out to the "hippies" and drug users of the California beach culture. He was a leader of the "Jesus Freak" movement that encouraged people to "turn off to drugs and on to Jesus." Smith founded over a hundred "community houses" modeled on the original "House of Miracles" for recent converts who needed a supportive environment.

Smith was a pioneer in the adaptation of secular rock and roll music for Christian worship. He established the Maranatha Music and Calvary Chapel recording companies, which have had a major impact on contemporary Protestant music. This "praise music" uses guitar and piano rather than traditional church instruments and has an upbeat tempo that has become very popular on Christian radio stations. This informal, lively music corresponds to the practice of wearing casual clothing and following very informal worship. Worship, fellowship, and study times may be very emotional since members are encouraged to express their love for Christ, love for one another, and offer their personal testimonies of salvation.

Calvary Chapels emphasize evangelism, conversion, and personal experience of the Holy Spirit, but they try to do so in an invitational rather than confrontational way. Slightly fewer than 15 percent of the members report that they had no previous church connection before joining a Calvary Chapel.

For more information: www.calvarychapel.com

INTERNATIONAL COUNCIL
OF COMMUNITY CHURCHES

Founded: 1950
Membership: 115,812 in 192 churches (2002)

Not a denomination in the traditional sense, the International Council of Community Churches provides services to several hundred independently organized and operated community churches in the U.S. and around the world. There are probably another one hundred thousand members in community churches that are not part of the International Council.

The stated purposes of the council are (1) to be an answer to Christ's prayer: "That they may all be one" (John 17:21 NRSV); (2) to affirm the worth and dignity of every person; (3) to attend to human need and suffering throughout the world; (4) to seek and share the truth; (5) to build toward a new world of peace.

The current organization resulted from a 1950 merger of two other councils: one composed of predominantly black congregations, the other of churches with predominantly white memberships. The council holds an annual conference to which every member church can send two voting members, at least one of whom must be a lay person. This conference elects a president, an executive director, a board of trustees, and other officers who carry on the business of the Council between conferences. The executive director and a small staff oversee the projects of the Council on a daily basis; headquarters are in Frankfort, Illinois.

The Council's services include ecclesiastical endorsement, personnel placement, continuing education, direct and brokered consultation for help in various areas, and supportive networks for clergy and their spouses and children. Publications include *The Christian Community,* a monthly newspaper; *The Pastor's Journal,* a quarterly for professionals; and materials from the Community Church Press.

It should be noted that many of the Council's member churches do not use the word *Community* in their names. Moreover, many churches that do include this term in their names are affiliated with a denomination, are members of a national organization outside the historic movement, or are independent congregations.

For more information: www.akcache.com/community/icccnat.html

Headquarters: 21116 Washington Parkway, Frankfort, IL 60423

THE POTTER'S HOUSE

Founded: 1996
Membership: 28,000 in 1 church

Thomas D. Jakes, Sr. is one of the most prominent figures in the history of African-American Pentecostalism.* His website describes him as a "pastor, community advocate, humanitarian, author, songwriter, playwright, conference speaker and broadcaster." Like many Pentecostal preachers, Jakes started with a storefront church, but his keen entrepreneurial and preaching skills helped him create one of the largest interracial faith communities in American history. His Potter's House specializes in "ministry to the shattered," and has a number of vibrant ministries to the homeless, hopeless, and addicted in the Dallas area.

324

Jakes is probably best known for his television broadcasts on cable TV networks such as BET (Black Entertainment Television). The church's distinctive blending of economics and spirituality is evident in the mission statement which includes the desire "to become a global voice, along a lifelong journey of spiritual and economic hope, encouragement and empowerment to people locally, nationally and around the world." Theologically, the church affirms many common elements of conservative evangelicalism including the inerrancy of Scripture, the premillenial return of Christ, and everlasting punishment for unbelievers. Jakes leads an extensive network of like-minded pastors who have partnered with the Potter's House and use resources provided by the organization.

For more information: www.thepottershouse.org

Headquarters: 6777 W. Kiest Blvd, Dallas, TX 75236

SADDLEBACK CHURCH

> Founded: 1980
> Membership: 20,000 in 1 church

Saddleback Church has become a legend in American Protestantism. In 1980 it was founded by a recent seminary graduate named Rick Warren in the Saddleback Valley of California with two hundred people and has since grown to be one of the largest mega-churches in the country. Warren described his goal for the church as "a place where the hurting, the depressed, the confused can find love, acceptance, help, hope, forgiveness and encouragement." An average of twenty thousand people attend worship services, and the church has more than two hundred ministries locally. Saddleback has helped establish thirty-four "daughter congregations" around the country and appears to be moving towards becoming its own denomination.

Warren's 1995 book, *The Purpose Driven Church,* made Saddleback and its pastor internationally famous. The church reports that over 350,000 church leaders have been trained in his model of church growth. The book was praised in business journals as a guide to entrepreneurship. Another of Warren's books, *The Purpose Driven*

Life, is the fastest selling book of all time with more than 20 million sold in less than two years. Warren also established Internet resources to mentor pastors in his his approach to church building and ministry. In this way, the Saddleback network of Rick Warren stretches across many denominations.

For more information: www.saddleback.com

Headquarters: 1 Saddleback Pkwy, Lake Forest, CA 92630

SOUTHEAST CHRISTIAN CHURCH (CHRISTIAN)

Founded: 1962
Membership: 18,000 in 1 church

The Southeast Christian Church started in 1962 as a fairly typical new church start in the Christian Church,* but when Robert Russell took over as pastor four years later the church developed a vision for expansion of the facilities. After having outgrown two sanctuaries, the congregation decided to build a massive campus off a major parkway in the 1990s. Over $30,000,000 was raised for the project, and now Southeast is one of the largest congregations in the U.S. and is a major economic force in Louisville. The congregation's spectacular Christmas and Easter performances attract thousands of visitors each year. Over 850 members have participated in short-term mission programs.

The church offers a variety of ministries to all age groups as well as special programs for blended families, disabled and deaf persons, and Spanish-language services. Their mission program includes an assertive Messianic mission to Jews. The church's mission statement is "to evangelize the lost; edify the saved; minister to those in need; and be a conscience in the community." The statement of faith includes much of the Apostles' Creed, but adds a number of beliefs important to the Christian Church,* such as believers' baptism by immersion and local congregational autonomy.

For more information: www.southeastchristian.org

Headquarters: 920 Blankenbaker Parkway, Louisville, KY 40243-1845

UNIVERSAL FELLOWSHIP
OF METROPOLITAN COMMUNITY CHURCHES

Founded: 1970
Membership: est. 44,000 in 300 churches (1998)

This Protestant body is unique among Christian bodies in that it was founded specifically to reach out to and affirm homosexual persons. The church's theology is based on the idea that God's love should be preserved to a segment of society often excluded from, and sometimes ridiculed for, participation in church life. This awareness prompted Troy D. Perry (b. 1940) to create a denomination in which such marginalized people could find genuine acceptance in a context of Christian worship and service. Perry, himself a homosexual, had been discharged from the Baptist* church he served as pastor and was ostracized from his denomination. He called a congregation into being in Los Angeles, and soon churches were organized in other cities. In the summer of 1970, the first general conference was held.

Heterosexuals may and do belong to the church, but a large percentage of the membership is homosexual. The denomination describes its ministry as a shared one—lay and clergy, women and men, privileged and underprivileged, lesbian, gay, and heterosexual. Forty-three percent of its clergy are women.

The church professes traditional Christian theology on such doctrines as Scripture, the Trinity, and the sacraments. The Bible, "interpreted by the Holy Spirit in conscience and faith," is the guide for faith and discipline. Since its members come from all types of Christian churches, the worship style, liturgy, and practice of congregations is eclectic and varied. Some congregations are more or less Pentecostal* while others are very liturgical. Baptism and Holy Communion are the sacraments.

The membership of this denomination is active in a variety of ministries, reflecting its primary orientation to the social gospel and liberation theology. In particular, it has sought to address the needs of the hungry, the homeless, and the powerless. It supports a freeze on nuclear weapons and is committed to eradicating sexism in its theology and in society at large. The civil rights of all people are a major concern. It also addresses the AIDS epidemic as a major social issue, partly because incidences of the disease are so prevalent among its own membership.

The church faces the controversial nature of its existence by stating that its members accept homosexuality as "a gift from God," just as heterosexuality is "a gift from God." Nonetheless, it holds that "our sexuality is not and should not be the focal point of our lives. The MCC emphasizes that everything in our life, including our sexuality, must center on our relationship with God, through faith in Jesus Christ."

The government of the church is vested in a General Council, consisting of Elders and District Coordinators, clergy, and lay delegates. The body applied for membership in the National Council of the Churches of Christ in the U.S.A. in 1983 and was declined, but it hopes eventually to become a part of that ecumenical organization, with which it remains in dialogue. It does participate as an official observer in World Council of Churches events.

For more information: www.mccchurch.org

Headquarters: 8704 Santa Monica Blvd. 2nd Floor, West Hollywood, CA 90069

WILLOW CREEK COMMUNITY CHURCH

Founded: 1975
Membership: est. 20,000 in 1 church

Willow Creek is one of the most successful and famous community churches, and it is developing its own national network of similar growth-oriented, non-denominational congregations. It developed out of a popular youth ministry (Son City) of the South Park Church in Park Ridge, Illinois, which grew to some 1,000 teenagers. The group was led by Bill Hybels, the founding pastor of Willow Creek, who employed contemporary music and drama as a way to apply the Bible to the lives of American teenagers. In 1975 Hybels and his co-workers rented a movie theater to hold services directed toward youth. As attendance grew to over 2,000, the members purchased ninety acres of undeveloped land in South Barrington and built a state-of-the-art auditorium in 1981.

The Willow Creek model for church development includes hundreds of small groups within the congregation that focus on different needs. Among them are "seeker groups" and discipleship groups. Evangelism is seen as the work of the entire congregation, and the large gatherings use the latest in stagecraft and musical technology. The doctrine of the church is basically evangelical Protestant. They practice believers' baptism but offer infant dedication ceremonies for children of baptized parents. Through the Willow Creek Association, the church is developing its own denominational identity, but the distinguishing characteristics are those of style and structure rather than doctrine or history. Currently there are about eight thousand congregations in the Association, but many of them have denominational affiliations as well. Tens of thousands of church leaders have been trained in the Willow Creek method.

For more information: www.willowcreek.org; www.willowcreek.com

Headquarters: Willow Creek Church, 67 East Algonquin Road in South Barrington, IL 60010.

WORLD CHANGERS MINISTRIES

Founded: 1986
Membership: 18,000 members in one church

Since their marriage in 1986, Creflo Dollar and his wife Taffi have become one of the most popular ministry teams of the electronic church. They are attractive, charismatic, and engaging on television and in person. These qualities contributed greatly to the stunning growth of the World Changers Ministry they first established in the cafeteria of a Georgia elementary school that Dollar attended as a child. A decade later he dedicated the World Dome, an 8,500-seat worship facility complete with state of the art audio and video equipment. Dollar boasts that the facility "had not only been prayed for, but ... was paid for."

Dollar is most famous for his vigorous promotion of "Prosperity Theology" in addition to the more traditional Pentecostal* gifts of healing and speaking in tongues. A major theme of his addresses and his educational programs is that believers who tithe and live according to the Scripture will not only get out of debt but will grow financially prosperous. He points to his own prosperity, which includes two Rolls Royce cars and tailor-made suits, as evidence of the blessings of God on the faithful. The congregation's most famous member is the former heavy-weight boxing champion Evander Hollifield. A significant portion of the congregation's $80,000,000 annual budget goes to purchase television time on cable networks such as BET (Black Entertainment Television).

For more information: www.worldchangers.org

Headquarters: P.O. Box 490124, College Park, GA 30349.

ISLAM

Islam is second only to Christianity in size and geographical scope among world religions, but it is only in the last quarter of the twentieth century that Muslims have been a significant presence in the United States. At the beginning of the twenty-first century Muslims outnumber Episcopalians and many other denominations in the U.S. If current trends keep up, there will be more Muslims than Jews or Lutherans in a generation. Despite this increasing presence in American religious and social life, Islam is poorly understood in the U.S., and Muslims have been subject to unfair stereotyping. This has been particularly the case since the militant attacks of Al Qaida, which promotes a violent fundamentalist ideology. It is important to keep in mind that such militants are a small percentage of Muslims. Islam is a monotheistic religion that has close historical and theological ties to Christianity and Judaism. Like them, it seeks to build a just and peaceful society based on a rational moral code. Islam has had a long and glorious tradition. In fact, when the Christian West was in its so-called Dark Ages, Islamic countries were renowned for their science, art, and philosophy.

But in the nineteenth and twentieth centuries, many Islamic regions were colonized by the industrialized Western nations. Their development was impaired by colonial rule, and for many Muslims anti-Western sentiment grew strong. For Muslims living in the U.S., there is the ever-present question of how much one can live like an American and remain faithful to the commandments of Allah. The question of how fully one can embrace American culture while remaining true to one's religious faith is, of course, common to all devout people in America, regardless of their religion.

331

History. The words "muslim" and "islam" are based on an Arabic root meaning obedience. A Muslim is one who is obedient to God in his or her thoughts and deeds. According to Muslims, Islam actually began with the Patriarch Abraham (Ibrahim), with whom God made a covenant. Abraham was obedient to God; therefore, Abraham was a Muslim—one who submits to the will of Allah. His was the true religion that later suffered corruption. The oldest son of Abraham was Ishmael (Ismail), whom the Arabs claim as their forebear. In Islam, it was Ishmael, the first born, whom Abraham willingly offered to God rather than Isaac. According to the sacred text of Islam, the Quran, Abraham and Ishmael built the first Ka'ba in Mecca as a place of worship for the one true God.

Historically, though, Islam as an organized religion developed out of Judaism over six hundred years after the birth of Jesus. Within a hundred years of the Hijrah in 622, Muslims conquered much of the ancient Christian world: Syria, Palestine, Egypt, North Africa, and Spain. In addition to the astounding military success of the early Muslim armies, this represents one of the most rapid expansions of any new religious movement. After the initial expansion of Islam, though, the various Muslim principalities and sultanates became divided among themselves. Eventually many were conquered by the Mongols who in turn were conquered by the Turks. In 1453 the great Christian city of Constantinople fell to the Turks and became an Islamic capital whose name was eventually changed to Istanbul. Now Muslims pray in mosques in Africa, Europe, America, much of Asia, and Indonesia. But it all began with one man.

Origins: Muslims around the world still proclaim, "There is no God but Allah, and Muhammad is his prophet." This greatest prophet of Islam was a member of the Quraysh tribe of Mecca, which was an important center for trade and religion in Arabia. Mecca housed the Ka'ba, a very important shrine among the people of Arabia. Thousands made pilgrimage each year to visit the Ka'ba and to see or to touch the holy stone contained therein. They also left gifts before the idols located at that time in the shrine.

When he was twenty-five years old, Muhammad married a wealthy widow, Khadijah, and managed her extensive holdings and trade. Every year during the month of Ramadan the family would leave the heat of the city to live in one of the cool caves nearby. During one of these family retreats, Muhammad received a call to be a prophet. He heard a voice that told him to read. When he protested that he could not read, the voice commanded him again. He then left the cave and saw the angel Gabriel (Jibril), who told him that he was to be God's messenger.

Later the angel revealed to Muhammad that he was called to reform the religion of the people of Mecca. They must get rid of their idols and worship only the true God of Abraham, Isaac, and Ishmael. Muhammad's first converts were Khadijah, his cousin Ali, and his friend Abu Bakr. Muhammad's reform offended his own tribe, who profited from the pilgrimages and gifts to the idols in the Ka'ba. After some thirteen years of struggling to convert the people of Mecca, a group of pilgrims from Yathrib, now known as Medina, heard Muhammad preach and accepted him as Allah's prophet. Messianic hopes were high among the Jews in Yathrib, and for a brief period early Muslims and Jews were united in their hope for the millennial kingdom.

In Mecca, though, the anger against the prophet increased, and in 622 C.E. Muhammad fled to Yathrib in order to avoid assassination. This flight to Yathrib is known as the *Hijrah*, and it begins the Muslim calendar. Dates in Islamic lands are counted in years after the *Hijrah* (A.H.), just as Christian lands date events before and after the birth of Jesus. Because of its importance in the development of Islam, Yathrib became known as Al-Medina (*the city*). It was in Medina that Muhammad laid the foundation for the religion of Islam and became a great chieftain. Medina remains one of the sacred cities of Islam and is visited by millions of pilgrims.

Over the years Muhammad received many divine messages in a state of trance. These prophecies, called *surahs,* were written down by his hearers and later collected and edited in the book we know as the Quran, or simply the Reading. They are organized according to length rather than content or chronology. Islam teaches that the Quran is the faithful recording of the word of God as it was delivered to Muhammad. It is written in the beautiful and poetic Arabic of the time of Muhammad.

After several years organizing his followers in Medina, Muhammad entered Mecca as a victor. The residents converted, and the idols were destroyed. Soon afterward Muhammad became the virtual emperor of Arabia and outlawed all forms of idolatry. Only monotheists—Muslims, Jews, and Christians—were tolerated. Before Muhammad died in 632 C.E., it is said that he was taken by Gabriel to Jerusalem where he visited the temple site. There

Muhammad ascended into heaven and met Moses and Jesus. The rock from which he ascended remains a holy site. One of the most beautiful buildings in the world, the Dome of Rock, was built in 687 over the rock.

Shortly after this journey by night, Muhammad died. His death was a blow to his followers, but they remembered that he was a mortal and not a god. Muslims follow the teachings of Muhammad; they do not worship him or view him as divine. The prophet was succeeded by his close companion and relative Abu Bakr. The early successors of the prophet are known as the Caliphs, which has much the same meaning as the English word "steward." A caliph (*khalifah*) acts on behalf of another. The first four Caliphs were instrumental in defining the nature of Islam and ensuring its long-term survival, and they are known to Muslims as the four "rightly guided" Caliphs.

One of the early tasks of the Caliphs was to insure that the Quran was written in an authentic and unalterable form so that the words of the prophet would not be corrupted through the years. A single version of the Quran was approved and all others destroyed. Even today, there are not different versions of the Quran. Translations into modern languages are all considered interpretations of the Quran rather than the Quran itself. Devout Muslims, who no longer speak this form of Arabic even in Arabia, learn the language of the Quran and commit much of the book to memory. Arabic, like Hebrew in Judaism, is one of the things that bind the worldwide Islamic community (the *Umma*) together.

During the period of the Caliphs, other sayings of Muhammad and remembrances of the prophet were collected and classified. These sayings or *sunnahs* are recorded in the *Hadith*. Though they are not considered Scripture equal to the Quran, they play an important role in helping to define Islamic practices and laws. The period of the "rightly guided" Caliphs was crucial in defining Islam, but in 662 C.E. it ended with the assassination of Ali, the last of Muhammad's original companions to lead the Muslims. The leadership of Islam passed to the Umayyad dynasty after a period of internal dispute, but their rule was rejected by many supporters of Ali. It was at this point that Shi'ite* Islam was born.

The basic idea of Islam is submission to the will of Allah. The will of God was expressed through the prophets, many of whom are common to Judaism and Christianity. According to Islam, there were five great prophets: Noah, Abraham, Moses, Jesus, and Muhammad.

Many Christians are surprised to learn that the Quran teaches that Mary was a virgin when Jesus was conceived and that Jesus worked miracles. Muslims, like most Christians, believe that Jesus will return at the end of human history, but they do not believe that Jesus was divine nor do they accept the idea of the crucifixion and resurrection of Jesus.

Though there are different branches of Islam, some of which have been in conflict with each other, there are some things basic to all forms of Islam (excluding the Nation of Islam*). There are five major beliefs in Islam: (1) There is only one God; (2) there are angels; (3) there have been many prophets, but there is only one message; (4) there will be a final judgment; (5) it is possible to have knowledge of God and God's will. Islam emphasizes the ability of ordinary people to know and understand the teachings of God; therefore, Islam emphasizes the intellect. Every faithful Muslim is a student. There is a Muslim saying that God's first creation was the pen. The first word God revealed to Muhammad was read. It is obligatory in Islam to read, study, and seek knowledge; therefore, the ink of the scholar is considered to be more valuable than the blood of a martyr.

Even more important than these five fundamental beliefs are the Five Pillars of Islam. Every Muslim must follow these five pillars in order to attain heaven, but provisions are made for the weak, the poor, and the infirm. The demands of religion, in Islam, should never imperil the health of one's spouse and children. The Five Pillars are:

(1) *Shahada*: "There is no God, but Allah and Muhammad is his prophet." This is the foundation of Islamic monotheism combined with confidence that the words Muhammad spoke were a true revelation of the will of the one God.

(2) *Salat*: five prayers daily facing Mecca. The prayers are proscribed, as is the bodily posture. By praying five times a day and humbling oneself physically before God, Muslims are reminded that humans are to submit to God in all things, at all times, and in all places.

(3) *Zakat*: ritual almsgiving. Muslims are expected to give 2.5 percent of their income to the needy. This is beyond the obligation to pay taxes, and the money must go to those in need rather than just any charitable organization.

(4) *Siyam*: a one-month fast during Ramadan. This is in imitation of the practice of Muhammad, and it makes Ramadan the holi-

est time of the year for Muslims. The fast is a daytime fast, but exceptions are made for those who are elderly, pregnant, or in poor health. The Ramadan fast emphasizes that the true fast is to refrain from evil and to be humble enough to ask forgiveness from those one has wronged.

(5) *Hajj*: a pilgrimage to Mecca. Each Muslim is espected to make at least one journey to Mecca to pray at the Ka'ba during his or her life. Today more than two million do so each year, at great cost to the Saudi Arabian government, which provides hospitality. Muslims are forbidden to borrow money for their Hajj or to impoverish their families.

The Five Pillars and the five basic tenets form the foundation of Islam, but there is much more to the Muslim life than these. Islam, like Judaism,* is an all-encompassing religion, and Islamic scholars through the centuries have offered guidance in how to live according to the commands of God. Muslims have always needed teachers to educate people about the law and to interpret the law so that it may be applied to every circumstance of life. These teachers and interpreters of the law are called *Muftis*. Those who help worshipers in the mosque understand and apply the law are sometimes called Imams; others are known as Mullahs.

Islam is a practical religion that gives guidance for daily life rather than encouraging asceticism. Moderation in all things, even religion, is stressed. Some things, like images, alcohol, and pork, are forbidden. Other things, like divorce, are permitted but discouraged. Thus there is some variation in Muslim customs because they reflect local traditions. Islam in the U.S. is different from Islam in Pakistan, for instance, but the Islamic ideal is that the whole world will become submissive to the will of God.

Islamic law is known as the *Sharia*, and it includes not only what Americans would consider criminal matters, such as theft, but also instructions on how family life and society should be organized. It also includes laws regarding religious observance, devotion, and worship. Sharia is based on the Quran and the Hadith of the prophet, but it also includes the work of legal scholars who faced the difficult task of applying teachings originally given in Arabia to the quite different situation of Muslims in many cultures. This process of interpretation of Sharia is called *ijtihad*. Sunni* and Shi'ite* Islam differ on important aspects of Sharia.

Islam in the United States: There were Muslims in America from the earliest days of European exploration and colonization. Some of these were Moors employed by the Spanish conquistadores; others were Africans brought as slaves. In the colonial period enslaved Africans in America were more likely to be Muslim than Christian. After the Civil War, Syrian and Lebanese immigrants left their farms in the Middle East in order to work in America's burgeoning metropolises. Some of the new arrivals were Christians, but many were Muslims. Muslim neighborhoods developed in New York City, Chicago, Detroit, and other major northern cities. As the Ottoman Empire slowly collapsed in the years leading up to World War I, more immigrants from the Middle East fled to America.

The most celebrated conversion of an American of European descent to Islam came in 1888 when Alexander Russell Webb, the U.S. Council to the Philippines spoke the *Shahada*. He promoted his new faith and worked for greater toleration of Islam through his journal *The Moslem World*. He was also a featured speaker at the famous World's Parliament of Religions in Chicago in 1893, which brought the world's great religious traditions to the American public's attention.

Immigration laws enacted after World War I to restrict the immigration of non-whites slowed the growth of Islam in the U. S. With the changes made in American immigration policy in 1965, an average of thirty thousand Muslims a year have immigrated to this country. Muslim immigrants, like their Catholic and Jewish predecessors, have located primarily in the urban centers of the Northeast, the Midwest, and the West Coast. American Muslims come from over sixty different nations; therefore, there has been some difficulty in relating divergent cultural expressions of the religion. Slightly over one-fourth of U.S. Muslims immigrated from the Middle East, but almost as many came from Eastern European countries, especially the Balkans.

Because of the diversity of national origins, the architectural style of mosques, leadership styles, and attitudes toward gender roles differ widely among American Muslims. Despite the diversity of American Islam, certain things, such as learning Arabic, reciting the prayers, and reading the Qur'an, unite Muslims of all national origins. Muslims in general are much more conservative than mainstream American culture. In terms of personal behavior in public Muslims share the values of conservative Jews and Christians. They

337

urge men and women to be modest in dress, monogamous in sex, respectful to others, and generous to the poor.

The major branches of Islam are represented in the U.S., but they are not organized as institutions the way Christian denominations are. There are Sunni mosques and organizations to promote and defend Sunnism, and there are similar organizations for the Shi'ites, but there are no headquarters for the different branches that maintain membership lists or statistics.

African-American Muslims: In the twentieth century, Islam began attracting significant numbers of African-American converts. Estimates range from five hundred thousand to over a million African-American Muslims in the U.S. today. For many converts, Islam represented an alternative to Christianity, which they associated with slaveholders. Further, Islam represented a connection with their ancestors; for at least some of the Africans brought in bondage to these shores had been Muslims in their homeland. Finally, Islam offered a practical discipline and control over one's destiny that many felt was denied to them in the dominant culture.

It was Malcolm X (1925–65) who did the most to spotlight Islam in the African-American community. He had originally been a leader in the Nation of Islam;* however, he rejected that organization when he made his *hajj* to Mecca and encountered Sunni Islam in its full international and interracial character. He saw that racism of every kind is condemned in Islam; all Muslims are equal in the eyes of God and will face the same judgment, just as all Muslims on hajj wear the same white robes of penitence and submission to Allah.

Malcolm X brought this message of racial equality back to the United States, but he was murdered just as he was establishing his own Islamic organization for African-Americans. After his death, others followed his example and continued his cause. Among them were notable athletes who took Muslim names, such as Muhammad Ali and Kareem Abdul Jabbar. African-American Muslims tend to establish their own mosques and publishing houses, but the same is true of Muslims who have recently immigrated. Perhaps twenty-five percent of American Muslims today are of African descent.

Islamic Circle of North America, 166-26 89th Ave., Jamaica, NY 11432

The Muslim American Society (The ministry of W. Deen Muhammad); PO Box 1944, Calumet City, IL 60409.

American Muslim Council; 1212 New York Ave. NW, Washington, DC 20005;

Suggestions for further reading:

Armstrong, Karen. *Islam: A Short History.* New York: Modern Library, 2000.

Esposito, John L. *Islam: The Straight Path.* New York: Oxford University Press, 1988.

Esposito, John L, ed. *The Oxford Encyclopedia of the Modern Islamic World.* 4 vols. New York: Oxford University Press, 1995.

Haddad, Yvonne Yazbeck. *The Islamic Impact.* Syracuse, NY: Syracuse University Press, 1984.

Haddad, Yvonne Yazbeck and Jane L. Smith, eds. *Muslim Communities in North America.* New York: Oxford University Press, 1993.

Malcolm X, with Alex Haley. *The Autobiography of Malcolm X.* New York: Ballantine, 1973.

McCloud, Aminah Beverly. *African American Islam.* New York: Routledge, 1995.

Nu'man, Fareed H. *The Muslim Population in the United States.* Washington, DC: The American Muslim Council, 1992.

Turner, Richard B. *Islam in the African-American Experience.* Bloomington: Indiana University Press, 1997.

SUNNI ISLAM

Founded: 622 C.E (major influx in the U.S. after 1965)
Membership: est. between 3.5 and 6 million
in approx. 1,500 mosques

Ninety percent of the world's one billion Muslims are in one of the four orthodox branches of Sunni Islam.* The Sunni teach that the "gate of *ijtihad*," the process of interpretation of the law, was closed in the tenth century. Before the gate of *ijtihad* was closed, four major schools of legal thought had developed in Sunni Islam. They are the Hanafi, Maliki, Shafi, and Hanbali legal traditions. This is not the place to discuss the technicalities of the different schools, but it is important to recognize that the different schools impacted different areas of the Muslim world. The schools also differ in their level of strictness.

Hanafi is the oldest school and was the official teaching of the Abbasid dynasty, and it continues to influence regions once controlled by the Abasids, such as Egypt, Syria, Jordan, India, and Turkey. The jurist Malik B. Anas placed great weight on the Hadith in interpreting the law, and he also emphasized the law's role in promoting the common good. *Maliki* law has been influencial in parts of Egypt, the Persian Gulf countries, and North Africa. Sharifi law is based on a more strict interpretation of the Quran and Hadith than the previous two, and it is suspicious of human legal reasoning. It has been influencial in southern Arabia and Southeast Asia as well as East Africa. The latest and strictest interpretation of the law, the *Hanbali*, is also the smallest. But it has become very influential since it is promoted in central Arabia and forms the basis of Saudi Arabia's legal system.

Theoretically, each school accepts the others as orthodox, but from time to time charismatic religious reformers will promote one view to the exclusion of the others. Sunni Muslims are expected to follow the teachings of one of the four traditions faithfully rather than mixing them. This has been difficult in Western countries, such as the United States, because Muslims from different regions of the world, following different schools of *Sharia*, often participate in the same mosques.

Membership figures for the Sunni in the U.S. are very rough estimates, since there are no central organizations for Muslims. Mosques are primarily places of prayer and study and generally do not keep or report statistics. The Islamic Society of North America (ISNA), located in Plainfield, Indiana, is the largest organization that provides support for Muslim ministries. In particular, it helps to establish full-time Islamic schools and reviews textbooks for Muslims. It also helps Muslims observe dietary laws while under U.S. government control (e.g., in the military or prison). The ISNA also has programs aimed at keeping youth involved in Islam and in training Islamic workers.

For more information: www.isna.net; www.amermuslim.org

Islamic Society of North America, P.O. Box 38, Plainfield, IN 46168

www.icna.org

SHI'ITE ISLAM

Founded: 662 C.E.
Membership: perhaps 100,000 in U.S. (2000)

About 10% of the world's one billion Muslims (roughly one hundred million) are Shi'ite instead of Sunni. The split between the Shi'a and the Sunni came when the fourth Caliph, Ali, was assassinated by extremists who believed that he had fallen into unbelief because he had accepted human arbitration during a dispute rather than letting God settle the matter through warfare. With the sudden death of Ali, the Umayyad family seized power and established the first Muslim ruling dynasty.

Ali was a very pious man, and his followers rejected the worldliness of the Umayyads. The Shi'is, as his followers were called, viewed Ali as the First Caliph, rather than the Fourth, and they traced the line of true Caliphs through Ali's family. Ali's second son, Husain, was put forward as the true successor when the first Umayyad ruler, Muawiyyah died in 680 C.E. In that year the Umayyad army surrounded Husain and his family on the plain of Kerbala near Kufa in modern day Iraq. Though it was a holy day of fasting, they were all murdered, with Husain dying while holding his infant son.

The murder of Husain and his family became a central aspect of Shi'ite devotion, and the shrine of Husain in Kerbala remains one of the most holy sites to Shi'ites. For centuries the story has been retold and even acted out as a "passion play," reminding Shi'ites of the importance of martyrdom. The Shi'ites grew strong in Iraq and Iran and developed a distinctive form of Islam.

The Shi'ites use the title "Imam," rather than "Caliph," to refer to the true leader of Islam. Many Shi'ites expect a "Twelfth Imam" to appear at the start of the messianic age. The clergy in Shi'ism generally have more authority to interpret Islamic law and observances than in Sunni Islam. Shi'ism has tended to be more flexible and more volatile than Sunni'ism since it allows for greater adaptation to changing social and historical conditions. In Yemen, the Zaydi legal tradition has been a force for moderation and social justice, but the last Zaydi Imam was overthrown by revolution in 1962.

Shi'ites have tended to promote greater separation between politics and religion than the Sunni, and there is a strong mystical element to Shi'ite faith. However, over the centuries, Shi'ite religious

341

leaders often led popular resistance movements against regimes they found to be unjust. In 1979 the Shi'ites in Iran rebelled against the oppressive rule of the last Shah of Iran, whom many viewed as a pawn of Western powers.

Shi'ite Islam has produced a number of interesting sects that are not very visible in the U.S. The most important are the Ismali who believed that the true line of Imams ran through the line of Ismail, the sixth Imam rather than his brother. Over time the Ismaili (or Seveners) developed an esoteric religious faith often accused of antinomianism. In Turkey, the Druze sect developed as a millenialist movement in the eleventh century. The Druze teach reincarnation and other ideas taken from Persian Zoroastrianism that are contrary to traditional Islamic teaching.

SUFISM

Founded: 8th century C.E.
Membership: statistics not available

Sufism is a mystical tradition in Islam that originated sometime before the tenth century. It has been most popular in regions with large Christian populations because of its fundamental message of religious toleration. Jesus plays a major role in all Islamic thought, but the Sufi view him as the true founder of their order. For the Sufi, Jesus was the great ascetic teacher of mystical union with God. Those who follow the path of Jesus can achieve a union with the divine similar to his own. The Sufi called upon Muslims to live and pray more like Jesus rather than focusing on external observation of the law. They called on Christians to focus less on worshiping Jesus and instead to seek the same mystical path of Jesus. For the Sufi, religion is essentially an interior matter of the soul purified by God rather than outward observance.

Sufism is similar to Hasidic Judaism* in its teaching that God is in all things, its focus on divine joy at all times, and its use of dancing to help induce religious experience. In Turkey, the Dervish developed Sufi mystical dance as the centerpiece of prayer. Unlike the Hasidim, though, the Sufi do not establish separate communities. Rather, Sufi masters teach the Sufi arts in any number of schools or religious orders. The Sufi do not believe that their way is the right way for all Muslims. It is for those who are specially called.

However, the teachings of the Sufi are available to all. In general, Sufism places less emphasis on legalism and more on religious experience and an embrace of all people in divine love. Sufi masters have been executed because of their public violations of Islamic law.

Sufi texts have become popular in the U.S., and there is a Sufi Order of the West, but it is not accepted as orthodox by most Muslims. Unlike the rationalism of most Islamic schools of thought, the Sufi self-consciously embrace paradox and parable. Sufi wisdom is often communicated through stories in which the fool is the one who is truly wise because he sees through the hypocrisy of the world. Poetry rather than didactic writing is the major medium of the Sufi.

WAHHABISM

Within Sunni* Islam, the Hanbali legal tradition is the most conservative, but the Wahhabi movement of eighteenth century made the Hanbali law even more rigid. Muhammad Ibn "Abd al-Wahhab (1703-1792) was the leader of an Arabian revivalist movement that sought to restore Islam to its original condition before various "corruptions" entered in. The Wahhabis viewed those who disagreed with their interpretation of Islam and Sharia as unbelievers. As such, they were a threat to true Islam. Convinced that Islam had become idolatrous, the Wahhabis violently attacked popular shrines, such as the tombs of Sufi saints and the sites sacred to the Shi'ites. They even tried to destroy the Ka'ba and its central stone. The Wahhabis were only concerned about Arabic Muslims and creating a true Islamic country. Through their alliance with the Saud family, the Wahhabis were able to make Saudi Arabia into a Wahhabbi state.

ISLAMIC FUNDAMENTALISM

"Fundamentalism" is a term taken from American Protestantism to describe several diverse extremist religious movements that arose in many parts of the world during the twentieth century. Some of these extremist movements have engaged in acts of violence that shocked the world. Unlike Christian and Jewish fundamentalism, Islamic fundamentalism developed as a response to the control of traditionally Muslim countries by Western commercial empires, especially Britain and the United States. As the Ottoman Empire decayed, the British Empire expanded into the Middle East and North Africa, often with the complicity of the local rulers. Trade agreements were established that were more advantageous to Europeans and the ruling elites than to the general populations, and many of these countries grew weaker and poorer during the economic boom of the twentieth century. The Western powers encouraged, and at times, required that the traditional religious law be replaced by Western laws.

Inspired in part by the example of the Wahhabi movement in Arabia, a number of zealous young scholars and activists in Egypt, Iran, and elsewhere turned to a strict interpretation of Islam as the only hedge against Western hegemony. These early theorists, such as the Egyptian Abul Ala Mawdudi (1903-1979) tended to be more moderate and democratic than their followers, in part because the despotic secularist regimes often responded brutally to their criticisms. Many fundamentalist leaders forged their extremist theories and agenda in prisons, labor camps, or in exile. Ironically, they often drew upon Western revolutionary ideology in formulating their ideas.

Mawdudi introduced a radical new element in Islamic thinking. He argued that the *jihad,* or struggle, was the central tenet of Islam. In traditional Islamic theology there are two *jihads.* The lesser *jihad* is the holy war that is sometimes required against idolatry, such as Muhammad had fought. The greater *jihad*, though, is the struggle against sin in oneself. Mawdudi, in contrast, argued that Muslims are required to engage in a *jihad* against the secular forces of oppression. The faithful must seize power from those who blaspheme against Allah and his laws, and then they must impose the *Sharia* on the nation. He founded the Muslim Brotherhood in order to resist the rule of General Nasser in Egypt.

Sayyid Qutb (1906-1966) was a devout young man who was profoundly influenced by Mawdudi. Qutb was able to study in an American university after World War II, and he was disgusted at the hedonism and unbelief he saw displayed in America. He became convinced that the West was intent on destroying the very basis of Islam: the belief in God and the desire to do God's will instead of pursuing one's own selfish pleasures. After returning to Egypt, he joined the radical opposition to Nasser, was arrested, and spent several years in prison where he wrote many of his most important works. Later Muslim extremists built on Qutb's critique of the West and his proposal to restore Islamic law in all Muslim lands.

In the 1970s and 1980s Islamic fundamentalism grew more radical and violent as it was adopted by some Palestinian groups as a weapon in their struggle for an independent state. In the struggle with Israel, Islamic extremists adopted a virulent anti-Semitism borrowed from Europe. Islamic radicals also adopted the terrorist tactics that had been employed in the Catholic-Protestant conflict in Northern Ireland. However, it was the Soviet invasion of Afghanistan that led to the most violent forms of Islamic extremism. The resistance to the Soviet Union was defined as a *jihad* by many of the mujahedeen, and their success against one of the world's most powerful armies emboldened the radicals.

By the end of the twentieth century, Islamic fundamentalism identified the United States as the great enemy of God's law in the world. American television and movies brought images of lust, violence and self-destruction into Muslim homes and villages. Americans controlled the world's economy to the detriment of Muslim countries, and American troops were stationed in Saudi Arabia. Osama Bin Laden, a member of a wealthy Saudi Arabian family, was a veteran of the anti-Soviet *jihad*, and in the 1990s he turned his attention to the United States. In 2001, members of his international terrorist organization, Al Qaida, launched suicide attacks on the World Trade Center and the Pentagon, killing nearly three thousand people.

LATTER-DAY SAINTS
(MORMONS)

Popularly known as Mormons, the Latter-day Saints are one of the most distinct religious groups in the Abrahamic tradition.* Their roots are clearly in the Christian tradition, but their scriptures, doctrine, and practices mark them as a unique religious tradition in their own right. They were also one of the fastest-growing religious movements of the twentieth century.

The Saints believe that the authentic church, having gone underground for many centuries, was restored with the revelations given to their great prophet Joseph Smith, Jr. (1805–44), who published the *Book of Mormon* in the 1820s. In addition to the sacred Scriptures of Judaism and Christianity (the Old and New Testaments), the Latter-day Saints base their beliefs on the *Book of Mormon* and two later works by Smith, *Doctrine and Covenants* and *The Pearl of Great Price*. In the Utah territory, they founded a religious community in what was once a desert and have established themselves as one of the outstanding religious groups in the nation. Few churches live with such clear identity and maintain such a high degree of loyalty and dedication. Today, the Saints are conservative politically and morally, giving a predominant place to family life.

History. The early years of the Latter-day Saints centered on the prophet Joseph Smith, Jr., who organized the movement with six charter members at Fayette, New York, in 1830. Smith grew up in the famous "Burned-over District" of upstate New York, so called because of the frequency and intensity of the religious revivals there during the Second Great Awakening. Smith claimed to have experi-

346

enced a series of heavenly visitations, beginning with the appearance of God and Jesus Christ in 1820. During these visits he was informed that all existing churches were in error and that the true gospel was yet to be restored. It would be revealed to him, and he was to reestablish the true church on earth.

An angel named Moroni led Smith to a hill called Cumorah near Manchester, N. Y. where he found a book written on gold plates left there by an ancient prophet named Mormon. The angel also gave Smith a "seer stone" that gave him the knowledge to translate the mysterious hieroglyphic writings. The plates contained the sacred records of the ancient inhabitants of North America, righteous Jews who had fled from Jerusalem in 600 B.C.E. and sailed to North America in a divinely designed ark. Smith returned the metal plates to the angel, but eleven other persons besides Smith claimed they had seen the book before it was returned.

The "priesthood of Aaron" was conferred upon Smith and his scribe, Oliver Cowdery (1806–50), by a heavenly messenger, John the Baptist, who instructed them to baptize each other. In 1829, a year before the founding of the church, three other divine visitors, Peter, James, and John, bestowed upon Smith and Cowdery the "priesthood of Melchizedek" and gave them the keys of apostleship. Opposition arose as the church gained strength, and in 1831 the Mormons left New York for Ohio, where headquarters were established at Kirkland. In 1838 Smith moved on to Independence, Missouri, where he and his followers planned to build the ideal community with a temple at its heart. Friction with other settlers there became so acute that they soon left Missouri and settled at Nauvoo, Illinois. Violence followed them and reached its peak when Joseph Smith announced his intention to run for the U.S. presidency. He and his brother, Hyrum Smith (1800–44), were murdered by a mob at Carthage, Illinois, in 1844.

With Smith's death, the Quorum of the Twelve Apostles was accepted as the head of the church, and Brigham Young (1801–77) was made president of the Quorum. Some objected that Young was not the legal successor to Smith, and they withdrew to form other churches. Some followed James J. Strang (1813–56) to Wisconsin. The largest body of "anti-Brighamites" believed that the leadership belonged to direct descendants of Joseph Smith, and in 1847 these people, led by Joseph Smith III (1832–1914), formed the Reorganized Church of Jesus Christ of Latter-day Saints.

The majority of Saints followed Young, whose administrative ability saved the church from disruption and further division. He led the Saints in February 1846 when they were driven out of Nauvoo and began their epic march to what is now Utah. They arrived in Salt Lake Valley in July 1847, and there they built the famous Mormon Tabernacle.

Some sources indicate that Joseph Smith, Jr., informed his associates in the 1840s that polygamous marriages were sanctioned and even commanded by God. Such marriages had been contracted secretly for some time before the practice was announced publicly by Brigham Young in 1852. Following the Civil War, the U.S. federal government mounted an increasingly intense campaign against Mormon polygamy. In 1882 the Edmunds Act provided stringent penalties against polygamy, and in 1887 the church was unincorporated and its properties confiscated. In 1890 the church's president issued a manifesto that officially discontinued the contracting of new polygamous marriages, paving the way for Utah to be granted statehood.

Beliefs and Practices. In some respects the Latter-day Saints today resemble conservative Protestant churches; but certain aspects of their doctrine depart dramatically from traditional Christian theology. The Saints believe that before his ascension into heaven, Jesus Christ appeared in North America, where he preached to the Judeans who had fled before the Babylonian Captivity. The Saints teach that there are three persons who comprise the Godhead: the Father, the Son, and the Holy Ghost; but the Father and the Son have bodies of flesh and bone. It is also maintained that persons will be punished for their own individual sins, not for Adam's transgression; however, those who have died may yet be saved through the atonement of Christ

Ordinances include faith in Christ, repentance, baptism by immersion for the remission of sins, the laying-on of hands for the gift of the Holy Ghost, and the observance of the Lord's Supper each Sunday. Baptism is necessary for salvation. Like Pentecostal churches, they believe in the gift of tongues and of interpretation of tongues, visions, prophecy, and healing.

The Latter-day Saints also practice baptism for the dead, which is based on the conviction that persons who died without a chance to hear or accept the gospel cannot possibly be condemned by a just and merciful God. They find authority for this practice in the New Testament (1 Peter 4:6). The ceremony is performed with a living person standing proxy for the dead. The practice of baptizing Holocaust victims has become a source of controversy with Jewish groups.

Suggestions for Further Reading:

Allen, James B. and Glen M. Leonard. *The Story of the Latter-day Saints,* rev. ed. Salt Lake City: Desseret Book, 1992.

Arrington, Leonard J. *Brigham Young: American Moses.* New York: Knopf, 1985.

Brodie, Fawn. *No Man Knows My History: The Life of Joseph Smith.* New York: Knopf, 1945.

Hansen, Klaus J. *Mormonism and the American Experience.* Chicago: University of Chicago Press, 1981.

Ludlow, Daniel, ed. *The Encyclopedia of Mormonism,* 4 vols. New York: Macmillan, 1992.

Shipps, Jan. *Mormonism: The Story of a New Religious Tradition.* Urbana: University of Illinois Press, 1985.

CHURCH OF CHRIST (TEMPLE LOT)

Founded: 1867, with roots to 1830
Membership: est. 2,400 in 32 congregations (2000)

Though under 5,000 members, the Temple Lot body is included in this *Handbook* because of its significance in Saints' history. It was formed after the death of Joseph Smith, Jr., in 1844, when some of the Saints who remained in the Midwest became convinced that the church leaders were advocating new teachings quite at variance with the original doctrines. The group centered in Crow Creek, Illinois, functioned under the name Church of Christ, and they returned to Independence, Missouri, in response to a revelation given in 1864 through the presiding elder, Granville Hedrick, in the "appointed year" of 1867. They took possession of the land originally dedicated in 1831 by Joseph Smith, Jr., for the building of the Lord's Temple. They believe that the church cannot build until the appointed time, but they have a sacred obligation to "hold and keep this land free; when the time of building comes. The Church of Christ won court battles with other Saints' bodies to maintain control of these lots.

The church accepts the King James Version of the Bible and the *Book of Mormon* as its standards. It holds that all latter-day revelation, including that of Joseph Smith, Jr., must be tested by these Scriptures; thus it does not accept all that was given through Smith. They prefer *The Book of Commandments* to *Doctrine and Covenants,* which includes changes in the original doctrine. For this reason, the doctrines of plural marriage, baptism for the dead, celestial marriage, and plurality of gods are not accepted.

For more information: www.churchofchrist-tl.org

Headquarters: P.O. Box 472, Independence, MO, 64051-0472

THE CHURCH OF JESUS CHRIST OF LATTER-DAY SAINTS

Founded: 1830
Membership: 5,700,000 (est.) in 12,100 congregations (2003)

The main body of Latter-day Saints is headquartered in Salt Lake City, Utah, where the Salt Lake Temple and Tabernacle are located. They believe that Christ will return to earth to rule from his capitals in Zion and Jerusalem following the restoration of the tribes of Israel. For this group, revelation is not to be regarded as confined to either the Bible or the *Book of Mormon;* it continues today in the living apostles and prophets of the Latter-day Saints church. Members are to adhere to the official pronouncements of the living president (prophet) of the church. Subjection to civil laws and rules is advocated, together with insistence on the right of the individual to worship according to the dictates of conscience.

A distinctive teaching of LDS church is that marriage has two forms: marriage for time and marriage for eternity (celestial marriage). Members who are married by only civil authority still remain in good standing in the church, but marriage for time and eternity in one of the church's 117 temples is regarded as a prerequisite for the highest opportunity for salvation.

Latter-day Saints recognize two priesthoods: (1) the higher priesthood of Melchizedek, which holds power of presidency and authority over offices of the church and whose officers include apostles, patriarchs, high priests, seventies, and elders, and (2) the lesser priesthood of Aaron, which guides the temporal affairs of the church through its bishops, priests, teachers, and deacons. The presiding council of the church is the First Presidency, made up of three high priests—the president and two counselors. Its authority is final in both spiritual and temporal affairs. The president of the church is the "mouthpiece of God"; through him come the laws of the church by direct revelation.

Next to the presidency stands the Council of the Twelve Apostles, chosen by revelation to supervise, under the direction of the First Presidency, the whole work of the church. The church is divided into areas and stakes (geographical divisions) composed of a number of wards (local churches or parishes). Members of two quorums of seventy preside over the areas, under the direction of the Twelve. High priests, assisted by elders, are in charge of the stakes and wards.

Members of the Melchizedek priesthood, under the direction of the presidency, officiate in all ordinances of the gospel. The stake presidents, ward bishops, patriarchs, high priests, and elders supervise the work within the stakes and wards of the church. The Aaronic priesthood is governed by three presiding bishops, known collectively as the Presiding Bishopric, who also supervise the work of the members of the priesthood in the stakes and wards. In 1978, it was ruled that "all worthy male members of the church may be ordained to the priesthood without regard for race or color."

Mission. The church influences all aspects of the life of every member; it supplies relief in illness or poverty and assists with education and employment when necessary. This church maintains, as part of a self-help welfare system, storehouses for community food and clothing. Members operate vegetable, seed, and wheat farms; orchards, dairies, and cannery processing facilities; sewing centers; soap-processing plants; and several grain elevators. Through this system the church donates thousands of tons of surplus clothing annually to needy populations around the world and sponsors water and agricultural projects in underdeveloped countries. The welfare system also includes sheltered workshops for persons with handicapping conditions and a variety of social services, including adoption and foster-care agencies.

Some 55,000 young persons currently serve as full-time missionaries throughout the world without compensation; they devote eighteen months to two years to spreading the teaching of their church at home and abroad at their own expense. Only about one hundred persons in full-time leadership positions receive a salary or living allowance.

351

The Latter-day Saints grew tremendously in the twentieth century and in the last half of the century became influential in national politics. The church is strongest in the western U.S., but now has more members outside the U.S. than in it. The church's largest institutions are Brigham Young University in Provo, Utah, and Brigham Young University in Rexburg, Idaho. Some 525,000 secondary and post-secondary students worldwide are enrolled in seminary and institute classes, which provide religious instruction.

For more information: www.lds.org

Headquarters: Joseph Smith Memorial Building, 15 East South Temple St., Salt Lake City, UT 84150.

COMMUNITY OF CHRIST

Founded: 1860, with roots to 1830
Membership: 142,106 in 951 congregations (2002)

Formerly know as the Reorganized Church of Jesus Christ of the Latter Day Saints, this church claims to be the true continuation of the original church organized by Joseph Smith, Jr., with leadership passing to his son Joseph Smith III in 1860. It bases this claim of succession on the book of *Doctrine and Covenants.* Court actions on two occasions, in Ohio in 1880 and in Missouri in 1894, are cited in naming it the legal continuation of the original church.

The Reorganized Church rejected the claims of the group led by Brigham Young because of its abandonment of this rule of succession, along with other doctrinal disagreements. Those holding to the lineal succession eventually reorganized, and the first collective expression of this movement was a conference in Beloit, Wisconsin, in 1852. Joseph Smith III was chosen president in 1860 at Amboy, Illinois. All of his successors have been descendants of the founder. Since 1920 headquarters have been located in Independence, Missouri, where a temple was built late in the twentieth century.

The Reorganized Church held polygamy to be contrary to the teachings of the *Book of Mormon* and the book of *Doctrine and Covenants* of the original organization. It also differs from the larger body over the doctrine of the Godhead, celestial marriage, and baptism of the dead. Basic beliefs include faith in the universality of God the Eternal Father, Jesus Christ as the only begotten Son of the

352

Father, the Holy Spirit, the worth and dignity of persons, repentance of sin, baptism by immersion, the efficacy of various sacramental ordinances, the resurrection of the dead, the open canon of Scriptures and the continuity of revelation, the doctrine of stewardship, and the accountability of all people to God.

The work of the church is supported by tithes and free-will offerings. This is regarded as a divine principle, and the tithe is calculated on a tenth of each member's annual increase over needs and just wants. Church doctrines, policies, and matters of legislation must have the approval and action of a delegate conference held biennially in Independence. General administration of the church is by a First Presidency of three high priests and elders, a Quorum of Twelve Apostles who represent the presidency in the field, and a pastoral arm under the high priests and elders. Bishops are responsible for church properties, the stewardship of members, and church finances. The Community of Christ has been active in developing ministries and understanding as it has expanded since 1960 into non-Western cultures. With work in over thirty countries, it has a worldwide membership of nearly 250,000. It sponsors several homes for the elderly, medical clinics, and educational facilities both in the U.S. and abroad. It seeks to dedicate itself to the pursuit of world peace and reconciliation. The ordination of women was approved in 1984, and by 2000 more than 3,500 women had been ordained to ecclesiastical orders

For more information: http://cofchrist.org

Headquarters: 1001 W. Walnut, Independence, MO 64050-3562

ESOTERIC, SPIRITUALIST, AND NEW THOUGHT BODIES

Some of the more interesting and controversial religious organizations in the U.S. endorse esoteric doctrines and practices. The word "esoteric" refers to hidden or secret teachings, and it is a common feature of esoteric groups that it is difficult for outsiders to gain a clear understanding of them. One needs to be initiated in order to fully understand their teachings. Despite this, estoteric bodies in the United States have been able to present some of their central beliefs publicly in an effort to recruit members or defend themselves from prejudice. With the Internet, there has been an explosion of estoteric religious websites and discussion groups. Complicating study of esoteric bodies is the great diversity of groups as well as their inter-relatedness.

Esoteric groups generally trace their origins back to the ancient world, especially to Egypt and Solomon's temple. They believe that some of the original wisdom of God was transmitted by Egyptian and Israelite priests in their temple rituals, but much of that wisdom was lost. According to esotericists, some of the important secret knowledge was passed down through various individuals and organizations, such as Hermes Trismagistis, the Templars, Paracelsus, and the Rosicrucians. Esotericism often draws from Renaissance neoplatonic philosophy, medieval alchemy, and ancient magic. Some of the radical Pietist sects used esoteric thought, as did the Masons, but for the most part, esotericism has remained in the shadows of the Abrahamic tradition.

Closely related to esotericism is Theosophy, or divine wisdom. Theosophists view divine wisdom as the universal perennial philosophy that underlies all religions. Thus it draws from both Eastern and

Western philosophy and religious teachings. The chief founder of the modern theosophical movement was Helena Petrovna Blavatsky (1831–91), who was born in Russia and traveled over the world in search of "knowledge of the laws which govern the universe." She arrived in the U.S. and founded the Theosophical Society of New York in 1875. Her aim was "to form a nucleus of the Universal Brotherhood of Humanity, without distinction of race, creed, sex, caste, or color; to encourage the study of comparative religion, philosophy, and science; and to investigate the unexplained laws of nature and the powers latent in man." Blavatsky held that all religions stem from a hierarchy that includes Jesus, Buddha, and other master thinkers who experienced a series of rebirths, or reincarnations, ultimately to attain divinity.

Reincarnation is a central theme in Theosophy. It is the method through which persons rid themselves of all impurities and unfold their inner potentials through varied experiences. Closely connected with the concept of reincarnation is that of karma, the law of cause and effect; each rebirth, then, is seen as the result of actions, thoughts, and desires brought from the past. The movement split after the death of Blavatsky in 1891. Spiritualism and Theosophy generated great excitement and controversy early in the twentieth century, but its appeal declined significantly over the course of the century. This was due in part to the spread of unlicensed mediums and psychics whose unethical practices brought the movement into disrepute. It was also due to the dramatic rise of New Age religious groups among the "baby boomers."

Theosophy and esotericism influenced a number of nineteenth and twentieth century religious thinkers and organizers, some of whom promoted less exotic and more practical versions of these beliefs. New Thought was influenced by New England Transcendentalism and draws upon both eastern and Abrahamic esoteric traditions to help individuals learn new ways of thinking in order to overcome the dualism of mind and body. The key idea in the various forms of New Thought is that a person's physical, emotional, and spiritual health are interrelated. In other words, faith and right thinking are the path to health.

Suggestions for Further Reading:

Benz, Ernst. *Emanuel Swedenborg: Visionary Savant in the Age of Reason.* Tr. Nicholas Goodrick-Clarke. West Chester, MA: Swedenborg Foundation, 2002.

De Witt, John. *The Christian Science Way of Life*. Boston: Christian Science Publishing Society, 1971.

Esoterica: The Journal. Published by the Michigan State University, East Lansing, MI

Fuller, Robert. *Mesmerism and the American Cure of Souls*. Philadelphia: University of Pennsylvania Press, 1982.

Gibbons, B.J. *Spirituality and the Occult from the Renaissance to the Modern Age*. London: Routledge, 2001.

Nelson, Geoffrey K. *Spiritualism and Society*. New York: Schocken Books, 1969.

Toksvig, Signe. *Emanuel Swedenborg, Scientist and Mystic*. New Haven: Yale University Press, 1948.

CHURCH OF CHRIST, SCIENTIST
(CHRISTIAN SCIENCE)

Founded: 1879
Membership: approx. 2,200 churches (1998)

The Church of Christ, Scientist is one of the few denominations founded by a woman, and for a time it was very influential in American society. Generally described as "a religious teaching and practice based on the words and works of Christ Jesus," Christian Science was regarded by the founder, Mary Baker Eddy (1821–1910), as "the scientific system of divine healing," and the "law of God, the law of good, interpreting and demonstrating the divine Principle and rule of universal harmony." She believed that God is "the Principle of all harmonious Mind-action." Eddy's *Science and Health with Key to the Scriptures* (1875, 1883) and the Bible are the twofold textbooks of Christian Science.

Christian Science originated from Eddy's personal experience. Eddy had suffered from a form of paralysis much of her life until 1866, when, after reading the account of Christ's healing of a man with a form of palsy (Matt. 9:1-8), she recovered almost instantly. Convinced that God was the source of her healing, Eddy found confirmation of her ideas in the writings of both Emanuel Swedenborg and Phineas Quimby. She became an advocate for spiritual causation and mental healing, and she quickly demonstrated a rare ability to recruit and organize followers. Under her direction, the Church of

Christ, Scientist, was established in her hometown of Lynn, Massachusetts in 1879. In 1892 she built a large "Mother Church" in Boston, which became the headquarters for her rapidly expanding denomination.

Christian Science is more closely connected to traditional Christianity than many bodies in this section of the *Handbook*. It teaches that God is the only might, or "Mind"; God is "All-in-all," the "divine Principle of all that really is," and "the all-knowing, all-seeing, all-acting, all-wise, all-loving, and eternal; Principle; Mind; Soul; Spirit; Life; Truth; Love; all substance; intelligence." The Bible is seen as sacred Scripture, and the church proclaims faith in the Father, Son, and Holy Spirit. The crucifixion and resurrection of Jesus are held as serving "to uplift faith to understand eternal Life, even the allness of Soul, Spirit, and the nothingness of matter."

The "allness" of spirit and "nothingness of matter" involve the basic teaching of Christian Science concerning reality. As *Science and Health* explains, "All reality is in God and His creation, harmonious and eternal. That which He creates is good, and He makes all that is made. Therefore the only reality of sin, sickness, or death is the awful fact that unrealities seem real to human, erring belief, until God strips off their disguise. They are not true, because they are not of God."

In Christian Science belief, God forgives sin through destroying it with "the spiritual understanding that casts out evil as unreal." The punishment for sin lasts as long as one's belief in sin endures. Adherents of Christian Science do not ignore what they consider "unreal"; rather, they seek to forsake and overcome error and evil through Christian discipleship, prayer, and progressive spiritual understanding of God's "allness" and goodness; they strive to see the spiritual "body," created in God's likeness, as the only real body.

Christian Scientists commonly rely wholly on the power of God for healing rather than on medical treatment. Healing is not held to be miraculous, but divinely natural. Disease is understood to be basically a mental concept that can be dispelled by active Christian discipleship, spiritual regeneration, and application of the truths to which Jesus bore witness. Prayer is "an absolute faith that all things are possible to God—a spiritual understanding of Him, an unselfed love." Baptism is not observed as a traditional ceremony, but is held to be a continuing individual spiritual experience, "a purification from all error."

The local Churches of Christ, Scientist, enjoy their own forms of democratic government within the general framework of bylaws laid down by Eddy in the *Manual of the Mother Church*. Reading rooms, open to the general public, are maintained by all churches. The affairs of the Mother Church are administered by the Christian Science Board of Directors, which elects a president and other officers of the church. There are two Readers in each branch church, usually a man and a woman, who are elected by the church members. In all services on Sundays and Thanksgiving Day, they read alternately from the Bible and from *Science and Health*. The "lessonsermons" of Sunday services are prepared by a committee and are issued quarterly by the Christian Science Publishing Society.

Practitioners devote their full time to healing and are listed in a directory in the monthly *Christian Science Journal*. A board of education consists of three members: a president, a vice president, and a teacher of Christian Science. Under the supervision of this board, a Normal class is held once every three years. Teachers are duly authorized by certificates granted by the board to form classes. Women practioners outnumber male practioners ten to one. Since World War II, the denomination has experienced a significant decline in membership and a corresponding increase in average age of membership.

For more information: www.tfccs.org

Headquarters: 175 Huntington Avenue, Boston, MA 02115

DIVINE SCIENCE

Founded: 1898
Membership: 16 churches (2000)

The principles and practice of Divine Science were developed in the late nineteenth century through the work of Aletha Brooks Small, Fannie Brooks James, Nona Lovell Brooks (all sisters), and Malinda E. Cramer. When the sisters, who lived in Denver, Colorado, met Cramer, of San Francisco, California, they all realized they had developed similar ideas independently. They joined forces in 1898 and organized the Divine Science College and the First Divine Science Church of Denver.

The core of Divine Science teaching is the principle of the all-inclusive God-mind: "The principle of the omnipresence of God means He is the One Presence containing all Wisdom, Power, and Substance." Human beings are understood to be the children of God, to be of God, and to be like God; knowledge of this truth frees persons to attain a larger concept of God and the understanding of one's higher nature.

All of the founders had the experience of divine healing, and the emphasis on healing naturally persists. Healing comes through an understanding of the nature of God and the Universal Law and is "the cleansing of the inner man from all that is unlike God." Divine Science does not deny the existence of visible matter but interprets form and substance as manifestations of God. Thoughts, feelings, words, and actions have an impact on one's life, health, and circumstances. Prayer is therefore seen as a way to transform one's own mind, not as a way to change the mind of God. Jesus is recognized as a man who realized his full divine potential and shows the way for others to do likewise.

In 1957 some of the ministers and key workers met and organized the Divine Science Federation International. This organization serves its member churches and centers and cooperates with Brooks Divinity School in Denver, which trains clergy, teachers, and practitioners, and with Divine Science School in Washington, D.C. Churches, centers, and study groups are found in several major U.S. cities and abroad.

For more information: www.divinescience.org

Headquarters: 8084 Watson Rd. Suite 236, St. Louis, MO, 63119

GNOSTICISM

Founded: 20th century with roots to 1st century
Membership: statistics unavailable

One of the major competitors of orthodox-catholic Christianity until the rise of Islam was Gnosticism, so called because of its emphasis on esoteric "gnosis" (Greek for "knowledge"). There were many versions of ancient Gnosticism, most of which had roots in neoplatonic philosophy. Gnosticism was declared heretical by early Christian bishops and councils, and most Gnostic writings were lost. From time to time there were unsuccessful attempts to revive ancient Gnosticism based on fragmentary evidence, but interest in

Gnosticism as a living religion increased dramatically after the discovery of numerous Gnostic manuscripts at Nag Hammadi in Egypt in the 1940s.

By the end of the twentieth century, there were a number of groups advocating Gnosticism as an ancient faith that combines faith in Jesus and esotericism. Most Christian Gnostic groups teach that Jesus revealed secret teachings to his disciples. Mary Magdalene figures prominently in Christian Gnosticism, and many Gnostics believe that she was the physical and spiritual spouse of Jesus. Dan Brown's best-selling and highly imaginative novel, *The DaVinci Code* made the marriage of Jesus and Mary central to the plot, generating great interest in Gnosticism. Unlike ancient Gnosticism, which tended to be ascetic, American Gnosticism often celebrates sexuality as part of spirituality. Many Gnostic groups are served by "wandering bishops," who claimed an apostolic succession from Jesus and Mary Magdalene parallel to that of the Catholic Church.*

For more information: www.gnosis.org

LIBERAL CATHOLIC CHURCH INTERNATIONAL

Founded: 1918
Membership: est. 6,000 in 9 churches

This church originated in 1916 in Great Britain as a branch of the Old Catholic Church* movement that began in Holland in the eighteenth century. The group took the name "Liberal Catholic Church" in 1918. It won a legal dispute over the name with the other Liberal Catholic Church that separated in the 1940s. Tracing its orders to an apostolic succession that runs back to the Roman Catholic Church under the reign of Pope Urban VIII (1568–1644), the Liberal Catholic Church aims at a combination of traditional Catholic forms of worship with the utmost freedom of individual conscience and thought.

The church endorses certain theosophical and esoteric principles, and its worship incorporates many basic tenets of Eastern mysticism. Paramount in the thinking is a central inspiration from faith in the living Christ based on the promises of Matt. 18:20 and 28:20, which are regarded as "validating all Christian worship." But special channels of Christ's power are found in the traditional seven sacraments of the church. Through such "spiritual labor" believers are able to come into a full realization of the divine presence and grow into the true likeness of God.

The Nicene Creed is generally used in Liberal Catholic services, but there is no requirement of submission to any creed, Scripture, or tradition. Members seek to serve humanity through corporate worship in a common ritual rather than doctrinal uniformity. The church operates St. Alban Theological Seminary in Frisco, Texas, while the St. Alban Press is located in San Diego.

For more information: www.liberalcatholic.org

Headquarters: 741 Cerro Gordo Avenue, San Diego, CA 92102

LIBERAL CATHOLIC CHURCH, PROVINCE OF THE UNITED STATES

Founded: 1940s
Membership: est. 6,500 in 24 churches (2002)

This Liberal Catholic body separated from the international body in the 1940s in a dispute over episcopal jurisdiction and theosophical beliefs. Most of the American Liberal Catholic clergy left the London-based church and formed a separate province. It remains very similar to the LCCI, but requires that clergy accept basic theosophical principles including reincarnation and ascended masters in additional to Nicene Christianity. It also encourages members to adopt a vegetarian and alcohol-free lifestyle. Its liturgy expresses basic esoteric beliefs.

As with the Old Catholic* churches, Liberal Catholic priests and bishops may marry, and they exact no fee for the administration of the sacraments; LCC priests are employed in secular occupations, but LCCI churches may offer a salary to their priests if financially able. Liberal Catholics permit the remarriage of divorced persons and are open to gay and lesbian persons. However, neither church ordains women. The presiding bishop of the LCC churches is headquartered in Ojai, California.

For more information: www.lcc.cc/tlc/thelcc.htm

Headquarters: P.O. Box 598, Ojai, CA 93023

361

SPIRITUALISM

NATIONAL SPIRITUAL ALLIANCE OF THE U.S.A.

Founded: 1913
Membership: statistics not available

NATIONAL SPIRITUALIST ASSOCIATION OF CHURCHES

Founded: 1893
Membership: est. 3,000 in 136 churches (1999)

These are two of the oldest and largest Spiritualist organizations, but Spiritualism has had a broader impact on American culture than is evident from its institutional forms. The Spiritualist movement in the U.S. began in 1848 with the activities of Margeretta and Kate Fox in Hydesvill, N.Y. The sisters claimed that they had succeeded in contacting the dead, who communicate through strange "rappings." Central to the beliefs and practices of Spiritualism in its many forms is the ability to communicate with the spirits of those who have departed this earthly life. This may be done through such things as mediums, séances, and mystical rites. In recent years there has been greater interest in psychic experiments and extrasensory perception. Many Spiritualists hold to a belief in reincarnation and seek to reconnect with past-life experiences.

The older Spiritualist organizations in the U.S. remain closer to the Abrahamic tradition than the more recent New Age spiritual movements. Christ is often recognized as a medium; the annunciation is seen as a message from the spirit world; the transfiguration was an opportunity for materialization of the spirits of Moses and Elijah; and the resurrection was evidence that all people live on in the spirit world.

Spiritualists often call the soul the astral body. At death the material body dissolves, and the soul, or the body of the spirit, progresses through a series of spheres to a higher and higher existence. In two lower spheres, persons of bad character or sinful record are purified and made ready for higher existences. Most of the departed are to be found in a third sphere, the summer land. Beyond this are the philosopher's sphere, the advanced contemplative and intellectual sphere, the love sphere, and the Christ sphere. All reach the higher spheres eventually; Spiritualists do not believe in heaven or hell or that any are ever lost.

Spiritualists in general profess belief in Infinite Intelligence and that natural phenomena are expressions of that Intelligence. True religion includes a correct understanding of the expressions of the Infinite Intelligence and learning how to live in accordance with the Infinite Intelligence. The personality of each individual lives on after death, which is just a change in state, and the living can and do contact those who have passed beyond. The moral code of Spiritualism is Jesus' Golden Rule, and happiness or unhappiness depends on whether people obey or disobey Nature's physical and spiritual laws. Spiritualism, like Pentecostalism,* believes that prophecy and healing are still spiritual gifts.

Services or séances are held in private homes, rented halls, or churches. Most Spiritualist churches have regular services with prayer, music, selections from writings by various spiritualists, a sermon or lecture, and spirit messages from the departed. Churches and ministers are supported by free-will offerings; mediums and ministers also gain support from classes and séances in which fees are charged. Attendance at church services is invariably small, averaging twenty to twenty-five.

Administration and government differ slightly in the various groups, but most have district or state associations and an annual general convention. All have mediums, and most have ministers in charge of the congregations. Requirements for licensing and ordination also differ, but a determined effort is being made to raise the standards of education and character in the larger groups.

The National Spiritualist Association of Churches was organized in Chicago around the time of the World's Parliament of Religions, which had heightened American interest in Eastern religions and esoteric philosophies. This association furnishes literature for the whole American Spiritualist movement. In 1994, the Association established the Center for Spiritual Studies, NSAC in Lily Dale, New York, that offers a course of study for members, licentiates, healers, mediums, National Spiritualist Teachers, and ordained ministers, leading to an Associate of Arts in Religious Studies.

The National Spiritualist Alliance separated from the NSAC in 1913 in a dispute over reincarnation. TNSA is primarily located in New England, but its influence is broader than its membership. The alliance stresses paranormal and impersonal manifestations and intercommunication with the spirit world. An official board of directors steers the work of ministers and certified mediums; college training is not required, but a minister must have passed a course of study arranged by the alliance. Mediums may baptize, but only ministers may officiate at ceremonies of ordination and marriage. Work of the alliance involves benevolent, literary, educational, musical, and scientific activities. A distinctive feature of the Alliance is its Psychic Fairs, held in various locations, which display psychic literature and phenomena.

For more information: www.nsac.org; www.thenationalspiritualalliance.org

Headquarters: NSAC, P.O. Box 217, Lily Dale, NY 14752-0217

TNSA, P.O. Box 88, Lake Pleasant, MA 01347

SWEDENBORGIAN CHURCHES

THE GENERAL CONVENTION
OF THE NEW JERUSALEM IN THE U.S.A.

Founded: 1817
Membership: 2,104 in 44 churches (2000)

THE GENERAL CHURCH OF THE NEW JERUSALEM

Founded: 1897
Membership: 6,444 in 35 churches (2002)

One of the primary figures in both Spiritualism and Theosophy was Emanuel Swedenborg (1688–1772). He was born in Stockholm, Sweden, and was an Enlightenment-era scientist distinguished in the fields of mathematics, geology, cosmology, and anatomy before he turned seriously to theology. Although certain he was divinely commissioned to teach the doctrines of the "New Church," Swedenborg never preached or founded a church. His followers, however, felt that the need for a separate denomination was implicit in the new revelation given in Swedenborg's monumental work *Arcana Celestia,* in which, they believed, he unlocked the hidden meaning of Scripture and recorded his conversations with great figures long dead.

The Swedenborgian church centers its worship on the risen and glorified present reality of Christ and looks for the establishment of the kingdom of God in the form of a universal church on earth. In this new church all people will strive for peace, freedom, and justice. Swedenborgian bodies have often used the name "Churches of the New Jerusalem" to indicate the in-breaking of the eschatological reality described in the New Testament.

The New Church as an organization arose in London in 1783 when Robert Hindmarsh (1759–1835), a printer, gathered a few friends to discuss the writings of Swedenborg. They formed a general conference of their societies in 1815. The first Swedenborgian Society in the U.S. was organized at Baltimore, Maryland, in 1792, and in 1817 the General Convention of the New Jerusalem in the U.S.A. was established. It was incorporated in 1861.

The Faith and Aims of the church state that the "Lord Jesus Christ has come again, not in a physical reappearance, but in spirit and in truth; not in a single event only, but in a progressive manifestation of his presence among men." Adherents claim that tokens of Christ's coming appear in the burst of scientific development, the rise of the spirit of inquiry, the progress toward political and intellectual freedom, and the deepening sense of national and international responsibility that has characterized the modern era.

The doctrines of the General Convention of the New Jerusalem are founded on the Bible, which is understood to have both a literal, historical meaning and a deeper, spiritual meaning. The church teaches that there is one God, known by many names, and that the Christian Trinity denotes aspects of this God. Human beings are believed to be essentially spirits clothed in material bodies, which are laid aside at death; the human spirit lives on in a spirit world, in a manner determined by its attitudes and behavior on earth. Therefore, Swedenborgians hold that adherents are to live out their religious beliefs in all aspects of life.

Societies are grouped into a General Convention that meets annually. Each society is self-regulating, with ministers and general pastors (in charge of state associations). Services are liturgical, based on

365

the *Book of Worship* issued by the General Convention. A theological school is in Newton, Massachusetts, and the Swedenborg Foundation is in West Chester, Pennsylvania. The most famous Swedenborgian evangelist was John Chapman (Johnny Appleseed), and today J. Appleseed & Co. distributes books and pamphlets based on Swedenborg's writings.

Another Swedenborgian body, The General Church of the New Jerusalem, broke away from the older group in 1890. It shares many of the doctrines of the larger body, but acknowledges the writings of Swedenborg as divinely inspired. Headquarters are at Bryn Athyn, Pennsylvania, where a cathedral has been built. At the end of the twentieth century, a new Swedenborgian church, the Lord's New Church, was established in South Africa and now has a handful of congregations in the U.S.

For more information: www.newchurch.org; www.sweden borg.org

Headquarters: Swedenborgian Church, 11 Highland Ave., Newtonville, MA 02460-1852.

New Church, P.O. Box 743, Bryn Athyn, PA 19009

UNITY SCHOOL OF CHRISTIANITY AND ASSOCIATION OF UNITY CHURCHES

Founded: 1886
Membership: est. 31,000 in 664 churches (1995)

Unity is a religious educational institution devoted to demonstrating that following the teaching of Jesus Christ is a practical, seven-day-a-week way of life. Unity teaches that "the true church is a state of consciousness in man." The Association of Unity Churches helps provide resources for congregations dedicated to Unity teachings. Unity has been described as "a religious philosophy with an 'open end,' seeking to find God's truth in all of life, wherever it may be." Unity has no strict creed or dogma; it finds good in all religions and teaches that people should keep their minds open to receive that goodness. Unity teaches that reality is ultimately spiritual and that realization of spiritual truth will illuminate, heal, and prosper humanity. Cultivation of health-conducive emotions such as love, confidence, and joy is encouraged. Overcoming health-inhibiting emotions such as anger, hatred, and despair is also encouraged. Unity has no rules concerning health but concentrates on spiritual goals, knowing that healthful living habits will follow. Some Unity students are vegetarians in the interest of health.

Unity began in 1886 when Charles Fillmore (1854–1948), bankrupt and crippled, and his wife, Myrtle (1845–1931), seriously ill with tuberculosis, discovered a way of life based on affirmative prayer. They studied a variety of Christian and Eastern theosophical and esoteric systems in creating their new approach to healing. The Fillmores held that "whatever man wants he can have by voicing his desire in the right way into the Universal Mind." It is through Christ, or the Christ consciousness, that the human gains eternal life and salvation. Salvation means the attainment of true spiritual consciousness, becoming like Christ. This transformation takes place not in any hereafter, but "here in this earth" through a process of unfolding and regeneration. A person suffers no final death, but changes into increasingly better states until finally becoming like Christ.

Prayer and meditation are suggested for every human want and illness. The Unity way of prayer and meditation involves relaxation and affirmation of spiritual truth to develop the consciousness of the individual and silent receptivity to the "Divine Mind" for whatever the seeker needs. The Bible is used constantly and is highly valued, but is not considered the sole or final authority in faith and practice. People must be in direct, personal communion with God, not dependent upon such secondary sources as the scriptures.

The Association of Unity Churches ordains ministers, provides educational and administrative support, and is self-supporting. Unity School trains ministers in a two-year program. It also educates teachers and offers retreat programs. A large staff in Unity Village, near Kansas City, Missouri, is available to pray with people day and night. Workers answer an average of one million calls and nearly two million letters annually. Most calls come from members of various Christian churches, but correspondents are never asked to leave the churches to which they belong. Unity School publishes some seventy-five million copies of booklets, brochures, and magazines annually. These materials are used by many who never contact headquarters or become members of a Unity church.

For more information: www.unity.org

Headquarters: Unity Village, MO 64065

UNITARIANS AND UNIVERSALISTS

Unitarianism and Universalism represent two quite distinct theological ideas that were brought together with the formation of the Unitarian Universalist Association of Congregations in 1961. It is helpful to look at the separate history of these two movements before discussing the new institution that was established in the twentieth century.

Unitarian: The basic tenet of Unitarianism is that there is only one God; thus, Jesus was not divine in essence. Unitarians often claim that their thought reaches back into the early Christian centuries, before the concept of the Trinity was developed. Unitarianism as we know it today, however, began with the Protestant Reformation, among anti-trinitarians such as Michael Servetus (ca. 1511–53) and Faustus Socinus (1539–1604). Some Anabaptists* in Switzerland, Hungary, Transylvania, Holland, Poland, and Italy held ideas similar to Unitarianism. In England, Unitarianism was championed by the scientist and mathematician Isaac Newton (1642–1727), the philosopher John Locke (1632–1704), and the poet John Milton (1608–74), but no attempt was made to organize the movement until late in the eighteenth century.

American Unitarianism developed in New England Congregational (see UNITED CHURCH OF CHRIST) churches that were known as Liberal Christian. The split within Congregationalism came into the open in 1805 when Henry Ware (1764–1845), a Unitarian, was appointed professor of theology at Harvard University, the bastion of Congregationalist education. The split widened in 1819 when William Ellery Channing (1780–1842) of Boston preached his famous Baltimore sermon outlining the

Unitarian view. Channing defined the true church in these words: "By his Church our Savior does not mean a party bearing the name of a human leader, distinguished by a form or an opinion.... These are the church—men made better, made holy, virtuous by his religion—men who, hoping in his promises, keep his commands."

There are several Pentecostal* bodies, known as "Jesus Only" churches that espouse a form of unitarian theology, but they are to be distinguished from Unitarians. Unitarians are generally very liberal theologically, politically, and socially. They reject the idea of the divinity of Jesus in favor of the oneness of God unlike the "Jesus only" Pentecostals, who proclaim that the one God was incarnate in Jesus.

Unitarians played a prominent role in nineteenth-century reform movements such as abolition, women's suffrage, prison reform, and inter-religious dialog. Prominent Unitarians include Elizabeth Cady Stanton, Susan B. Anthony, John and Abigail Adams, Dorothea Dix, and Oliver Wendell Holmes. Almost half the signers of the famous *Humanist Manifesto* were Unitarians, causing a division within the movement between theists and non-theists that was eventually healed.

Eventually, Unitarian Congregationalists organized the American Unitarian Association in 1825 in order to "better work for the Kingdom of God" and "and promote the interests of religion that Jesus taught as love to God and love to man." Included in the plan was the expansion of liberal religion around the world. Independent local churches were grouped in local, county, district, state, and regional conferences and were united in an international association for purposes of fellowship, counsel, and promotion of mutual interests. In 1961 there were four Unitarian seminaries, two preparatory schools, 386 churches, and approximately 115,000 members.

Universalist. There are many forms of universalism, but in general the term refers to the belief that all persons will be saved regardless of religious belief or non-belief. Universalists find evidence of their thinking and philosophy in many cultural streams, and the teaching has much in common with several religions throughout the world. Universalists claim roots in the early Christian Gnostic, Origen of Alexandria (185-254), certain Anabaptists, and radical Pietist* mystics such as Jacob Boehme (1575–1624).

In 1759 James Relly (1722–78) of England wrote *Union*, in which he opposed the Calvinistic doctrine of election of the few. Relly's conviction of universal salvation deeply influenced John Murray

(1741–1815), a Wesleyan evangelist who came to New Jersey in 1770 and found groups of Universalist-minded people scattered along the Atlantic coast. He became minister to one such group in Gloucester, Massachusetts, and later served briefly as a Revolutionary War chaplain in the armies of Washington and Greene. His Independent Christian Church of Gloucester became the first organized Universalist church in the U.S. in 1779.

A group of Universalists met at Philadelphia in 1790 to draft their first declaration of faith and plan of government. They promoted pacifism, abolition of slavery, testimony by affirmation rather than by oath, and free public education. This Philadelphia declaration was adopted by a group of New England Universalists in 1793.

At about the same time, Hosea Ballou (1771–1852), a school teacher and itinerant preacher in Vermont, was ordained in the Universalist ministry. He broke radically with Murray's thought. His 1805 *Treatise on Atonement* gave Universalists their first consistent philosophy. In addition to the rationalist rejection of endless punishment in hell, the Trinity, and miracles, Ballou taught that God recognized humanity's heavenly nature and loved the human race as God's own offspring. The meaning of the atonement was not found in bloody sacrifice to appease divine wrath, but in the heroic sacrifice of Jesus, who wanted to win all persons to God's love.

Like the Unitarians, Universalists in the nineteenth century were active very early in reform movements for prison inmates and working women. They opposed slavery, stood for separation of church and state, and have maintained a continuing interest in the fields of science, labor, management, civil rights, and human concern. Universalists founded several non-sectarian colleges and universities, including Tufts, St. Lawrence, Goddard, and the California Institute of Technology. At the time of the merger, there were 68,949 members in 334 churches.

Suggestions for further reading:

Buehrens, John A., et al. *A Chosen Faith: An Introduction to Unitarian Universalism.* Boston: Beacon, 1998.

Robinson, David. *The Unitarians and the Universalists.* Westport, Conn.: Greenwood, 1985.

Williams, George H. *American Universalism: A Bicentennial Historical Essay.* Boston: Universalist Historical Society, 1971.

AMERICAN UNITARIAN CONFERENCE

Founded: 2000
Membership statistics not available

This organization represents a rare institutional split in American Unitarianism, and it is still unclear how this new denomination will develop as an institution. The AUC developed from Carl Scovel's concern that the Unitarian Universalist Association's embrace of humanism and eastern religious beliefs was crowding out Unitarian theism, which was the traditional understanding of the denomination. The AUC remains committed to the Unitarian principle of freedom of religion and toleration of a wide variety of religious beliefs while promoting monotheism. Central to the ethos of the AUC is that faith, reason, science, and religion should be seen as collaborative rather than competitive activities.

Among the denomination's principles are that God's presence is known in different ways and that revelation is continuing; religion should be a responsible search for meaning; free will is a gift from God and religion should assist in the development of human ethics; both reason and faith lead to humility and humility leads to tolerance; and finally, the religious quest should lead to greater mercy and compassion in a world filled with suffering.

For more information: www.americanunitarian.org

Headquarters: 6806 Springfield Dr., Mason Neck, VA 22079.

UNITARIAN UNIVERSALIST ASSOCIATION

Founded: 1961
Membership: 219,715 in 1,042 churches (2003)

In May 1961 the Unitarian and Universalist churches in the U.S. and Canada were consolidated as the Unitarian Universalist Association of Congregations in North America, one of the most influential liberal churches. The two bodies had separate and interesting origins and history (see above). In this association, flexibility, freedom of conscience, and local autonomy are prime values. No minister, member, or congregation "shall be required to subscribe to

371

any particular interpretation of religion, or to any particular religious belief or creed."

The aims of the association were set forth in 1985 in a revised statement that promotes human dignity, social justice and compassion, the free and responsible search for truth, democracy, the goal of global community, and respect for the environment. Increasingly, since the merger in 1961, the UUA has embraced eastern as well as western religious practices, beliefs, and traditions.

In recent years the Association has been heavily involved in numerous causes and concerns: the issue of racial and cultural diversity in what have been historically white congregations; the rise of feminist consciousness; scholarship in church history and process theology; inner-city ministries; and the rights of gay, lesbian, and bisexual persons. The Unitarian Universalist Service Committee provides leadership and materials in the field of social change. The denomination has dozens of independent affiliate organizations that advocate and provide resources for various causes.

A General Assembly, with clergy and lay representatives, is the overall policy-making body, meeting annually. The officers of the Association are elected for four-year terms and serve together with other elected members as a Board of Trustees that appoints the executive and administrative officers and generally carries out policies and directives. In 2001 the UUA elected William Sinkford as its first African-American head.

The headquarters are in Boston, and twenty-three district offices have been established. Principal numerical strength lies in the Northeast, the Midwest, and the Pacific West Coast. Foreign work is now conducted through the International Association for Religious Freedom. Beacon Press, which produces fifty new titles each year, is one of the most distinguished independent publishing houses in the U.S.

For more information: www.uua.org

Headquarters: 25 Beacon St., Boston, MA 02108

BAHÁ'Í

Founded: 1844 (came to the U.S. in 1894)
Membership: 151,172 registered in
1,178 assemblies (2004)

The Bahá'í Faith is one of the few religions to emerge in modern times; however, like many other religious bodies, it has roots in the ancient traditions of Western monotheism that can be traced back to the biblical patriarch Abraham. Now recognized as an independent religion, the Bahá'í faith was born as an offshoot of Shi'a Islam in mid-nineteenth century Persia (present-day Iran).

Bahá'ís see all of the great religions of the world, eastern as well as western, as part of a single process of "progressive revelation" through which God reveals his will to humanity. The founders of the world's major religions, including Abraham, Krishna, Moses, Zoroaster, Buddha, Jesus and Muhammad, are recognized as "Manifestations of God," peerless individuals who are seen as reflections of God's attributes who appear in each age to guide and educate humanity. The founder of the Bahá'í faith, Bahá'u'lláh, claimed to be the most recent, but not the final, manifestation of God in this ongoing process of divine revelation.

According to Bahá'í teachings, claims of exclusivity and finality by the followers of the various religions have been a prolific source of violence and contention in the world. These conflicts can be resolved through the recognition of the progressive nature of religious truth. Throughout the ages, all the religions have reaffirmed the same core spiritual and ethical principles, but their social and

373

temporal teachings have differed in response to the evolving needs of an ever-advancing civilization.

Bahá'ís believe that there is only one God and one human race, and all the manifestations of God have come to help move humankind gradually closer to God. Bahá'u'lláh taught that in this day humankind is reaching its long-awaited stage of maturity, when the global unity and oneness of the human race can be recognized and established. He laid down principles, laws, and institutions for a world civilization, including the abandonment of all forms of prejudice, the full equality of men and women, the elimination of the extremes of poverty and wealth, universal compulsory education, the abolishment of the clergy and the responsibility of each person to search independently for truth, the harmony of science and religion, and the establishment of a world federal system based on the principles of collective security.

The Bahá'í Faith originated with the teachings of Mirza Ali Muhammad (1819-50), called "the Báb" (Arabic, for "gate" or "door"), who suffered persecution and was martyred in 1850. The Báb emphasized a messianic theme in Islamic thought: that the Madhi (or "Messiah") would soon appear to inaugurate an age of peace and justice on earth. It was a message of hope for thousands of the disenfranchised in Iran, but the Báb's preaching threatened the Persian authorities, who feared that the prophecies about the Madhi might inspire revolution. Thus the Báb was arrested, tortured, and executed. As many as twenty thousand of his followers, known as Bábis, were also slain during the early years of the new faith.

As so often happens in the history of religious persecution, the death of the prophet did not stop his message. One of the Báb's followers was a nobleman, Mirza Husayn-'Ali Nuri (1817-1892), long admired for his philanthropy and selflessness. In 1852 he was stripped of his possessions and cast into an underground dungeon in Tehran. While in prison, he experienced the descent of the Holy Spirit, an event that Bahá'í's compare to God's revealing himself to his earlier messengers: Moses before the burning bush; the Buddha under the Bodhi tree; when the Holy Spirit, in the form of a dove, descended upon Jesus; and when the archangel Gabriel appeared to Muhammad. When he was released, he was banished from Persia and spent the rest of his life as a prisoner and exile, first in Baghdad, then in Istanbul, and finally in the prison-city of Akko in Ottoman

Palestine. He took the title "Bahá'u'lláh," which means "the Glory of God" in Arabic.

In 1863 Bahá'u'lláh announced publicly that he was the one about whom the Báb had prophesied, the messenger sent by God with a new revelation for the coming age. His words were to prepare a new world order. Beginning that year Bahá'u'lláh issued a series of weighty letters to the kings and rulers of the world to inform them of the coming new world order and urge them to assist in the next stage of human development. He maintained that the nations of the world should reduce their armaments, reconcile their differences, and seek justice for all of the world's people. In addition to these letters to the kings and rulers, Bahá'u'lláh revealed a vast number of books, epistles, prayers and meditations that address every aspect of human existence and which are considered the revealed Word of God.

When Bahá'u'lláh passed away in 1892, his remains were buried in a small room near the mansion of Bahji, an estate just north of Akko. Known as the Shrine of Bahá'u'lláh, this burial place is a pilgrimage site for Bahá'ís today. Before his passing, Bahá'u'lláh appointed his eldest son, Abbas Effendi (1844-1921), as the Center of His Covenant, to whom his followers would turn for guidance after his passing.

While efforts have been made to create breakaway sects, the vast majority of Bahá'ís today are part of a single world community united by an administrative structure ordained by Bahá'u'lláh. This structure consists of consultative assemblies elected from among the adult believers at the local, national, and international levels. The international governing body of the Faith is an elected council of nine members known as the Universal House of Justice, which operates from its seat at the Bahá'í World Center in Haifa, Israel. There are 182 National Spiritual Assemblies and more than eleven thousand Local Spiritual Assemblies around the world.

Abbas Effendi, known to Baha'ís as Abdu'l-Bahá, was released in 1908 when the Ottoman Empire collapsed in the aftermath of the Young Turk Revolution. Between 1911 and 1913 he undertook a series of historic journeys to Egypt, Europe, and North America to proclaim his father's message. At Wilmette, Illinois, in 1912, he laid the cornerstone of the first Bahá'í house of worship in the West. The headquarters of the National Spiritual Assembly, the administrative body in the United States, is in that vicinity.

In 1953 the building was dedicated to the unity of God, the unity of the prophets, and the unity of humankind. Worship services are conducted frequently and are not restricted to weekly programs. Bahá'í houses of worship follow a design principle in which the number nine, the Bahá'í symbol of unity, is repeatedly emphasized. The temples have nine entrances on nine sides surmounted by a single dome. While in the future these temples will be built in every locality where Bahá'ís reside, at present there are only seven in the world. In addition to the Wilmette temple, Bahá'í houses of worship are located in Panama, Uganda, Germany, Australia, Western Samoa, and India.

These temples are mostly used for private prayer and meditation, and there are no rituals, sacraments, sermons, or regular worship services. Devotional programs are held to commemorate Bahá'í holy days and other occasions, during which selections from the scriptures of all the major religions may be recited. The display of pictures or statues is forbidden, as is the use of musical instruments. Only the human voice may be used to sing, chant or recite.

The chief purpose of the Bahá'í faith is to help unite humanity in a peaceful and just world order; hence, its chief principle is the oneness and the wholeness of the human race. Other dominant principles are independent investigation of the truth, the essential harmony of science and religion, recognition of the divine foundation of all religions, universal compulsory education, equality of all men and women, a spiritual solution for economic problems, the need for a universal auxiliary language, universal peace based on a world federation of nations, elimination of all prejudice, and recognition of the essential unity of humanity. Not surprisingly, Bahá'ís view the creation of the United Nations as a significant step toward the establishment of universal peace and justice.

Unlike many new religious movements, the Bahá'í Faith stresses the importance of secular education and the equality of women with men. The oppression of women around the world, Bahá'u'lláh declared, is the cause of much of the world's suffering, and he made the education of women a cardinal teaching. Bahá'ís see the achievement of equality between the sexes and the integration of women into every field of human endeavor—in government, academia and professional life—as an essential prerequisite to peace and human progress. In fact, Bahá'ís hold that if a family has the means to send only one child to school, the daughter should be given precedence since the daughter will be the first educator of the future generations.

When it comes to family life, though, the Bahá'í are rather traditional and conservative. Sex is to be only within the confines of a marriage between a man and a woman, and divorce is discouraged.

Bahá'ís are also instructed to obey their government, to avoid alcohol and narcotics except for medicinal purposes, and to use prayer and fasting as a means of elevating the soul. Bahá'í teachings condemn idleness, exalt any work performed in the spirit of service, and prohibit slavery and other forms of oppression. Bahá'í teachings also prohibit religious practices common to other religious groups, such as confession of sins, asceticism, and monasticism. Each man and woman is expected to live in a happy and productive family, working for the cause of peace and harmony.

The Bahá'í faith has no prescribed rituals or clergy. Marriage and funeral services are simple and flexible. Bahá'í communities organize devotional and prayer services, public lectures, study classes, and discussion groups for inquirers, which are offered by unpaid teachers and pioneers. Other Bahá'í community meetings include electoral conventions for the election of the National Spiritual Assembly and summer and winter schools and institutes. Permanent Bahá'í schools and institutes are located in Maine, California, Michigan, Arizona, and South Carolina.

The Bahá'í calendar is composed of nineteen months of nineteen days each, with four "intercalary days" from February 26 to March 1. The final month of the year, from March 2 to 20, is a time of spiritual renewal and fasting, when Bahá'ís avoid food and drink between sunrise and sunset. The fast is followed by the Bahá'í New Year on the vernal equinox. The Bahá'í day starts and ends at sunset. The focal point of Bahá'í community life is the Nineteen-Day Feast, held on the first day of each Bahá'í month, which contains three central elements: spiritual devotion, administrative consultation, and fellowship. Other than these, the details of the Feast embody local cultural norms for food and celebration. The central aspect of the Nineteen-Day Feast is not food, however, but rather spiritual fellowship and communion.

Although forbidden from aggressively seeking converts, Bahá'ís do enthusiastically teach their religion to others as part of the effort to foster an ever-advancing civilization. Since 1963 there has been marked growth in the number of adherents to the religion around the world. The Bahá'í grew rapidly in the United States during the 1960s and 1970s as many youth sought out non-Western spiritualities, but numbers declined as many of thoses converts moved on to more exotic religions.

Although still a small movement in the United States, the Bahá'í Faith claims five million believers in some 230 countries, making it one of the most geographically diverse religions in history. There are approximately 11,740 local assemblies and 182 national assemblies. Within this world fellowship are people of all races, nationalities, and creeds, including former Muslims, Hindus, Christians, and Jews. The writings of the Bahá'í faith have been translated into more than eight hundred languages.

For more information: www.bahai.org

Headquarters: Institute for Bahá'í Studies, 1233 Central St., Evanston, IL 60091

Suggestions for further reading:

Ferraby, Richard John. *All Things Made New: A Comprehensive Outline of the Baha'í Faith,* rev. ed. London: Bahá'í Publishing Trust, 1975.

Cole, Juan R. and Moojan Momen, eds. *From Iran East and West.* Los Angeles: Kalimat, 1984.

Stockman, Robert. *The Baha'I Faith in America: Origins, 1892-1900.* Wilmette, IL: Bahá'í Publishing Trust, 1985.

NATION OF ISLAM

Founded: 1920s
Membership: est. 20,000-40,000 (2000)

The Nation of Islam is an expression of the African pride movement of Marcus Garvey (1887–1940) and others in the first decades of the twentieth century (see AFRICAN ORTHODOX CHURCH). Timothy Drew (1886–1920) became convinced that Islam was the true religion of black people, founded Moorish Science Temple in Newark, New Jersey, and took the name Noble Drew Ali. According to Drew, African-Americans were Moors whose forebears had lived in Morocco. Only by leaving the distorted white religion of Christianity could African-Americans be free. His followers divided into several groups when he died in 1920.

Wallace D. Fard (1877-1933) led a group in Detroit, Michigan. He called himself the reincarnation of Noble Drew Ali and taught "The Religion of the Black Men of Asia and Africa," based at first on the Bible and the Qur'an. Fard's ideas eventually became more radical, attacking the Bible as a book of lies and claiming that African-Americans were gods while the white race was the serpent devil that would ultimately be destroyed. Fard announced that he was a tool in the hands of Allah, called to tell the truth about the races and prepare for the final judgment. After his mysterious disappearance in 1933, his followers claimed that he had been Allah personified.

Fard was succeeded by Elijah Poole (1897–1975), known as Elijah Muhammad. Elijah Muhammad continued to preach Fard's gospel of black revolution by which African-Americans would end white domination. He called for the creation of an independent Black

Nation of Islam within the U.S. Building on the desperate conditions of poverty in the inner-city ghettos, the movement spread across the country and became increasingly militant after World War II.

Elijah Muhammad encouraged his members to spread his teachings among the millions of African-American males imprisoned in the U.S. Among his prison converts was Malcolm X (1925–65), one of the towering figures of the Black Power movement of the 1960s. Malcolm used the symbol X to reject the name acquired during slavery. He urged African-Americans to take charge of their own destiny rather than relying on the charity of white liberals. He also rejected the pacifist Christian approach of Martin Luther King, Jr., during the civil rights movement. Rather than calling for integration of African-Americans into white society, Malcolm X and the Nation of Islam promoted a separate culture. His preaching helped to build membership in the Nation of Islam, but disagreements developed between Malcolm X and Elijah Muhammad after Malcolm discovered orthodox Islam. Malcolm was murdered in New York City in 1965, but his ideas have remained influential.

After his death in 1975, Elijah Muhammad was succeeded by his son, Warith Deen Muhammad who reoriented and decentralized the movement. He also moved the organization closer to the normative Islamic tradition. Meanwhile, a splinter group led by Louis Farrakhan, based in Chicago, Illinois, continued to emphasize the more radical aspects of the Nation of Islam, especially black nationalism and the racial theories of Fard. Farrakhan's statements and actions have evoked both admiration and condemnation. Warith Deen Mohammad, meanwhile, joined with other Muslim leaders in 1992 to form the Muslim American Society, which is basically orthodox Sunni Islam* and claims a membership of two hundred thousand.

Although subject to controversy and occasional violence, the Nation of Islam has achieved some definite accomplishments. It established a chain of industries, such as barbershops, supermarkets, bakeries, restaurants, cleaning establishments, and farms to relieve poverty among African-Americans. Black Muslims do not gamble, smoke, drink, overeat, or buy on credit. They arrange parole for convicts and offer guidance for those released. They claim to give blacks self-respect and a sense of identity, and they have reached many persons whom the mainstream Christian churches have been unable to reach.

For more information: www.noi.org

Headquarters: 7351 South Stoney Island Avenue, Chicago, IL 60649.

Suggestions for further reading:

Clegg, Claude Andrew III. *An Original Man: The Life and Times of Elijah Muhammad*. New York: St. Martin's Press, 1997.

Lee, Martha F. *The Nation of Islam: An American Millenerian Movement. Studies in Religion and Society,* Vol. 21. Lewiston, NY: Edwin Mellen, 1988.

Lincoln, C. Eric. *The Black Muslims in America*. Boston: Beacon, 1961.

UNIFICATION CHURCH

Founded: 1954
Membership: statistics not available

One of the most controversial churches born in modern times is the Unification Church of the Rev. Sun Myung Moon (1920–). This church originated in Korea and burst upon the American scene in the 1970s. Its teaching is a blend of Eastern traditional philosophy and evangelical Christianity. Members hold that Satan distorted the original harmony of creation, but through the sacrifice of Jesus and revelations given to the Rev. Moon that harmony is being restored. Central to Moon's teaching is that God is a balance of masculine and feminine traits (basically the yin and yang of Taoism) and that humans can restore this harmony of polarities through spiritual marriage. Humans can also connect with the spiritual world and experience spiritual growth through proper actions, attitudes, and devotions that blend Eastern and Western elements.

Sun Myung Moon was born in 1920 in Korea and studied at a Confucian school. During the 1930s his parents became fervent Presbyterians, and the young Moon became a Sunday school teacher. At Easter 1935, as he was praying in the Korean mountains, Moon had a vision of Jesus, who asked him to continue the work Jesus had begun on earth nearly two thousand years before. Sun Myung Moon studied the Bible and many other religious teachings in order to unravel the mysteries of life and human history. Embracing asceticism, he came to an understanding of God's own suffering and longing to be reunited with God's children.

By 1945 Moon had organized the teachings that came to be known as the Divine Principle, and he began his public ministry. On May 1, 1954, in Seoul, Moon founded the Holy Spirit Association for the Unification of World Christianity, popularly called the Unification Church. Despite opposition from other churches and the government, including imprisonment of Moon and other leaders, the church quickly spread throughout South Korea. In 1959 the first missionaries arrived in the U.S.

Marriage is central to the teachings of the church, and the wedding of Moon to Hak Ja Han in 1960 was seen by his followers as the marriage of the Lamb foretold in the book of Revelation, marking the beginning of the restoration of humankind back into God's lineage. Sun Myung Moon and Hak Ja Han established the position of True Parents and are considered the first couple to have the complete blessing of God and to be able to bring forth children with no original sin. The church teaches that all people, whether previously married or single, can receive the blessing of God upon their marriages through the Moons' standing as the True Parents. The number of couples who have received this blessing in large wedding ceremonies was 360,000 by 1995.

In 1971 Moon expanded his ministry by coming to the United States. He conducted a "Day of Hope" speaking tour throughout the U.S. in the early 1970s with the purpose of reviving traditional Judeo-Christian values. He was invited to the White House, where he met with President Richard Nixon. On two occasions, Moon addressed members of the U.S. Congress from both the House and the Senate. In 1975 Reverend Moon sent missionaries to 120 countries, making the Unification Church a worldwide faith. Controversy followed Moon and his followers, however, and in the 1980s he was convicted of tax evasion and imprisoned in the U.S. for thirteen months.

In 1992 Reverend Moon declared that he and his wife are the Messiah and True Parents of all humanity. For adherents, this marks the beginning of the Completed Testament Age. Since then, Mrs. Moon has taken a more active role in the worldwide work of the church. In a speech at a U.S. Congressional reception in 2004, Rev. Moon was officially crowned, and he then declared that he "is none other than humanity's Savior, Messiah, Returning Lord, and True Parent." Rev. Moon's organization owns the *Washington Times* newspaper in the nation's capital.

For more information: www.unification.net, www.ffwpui.org

Suggestions for further reading:

Barker, Eileen. *The Making of a Moonie*. Oxford: Basil Blackwell, 1984.

Bromley, David G., and Anson Shupe. *"Moonies" in America*. Beverly Hills, Calif.: Sage, 1979.

Chryssides, George D. *The Advent of Sun Myung Moon: The Origins, Beliefs, and Practices of the Unification Church*. New York: Saint Martin's Press, 1991.

APPENDIX

Appendix 1
Members of the National Association of Evangelicals
(and date they joined)

Advent Christian General Conference (1986)
Assemblies of God (1943)
Association of Life-Giving Churches
Association of Vineyard Churches—U.S.A.
Baptist General Conference (1966)
The Brethren Church (1968)
Brethren in Christ Church (1949)
Christ Community Church
Christian Catholic Church (Evangelical Protestant) (1975)
Christian Church of North America (1953)
Christian Evangelical Churches of America, Inc.
Christian Reformed Church in North America (1943-51; 1988)
Christian Union (1954)
Church of God (1944)
Church of God (Holiness)
Church of God, Mountain Assembly, Inc. (1981)
Church of the Nazarene (1984)
Churches of Christ in Christian Union (1945)
Congregational Holiness Church (1990-92, 1994)
Conservative Baptist Association of America (1990)
Conservative Congregational Christian Conference (1951)
Conservative Lutheran Association (1984)
Elim Fellowship (1947)

Evangelical Church of North America (1969)

Evangelical Congregational Church (1962)

Evangelical Fellowship Chapel

Evangelical Free Church of America (1943)

Evangelical Friends Church Eastern Region

Evangelical Methodist Church (1952)

Evangelical Presbyterian Church (1982)

Evangelistic Missionary Fellowship (1982)

Fellowship of Evangelical Bible Churches (1948)

Fellowship of Evangelical Churches

Fire Baptized Holiness Church of God of the Americas (1978)

Free Methodist Church of North America (1944)

General Association of General Baptists (1988)

International Church of the Foursquare Gospel (1952)

International Pentecostal Church of Christ (1946)

International Pentecostal Holiness Church (1943)

Midwest Congregational Christian Fellowship (1964)

Missionary Church, Inc. (1944)

Northland, A Church Distributed

Open Bible Standard Churches (1943)

Pentecostal Church of God (1954)

Pentecostal Free Will Baptist Church, Inc. (1988)

Presbyterian Church in America (1986)

Primitive Methodist Church U.S.A. (1946)

Reformed Episcopal Church (1990)

Reformed Presbyterian Church of North America (1946)

Regional Synod of Mid-America (Reformed Church in America) (1989)

The Brethren Church

The Christian and Missionary Alliance

The Salvation Army (1990)

The Wesleyan Church (1948)

United Brethren in Christ

U.S. Conference of the Mennonite Brethren Churches

Worldwide Church of God (1997)

Appendix 2
Member Communions of the National Council
of the Churches of Christ in the U.S.A.

African Methodist Episcopal Church
African Methodist Episcopal Zion Church
The Alliance of Baptist Churches in the U.S.A.
American Baptist Churches in the U.S.A.
The Antiochian Orthodox Christian Archdiocese of North America
Diocese of the Armenian Church of America
Christian Church (Disciples of Christ)
Christian Methodist Episcopal Church
Church of the Brethren
The Coptic Orthodox Church in North America
The Episcopal Church
Evangelical Lutheran Church in America
Friends United Meeting
Greek Orthodox Archdiocese of North and South America
Hungarian Reformed Church in America
International Council of Community Churches
Korean Presbyterian Church in America
Malankara Orthodox Syrian Church
Mar Thoma Church
Moravian Church in America Northern Province and Southern
    Province
National Baptist Convention of America
National Baptist Convention, U.S.A., Inc.
National Missionary Baptist Convention of America
Orthodox Church in America
Patriarchal Parishes of the Russian Orthodox Church in the U.S.A.
Philadelphia Yearly Meeting of the Religious Society of Friends
Polish National Catholic Church of America
Presbyterian Church (U.S.A.)
Progressive National Baptist Convention, Inc.
Reformed Church in America
Serbian Orthodox Church in the U.S.A. and Canada
The Swedenborgian Church
Syrian Orthodox Church of Antioch
Ukrainian Orthodox Church of America
United Church of Christ
The United Methodist Church

Appendix 3: Relationships of Church Bodies to One Another

The Early Church

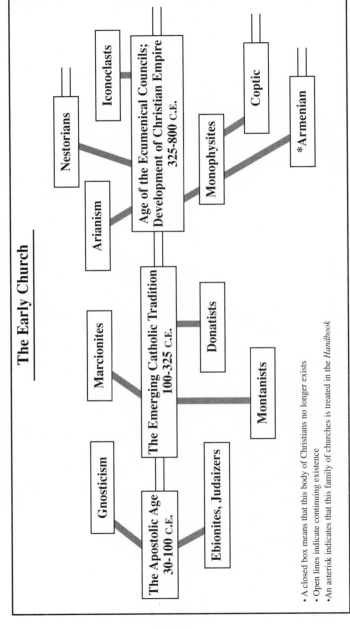

- A closed box means that this body of Christians no longer exists
- Open lines indicate continuing existence
- An asterisk indicates that this family of churches is treated in the *Handbook*

The Apostolic Age 30-100 C.E.

Gnosticism

Ebionites, Judaizers

The Emerging Catholic Tradition 100-325 C.E.

Marcionites

Donatists

Montanists

Age of the Ecumenical Councils; Development of Christian Empire 325-800 C.E.

Arianism

Nestorians

Iconoclasts

Monophysites

Coptic

*Armenian

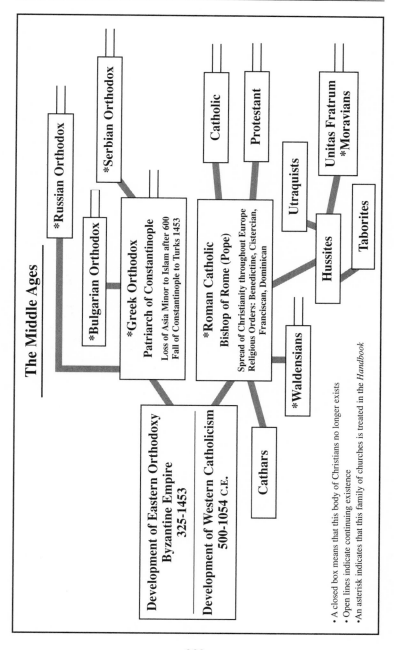

The Middle Ages

*Russian Orthodox

*Serbian Orthodox

*Bulgarian Orthodox

*Greek Orthodox
Patriarch of Constantinople
Loss of Asia Minor to Islam after 600
Fall of Constantinople to Turks 1453

Catholic

Protestant

Utraquists

Unitas Fratrum
*Moravians

Hussites

Taborites

*Roman Catholic
Bishop of Rome (Pope)
Spread of Christianity throughout Europe
Religious Orders: Benedictine, Cistercian,
Franciscan, Dominican

*Waldensians

Development of Eastern Orthodoxy
Byzantine Empire
325-1453

Development of Western Catholicism
500-1054 C.E.

Cathars

• A closed box means that this body of Christians no longer exists
• Open lines indicate continuing existence
•An asterisk indicates that this family of churches is treated in the *Handbook*

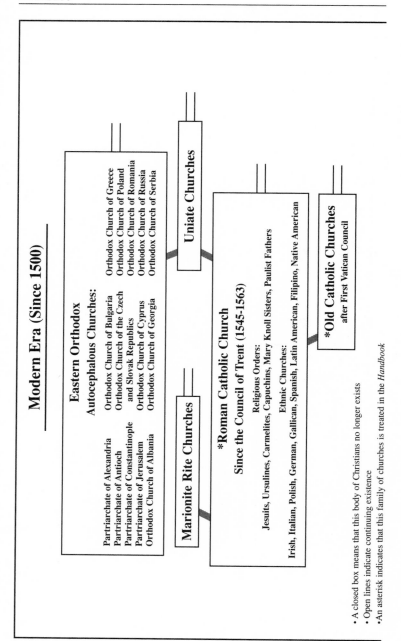

Modern Era (Since 1500)

Eastern Orthodox
Autocephalous Churches:

Partriarchate of Alexandria
Partriarchate of Antioch
Partriarchate of Constantinople
Partriarchate of Jerusalem
Orthodox Church of Albania

Orthodox Church of Bulgaria
Orthodox Church of the Czech
and Slovak Republics
Orthodox Church of Cyprus
Orthodox Church of Georgia

Orthodox Church of Greece
Orthodox Church of Poland
Orthodox Church of Romania
Orthodox Church of Russia
Orthodox Church of Serbia

Marionite Rite Churches

Uniate Churches

*Roman Catholic Church
Since the Council of Trent (1545-1563)

Religious Orders:
Jesuits, Ursulines, Carmelites, Capuchins, Mary Knoll Sisters, Paulist Fathers

Ethnic Churches:
Irish, Italian, Polish, German, Gallican, Spanish, Latin American, Filipino, Native American

*Old Catholic Churches
after First Vatican Council

• A closed box means that this body of Christians no longer exists
• Open lines indicate continuing existence
• An asterisk indicates that this family of churches is treated in the *Handbook*

390

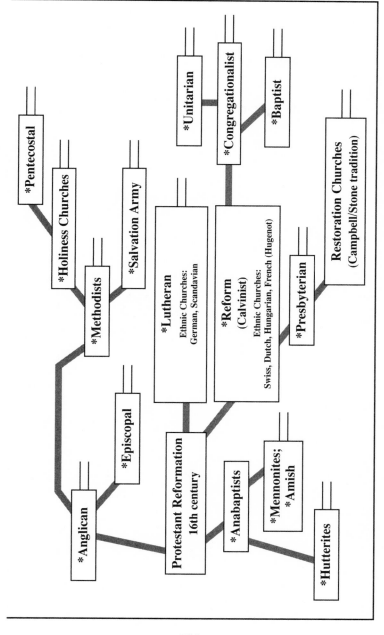

Appendix 4: Directory of Denomination and Headquarters Web Sites

Church	Address	Web Site
Advent Christian Church	14601 Albemarle Road, P.O. Box 23152, Charlotte, NC 28227	www.adventchristian.org
African Methodist Episcopal Church	1134 11th Street NW, Washington, D.C. 20001	www.amecnet.org
African Methodist Episcopal Zion Church	P.O. Box 32843, Charlotte, NC 28323	www.amezion.org
African Orthodox Church	137 Alston Street NW, Cambridge, MA 02139	
Albanian Orthodox Archdiocese in America	523 East Broadway, South Boston, MA 02127	www.oca.org/oca/al
American Association of Lutheran Churches	801 West 106th St., #203, Minneapolis, MN 55420	www.taalc.org
American Baptist Association	4605 N. State Line Avenue, Texarkana, TX 75503	www.abaptist.org
American Baptist Churches in the U.S.A.	P.O. Box 851, Valley Forge, PA 19482-0851	www.abc-usa.org
American Carpatho-Russian Greek Catholic Church	312 Garfield Street, Johnstown, PA 15906	www.goarch.org
American Catholic Church	P.O. Box 725, Hampton Bays, NY 11946	www.geocities.com/westhollywood/4136
American Evangelical Christian Churches	P.O. Box 47312, Indianapolis, IN 46277	www.aeccministries.com
American Jewish Committee	165 East 56th Street, New York, NY 10022	www.ajc.org
American Rescue Workers	643 Elmira Street, Williamsport, PA 17701	www.arwus.com
Anglican Catholic Church	107 West Broadway, Gettysburg, PA 17325	www.anglicancatholic.org
Anglican Rite Synod in the Americas	875 Berkshire Valley Road, Wharton, NJ 07885	www.anglicanrite.org
Antiochian Orthodox Christian Archdiocese of North America	550 West 50th Street, New York, NY 10019	www.antiochian.org
Apostolic Christian Church (Nazarene)	1135 Sholey Road, Richmond, VA 23231	
Apostolic Christian Church of America	3420 North Sheridan Road, Peoria, IL 61604	www.apostolicchristian.org
Apostolic Episcopal Church — Order of Corporate Reunion	P. O. Box 2401, Apple Valley, CA 92307	www.celticsynod.org/aec.htm
Apostolic Faith Mission of Portland, OR	6615 SE Duke Street, Portland, OR 97206	www.apostolicfaith.org
Apostolic Lutheran Church of America	332 Mt. Washington Way, Clayton, CA 94517-1546	www.apostolic-lutheran.org
Apostolic Orthodox Catholic Church	P.O. Box 1834, Glendora, CA 91740-1834	www.pe.net/~idyll/para1.htm (unofficial)
Apostolic Overcoming Holy Church of God, Inc.	1120 North 24th Street, Birmingham, AL 35234	www.prairienet.org/staoh
Armenian Apostolic Church of America	138 E. 39th Street, New York, NY 10016-4885	www.armprelacy.org

Church	Address	Web Site
Assemblies of God International	1445 Boonville Avenue, Springfield, MO 65802	www.ag.org
Assemblies of God International Fellowship	P.O. Box 22410, San Diego, CA 92192-2410	www.agifellowship.org
Assemblies of the Lord Jesus Christ	875 N. White Station Road, Memphis, TN 38122	www.aljc.org
Associate Reformed Presbyterian Church	3132 Grace Hill Road, Columbia, SC 29204	www.arpsynod.org
Association of Free Lutheran Congregations	3110 E. Medicine Lake Boulevard, Minneapolis, MN 55441	www.aflc.org
Baha'i	866 UN Plaza, Suite 1202, New York, NY 10017	www.bahai.org
Baptist Bible Fellowship International	P.O. Box 191, Springfield, MO 65801	www.bbfi.org
Baptist General Conference	2002 South Arlington Heights Road, Arlington Heights, IL 60005	www.bgc.bethel.edu
Baptist Missionary Association of America	P.O. Box 193920, Little Rock, AR 72219-3920	www.bmaa-missions.com
Beachy Amish Mennonite Churches	3015 Partridge Road, P.O. Box 73, Partridge, KS 67566	www.mhsc.ca (unofficial)
Berean Fundamental Church	P.O. Box 6103, Lincoln, NE 68506	
Bible Fellowship Church	3000 Fellowship Dr., Whitehall, PA 18052	www.bfc.org
Bible Way Church of Our Lord Jesus Christ World Wide, Inc.	4949 Two-Notch Road, Columbia, SC 29204	www.biblewaychurch.org
Brethren Church (Ashland)	524 College Avenue, Ashland, OH 44805	www.brethrenchurch.org
Brethren in Christ Church	P.O. Box A, Grantham, PA 17207-0901	www.bic-church.org/index.htm
Bulgarian Eastern Orthodox Church	550-A West 50th Street, New York, NY 10019	
Charismatic Episcopal Church	46797 Trailwood Place, Potomac Falls, VA 20165	www.diochi.org
Christadelphians	1000 Mohawk Drive, Elgin, IL 60120-3148	www.christadelphia.org
Christian and Missionary Alliance	P.O. Box 35000, Colorado Springs, CO 80935-3500	www.cmalliance.org
Christian Brethren	327 Prairie Avenue, Wheaton, IL 60187-3408	
Christian Catholic Church	Dowie Memorial Drive, Zion, IL 60099	
Christian Church (Disciples of Christ)	130 East Washington Street, P.O. Box 1986, Indianapolis, IN 46206	www.disciples.org
Christian Church of North America, General Council	1294 Rutledge Road, Transfer, PA 16154-9005	www.ccna.org
Christian Churches and Churches of Christ	4210 Bridgetown Road, P.O. Box 11326, Cincinnati, OH 45211	www.cwv.net/christ'n (unofficial)
Christian Congregation, Inc.	804 West Hemlock Street, LaFollette, TN 37766	
Christian Methodist Episcopal Church	4466 Elvis Presley Blvd., Memphis, TN 38116	www.c-m-e.org
Christian Reformed Church in North America	2850 Kalamazoo Avenue SE, Grand Rapids, MI 49560	www.crcna.org
Church of Christ (Holiness) U.S.A.	329 East Monument Street, P.O. Box 3622, Jackson, MS 39207	www.cochusa.com/main.htm

Church	Address	Web Site
Church of Christ (Temple Lot)	200 S. River Boulevard, P.O. Box 472, Independence, MO 64501-0472	www.church-of-christ.com
Church of Christ, Scientist	175 Huntington Avenue, Boston, MA 02115	www.tfccs.com
Church of God and Saints of Christ	3825 Central Avenue, Cleveland, OH 44115	www.churchofgod1896.org
Church of God (Anderson, IN)	P.O. Box 2420, Anderson, IN 46018-2420	www.chog.org
Church of God (Cleveland, TN)	2490 Keith St., P.O. Box 2430, Cleveland, TN 37320-2430	www.churchofgod.org
Church of God (General Conference)	P.O. Box 100,000, Morrow, GA 30260	www.abc-coggc.org
Church of God (Holiness)	7407 Metcalf, P.O. Box 4711, Overland Park, KS 66204	www.kccbs.edu/cogh
Church of God (Seventh Day)	330 West 152nd Avenue, P.O. Box 33677, Denver, CO 80233	www.cog7.org
Church of God by Faith, Inc.	1315 South Lane Avenue, Suite 6, Jacksonville, FL 32206	www.cogbf.org
Church of God in Christ	272 South Main Street, Memphis, TN 38101	
Church of God in Christ, International	170 Adelphi Street, Brooklyn, NY 11205	www.bibleviews.com
Church of God in Christ, Mennonite	P.O. Box 230, Moundridge, KS 67107	
Church of God of Prophecy	3720 North Keith Street, P.O. Box 2910, Cleveland, TN 37320-2910	www.cogop.org
Church of Jesus Christ	P.O. Box 1414, Cleveland, TN 37311	
Church of Jesus Christ (Bickertonites)	2007 Cutter Drive, McKees Rocks, PA 15136	
Church of Jesus Christ of Latter-day Saints	15 East South Temple Street, Salt Lake City, UT 84150	www.lds.org
Church of Our Lord Jesus Christ of the Apostolic Faith	444 W. Penn Street, Philadelphia, PA 19144	www.apostolic-faith.org
Church of the Brethren	1451 Dundee Avenue, Elgin, IL 60120	www.brethren.org
Church of the Living God (Christian Workers for Fellowship)	430 Forest Avenue, Cincinnati, OH 45229	
Church of the Living God, the Pillar and Ground of Truth, Inc.	4520 Ashland City Hwy., Nashville, TN 37208	www.clgpgt.org
Church of the Lutheran Brethren of America	P.O. Box 655, Fergus Falls, MN 56538	www.clba.org
Church of the Lutheran Confession	501 Grover Road, Eau Claire, WI 54701	www.clclutheran.org
Church of the Nazarene	6401 The Paseo, Kansas City, MO 64131	www.nazarene.org
Church of the United Brethren in Christ	302 Lake Street, Huntington, IN 46750	www.ub.org
Churches of Christ	P.O. Box 726, Kosciusko, MS 39090	www.church-of-christ.org
Churches of Christ in Christian Union	1426 Lancaster Pike, Box 30, Circleville, OH 43113	www.bright.net/~ccuhq

394

Church	Address	Website
Churches of God, General Conference	700 Melrose Ave., P.O. Box 926, Findlay, OH 45839	www.cggc.org
Congregational Christian Churches	P.O. Box 1620, Oak Creek, WI 53154	www.naccc.org
Congregational Holiness Church	3888 Fayetteville Hwy., Griffin, GA 30223	www.ch.church.com
Congregational Methodist Church	P.O. Box 9, Florence, MS 39073	
Conservative Baptist Association of America	1501 West Mineral Ave., Suite B, Littleton, CO 80120-5612	www.cbamerica.org
Conservative Congregational Christian Conference	7582 Currell Boulevard, Suite 108, St. Paul, MN 55125	www.cccusa.org
Conservative Mennonite Conference	9910 Rosedale-Milford Center Road, Irwin, OH 43029	www.cmcrosedale.org
Cooperative Baptist Fellowship	P.O. Box 450329, Atlanta, GA 31145-0329	www.cbfonline.org
Coptic Orthodox Church	P.O. Box 384, Cedar Grove, NJ 07009	www.nacopticchurch.org
Cumberland Presbyterian Church	1978 Union Avenue, Memphis, TN 38104	www.cumberland.org
Cumberland Presbyterian Church in America	226 Church Street, Huntsville, AL 35801	www.cumberland.org/cpca
Divine Science	2025 35th Street NW, Washington, D.C. 20007	www.divinescience.org
Elim Fellowship	1703 Dalton Road, Lima, NY 14485	www.elim.edu
Episcopal Church	815 Second Avenue, New York, NY 10017	www.ecusa.org
Episcopal Missionary Church	600 Oak Hollow Lane, Fort Worth, TX 76112	www.emchome.org
Evangelical Church	7733 West River Road, Minneapolis, MN 55444	
Evangelical Congregational Church	100 West Park Avenue, Myerstown, PA 17067	www.eccenter.com
Evangelical Covenant Church	5101 North Francisco Avenue, Chicago, IL 60625	www.covchurch.org
Evangelical Free Church of America	901 East 78th Street, Minneapolis, MN 55420-1300	www.efca.org
Evangelical Friends International	1975 Raisin Center Hwy., Adrian, MI 49221	www.evangelical-friends.org
Evangelical Lutheran Church in America	8765 West Higgins Road, Chicago, IL 60631	www.elca.org
Evangelical Lutheran Synod	6 Browns Court, Mankato, MN 56001	www.evluthsyn.org
Evangelical Mennonite Church	1420 Kerrway Court, Fort Wayne, IN 46805	www.brookside.org
Evangelical Methodist Church	P.O. Box 17070, Indianapolis, IN 46217	www.emchurch.org
Evangelical Presbyterian Church	29140 Buckingham Avenue, Suite 5, Livonia, MI 48154	www.epc.org
Fellowship of Evangelical Bible Churches	5800 South 14th Street, Omaha, NE 68107	
Fellowship of Grace Brethren Churches	P.O. Box 386, Winona Lake, IN 46590	www.fgbc.org
Free Methodist Church of North America	P.O. Box 535002, Indianapolis, IN 46253	www.fmcna.org
Free Will Baptists, National Association	P.O. Box 5002, Antioch, TN 37011-5002	www.nafwb.org

Church	Address	Web Site
Friends General Conference	1216 Arch St, #2, Philadelphia, PA 19107	www.fgcquaker.org
Friends United Meeting	101 Quaker Hill Drive, Richmond, IN 47374-1980	www.fum.org
Full Gospel Assemblies International	P.O. Box 1230, Coatesville, PA 19320	
Full Gospel Fellowship of Churches and Ministries, International	4325 W. Ledbetter Drive, Dallas, TX 75233	www.fgfcmi.org
General Association of General Baptist Churches	100 Stinson Drive, Poplar Bluff, MO 63901	www.angelfire.com
General Association of Regular Baptist Churches	1300 North Meacham Road, Schaumburg, IL 60173	www.garbc.org
General Church of the New Jerusalem	P.O. Box 711, Bryn Athyn, PA 19009	www.newchurch.org
Grace Gospel Fellowship	2125 Martindale SW, P.O. Box 9432, Grand Rapids, MI 49509	www.ggfusa.org
Greek Orthodox Archdiocese of America	8-10 East 79th Street, New York, NY 10021	www.goarch.org
Holy Eastern Orthodox Catholic and Apostolic Church	HC74, Box 419-2, Mountain View, AR 72560	www.theocacna.org
House of God, Which is the Church of the Living God, the Pillar and Ground of the Truth	866 Georgetown Street, Lexington, KY 40508	www.houseofgod.org
Hungarian Reformed Church in America	13 Grove Street, Poughkeepsie, NY 12601	www.calvinsynod.org
Hutterian Brethren	Crystal Spring Colony, Box 10, Ste Agathe, MB R0G 1Y0 Canada	www.hutterianbrethren.com (unofficial)
Independent Fundamental Churches of America (IFCA International, Inc.)	3250 Fairlanes, P.O. Box 810, Grandville, MI 49468	www.ifca.org
International Church of the Foursquare Gospel	1910 W. Sunset Blvd., Suite 210, P.O. Box 26902, Los Angeles, CA 90026-0176	www.foursquare.org
International Council of Community Churches	21116 Washington Parkway, Frankfort, IL 60423-3112	www.akcache.com/community/iccc.html
International Pentecostal Church of Christ	2245 State Route 42 SW, P.O. Box 439, London, OH 43140	http: members.aol.com/hqipcc/
International Pentecostal Holiness Church	P.O. Box 12609, Oklahoma City, OK 73157	www.iphc.org
Islamic Center of Washington	2551 Massachusetts Avenue NW, Washington, D.C. 20008	
Islamic Society of North America	P.O. Box 38, Plainfield, IN 46168	www.isna.net
Jehovah's Witnesses	25 Columbia Heights, Brooklyn, NY 11201-2483	www.watchtower.org
Jewish Reconstructionist Federation	78 Montgomery Avenue, Suite 9, Elkins Park, PA 19027	www.jrf.org
Korean Presbyterian Church in America	P.O. Box 457, Morganville, NJ 07951	
Korean-American Presbyterian Church	2853 W. 7th Street, Los Angeles, CA 90005	www.kapc.org

Church	Address	Web Site
Liberal Catholic Church International	1206 Ayers Ave., Ojai, CA 93023	www.thelcc.org
Lubavitch World Headquarters	7700 Eastern Parkway, Brooklyn, NY 11213	www.chabad-centers.com
Lutheran Church—Missouri Synod	1333 South Kirkwood Road, St. Louis, MO 63122-7295	www.lcms.org
Malankara Orthodox Syrian Church	80-34 Commonwealth Boulevard, Bellerose, NY 11426	www.malankara.org/american.htm
Mar Thoma Orthodox Syrian Church of India	2320 S. Merrick Avenue, Merrick, NY 11566	www.marthomachurch.org
Mennonite Brethren Churches, General Conference	4824 Butler Avenue, Fresno, CA 93727-5097	www.mbconf.org
Mennonite Church USA	421 South Second Street, Suite 600, Elkhart, IN 46516	www.mennonites.org
Missionary Church	3811 Vanguard Drive, P.O. Box 9127, Fort Wayne, IN 46899-9127	www.mcusa.org
Moravian Church (Unitas Fratrum)	1021 Center Street, P.O. Box 1245, Bethlehem, PA 18016-1245	www.moravian.org
Muslim American Society (W. Deen Muhammed)	P.O. Box 1944, Calumet City, IL 60409	www.taqwa-annur.com/information.htm
National Baptist Convention of America	777 S. R.L. Thornton Freeway, Suite 205, Dallas, TX 75203	http://members.aol.com/nbyc1/nbca.htm
National Baptist Convention U.S.A., Inc.	1700 Baptist World Center Dr., Nashville, TN 37207	
National Missionary Baptist Convention of America	P.O. Box 512096, Los Angeles, CA 90051-0096	www.natl-missionarybaptist.com
National Primitive Baptist Convention U.S.A.	6433 Hidden Forrest Drive, Charlotte, NC 28213	www.natlprimbaptcorv.org
National Spiritual Alliance of the U.S.A.	67 Mine Road, Winchester, NH 03470	
National Spiritualist Association of Churches	P.O. Box 217, Lily Dale, NY 14752	www.nsac.org
Netherlands Reformed Congregations	1261 Beckwith N.E., Grand Rapids, MI 49505	http://home.earthlink.net/~vogelaar /nrc/church.htm (unofficial)
New Apostolic Church of North America	3753 North Troy Street, Chicago, IL 60618	www.nak.org
North American Baptist Conference	1 South 210 Summit Avenue, Oakbrook Terrace, IL 60181	www.nabconference.org
Old Catholic Church of America	409 N. Lexington Parkway, DeForest, WI 53532	www.oldcatholic.org
Old German Baptist Brethren	6952 N. Montgomery County Line Rd, Englewood, OH 45322-9748	www.cob-net.org/docs/groups.htm (unofficial)
Old Roman Catholic Church of North America	1207 Potomac Place, Louisville, KY 40214	www.orccna.org
Open Bible Standard Churches	2020 Bell Avenue, Des Moines, IA 50315	www.openbible.org
Orthodox Church in America	P.O. Box 675, Sysosset, NY 11791-0675	www.oca.org
Orthodox Presbyterian Church	607 North Easton Road, Bldg. E, Box P, Willow Grove, PA 19090-0920	www.opc.org
Orthodox Union in America	333 Seventh Ave, New York, NY 10001	www.ou.org
Pentecostal Assemblies of the World, Inc	3939 Meadows Drive, Indianapolis, IN 46205	http://members.tripod.com/paw_inc/ index.html

397

Church	Address	Web Site
Pentecostal Church of God	4901 Pennsylvania, P.O. Box 850, Joplin, MO 64802	www.pcg.org
Pentecostal Free Will Baptist Church, Inc		www.pfwb.org
Pillar of Fire	P.O. Box 9159, Zarephath, NJ 08890	www.gospelcom.net/pof
Polish National Catholic Church of America	1006 Pittston Avenue, Scranton, PA 18505	www.pncc.org
Presbyterian Church (U.S.A.)	100 Witherspoon Street, Louisville, KY 40202	www.pcusa.org
Presbyterian Church in America	1852 Century Place, Atlanta, GA 30345-4305	www.pcanet.org
Primitive Baptists		www.pb.org (unofficial)
Primitive Methodist Church in the U.S.A.	1045 Laurel Run Road, Wilkes-Barre, PA 18702	www.primitivemethodistchurch.org
Progressive National Baptist Convention, Inc.	601 50th Street, NE, Washington, DC 20019	www.pnbc.org
Protestant Reformed Churches in America	4949 Ivanrest Avenue, Grandville, MI 49418	www.prca.org (unofficial)
Reformed Church in America	Office of the General Secretary, 475 Riverside Dr., 18th Floor, New York, NY 10115	www.rca.org
Reformed Church in the United States	6121 Pine Vista Way, Elk Grove, CA 95758	www.rcus.org
Reformed Episcopal Church	826 Second Ave, Blue Bell, PA 19422-1257	www.recus.org
Reformed Methodist Union Episcopal Church	1136 Brody Ave.., Charleston, SC 29407	
Reformed Presbyterian Church of North America	7408 Penn Avenue, Pittsburgh, PA 15208	www.reformedpresbyterian.org
Religious Society of Friends (Conservative)		www.quaker.org
Reorganized Church of Jesus Christ of Latter-day Saints	P.O. Box 1059, 1001 Walnut Street, Independence, MO 64501	www.rlds.org
Roman Catholic Church Council	3211 Fourth Street, Washington, DC 20017	www.vatican.va
Romanian Orthodox Episcopate of America	2535 Grey Tower Road, Jackson, MI 49201-9120	www.roeg.org
Russian Orthodox Church outside of Russia	75 East 93rd Street, New York, NY 10128	www.rocor.org
The Salvation Army	615 Slaters Lane, Alexandria, VA 22313	www.sarmy.org
Schwenkfelder Church	105 Seminary St., Pennsburg, PA 18073	www.schwenkfelder.org
Separate Baptists in Christ	10102 N Hickory Lane, Columbus, IN 47203	www.separatebaptist.org
Serbian Eastern Orthodox Church in the U.S.A. and Canada	Office of External Affairs, 2311 M St, NW (Suite 402), Washington, DC 20037	http://oca.serbian-church.net
Seventh Day Baptist General Conference	P.O. Box 167, Janesville, WI 53547-16788	www.seventhdaybaptist.org
Seventh-day Adventist Church	12501 Old Columbia Pike, Silver Spring, MD 20904-6600	http://northamerica.adventist.org
Southern Baptist Convention	901 Commerce Street, Suite 750, Nashville, TN 37203	www.sbc.net

Church	Address	Web Site
Southern Episcopal Church	234 Willow Lane, Nashville, TN 37211-4945	www.angelfire.com/biz/Southern
Southern Methodist Church	P.O. Box 39, Orangeburg, SC 29116-0039	www.southernmethodistchurch.org
Swedenborgian Church	11 Highland Avenue, Newtonville, MA 02460	www.swedenborg.org
Syrian (Syriac) Orthodox Church of Antioch (Archdiocese of the Eastern United States)	260 Elm Avenue, Teaneck, NJ 07661	www.syrianorthodoxchurch.org
Theosophical Society in America	P.O. Box 270, Wheaton, IL 60189	www.theosophical.org
Triumph the Church and Kingdom of God in Christ Inc. (International)	213 Farrington Ave SE, Atlanta, GA 30315	
Ukrainian Orthodox Church of the USA	135 Davidson Avenue, Somerset, NJ 08873	www.uocofusa.org
Unification Church	4 West 43rd St., New York, NY 10036	www.unification.org
Union of American Hebrew Congregations	838 Fifth Avenue, New York, NY 10021	www.uahc.org
Unitarian Universalist Association of Congregations	25 Beacon Street, Boston, MA 02108	www.uua.org
United Church of Christ	700 Prospect Avenue, Cleveland, OH 02108	www.ucc.org
United Holy Church of America, Inc.	312 Umstead Street, Durham, NC 27702	http://members.aol.com/newpent/nphca (unofficial)
United Methodist Church	P.O. Box 320, 810 Twelfth Ave. S., Nashville, TN 37202-0320	www.umc.org
United Pentecostal Church International	8855 Dunn Road, Hazelwood, MO 63042	www.upci.org
United Synagogues of Conservative Judaism	155 Fifth Ave, New York, NY 10010	www.uscj.org
Unity Churches, Association of	P.O. Box 610, Lee's Summit, MO 64063	www.unity.org
Unity of the Brethren		www.unityofthebrethren.org
Universal Fellowship of Metropolitan Community Churches	8704 Santa Monica Boulevard, 2nd Floor, West Hollywood, CA 90069	www.ufmcc.com
Vineyard Churches USA	5340 E. LaPalma Ave., Anaheim, CA 92807	www.vineyardusa.org
Volunteers of America	1660 Duke Street, Alexandria, VA 22314-3421	www.voa.org
Wesleyan Church	P.O. Box 50434, Indianapolis, IN 46250	www.wesleyan.org
Wisconsin Evangelical Lutheran Synod	2929 N Mayfair Road, Milwaukee, WI 53222	www.wels.net
Worldwide Church of God	300 West Green Street, Pasadena, CA 91123	www.wcg.org

INDEX

411

Houteff, Victor T., 261, 262
Huguenots, 19
Humanae Vitae, 85
Humanist Manifesto, 369
Hungarian Reformed Church in
America. See Reformed,
Congregationalist and Presbyterian
churches
Hus, John, 177
Husain, 341
Hussite, 177
Hutter, Jacob, 155
Hutterian Brethren, 155-6. See also
Mennonite and Anabaptist churches
Hutterites, 155-6
Hybels, Bill, 319, 328

IFCA International, 312-13. See also
Fundamentalist and Bible churches
Ignatius of Antioch, 78
Independent Assemblies of God,
International. See Pentecostal
churches
Independent Baptist Fellowship
International. See Fundamentalist
and Bible churches
Independent Christian Church, 370
Independent Fundamental Churches of
America (IFCA). See
Fundamentalist and Bible churches
Independent Fundamentalist Baptist
Churches. See Fundamentalist and
Bible churches
Independent Pentecostal Churches, 292
Indian Religious Freedom Resolution,
303
Inner Light, 159, 160, 161, 162
Inner Voice, 160
Institute of Reformed Baptist Studies,
211
Institute of Theology by Extension,
296
Interdenominational Theological
Center, 285
International Association for Religious
Freedom, 372
International Bible Students, 268
International Center, 123, 243
International Churches of Christ, 255-
56. See Christian and Restorationist
churches
International Church of the Foursquare
Gospel. See Pentecostal churches

International College and Graduate
School, 194
International Communion of the
Charismatic Episcopal Church. See
Episcopal and Anglican churches
International Council of Community
Churches. See Community and
New Paradigm churches.
International Mission Board, 214
International Pentecostal Church of
Christ. See Pentecostal churches
International Pentecostal Holiness
Church, 290, 294-95. See
Pentecostal churches.
International Voluntary Service, 172
Internet, 22, 165, 318, 326, 354
Interstate and Foreign Landmark
Missionary Baptist Association.
See Baptist churches
Irving, Edward, 246
Isabella (Queen), 31
Ishmael, 25, 332, 333
Islam, 331-39
Shi'ite Islam, 334, 336, 338,
341-42
Sufism, 342-43
Sunni Islam, 336, 338-40
Wahhabism, 343
Islamic Fundamentalism, 343-
45
Islamic Fundamentalism, See Islam.
Islamic Society of North America, 340
Italian Christian Church, 282

J. Appleseed & Co., 366
Jabbar, Kareem Abdul, 338
Jackson, Joseph H., 203, 209
Jacob, 25, 29, 45
Jakes, Thomas D., 324-25
James, apostle, 74
James I, 182
James, Fannie Brooks, 358
Jarratt, Devereux, 218
Jednota Bratrska, 177
Jefferson, Thomas, 17
Jehovah's Witnesses, 18, 259, 267-70.
See Adventist and Sabbatarian
churches
Jenkin, Jerry B., 306
Jericho City of Praise, The, 321
Jerome, 77
Jesuits, 79, 82, 98. See also Society of
Jesus

North American Mission Board, 214
North American Old Catholic Church.
    See Catholic churches
North American Old Roman Catholic
    Church. See Catholic churches
North American Teshuva, 39
North Park Theological Seminary, 175
North Park University, 175
North Phoenix Baptist Church, 321
Northern Baptist Convention. See
    Baptist churches.
Northwest Canada Conference, 227
Norwegian-Danish Evangelical Free
    Church Association. See Brethren
    and Pietist churches
Norwegian Lutheran Church. See
    Lutheran churches
Norwegian Lutheran Church of
    America. See Lutheran churches
Notre Dame University, 82

Oakland City University, 198
Office of Communication, 251
Official Catholic Directory, The, 81
O'Kelly, James, 248
Old Catholic Church. See Catholic
    churches
Old Catholic Church of America. See
    Catholic churches
Old German Baptist Brethren (Old
    Order Dunkers). See Brethren and
    Pietist churches
Old Hungarian Reformed Church, 129
Old Lights (Baptist). See Baptist
    churches
Old-Line Primitive Baptists, 208
Old Missionary Baptist Associations.
    See Baptist churches
Old Order Amish Churches. See
    Mennonite and Anabaptist churches
Old Order Amish Mennonite Church.
    See Mennonite and Anabaptist
    churches
Old Order Dunkers (Old German
    Baptist Brethren). See Brethren
    and Pietist churches
Old Order (Wisler) Mennonite Church.
    See Mennonite and Anabaptist
    churches
Old Regular Baptists. See Baptist
    churches
Old Roman Catholic Church (English
    Rite). See Catholic churches

Old Roman Catholic Church of North
    America. See Catholic churches
Old Time Religion (television show),
    306
Olha, Princess, 75
Olsen, Ivan E., 308
Open Bible Evangelistic Association,
    295
Open Bible Standard Churches, Inc.
    See Pentecostal churches
Oriental Orthodox Church, 51-55, 63-
    64
Origen, 65, 369
Original Free Will Baptist Convention.
    See Baptist churches
Orthodox and Oriental Orthodox
    churches, 51-76
        African Orthodox Church, 56-
            67
        Albanian Orthodox Archdiocese
            in America, 57-58
        American Carpatho-Russian
            Orthodox Greek Catholic
            Church, 58-59
        Antiochian Orthodox Christian
            Archdiocese of North
            America, 59-61, 387
        Apostolic Catholic Assyrian
            Church of the East, North
            American Diocese, 61
        Apostolic Episcopal Church,
            61-62
        Armenian Apostolic Church,
            Diocese of America, 62-64
        Armenian Church, 51, 62, 63,
            88
        Bulgarian Eastern Orthodox
            Church, 64
        Coptic Orthodox Church, 51,
            56, 64-66, 387
        Greek Orthodox Archdiocese of
            North America, 66-67, 387
        Holy Eastern Orthodox and
            Apostolic Church in North
            America, Inc., 71
        Malankara Orthodox Syrian
            Church, 67-68, 387
        Mar Thoma Orthodox Syrian
            Church, 67-68, 387
        Orthodox Church in America
            (Russian Orthodox), 69-72,
            387

St. Herman's Theological Seminary, 72
St. John of Damascus Orthodox
    Theological Academy, 60
St. John of Damascus Sacred Art
    Academy, 61
St. Lawrence University, 370
St. Louis University, 82
St. Mari, 61
St. Sophia Seminary, 76
St. Tikhon's Theological Seminary, 72
St. Vladimir's Orthodox Theological
    Seminary, 60, 72
St. Volodymyr (Vladimir) the Great
    (Basil), 76
Scalabrini Fathers, 98
Scandinavian Assemblies of God, 292
Schechter, Solomon, 43
Schlatter, Michael, 128
Schleitheim Articles, 156
Schmalkald Articles of Faith, 113, 115
Schmiedeleut, 156
Schneerson, Menachem, 41
School for Officers' Training
    (Salvation Army), 230
School Sisters of Notre Dame, 98
Schwarz, Bishop, 246
Schwenkfeld von Ossig, Caspar, 180
Schwenkfelder Church, 180-1. See
    also Brethren and Pietist churches
Science and Health with Key to the
    Scriptures (Mary Baker Eddy),
    356, 357, 358
Scofield, Cyrus, 305
Scofield Study Bible, 305
Scopes "Monkey Trial," 306
Scots Confession, 143
Scott, Orange, 247
Scovel, Carl, 371
Seabury, Samuel, 103
Second Baptist Church (Houston,
    Texas), 321
Second Cumberland Presbyterian
    Church, 137
Second Great Awakening, 18, 136,
    206, 248, 257, 346
Second Vatican Council, 80, 85, 87, 92,
    95, 100, 101
Second World Conference of Friends,
    163
Semple, Robert, 292
Separate Baptist Missions, Inc., 212
Separate Baptists, 197, 216

Separate Baptists in Christ (General
    Association). See Baptist churches
Separatism/Separatists, 167, 182, 306
Sephardic Judaism. See Judaism
Serbian Eastern Orthodox Church, 73-
    74
Serbian Orthodox Church, 72-74, 387
    See Orthodox and Oriental
    Orthodox churches
Sergius, Metropolitan, 70
Serious Call to a Devout and Holy
    Life, A (William Law), 217
Servetus, Michael, 368
Seton, Elizabeth, 83
"Seven Articles of Faith," 308
Seven Keys, The, 266
Seventh-Day Adventist Church, 270-
    73. See Adventist and Sabbatarian
    churches
Seventh Day Baptist General
    Conference. See Baptist churches
Seymour, William J., 276
Shakers, 18
Sharia, 336, 340, 343, 344
Shenouda III, Pope, 66
Shepherd of the Hills, 322
Shepherd's Rod, The, 261
Shi'ites. See Islam, Shi'ism
Simons, Menno, 148
Simpson, A. B., 240
Sinkford, William, 372
Sisters of Charity, 83
Sisters of Mercy, 82, 83
Six Days War, 45
Small, Aletha Brooks, 358
Small Catechism (Martin Luther), 113
Smith, Church, 322-23
Smith, Hyrum, 347
Smith, Captain John,
Smith, Joseph, Jr., 346-48, 349-50, 352
Smith, Joseph, III, 347, 352
Smith, Samuel, 279
Smyth, John, 182, 197
Social Creed, 233
Social Gospel Movement, 106, 221,
    327
Society for the Propagation of the
    Faith, 96
Society for the Propagation of the
    Gospel, 103
Society of Jesus, 79, 82, 98. See also
    Jesuits
Society of Friends, 159-60